Western industrial societies have undergone a massive transformation since the 1980s, and this is particularly noticeable in the older cities whose economies were based on labour intensive industry. In the period following World War II, racial and ethnic minorities, who migrated from overseas or from the rural areas within the same country, formed a pool of low-paid labour upon which the prosperity of the industrial city depended. With the subsequent reorganisation of these economies industrial production shifted overseas, while the new technological industries expanded locally, requiring fewer, and better skilled workers. The consequence for those seemingly excluded from the prosperity of the post-industrial age has been disastrous.

In this collection of essays, edited by Malcolm Cross, leading authorities compare the situation of racial minorities in the post-industrial cities of Europe and North America, and examine ways in which their position can be ameliorated. The authors ask whether it is true that racial discrimination is no longer the main problem to be overcome in combating racial inequality, and consider whether racial minorities should remigrate in search of work, or concentrate their efforts in developing the kind of skills required by the new technology. They suggest that failure to find a solution that ensures greater equality for racial minorities may inevitably lead to a ghetto society where cities are the focus of unrest and urban rioting.

Comparative ethnic and race relations

Ethnic minorities and industrial change in Europe and North America

Comparative ethnic and race relations

Published for the Centre of Research in Ethnic Relations at the University of Warwick

Senior Editor
Professor John Rex *Emeritus Professor of Ethnic Relations, University of Warwick*

Editors
Professor Robin Cohen *Professor of Sociology, University of Warwick*
Mr Malcolm Cross *Principal Research Fellow, University of Warwick*

This series publishes works of original theory, empirical research, and texts on the problems of racially mixed societies. It is based on the work for the Centre of Research in Ethnic Relations, a Designated Research Centre of the Economic and Social Research Council, and the main centre for the study of race relations in Britain.

The books are intended for an international readership of scholars, students and professionals concerned with racial issues, across a wide range of disciplines (such as sociology, anthropology, social policy, politics, economics, education and law), as well as among professional social administrators, teachers, government officials, health service workers and others.

Other books in this series:
Michael Banton: *Racial and ethnic competition* (issued in hardcover and as a paperback)
Thomas Hammar (ed.): *European immigration policy*
Frank Reeves: *British racial discourse*
Robin Ward and Richard Jenkins (eds.): *Ethnic communities in business*
Richard Jenkins: *Racism and recruitment: managers, organisations and equal opportunity in the labour market*
Roger Hewitt: *White talk black talk: inter-racial friendships and communication amongst adolescents*
Paul B. Rich: *Race and Empire in British politics*
Richard Jenkins and John Solomos (eds.): *Racism and equal opportunity policies in the 1980s*
John Rex and David Mason (eds.): *Theories of race and ethnic relations*
John Solomos: *Black youth, racism and the state: the politics of ideology and policy*
Colin Clarke, Ceri Peach and Steven Vertovec (eds.): *South Asians overseas*
Harry Goulbourne: *Ethnicity and nationalism in post-imperial Britain*

Ethnic minorities and industrial change in Europe and North America

Edited by
MALCOLM CROSS

CAMBRIDGE
UNIVERSITY PRESS

Published by the Press Syndicate of the University of Cambridge
The Pitt Building, Trumpington Street, Cambridge CB2 1RP
40 West 20th Street, New York, NY 10011–4211, USA
10 Stamford Road, Oakleigh, Victoria 3166, Australia

First published 1992

Printed and bound in Great Britain by
Woolnough Bookbinding Ltd, Irthlingborough, Northamptonshire

A catalogue record for this book is available from the British Library

Library of Congress cataloguing in publication data

Ethnic minorities and industrial change in Europe and North America /
edited by Malcolm Cross.
    p. cm. – (Comparative ethnic and race relations)
  Includes bibliographical references (p.   ) and index.
  ISBN 0–521–37244–5 (hardback)
  1. Minorities – Employment – Europe. 2. Minorities – Employment – North America.
3. Europe – Race relations. 4. North America – Race relations.
I. Cross, Malcolm. II. Series: Comparative ethnic and race relations series.
HD8378.5.A2E85 1992
331.6 – dc20   91–32091 CIP

ISBN 0 521 37244 5 hardback

CE

Contents

Part II   The city and the underclass

Illustrations

Figures

Maps

Tables

Notes on contributors

STEPHEN CASTLES is Director of the Centre for Multicultural Studies, University of Wollongong. His publications include *Immigrant Workers and Class Structure in Western Europe* (1985), *Here for Good: Western Europe's New Ethnic Minorities* (1984), and *Mistaken Identity: Multiculturalism and the Demise of Nationalism in Australia* (1988).

ROBIN COHEN is Professor of Sociology at the University of Warwick. His most recent books are *The New Helots: Migrants in the International Division of Labour* (1988) and *Contested Domains: Debates in International Labour Studies* (1991).

MALCOLM CROSS is Principal Research Fellow in the Centre for Research in Ethnic Relations, University of Warwick. His recent publications include *Work and the Enterprise Culture* (1991) and *Beyond Law and Order* (1991).

KAY EHLERS has published a number of articles on urban change and labour market issues with John D. Kasarda.

DAVID EVERSLEY is Professor of Population and Regional Studies at the University of Sussex; he was Chief Strategic Planner at the Greater London Council.

NORMAN FAINSTEIN is Dean of Social Sciences at Baruch College at the City University of New York. His books include *Urban Policy under Capitalism* (1982) with Susan Fainstein.

JÜRGEN FRIEDRICHS is Professor of Sociology at the University of Hamburg. He is the author of *The Changing Downtown: A Comparative Study of Baltimore and Hamburg* (1987) and the editor of *Affordable Housing and the Homeless* (1988).

CHRIS HAMNETT is Professor in the Faculty of Social Sciences at the Open University, UK. His publications include *The Future of Cities* (1974), *Fundamentals of Human Geography* (1978) and *City, Economy and Society* (1981). He co-authored *Cities, Housing and Profits* (1988) with Bill Randolph.

RICHARD CHILD HILL is Professor of Sociology and Urban Affairs at Michigan State University. His most recent book is *Detroit: Race and Uneven Development* (1988).

JOHN D. KASARDA is Kenan Professor and Chairman of the Department of Sociology at the University of North Carolina at Chapel Hill where he also serves as Director of the Center for Competitiveness and Employment Growth. His books include *The Metropolis Era* (1988) and *Structuring in Organizations* (1987).

CYNTHIA NEGREY is an Assistant Professor of Sociology at the University of Louisville in Louisville, Kentucky.

ANNIE PHIZACKLEA is Lecturer in Sociology at the University of Warwick. Her last book was *Unpacking the Fashion Industry* (1990).

CERI PEACH is Fellow of St Catherine's College and Lecturer in Geography at Oxford University where he is a member of the Ethnic Geography Research Group. He is author of *West Indian Migration to Britain* (1986) and co-editor of *South Asians Overseas* (1990) with Adrian Mayer, Colin Clarke and Steven Vertovec.

BILL RANDOLPH is the Principal Research Officer at the National Federation of Housing Associations in London. He has recently completed a doctoral thesis at the London School of Economics on labour market change and residential polarisation in inner London and he is co-author of *Cities, Housing and Politics* (1988).

ALISDAIR ROGERS is a Demonstrator at the School of Geography, Oxford University, where he also lectures at Keble College and Lady Margaret Hall. He is co-editor of *Hollow Promises, Policy, Theory and Practice in the Inner City* (1991) with Michael Keith.

ROGER WALDINGER was Associate Professor of Sociology at City College Graduate Center at the City University of New York and is now Professor at the University of California, Los Angeles. He is author of *Through the Eye of the Needle: Immigrants and Enterprise in New York's Garment Trades* (1986) and co-editor of *Ethnic Entrepreneurs: Immigrant Business in Industrial Societies* (1990) with Howard Aldrich and Robin Ward.

Preface and acknowledgements

The 1980s witnessed an unprecedented concern for efficiency, industrial enterprise and new forms of economic activity on both sides of the Atlantic. Partly to sustain and increase profitability, partly to build on new technologies and partly to contend with a new world economic order, the industrial landscape changed out of recognition. In the process, some groups benefited while others were forced to the margins of the labour market and into unemployment or poorly paid work. This book is concerned with whether there is any pattern to the downside of economic change and, if so, what it reveals, with particular reference to ethnic and racial minorities.

I am most grateful to the contributors to this book and to the Economic and Social Research Council whose financial support made it possible. I should also like to thank Rose Goodwin and Gurbakhsh Hundal for their skill and patience in preparing the manuscript for publication.

MALCOLM CROSS

Introduction: migration, the city and the urban dispossessed

A newcomer to the field of racial inequality and migration could be forgiven for thinking that the issues and problems emerging in the United States and Europe were so dissimilar as to warrant quite separate approaches. In the United States, until relatively recently, migration was regarded as highly significant only as the way by which the original workforce was established, but as having only marginal relevance to the great struggle for racial equality. Migration may have created a mosaic of cultures, but ethnic boundaries were perceived as softening as all surrendered to the American Dream. Even with the wakening of the 1960s, the issue was conceived as one of *civil rights* and not one of labour or class relations.

In Europe, by contrast, inward labour migration since the Second World War has generated what is sometimes called the 'thirteenth state' of Europe; 16 million migrants and their descendants from old colonial territories or poor countries on the European periphery whose arrival has not been an invitation to the 'European Dream'. On the contrary, they have been carefully introduced as the 'new helots' from whose labours opportunities have opened up for others.

While it is far too glib to suggest that in the United States migration created the powerful while in Europe it has generated the powerless, there can be no denying that the social structure of advanced capitalist economies on both sides of the Atlantic has come now to look more similar than hitherto. In the recent past, racism in Europe triggered thoughts of the Holocaust, while references to 'ethnic minorities' were taken to refer to Bretons or Basques but not to migrant workers and their descendants. Britain has been the exception to this generalisation, but even there few have been prepared to accept that the North American experience was of any great relevance.

The first central point of this book, therefore, is to argue against these prejudices and to suggest that a structural convergence has occurred, the main feature of which has been the generation of minorities identifiable both by their class position and by a variety of processes of social and political exclusion. Because of this, comparison becomes imperative. A related point is that these are emergent processes; that is, as the economies of Western industrial nations have become further enmeshed in a reordered global network of capital and labour movements, so too have the fortunes of minorities come to look increasingly alike. In the first part of the book, these similarities are described. The central argument is that as Western economies have shed manufacturing jobs they have marginalised and excluded those whose low-cost labour was used to prop up the vestiges of the production processes on which the last Industrial Revolution depended. The first sense, therefore, in which the term 'dispossessed' is being used is to refer to the virtual labour market exclusion of those whose origins lay in the sharecroppers of the southern states, or the plantations of the Caribbean, or the peasantries of the Indian subcontinent or the Mediterranean and those who migrated for work. What they have lost is the chance to continue working in their chosen locations, mostly in the industrial centres of the central and north-eastern United States or the old industrial heartlands of northern Europe.

Stated as baldly as this, the proposition sounds overly deterministic and complete. In fact, economies do not change in this simple way from a total dependence upon manufacturing to an equally complete reliance upon services and new technology. Manufacturing is itself reborn, either in a new form or by assuming the contours of low wages and low costs that have led to such massive industrialisation in the 'new Japans' of South-East Asia. 'Post-industrialisation' is no less incremental, partial and uneven than its predecessor. Thus some minorities are reincorporated back into the labour market through 'Third World' doors, but that process itself again confirms their subordinate status. Others are introduced for the first time as a new, low-level service class to provide food, cleaning and transport to oil the wheels of finance capitalism.

A second theme is that with economic restructuring has come an enhanced salience of *space*. Just as the Industrial Revolution forever changed the face of some cities, so too has the Post-Industrial Revolution done the same. The cities of today are sites of hi-tech production, capital circulation and consumption, but they have for the most part been grafted uneasily onto the cities of yesterday. The result is the emergence or re-emergence of that shadowy zone around the central business district identified as the 'inner city'.[1] It is, of course, within this *cordon insanitaire* that a very large proportion of non-white minorities are forced to live. There is then a second sense in which the term 'dispossessed' is being used.

It refers to those who are excluded from the fruits of *consumption* and
forced to live in poor housing, often on run-down, crime ridden estates,
where the level of public services and facilities simply serves to confirm
their exclusion and subordinate position.

Once again, however, this is not a deterministic or simple process.
There is plenty of evidence of variation in this depressing picture. Not all
minorities are in 'inner cities' and those that are are occupy a variety of
positions. Indeed, there is considerable evidence to suggest that in some of
the most 'post-industrial' cities, minorities have become increasingly
differentiated as some find themselves able to exploit hitherto closed
options for advancement while others sink into the so-called 'ghetto
underclass' (Cross and Waldinger 1992).

This book is not directly concerned with economic and social *policy* but
more with identifying the issues with which new policies will have to
contend. There is, however, one key debate that has emerged out of the
issues raised herein and for that reason some comment has been included.
The final chapters of this book refer to what has come to be called the
'underclass debate' and in the last part of this opening chapter some of the
issues in that debate are discussed.

Migration and production

On both sides of the Atlantic, the 1970s and 1980s have witnessed an
unprecedented decline in manufacturing both in terms of share of GDP
and, more particularly, in employment. But is deindustrialisation a
reversible process or are we witnessing a seed change in which the
domestic division of labour is being supplanted by a form of international
specialisation which will remove for ever manufacturing and possibly
some service jobs? Theorists of the New International Division of Labour
(NIDL) school have no doubts. These effects are both permanent and
coincidental with national boundaries. What this means is a new form of
specialisation in which whole nations can become proletarianised as they
assume the role of manufacturers of the increasingly sophisticated goods
demanded by Western consumers.

The chapter by Robin Cohen is a very important corrective to the
NIDL thesis. As he points out, the phrase 'division of labour' is itself used
in different ways, and the thesis fails to take account of the major
migratory labour movements. Not only have new migratory streams been
generated by the mushrooming economies of the Middle East, but there is
evidence of new waves of migrant labour being drawn into those economies from which jobs are also being lost. It is this which constitutes the
so-called 'New Migration' which is as characteristic of current economic

restructuring as exclusion from the manufacturing sector. Two questions arise from this analysis. The first is whether NIDL theory can be reconstituted to account for these apparently contradictory phenomena and, second, whether these processes imply that the exclusion of existing racial and ethnic minorities from employment is temporary. The critique of NIDL theory does not itself answer the latter question. It is perfectly possible for so-called 'new migrants' to take the low-level, often part-time, service jobs without improving the prospects of those languishing on the economic sidelines.

The European experience of recent migration suggests a considerable variation in the responses of national governments. On the one hand, the apparently *laissez-faire* – or at least *ad hoc* – policy making of the British state can be contrasted with the interventionist planning of what was West Germany. Stephen Castles makes the point, however, that while modern Germany represents an extreme case, the politicisation of race and ethnicity is a wider phenomenon. Faced with white electorates clamouring for solutions for what appear to be intractable economic problems, no European government has been prepared to promote racial equality with any degree of conviction. In the German case the implicit message from the Bundestag has been one of complicity with those wishing to blame the pains of restructuring on the 'foreigner problem'. This is, of course, no isolated case; other European Community governments, too, have found it convenient, when faced with a total of 15 million unemployed, to imply that if only the same number of migrant workers could be sent home then the problem would be solved. Racism is a response of the fearful and uncertain, and there can be few times more potentially fearful and uncertain than those facing Europe at the present time. In addition to the dislocations of massive economic change, the political turmoil at the end of the last decade has added a new twist. On top of job losses and new forms of labour demand, often fed by undocumented workers, we now have the possibility of massive waves of migration from the East as the log jam of state suppression gives way. Already there are signs that these effects will be felt on both sides. The release of poor workers to the West may well further displace Turkish, Moroccan and other Islamic minorities but not itself be of a sufficient magnitude to prevent the resurgence of anti-Semitism in Poland, Czechoslovakia, or the USSR.

Economic change of the magnitude that has affected Western societies from the mid-1970s has had a pronounced impact on social class. If the nineteenth-century revolution led to two major contenders for political power and economic dominance, then the Post-Industrial Revolution has led to fracturing and regrouping. In the process, traditional working-class allegiances have changed as the primary and secondary features of the labour market have become reconstituted into an array of new sub-classes and social movements. As Stuart Hall, commenting on the political aspirations of the left in Britain, put it:

> Divisions, not solidarities, of class identification are the rule. There are large and significant sectors of the 'working class' as it really is today – the unemployed, semi-skilled and unskilled, part-time workers, male and female, the low paid, black people, the 'underclasses' of Thatcherite Britain – who no longer see themselves in a traditional Labour Way.   (Hall 1988: 266)

As a result political parties and trade unions on the left have to contend with either trying to appeal to old loyalties across an increasingly wide divide in the working class, or with rethinking their principles to appeal to groups outside the traditional working class. Either way this poses political problems for ethnic minorities who, because of their economic position, are faced with the choice between working-class politics that are increasingly irrelevant to their needs, or 'new-class' politics in which there is no coherent agenda. As Castles shows, this is a fertile terrain for the growth of new versions of old tendencies to blame innocent victims. Given the recent history of European racism, it would be unwise not to be concerned about the potential dangers in this volatile mix.

Industrial restructuring

The two chapters by Hill and Negrey and by Cross can be read in parallel. Both attempt to examine the impact on minorities of changes in those sectors of the US and UK economies in which the winds of change have been at their strongest. In the industrial heartland of the US, black workers had attained a powerful presence in the automobile industry. Rationalisation, exported production and disinvestment have had a dramatic effect on all workers, but none more so than blacks and Hispanics. The figures are astounding. More than half the minority production workers in Detroit, for example, lost their jobs between 1979 and 1984 with the result that poverty rose rapidly, and in some parts of the city infant mortality rates came to rival those in Third World countries. What is quite clear, both here and in those parts of the UK where a comparable collapse in labour markets has occurred, is that these changes are non-reversible. It is perfectly true that economic fortunes since the mid-1980s have greatly improved but the *relative* position of black workers has remained at the level to which it sank in the darkest days of the recession. In the Michigan case there is official recognition that new jobs will neither be as numerous nor as appropriate for black and migrant labour as the old. Changes in the labour process, together with automation, will ensure that there will be no return to a seller's market in labour except for those with higher levels of training and skill than former employees possess.

Another phenomenon with important implications for minority workers is that restructured economies may regenerate manufacturing by promoting Third World conditions in First World locations. Annie Phizacklea argues, for example, that parts of the clothing industry in the UK are able to exploit a malleable, largely female, workforce which can rival in cost terms the sweatshops of South-East Asia. The flexibility of home working, for example, minimises costs by depressing wages and by allowing for fluctuations in demand without the necessity to retain labour. Where fashion wear is concerned the benefits of proximity and speedy responses outweigh the rock bottom prices of workers overseas. A particularly important feature of this phenomenon is that the reincorporation of workers into production is mediated by both race and gender. This demonstrates the important point made by Robin Cohen in his critique of NIDL theory: where race and gender combine to fracture working-class communities, the relocation imperative is controlled, but only at the cost of reproducing those very divisions in a more extreme form.

The post-industrial city

The fortunes of racial minorities in all settings appear to be intimately bound up with the future of the city. But the city itself is dramatically changing as Western economies are reorganising to exploit new technologies and to profit from, rather than be undermined by, the new centres of manufacturing enterprise that have emerged so powerfully in South-East Asia and elsewhere.

The residential concentration of recent migrants in urban centres is not a new phenomenon. Earlier twentieth-century movements of Jews, for example, from Eastern Europe have shown how the twin pressures of limited opportunity and choice, born partially out of a desire to defend cultural traditions, have had a concentrating effect in key locations. In the British, Dutch and French cases, migrant labour in the period after World War II has often succeeded earlier immigrants in exactly the same streets and neighbourhoods. As Ceri Peach shows in his survey of European migrant segregation, the key issue is not so much the level of separation in space but the corollary of poor housing and urban blight. Despite common features, however, Peach reminds us that the specific histories of each country and each constituent group can make a considerable difference. Thus, a danger exists of assuming there is a 'European' pattern, let alone one which is common to North America *and* Europe. It is true that migrants have been drawn from vastly different countries and have been attracted for different reasons. It is also clear that the societies into which migrants have been incorporated differ considerably. However, the clear-cut succession, which typified migration to North America in the early years of the twentieth century, is not so evident. Also, when we look at the *social* position of migrants, much greater degrees of similarity become apparent. The message is, therefore, that low socio-economic incorporation produces similar patterns of exclusion regardless of significant and important differences of culture, aspiration and political setting. What it does not account for is the level of segregation of groups from indigenous majorities or from other minorities. Thus the position of migrants as they become more or less permanent minorities can only be explained by reference to both ethnicity or group cohesion on the one hand, and socio-economic position on the other.

The economic position of American blacks has been well documented for many years. The similar position of many new minorities in Europe has only become evident in the 1980s. The chapter by Eversley, for example, draws on a new analysis of 1981 census data for the UK to demonstrate that the vast majority of Afro-Caribbeans and Asian minorities live in areas of severe urban deprivation. The critical point, however, is that older industrial areas, which did not attract migrants in the 1950s and 1960s, are equally deprived on all the normal indices. The poverty and joblessness of minorities is a function, therefore, of changes in the fortunes of the places into which they initially moved, compounded by well-known processes of racial and ethnic exclusion. Thus we cannot expect to understand what is happening to minorities now without an appreciation of changes in the economies of Western societies. In particular, the plight of minorities has been profoundly deepened with the uneven development in cities and major urban centres. But, once again, we are reminded that it is folly to assume that minorities are passive victims. Groups differ in the responses they make to these worsening conditions. Some will respond politically by taking up the cudgels for state intervention to mitigate the worst consequences of economic restructuring; some will fall back on strong religious and cultural traditions to try and achieve what others did before by capturing 'middlemen' niches and specialised opportunities that emerge in any period of rapid economic change.

This picture is well described for London by Hamnett and Randolph who again are able to draw on a recently available data source. What their longitudinal study shows is precisely this complex pattern generated by the interaction of economic change and ethnicity. In the first place, it is a mistake to assume that there is a simple relationship between economic decline and minority job loss. In the London case, for example, the secondary position of black workers in manufacturing appears to have protected them from some of the worst job-shedding associated with reorganisation. In other words, the new economies are not necessarily those in which there is no demand for low-level workers. On the other hand, the deindustrialisation process lowers the proportion of total jobs in manufacturing and thus exposes those hitherto dependent on this sector to the potentially dangerous task of finding alternative economic activity. Afro-Caribbean women, for example, have led the movement into alternative jobs, but there is little evidence to suggest a move out of a secondary labour market position. What has happened is that ethnic minority women, particularly those of Afro-Caribbean origin, have pioneered the general change to more female employment, albeit part-time and poorly paid. While it is true, therefore, that economic restructuring has tended to dispossess minorities of their original economic positions, this does not mean that they have all been equally effected. There is strong evidence, for example, that those Asians who came to Britain as a result of the expulsion from East Africa have drawn on their entrepreneurial skills and community loyalties to seek out and exploit the opportunities generated by major economic reorganisation (cf. Cross and Waldinger 1992).

Arguments over the 'New Migration' have focussed on the so called 'global cities', or centres of the world economy which have the special role of lubricating the flow of information and providing financial services. Roger Waldinger demonstrates that in the case of New York at least two separable processes have been at work. Whites have left the city faster than the jobs they formerly occupied, with the effect of opening up opportunities for non-white labour. In the public sphere some native blacks have been the beneficiaries, but in private business new migrants from South-East Asia have gained employment. At the bottom, however, there has been a growth of menial jobs which have largely gone to the remaining new migrants – those from Puerto Rico, Haiti and the Dominican Republic. In other words, post-industrial transformation has led to a fracturing of minority groups themselves into a complex ethnic division of labour. This would not be predicted by most existing theory which tends to assume that all ethnic minority groups are equally displaced, or that all are destined to become the new helots in a polarised class structure. The fact that the picture is considerably more complex should not detract, however, from the critical point that for most native black Americans the post-industrial economy of New York has exacerbated their plight on the margins of a rapidly changing labour market.

The chapter by Alisdair Rogers makes it quite clear that the 'fourth wave' migration to the United States is quite unlike that which went before. In one sense, it is more akin to the post-war migration to Britain in which it was possible to identify a middle-class stream, mostly from India into the health service, and a much larger movement into very low-level, poorly paid jobs. The current inward movement is into the west and south-west sunbelts of America. The migration is also bimodal with Indians and Koreans finding niches in the burgeoning topography of silicon valleys, while the Mexican and Caribbean workers soak up these new menial jobs. The movements are urban but not 'inner city'. Rather, these new migrants find their way into suburbia where they generate business, rather than residential, enclaves. Unlike Peach, then, Rogers is more persuaded by the economic determinants of residential locations. What is particularly important about this phenomenon is that rather than seeing 'ethnicity' and 'class' as alternative perspectives in accounting for spatial distributions, ethnicity is understood as emergent in those locations where it mediates class relations. In other words, it is essential to view these two bases of structured division and inequality together and to explore their interrelations.

The underclass debate

While it is quite apparent, therefore, that all minorities are not affected in the same ways by industrial reorganisation, and that new migrants are incorporated at different levels, it is also clear that a significant proportion of native black Americans, and a growing proportion of some minorities in Britain, and possibly the rest of Europe, are becoming trapped in conditions of increasing poverty. In both Britain and North America there has been a reluctance by researchers to recognise this fact for fear of rekindling the 'culture of poverty' debate initiated in the 1960s by Daniel Moynihan (1965 and 1970). The vacuum created by this timidity was initially filled by those seeking to provide intellectual justification for the rolling back of the 'nanny state'. The most important example of this thinking was in the work of Charles Murray, whose book *Losing Ground* (1984) revived an earlier debate on the so-called 'urban underclass'. This is an important contribution which specifically challenges the central approach of this book. To Murray, the emerging evidence on the so-called 'underclass', or those who are termed here the 'dispossessed', signifies a change in family patterns and styles of parenting rather than a product of economic change. His initial statement stimulated a response by William J. Wilson (1987) which built on an earlier book showing the degree to which civil rights legislation in the United

States had stimulated class divisions within black America. Since the last two essays in this book offer extensions and correctives to Wilson's position, it is important to identify the main parameters of the debate itself.

Charles Murray's argument is that there are three key indicators of the underclass condition. These are, first, the levels of illegitimacy, the incidence of violent crime and the extent of labour market withdrawal. Illegitimacy is taken as an indicator of weak family life and poor parenting, which is itself thought to be a cause of violent crime and low labour market commitment. In other words, the other two indicators are *outcomes* of the underclass condition. Crime and unemployment do not create an underclass; rather, they are the way by which we know it.

As a later development of Murray's approach, where he seeks to apply it to Britain, makes clear, there are three key theses bound up in these propositions. The first is moral. It is to suggest that old distinctions between 'roughs' and 'respectables' are still salient; indeed, that they are more salient today than before because some forces, largely unspecified but linked to the family (weak parenting), have increased the proportion of the 'roughs', or those whose values differ from those of the Protestant ethic. Thus, it is how people *react* to their circumstances which is important, rather than the circumstances themselves:

> When I use the term 'underclass' I am indeed focussing on a certain type of poor person defined not by his condition, e.g. long-term unemployed, but by his deplorable behaviour in response to that condition, e.g. unwilling to take the jobs that are available to him.   (Murray 1990: 68)

A second thesis, quite unrelated to the first, suggests that the problem is related to how people behave when confronted by certain opportunities created by state intervention. For example, he dismisses the notion that his is a 'culture of poverty' thesis on the grounds that members of the underclass are not culturally delinquent. On the contrary, they are perfectly rational because what they are doing is exploiting opportunities (wrongly) put before them:

> How can people read my extensive descriptions of causation, all of which focus on the ways in which members are responding sensibly (at least in the short term) to policies that have been put in place around them, and then cite surveys regarding a 'culture of poverty' to refute me?   (Murray 1990: 69)

But, of course, not *all* members of the lower class do behave in this way, so the important question is why some do. We are back then to the moral theory of what poverty is.

The final element that Murray puts forward, but which is never developed in the main argument, is that environmental factors are crucial. Thus, we need to disaggregate national, or even regional, data since he argues ' … there is an ecology to poverty'. It follows from this that:

> Cross-sectional surveys of poor people or of the unemployed that detail population parameters are useless in either confirming or disconfirming this hypothesis.   (Murray 1990: 69)

In other words, the issue of the underclass is intimately bound up with a spatial analysis. The underclass is a community of delinquents rather than a social scientist's statistical creation. It is indeed true that in Britain most of the opponents of this view take a very traditional view of that poverty. Some, indeed, have simply co-opted the term 'underclass' to direct attention to those whose condition is weakest. Murray's argument is that there is a difference of *type*, rather than of degree.

Not unsurprisingly, a thesis which justifies the removal of state support on the apparent grounds that some cities possess within them communities which are by their nature composed of the feckless and amoral has stimulated a lively response. These fall into two main camps. There are those who deny the existence of the 'underclass' and those who accept that the term refers to an identifiable phenomenon but who oppose the aetiology which Murray advances. The evidence for the first approach hinges on whether or not the changes that Murray identifies are not simply part of more general social processes. For example, children across the social spectrum are increasingly born to parents who are not married; single parenting is as much a phenomenon of easier divorce as it is of non-marriage, and the white-collar crime rate is growing at least as fast as 'inner city crime'. Moreover, the reputed lack of enthusiasm for work, formerly most noticeable among the upper classes, has permeated down to the growing ranks of the prematurely 'retired' or 'resting' members of the middle classes, and is not simply a function of the poor. Indeed, one could argue that the association between work and wealth has never been so tenuous; many in employment fall well below the poverty line (however defined) while many above it have eschewed work for years while being fit and of pre-retirement age.

The second line of approach accepts that a new form of poverty has evolved but rejects the arguments put forward by Murray to explain it. It is here that William J. Wilson's thesis on what is occurring in the US is highly salient. Unlike other critics, his approach is premised on the collapse of specifically black 'inner city' communities:

> In the early years, the black middle and working classes were confined by restrictive covenants to communities also inhabited

> by the lower class; their very presence provided stability to inner city neighborhoods and reinforced and perpetuated mainstream patterns of norms and behavior.   (Wilson 1987: 7)

In this sense the modest advances made by the Civil Rights Act are responsible for leaderless communities; the ghetto might have been prevented if segregation had been sustained. This is one reason why Wilson's analysis is as controversial as Murray's.

Wilson cites as evidence of increasing ghetto problems the rise in births outside marriage and the proportion of families headed by women. In 1965, 25 per cent of black births were outside marriage; by 1980 the figure was 57 per cent. In 1965 a quarter of black families were headed by a woman; by 1980, the proportion was 43 per cent. Wilson also uses criminal data: ' ... the rate of black imprisonment in 1984 was 6.25 times greater than the rate of white imprisonment' (1987: 22). He singles out the demographic structure of inner urban communities as a relevant factor, too. Blacks are much younger on average than whites and it is amongst the young that most of the indices used to identify the so-called 'underclass' are at their highest.

It is the level of joblessness, however, that gives rise to increases in the proportion of children born to single mothers since, as unemployment rises, the proportion of marriageable men falls. When this is combined with differential imprisonment rates and rates of mortality that are higher than for whites, the numbers of black males falls still further. This process has been confused because the proportion of children in households headed by a woman has risen for white women, too. What Wilson argues, however, is that the aetiology of this phenomenon is quite different. For white women, the employment status of their menfolk is not the most important factor in determining marriage rates; rather, they are responding to opportunities for independence which arise from their improving occupational position. This is further shown by rates of remarriage and by earlier ages at first marriage:

> That the employment status of white males is not a major factor in white single motherhood or female-headed families can perhaps also be seen in the higher rate of remarriage among white women and the significantly earlier age of first marriage. By contrast, the increasing delay of first marriage and the low rate of remarriage among black women seem to be directly tied to the increasing labor-force problems of men.   (1987: 83–4)

It is these effects, rather than the consequences of welfare payments, which have devastated black families. A second key component of

Wilson's theory is that black Americans are increasingly divided by social class. As some upward mobility occurs amongst former ghetto residents, it is accompanied by suburban movement. The result is that those left behind are not only impoverished; they are also leaderless and isolated from the contacts which might permit opportunities to be realised:

> ... in a neighborhood with a paucity of regularly employed families and with the overwhelming majority of families having spells of long-term joblessness, people experience a social isolation that excludes them from the job network system that permeates other neighborhoods and that is so important in learning about or being recommended for jobs that become available in various parts of the city.   (1987: 57)

The thesis clearly implies that areas themselves make a difference. Blacks are in areas of concentrated trauma, cut off from contact with others whose example could redirect them towards avenues of greater hope and possibility:

> Unlike poor urban whites or even inner city blacks of earlier years, the residents of highly concentrated poverty neighborhoods in the inner city today not only infrequently interact with those individuals or families who have had a stable work history and have had little involvement with welfare or public assistance, they also seldom have sustained contact with friends or relatives in the more stable areas of the city or in the suburbs.
> (1987: 60)

He is particularly emphatic about separating this analysis from 'culture of poverty' arguments. The latter predispose governments to intervene directly to change behaviour. On the other hand he writes:

> The increasing social isolation of the inner city is a product of the class transformation of the inner city, including the growing concentration of poverty in inner-city neighborhoods. And the class transformation of the inner city cannot be understood without considering the effects of fundamental changes in the urban economy on the lower-income minorities, effects that include joblessness and that thereby increase the chances of long-term residence in highly concentrated poverty areas.
> (1987: 61–2)

In other words, the effects are cumulative and additive. Initial patterns of concentration, dictated by housing availability and employment chances, become ecological prisons as opportunities melt away in the face of profound transformations to urban political economy. The bars preventing social mobility are educational, while spatial movement is effectively excluded by poverty, social isolation and fear of the unknown and the unknowable.

It is important that Wilson does not regard the solution to these problems as likely to emanate from race-specific policies. Rather, race-specific policies open up opportunities to those who are in a position to benefit from lower barriers to advancement. Indeed, he accuses social scientists of being preoccupied with the argument that racism is the overwhelming problem to be resolved in combating racial inequality. His critique falls into two parts. First, since black poverty is much worse than before, this must mean that racism is worse at a time when all relevant measures show that some black Americans are better off than ever before. Second, the argument cannot account for emergent differentials between ethnic groups. In other words, the explanation must lie with causes that are specific to the urban poor, or those parts of it that are being worst affected.

> ... some liberals completely avoid any discussion of these problems, some eschew terms such as *underclass*, and others embrace selective evidence that denies the very existence of an underclass and behavior associated with the underclass or rely on the convenient term *racism* to account for the sharp rise in the rates of social dislocation in the inner city. The combined effects of these tendencies is to render liberal arguments ineffective and to enhance conservative arguments on the underclass ... (1987: 12)

By refusing to accept the emergence of the dispossessed, social scientists have left the terrain open to be filled by those campaigning for the minimal state and for cuts in welfare expenditure.

William Wilson's argument is clearly relevant to the central themes of this book. Although it is not a central part of his thesis, he borrows from another US author a parallel argument on the apparent 'mismatch' between urban jobs and the qualifications of those nearest to undertake them (Kasarda 1985). If cities are compared in terms of the education required for the jobs they contain, this shows a decline in low-education jobs relative to others. If blacks have low educational levels then they must be disadvantaged by this process.

The chapter by John Kasarda and his co-authors carries this debate forward onto a specifically international canvas. In comparing the US and Germany, Kasarda and his co-authors reveal very considerable similarities in the mismatch between new jobs and those who are unemployed, particularly those from a minority background. Moreover, the 'mismatch' argument is developed to account for the apparently puzzling fact that racial minorities are not as mobile as their recent history would suggest they might be in moving after the decentralising jobs. This raises the key policy question of what keeps the underclass going in the absence of regular employment. The answer they suggest is the growth of an informal economy and the existence of the welfare state. We are once again back into an area of crucial policy importance. If welfare provision, intended to ameliorate poverty and despair, leads to the maintenance of urban ghettos, then clearly it may be time for a review. It is one thing, however, to suggest the unanticipated functions of welfare; quite another to propose solutions which are equally humane but which stimulate recovery and revival.

There seems little doubt that some new jobs in cities are unlike those that preceded them. It is by no means clear, however, that as service jobs take over a pre-eminent position from those in manufacturing, they *necessarily* become more skilled. Indeed, the evidence suggests that a good proportion of jobs in the financial sector or in information technology are as low skilled or as mundane as any that went before. Sassen-Koob, for example, has shown how expansion of low-level jobs in high technology sectors of the New York economy has led to new immigration from the Caribbean and Asia (Sassen-Koob 1983 and 1984). It is also unclear why welfare payments should have the effect of lessening the wish to migrate internally, since in many countries they are available nationally so that city centre residence does not confer any special benefits. What is clear, and undisputed, is that minorities are likely to benefit from high-level, relevant training programmes. It is perhaps dangerous to regard the 'people' or 'places' argument as exclusive. The mismatch of people and jobs is both a quantitative and qualitative phenomenon.

The other line of critique which can be developed from the underclass debate concerns the relevance of race-specific policies. Is there not a danger that in moving away from the argument that racism is a key factor, we shall inadvertently maintain major racial differentials in access to both spheres of production and consumption? As Fainstein argues, unemployment rates for blacks are higher than for whites, even when controlling for skill levels. Blacks do much less well in terms of income and life style whether they live in or outside the inner city. Moreover, many of the supposed benefits which are claimed to have been set in train by the Civil Rights Act turn out to have benefited whites as well as blacks, leaving more or less intact the relative disadvantage with which the latter have to contend.

The answer to this conundrum is surely to suggest that racial equality is proving elusive partly because it is not being pursued with vigour on either side of the Atlantic, and also because it is a more complex phenomenon that has hitherto been realised. In addition to the continuation of high, and in some cases growing, levels of racism, racial minorities have been funnelled into particular class locations. They have also become deeply affected by economic restructuring which has imposed a new 'spatial division of labour' on advanced capitalist economies. This has tended to redistribute resources of consumption as well as production so that the quality of life has come to be as much influenced by *where* you live and work as by *what* work you do. Thus 'race', 'class' and 'place' are the triple buttresses to the inequalities of opportunity and outcome from which minorities suffer. It follows that progress on one front would need to be complemented by equal advances on the other two if genuine gains are to be made.

The coming of post-industrial cities within the restructured economies of Western capitalism is hardly good news, therefore, for established racial and ethnic minorities. Some new opportunities have opened up, but the overwhelming impression is one of double dispossession. Restructuring has had profound effects on the availability of the very jobs that blacks and migrant workers came to occupy. This is the primary reason for the continuation of high levels of unemployment in such groups. Where jobs have been regenerated, however, they are either in the most poorly paid, unprotected and irregular sectors of the economy, in which case they are filled by minority women or new migrants, or they are available in geographical zones or at skill levels which put them beyond the reach of the minority poor.

The picture is, then, one in which the post-industrial transformation is accompanied by new forms of social mobility opening up for some identifiable minorities *together with* the progressive exclusion of others as they appear to be increasingly marginal to the needs of the new economy. A key question that this raises is whether the welfare machinery set up to counteract the inequalities which appear to have been inherent in the development of earlier periods of industrialisation can apply unchanged to the new citizens of the industrial cities.

Note

1 The term 'inner city' is far from being ideologically neutral. For example, in many countries it has become a coded way of referring to areas of black and minority concentration (see Cross and Keith 1991).

Part I

Migration and economic
restructuring

1

Migration and the new international division of labour

Introduction

In this chapter, I will summarise a critique of theories of the new international division of labour developed elsewhere (Cohen 1987) before turning directly to issues of migration. It is perhaps important to emphasise that my critique is not meant as a total refutation of the pioneering work of Ernst (1980) or Fröbel and his colleagues (1980). Their work was crucial in recognising that global shifts in production facilities, particularly to South-East Asia, had fundamentally altered the shape and contours of the contemporary world economy. Indeed, the casual traveller to the four 'golden economies' of Asia – Hong Kong, Taiwan, Singapore and Korea – cannot fail to be impressed by the sudden evidence of modernity and industrialisation. Even using the appellation 'Third World' of such places sounds absurd, particularly when one is conscious of the transformation of great sections of the old industrial boom cities – like Cleveland, Detroit, Birmingham or Liverpool – into depressed slums and economic wastelands. Clearly, an economic transformation of some magnitude is taking place, as investment patterns alter and industrial plant becomes spatially redistributed.

Fröbel and his associates referred to this transformation as 'the new international division of labour' (henceforth NIDL). Their theory drew implicitly or explicitly on Warren's (1980) attack on dependency theory, on Wallerstein's (1979 and elsewhere) world systems analysis and, to a lesser degree, on the depiction of 'peripheral capitalism' suggested by Amin (1974).

The NIDL thesis

Taking over the vocabulary of world systems analysis, the NIDL theorists argued that industrial capital from the core was moving to the periphery as 'world-market factories' were established producing manufactured goods destined *for export*. The strategy of export-orientated manufacturing from newly industrialising countries, (NICs), was also adopted as an alternative to import-substitution strategies of development, which were held to have failed Third World countries. The movement of capital away from the core industrial countries was, in turn, necessitated by the difficulties in securing and realising high profits – as industrial conflict, increased reproduction costs and the growing organisation of migrant communities prevented the attainment of high levels of exploitation. These difficulties were particularly evident in European countries, where, at the beginning of the 1970s, the initial economic advantages that accrued to employers by importing large numbers of migrant workers, rapidly began to erode. On the one hand, many Third World countries had large supplies of cheap, unorganised labour. The oversupply of labour-power had occurred with the commoditisation of agriculture (accelerated by technological innovations like the 'green revolution'). As the rural poor were pushed off the land, unemployment, underemployment and, for some, the process of full proletarianisation had resulted. The NIDL theorists further observed that technical and managerial developments in the labour process now allowed the effective use of peripheral labour-power. The increasingly minute division of labour permitted the reorganisation of unskilled and semi-skilled tasks. With a minimal level of training, levels of productivity soon matched or exceeded metropolitan levels. The movement of manufacturing capital to parts of the periphery was also accelerated by an investment climate made more attractive by government policies. A number of governments in the Third World passed laws restricting the organisation and bargaining power of the unions. They provided freedom from planning and environmental controls, poor, and therefore cheap, health and safety standards, permission to repatriate profits without restriction, tax holidays and in some cases, like Singapore, a powerful paternal state, which seemed to guarantee political stability. At the level of transport and communications, international facilities had dramatically improved in the form of containerised shipping, cheap air cargo, and computer, telex and satellite links. Especially in the case of low-bulk, high-value goods, with a high value added at the point of production, it was often no longer necessary for the site of production to be near the end-market. Examples of goods of this kind include electrical or electronic goods, toys, shoes and clothes. Finally, the world market factories could be staffed predominantly by young women, who were particularly prone to exploitation given the difficulties of organising a group characteristically under patriarchal dominance and with a limited commitment to life-time wage labour (see Fröbel *et al.* 1980; Elson and Pearson 1981; Henderson and Cohen 1982; Henderson 1985).

In short, it looked as if metropolitan employers, having been frustrated in their countries in fully exploiting imported migrant labour, had alighted on another strategy. The import of cheap labour could be replaced by the export of capital. The empirical demonstration of the thesis was supported by some convincing data (Fröbel *et al.* 1980; 275, 276–90) from Federal Germany. After 1959, when restrictions on German companies investing abroad were lifted, a steep increase in the amount of direct foreign investment began to be noticed – from DM 3,291 million in 1961, to DM 19,932 million in 1971 and to DM 47,048 million in 1976. However, this investment did not, in general, represent a net expansion of German capitalist development on a world scale, but rather the integration of new sites and the relocation of certain manufacturing processes previously reserved for domestic manufacturing. Within Germany, this was bound to have consequences for the number of jobs available. A small rise over the period 1967 to 1973 was followed by a sudden drop of nearly a million jobs over the next three years. However, the loss of domestic jobs coincided with an *increase* in turnover and profit for key German firms. Simultaneously, an estimate for the number of jobs created abroad by German manufacturing firms by 1976 was 1.5 million. Fröbel and his colleagues (1980: 287) are properly cautious in saying that these figures alone 'do not allow us to deduce the extent to which employment abroad has replaced employment in Germany', but the inference is none-theless there for all to read. By the pattern of imports of manufactured goods, by the statements of the companies themselves and through an examination of the free production zones in Third World countries, we are led ineluctably to the conclusion that capital has migrated in search of its own comparative advantage, especially in respect of labour-power costs, and at the expense of domestic and imported workers, whose job chances have been correspondingly diminished.

The picture drawn by the NIDL theorists seemed to confirm observable reality in the NICs and also presents a powerful explanation for industrial decline in the other old centres. Part of the work undertaken by Henderson and myself (1982) on international restructuring was a replication study using British data. The basic contours of the German experience were evident, the ratio of overseas investment by British capital compared to the rate of investment within Britain (as measured by net domestic fixed capital formation) moving from 3:1 in 1969 to 4:1 by 1980. Again, although it is difficult to separate out the many factors producing unemployment (including government policy, automation, the loss of

international competitiveness and underinvestment), there is evidence to
suggest that in Britain, as in Germany, key firms added to their payroll
overseas while cutting their workforce in Britain. Thus, an ILO report
(1981: 82), surveying the operations of 118 major British firms over the
period 1971–5, showed that they had added 250,000 employees to their
payrolls abroad compared to only 80,000 in the UK. As the study
concluded, 'employment-wise they were clearly growing much faster
abroad than at home, both in absolute and relative terms'. The US also
revealed a similar picture. Bluestone and Harrison (1982) found that
between 1968 and 1976 there was a loss of approximately 15 million jobs
as a result of plant closures. The closures partly resulted from technological changes, but managers also saw the transfer of production abroad as
an attractive alternative to production at home, as risk was diversified,
greater control over labour was achieved and they could take advantage
of large international wage differentials (Nash and Fernandez-Kelly
1983: ix).

While accepting that NIDL theory provides a major key to understanding some of the processes of capital accumulation in the modern world
order, there are nonetheless some major limitations and omissions that
inhere in the theory. I will concentrate my critique of NIDL theory on
three aspects. First, *conceptual problems* – where I shall argue that the
variety of meanings attaching to the phrase 'division of labour' makes it
difficult to understand what precise phenomena are under investigation.
Second, *historical gaps* – where I maintain that NIDL theorists have
ignored or misconceived the historical evolution and successive phases of
the international division of labour. And third, *empirical omissions* –
where I shall show that NIDL theory tends to concentrate attention
exclusively on the growth of the manufacturing sector in the periphery,
ignoring other forms of restructuring, in peripheral and core countries
alike. These are best measured by shifts in labour, rather than shifts in
capital. This comment will serve to introduce my discussion on migration.

Critique of the NIDL thesis

When trying to understand the phrase, 'the new international division of
labour', it is necessary first to unscramble the good deal of conceptual
ambiguity arising in the prior expression, 'the division of labour'. The
notion has been used very differently to explain different phenomena. In
its earliest usage, it often was pressed into service to distinguish what are
now described as sectoral divisions in the economy – divisions, for
example, between industry, agriculture and services. It was used also to
define the occupational and skill structure of the labour force and the

differences between skilled and unskilled labourers, masters and appren-
tices, craftsmen and production workers. Additionally, the division of
labour referred to the organisation of tasks, characteristically dictated by
the management. Who is in the workplace, who is on the line, who is in
the office, who minds the machines and who sweeps the floors? Though
related to skill and occupational structure, the detailed specification of
tasks is by no means coincidental with skill as Braverman's (1974) contribution on the process of 'deskilling' testifies. To these three original
meanings of 'the division of labour' have been added others of more
recent vintage. First, the gender or racial division of labour – indicating
the new sensitivity to the ethnic composition of the labour force and to the
role of women in production and reproduction (Pahl 1984: 254–76).
Second, the spatial division of production and product (an aspect of the
division of labour which it may be argued is far from 'new'). And third,
perhaps the latest meaning attaching to the notion, the contracting out of
some elements of the production processes to well outside the factory
gates – into domestic, peasant or household units.

The changing definitions and meanings of the phrase 'division of
labour' impel different discussions and have different implications of a
more practical and political nature. For example, if it is argued that the
putting out system has now revived on an international scale and constitutes an important new feature of capitalist production, feminists who
argue for a politics of the home and of reproduction would have a strong
case against those who argue for a politics of the factory – from which
production would be putatively or potentially disappearing. Equally, if
the manufacturing sector in Third World countries is as significant a
feature of contemporary capitalism as the NIDL theorists argue, the
whole structure of workers' resistance to capital will have to undergo a
massive lateral shift if it is to succeed. This is particularly the case when
the question of international solidarity is considered. Metropolitan
workers are confronted with two diametrically opposed strategies. On the
one hand, a more nationalist posture would argue for the preservation of
jobs at home by the erection of high tariff walls and import duties
designed to keep out Third World manufacturers. On the other hand, an
internationalist position would dictate that bonds of solidarity should be
effected between metropolitan workers and Third World workers already
employed in branch plants so as to restrict the manœuvrability of multinational capital and spread the benefits of employment equally between
the participant partners.

In short, even only taking two possible meanings of 'the division of
labour' we end up with strongly differing pictures of the changing battle
lines between the old contestants, 'capital' and 'labour'. There is, of

course, no need logically to admit only one meaning of the division of labour as valid, but even if one accepts that a variety of meaning has now legitimately accrued to a particular label, this raises the posterior question of the relative weight, or significance, between the different phenomena grouped under this particular label. The last question is superficially one amenable to empirical enquiry – but behind the empirical question lies a paradox which inheres in the measurements so far characteristically deployed to evaluate changes in the international division of labour. The NIDL theorists use as their predominant data aggregate trade and investment figures – i.e. they use measures of the migration of *capital* to measure changes in the division of *labour*. This method can lead to some very misleading impressions. For example, it is likely that changes in the location of manufacturing enterprises are far less important in terms of employment (and in terms of profit) than changes between sectors (in particular the movement from industry and agriculture, to services and information) within the metropolitan economies. The possibilities for the deployment of subordinate and migrant sections of the metropolitan labour force in the service sector would thereby be easily and misleadingly missed. There does seem to be a case, on empirical as well as conceptual grounds, for using measurements of the movement of *labour* to indicate changes in the division of *labour*. In my discussion on migration below I point to additional sectors (in the oil-rich countries and in the service and sweatshop sectors of 'world cities') where significant employment of subordinate and professional labour-power has taken place without this being able to be easily accommodated in NIDL theory.

Not only is the use of movements of capital a limited means of understanding divisions of labour, the NIDL theorists have also imposed a self-denying ordinance in limiting their conceptual progenitors to nineteenth-century political economy. Thus they list as their mentors Adam Smith, Charles Babbage and Andrew Ure (Fröbel *et al.* 1980: 37–44). In addition to these three figures, NIDL theorists depend on another classical theory to underpin their argument – namely, Ricardo's basic law of comparative advantage. Ricardo's law can be simply stated as follows: the pattern of international trade is dependent on the principle of comparative labour costs 'which states that if two countries, A and B, entered into trade relations, each capable of producing commodities X and Y, A would sell the commodity in which its relative (rather than absolute) cost was lower and correspondingly B would sell the commodity in which its own comparative cost is low' (Bagchi 1982: 16).

This conceptual dependence on classical political economy unfortunately brings in its baggage train the limits of this tradition. In the nineteenth century, the state was not a significant actor on the industrial scene and again, in NIDL theory, it virtually disappears – except in the Third World case, where it appears only as a *bourgeoisie manquée* having to kowtow to the overwhelming power of metropolitan capital. In the nineteenth century, with the major exception of Marx, the rising power of the working class was ignored in economic theory. Again, this feature of the classical tradition reproduces itself in NIDL theory, with the social and political relations that surround the production process being almost wholly neglected in favour of discussion of aggregate trade and investment transactions, which reflect the power of capital. All that happens can, in such a view, be explained by the logic of capital without seriously taking into account independent institutional forces, the contradictions between merchants, national capitalists, transnationals and governments, or the political and social protests by those who fall victim to the logic of capital. Inter- and intra-class conflict within and between metropolitan and Third World societies hardly make an appearance.

A second critique of NIDL theory lies in its historical insensitivity. Proponents of the theory make a rather curious conceptual leap from nineteenth-century classical political economy to the late twentieth century – almost as if nothing of any great moment has happened over the last 100 years. It appears that NIDL theorists boarded a time-machine in the mid-nineteenth century to arrive at Hong Kong and Singapore late last night, without bothering to land at any of the intermediate airports – notably those marked on the historical maps as 'Imperialism' and 'Colonialism'. On prima-facie grounds, it would seem appropriate to assume that imperialism and colonialism had something to do with the evolution of the present-day international division of labour. Indeed, as I argue in an earlier paper (Cohen 1987), the historical patterns established by prior international divisions of labour are so much part of our contemporary reality that the distinction between the 'new' and 'old' international division of labour is not a very useful one. For this reason it is preferable to use the expression 'the *changing* international division of labour'.

Within this changing division of labour, from the point of view of the form of capital hegemonic in each phase, four sequential phases can be identified – the mercantile, industrial, imperial and transnational divisions of labour. The features of these phases are specified in detail in my earlier work already referred to. Here, five points can simply be noted by way of summary:

- First, the supposedly novel features of the contemporary division of labour to which the NIDL theorists draw attention are not really so novel. Even in the mercantile period, production sites were located abroad and elements of a global labour market were created and reproduced.

- Second, the appellation 'new' is further misleading in that it fails to recognise the indelible heritage of the past. Thus, it is more than plausible to argue that the mercantile, industrial and imperial phases have left deep scars on the face of the global population and production facilities. That there are Africans in the Caribbean and the US, Italians in Brazil and Indians in South Africa is a more salient and determinant datum informing the workings of modern capitalism than that export-processing zones have begun to employ Third World labourers.
- Third, there is a sense of a logical succession between the phases mentioned. Just as conventional Marxism adduces a logical end to successive modes of production as antagonistic contradictions emerge which make a prior mode obsolete, so an analogous sequence can be found in the case of the historical phases of the international division of labour.
- Fourth, and again the analogy with Marxist theory holds, there is a good deal of overlap between the sequential phases. This is obviously because once populations are displaced for reasons appropriate to one phase in the international division of labour, it is near impossible to return them (like the legendary genie) to the bottles from whence they came. The forms of labour deployed in an earlier phase thus continue to operate into the next phase or phases.
- Fifth, the current phase of the division of the labour (i.e. the transnational phase) should be conceived as embracing a number of different forms of labour utilisation not adequately depicted in NIDL theory. These all have implications for the patterning of migration flows.

The transnational division of labour: implications for migration

The phrase 'transnational division of labour' is used here to include the so-called NIDL, but is also wider than that. Essentially, this is the phase of the changing international division of labour marked by the collapse of the European colonial empires in the wake of the Second World War and the rise of transnational capital. The humiliating defeat of the European powers in Asia, the strength of the anti-colonial movements and the growth of competitive capital centred in the US, and later in Japan, hastened the end of the imperial order. The transnational phase left in place some neo-colonial relationships (which the French held on to notably better than the other European powers), but also led to a major restructuring of industrial production in the metropoles (allied to the importation of migrant labour) and the further internationalisation of leading fractions of capital, particularly the oil giants, the car companies and those firms producing consumer durables, electrical goods and electronic components.

In the post-1945 period, migration patterns have taken four main directions. First, the importation of large numbers of Third World workers to the European countries and to North America over the period 1945–75. Second, an internal movement of migrants within the Third World following long-established rural-to-urban routes, but now also directed to finding employment in the export-oriented industries in the NICs. Third, managerial, professional and unskilled labour attracted to the oil-rich countries to service the large-scale development projects which were initiated because of the new-found wealth of these countries. Fourth, and finally, recently noted growth of service employment in some metropolitan cities (so-called 'world cities') linked both to changes in the internal labour market and to illegal and contract migration.

The first mentioned migratory direction (from Third World to metropolitan country) is well covered in the established literature (Castles and Kosack 1985; Piore 1979; Power 1979). It needs no particular amplification here, other than to note that the lines of migration tended to follow earlier patterns of dominance established in prior international divisions of labour. Thus within Europe, migrants to France were often drawn from *départements*, colonies or ex-colonies like Algeria, Vietnam, Guadeloupe and Senegal. Britain drew its migrant labour-power predominantly from the West Indies, India and Pakistan, while The Netherlands attracted more than half the population of Surinam and substantial numbers from Indonesia and its other former colonies in the East Indies. By contrast, those labour-importing European countries without colonies (such as Germany and Switzerland) usually drew their migrants from poorer adjacent countries, a pattern observable, too, in respect of the US and its surrounding poorer periphery to the south and east. By the mid-seventies, migration of this type had outlived its usefulness for metropolitan employers and had engendered fierce political and social contestation with sections of the indigenous populations, particularly in Europe. The state responded by imposing severe immigration restrictions in all European countries, thus throttling off this form of migration.

According to the NIDL theorists, the restrictive practices of European states in respect of the import of labour-power now impelled a movement of capital to the Third World to take advantage of the available supplies of newly arrived migrants to Third World cities – the second migratory direction mentioned earlier. Again the basic contours of this movement are well known. As cash-cropping and commercial agriculture took a grip on the rural world in Asia, Africa and Latin America, economies of scale and more technological forms of agricultural production pushed workers off the land to swell the teeming cities. Cause and consequence should not, thus, be confused. The drift to the towns and cities was essentially a response to changes in the countryside, rather than a form of 'pull' migration to the newly established 'world market factories'. Of course, the establishment of such factories did act as an additional incentive to rural migrants. The border towns of northern Mexico, for example, where US corporations had established a strip of 800 assembly plants in the 1970s, became swollen with more and more Mexican migrants from central and northern states in the Mexican hinterland. US government officials who had hoped that the establishment of the Border Industrialisation Program (as it was called) would staunch the flow of illegal Mexican workers to the US were confounded. Not only did the program attract more migrants than could possibly be employed, but the plants also normally employed young females, who were entering the labour force for the first time, thus doing nothing to mop up the demand for male employment.

Nor should the absolute numbers, male and female, employed in the export-oriented factories, be exaggerated. According to Fröbel *et al.* (1980: 310) by 1975 about 725,000 workers were employed in world market factories and free production zones in the Third World. A wider picture can be gleaned from the ILO (1984: 20), which claims that employment generated by the multinationals – seen as the engine of growth by NIDL theorists – in *all* developing countries reached about 4 million people in 1980. The share of multinational employment in different countries varied from a low of 2 per cent in Thailand, to a high of 70 per cent in Singapore, with employment created by multinationals accounting for 20–30 per cent in countries like Korea, Brazil, Kenya and Mexico. The creation of 4 million jobs by the multinationals in Third World countries should be contrasted with their employment of 40 million workers in industrialised countries. It is possible to argue that multinational investment will create a positive spin-off in the creation of further ancillary industries, but this effect (which no doubt occurs) has to be set against the displacement effect multinational investment may have for local industry. I know of no attempt to quantify these contrasting tendencies in terms of job loss/creation.

To the quantitative estimate in employment must be added a more qualitative sense of who these workers in the NICs are. In this respect, the NIDL theorists provide a good general guide to the first cohort of workers (Fröbel *et al.* 1980: 344). The overwhelming majority of employees in the world market factories and free production zones are women, with an age-range between sixteen and twenty-five years, unskilled or semi-skilled and employed as production workers. A more recent study by Lin (1985: 76, 77) suggests that some of the features of the workforce are changing. While the majority is still young, an increasing number of female workers are getting older, becoming married while still working, better educated and acquiring a greater variety of work experience within and between companies. Women are increasingly 'realising that work means being valued as productive beings', ethnic particularities are breaking down and, according to Lin, there is a sense of having to 'build a new multi-cultural working class'.

Although the increased level of class organisation observed by Lin somewhat counters the strong bias in NIDL theory towards the power of capital, such a development could be predicted by assuming that time would permit a greater degree of self-organisation among workers. Much greater lacunae are the absence in NIDL discussions of two other sites for the deployment of subordinate and migrant labour, both of which provide salient aspects of the contemporary division of labour. I refer to the oil-rich countries and to the growth of a service sector in the metropolitan world cities, both of which, because they are less familiar, require separate treatment.

Migration to the oil-rich countries

In a number of Middle Eastern and other OPEC countries, oil revenues, accelerated in the period after 1973 for about a decade, allowed the initiation of ambitious development plans. In Venezuela, for example, following the oil-price boom which contributed some 70 per cent of national revenue, governmental policy switched to a pro-immigration stance, which legitimised and enhanced a flow of perhaps half a million undocumented foreign migrants flowing into Caracas in addition to the vast numbers of internal migrants. The Venezuelan Council for Human Resources planned to import another half million workers during the period 1976–80. The migrants arrived from Colombia, Argentina, Chile and Ecuador (amongst Latin American countries) and from Spain, Italy and Portugal (amongst European countries) (Sassen-Koob 1979: 455–64). Again, the Middle Eastern oil-producing countries have shown dramatic increases in imported labour-power. Workers from India, Bangladesh, Pakistan and Afghanistan poured into the oil-rich countries of the Middle East, their Muslim religion being regarded by the authorities as an important reason for permitting their import. In the mid-1970s, an estimated 748,000 workers from these countries arrived in Saudi Arabia, with other large numbers going to the United Arab Emirates, Qatar and Kuwait (Halliday 1977; Birks and Sinclair 1980; Kidron and Segal

1981: 38). Some of the large flows of migration were recorded in Arab countries (for example, Egyptians in Libya, and North Yemenis, Jordanians and Palestinians in Saudi Arabia). In other cases, the bulk of the labour force comes from outside the immediate area. For example, Sudan alone provides as many as 800,000 workers to the Arab OPEC countries (*Le Monde*, 3 February 1982). In some Middle Eastern countries before the Gulf War, the proportion of foreign to home workers has reached almost absurd levels: 50 per cent in Saudi Arabia, 80 per cent in Kuwait and no less than 85 per cent of the total population in the United Arab Emirates (*The Times* 'Special Report', 23 February 1981). If we turn next to West Africa, perhaps a million migrants from Upper Volta, Togo and other nearby countries entered Ghana during the period of its greatest prosperity in the 1950s and 1960s, though the adverse economic climate thereafter produced a strong reaction against 'the aliens' (Peil 1971). As the Ghanaian economy collapsed, workers and petty traders from that country streamed into oil-rich and development-crazy Nigeria – only in turn to be the subjects of mass expulsion orders in 1983 and 1985, harshly enforced by the Nigerian authorities. Despite the difficulties of aggregating figures collected by different authorities for different purposes, simply adding together the number of unskilled *foreign* labourers (alone) mentioned as migrating to oil-producing countries, yields a figure as great as the numbers employed in the export-processing zones.

An interesting pattern of *skilled* migration can also be observed as transnational companies expanded their operations abroad to OPEC countries. Although the numbers involved are not that high, Findlay (1986) has shown how, in the case of Britain, there has been a fundamental shift away from old Commonwealth (Australia, New Zealand and Canada) emigration, compared to other destinations. In 1984, only 22 per cent of those leaving the UK went to old Commonwealth destinations, compared to 45 per cent in 1973. Moreover, the form of migration was for a fixed-term contract, rather than for settlement overseas. This is reflected in the figure of 64 per cent of the 79,000 British citizens returning to the UK in 1984, who had been abroad for three years or less. These returnees came back not as 'failed migrants' but primarily as skilled, professional and managerial workers, having successfully completed their assignments abroad. In the Gulf states, there remained a continued demand for highly skilled expatriate staff even in 1985/6, when unskilled labour contracts were being cancelled. In a sample survey, Findlay (1986) draws attention to the case of a British construction company with about 200 staff in the UK and a staff of 110 employees in the Middle East alone (other overseas staff meant the company had far more on its overseas payroll than in its British base). Its Gulf employees included 25 per cent who were professional, 10 per cent managerial, 30 per cent technical and 35 per cent supervisory or foremen. The average length of residence in the Gulf was twenty months. Findlay does seem to be spotting an emerging trend when he remarks that 'British regions form a convenient village of return for the new nomads of the world economy'.

Service employment in 'world cities'

Another part of the employment world missed by the NIDL theorists is that part of the metropolitan economy marked by the switch of employment between different sectors. NIDL theory concentrates on the loss in employment in the manufacturing (or industrial) sector and the possible switch in these jobs from industrialised countries to Third World countries. However, even if all the jobs created by the transnationals can be said to be net losses for the industrialised countries and net gains for the NICs (a highly implausible assumption) we are only talking of perhaps 4 to 6 million jobs at stake. If, on the other hand, we look at switches between different sectors within industrial economies, an OECD study found that since 1950 the share of industrial country employment represented by 'information occupations', has increased by nearly 3 per cent in each five-year period. By 1975, these occupations accounted for more than one third of the total labour force. If we examine employment across the four sectors – agriculture, industry, services and information – we can see an anticipated shrinkage in agriculture over the period 1950 to the mid-1970s to a half or a third less people employed in France, Japan, Sweden, the United Kingdom, the United States and West Germany. With respect to industry, some shrinkage also occurs in these countries over the period mentioned (as is recognised in NIDL theory). But the most significant change is a spectacular growth (with the marginal exception of the United Kingdom) in the service sector (ILO 1984: 179–80).

The growth of employment demand in the service sector is a feature of a contemporary division of labour particularly highlighted in the work of Sassen-Koob (1983 and 1984). She advances a theory which, in important respects, should be laid side by side with NIDL, arguing that the 'technological transformation of the work process, the decentralisation of manufacturing and of office work, in part made possible by the technological transformation of the work process, and the transnationalisation of the economy generally, have all contributed to the consolidation of a new kind of economic center from where the world is managed and serviced' (1984: 140). Her analysis is concentrated on New York City and on Los Angeles, where she shows that there has been a pronounced increase in the domestic and international demand for services – which she identifies as legal, managerial, financial, technical, engineering, accounting, consulting and 'a large array of other such services'. She argues that the expansion of these advanced services is the fastest growing sector of the US economy in terms of 'its share of GNP, employment and exports'. The employment pattern and social structure characterising Los Angeles and New York City, despite the superficial differences, are moving in a similar direction – a notable expansion in the supply of very high income jobs, a shrinking of the traditional middle income blue and white collar jobs and an *expansion* of the low wage jobs available. It is this last characteristic that provides her most surprising and important finding in that conventional wisdom and other assumptions about restructuring and industrial decline had led many observers to assume that there would be a permanent shrinkage in the number of jobs available for the more dispossessed segments of the labour force (women, blacks and migrants). In fact Sassen-Koob argues just the opposite: 'The rate of growth of various earnings categories in the service industries from 1960 to 1975 shows a 35 per cent increase in jobs in the highest two earnings classes, an 11.3 per cent increase in jobs in the medium earnings class, and a 54 per cent increase in jobs in the two lowest earnings classes.' As she points out, both New York and Los Angeles contain the largest concentration of ethnic minorities – Hispanic and Asians in Los Angeles and Caribbean peoples in the case of New York City. Although migration from, for example, the Caribbean and Mexico has often been explained by push factors from the recipient countries, Sassen-Koob considers that demand factors in cities like New York provide an equally salient explanation for migration.

What Sassen-Koob's data as yet do not provide is some sort of global indication of this trend and it is therefore only somewhat speculative to argue that one could suggest a similar tendency occurring in other 'world cities'. These, according to some of Friedman's (1985) hypotheses, are cities integrating the world economy, providing the 'base points' for production and marketing, the sites for the accumulation and concentration of capital, the points of destination for internal and international migrants, and revealing precisely the occupational profile found in Los Angeles and New York by Sassen-Koob. Such cities are arranged in a complex spatial hierarchy, and include London, Paris, Rotterdam, Frankfurt, Zurich, Chicago and Tokyo in addition to the two fortuitously (in the sense of the world city hypothesis) examined by Sassen-Koob. Though the world city hypothesis still needs much greater empirical anchorage for its validation, the notion that there are such critical nodes in the world economy has great impressionistic appeal. These cities are where the professional and managerial classes meet, where the Inter-Continental, Sheraton and Hilton hotels are established, where frequent connecting flights by international airlines operate. The cities contain stock exchanges, theatres, sophisticated entertainment, town houses and international schools.

If it is right to suggest that Sassen-Koob's findings for New York and Los Angeles can be transposed to a world city context, we should also find a similar growth in the service industries that she describes. To generalise her argument it may be important to extend her list away from what she calls 'advanced services' into more prosaic activities which service the needs of the world's managers, professionals, financiers and consultants. She partly hints at a wider notion in her own work, but I think it is as well to be explicit that we are talking not only of the expansion of low-wage activities directly related to advanced services, but also the growth of ancillary occupations – the cleaners and porters in the world's airports, the waiters in the French restaurants, the prostitutes in the night clubs, the chamber maids in the hotels, the seamstresses manufacturing *haute couture* clothes in the back streets of Paris, New York or London.

What seems difficult at the moment to establish is what proportion of the new service sector jobs is being filled by transfers from internal areas of declining significance in the metropolitan countries (for example, the metal-bashing industries), and what proportion is being filled by new members of the workforce (for example, women entering part-time employment for the first time) or from external migrants, arriving either illegally or on a contractual basis. This lack of precision is frustrating in that it would help address the crucial underlying theme of this book – namely, can the ethnic minorities, previously drawn into the expanding factory employment of the 1950s and 1960s, profit from the more recent forms of economic restructuring? Or are they condemned to remain as permanent casualties in the old industrial boom cities?

A number of chapters in this book address this question with new data and hypotheses, and I would not, therefore, like to present my comments here as anything but the most general observations. If we turn to the US first, a sophisticated analysis of trends in racial occupational inequality over the four decades 1940–80 provides a basis for advancing some statistical generalisation. Using an updated index of inequality, Fosset *et al.* (1986) find that while racial inequality between black and white males between the ages of twenty-five and sixty-four of similar educational attainment increased in the 1940s, inequality decreased in the three subsequent decades. When, however, the authors move from the national to the regional level, they find that despite the large increase in economic opportunity in the South during the 1950s, the South also saw a sharp *increase* in the degree of racial inequality for matched black and white males. They demonstrate that gains made by blacks are importantly explained by public intervention in the labour market and in the educational system in respect of social policies aimed at eliminating discrimination and enhancing equality of opportunity. The conclusion I derive from this data is that despite the currently fashionable proposition that 'leaving it to the market' will solve all problems, the shift in labour market opportunities will not in itself produce employment for ethnic minority workers discarded from the manufacturing sector. Some sort of enabling public policy must be put in place to structure and create employment and transfer possibilities. This observation applies equally well to the case of London where it is apparent that ethnic minority workers are not able to take advantage of what changes in employment possibilities have occurred as a result of the shift from manufacturing to financial services. Massey (1986) reports that between 1966 and 1983 jobs in manufacturing in London fell by 700,000, whereas employment in the financial services sector grew by 100,000 between 1973 and 1984. However, workers within London discarded from manufacturing seem to be victims of a 'skills gap', combined sometimes with difficulties in transport costs. Workers outside London, say from the embattled Midlands, no more than 150 miles from London, are faced with an additional obstacle. The cost of housing in London is often twice the price of the Midlands equivalent. Workers have no or little equity and 'swaps' between public housing tenants in London and the Midlands are virtually impossible to arrange – few council tenants in the south wish to make such a move.

What the United States and London examples suggest is that the transfer of ethnic minority labourers from the old public sector or manufacturing labour market will be a very limited phenomenon, at least if left to market forces. The growth of the service sector in 'world cities', therefore, seems to have been accomplished largely by fresh external migration (in the US we can surmise much of it illegal) and by part-time, perhaps normally female, employment.

Conclusion

In developing a critique of NIDL theory, I laid emphasis on three aspects – the lack of conceptual clarity in the German theorists, the historical gaps apparent in their neglect of a century marked by colonialism and imperialism, and some empirical omissions in the contemporary period. The question of empirical omissions has been the one to tax me most in this chapter. In its current form, NIDL theory is too constrained by its nineteenth-century origins in classical political economy, and by its current reliance on radical trade theory and the logic of capital.

As soon as one widens 'the new international division of labour' into a discussion of the post-war transnational division of labour, and accords labour flows as important a place as capital flows, some of the limitations of NIDL theory become apparent. The theory accounts well for the limited movement of Third World workers into the world market factories (though it fails to recognise that phenomenon as part of a much longer rural–urban migration). It also implicitly deals with the end of the long migrant labour boom after World War II in Europe and the US (though not with its origins). What it fails to pick up is the statistically significant phenomenon of migration to the OPEC countries, and it is totally unable to account for the growth of service employment in metropolitan cities. It is this last manifestation of the contemporary division of labour that is potentially the most significant in respect of the employment of ethnic minorities. Though the data do not seem conclusive, they suggest that transfers of redundant migrant workers from the growth industries of the 1950s and 1960s will not occur through 'the invisible hand'; public policy will be needed to induce greater interregional mobility and to energise, resocialise and enskill a demoralised migrant workforce, whose native sons and daughters face bleak prospects in the intermediate future.

STEPHEN CASTLES

2

Migrants and minorities in post-Keynesian capitalism: the German case*

Migrant labour in the post-war expansion

Labour migration played a crucial role throughout the capitalist world in the period of industrial expansion from 1945 to the early seventies, which was marked by the concentration of the factors of production – capital, labour, raw material and machinery – in Western Europe, North America and Japan. In some respects this was a continuation of historical trends going back to the Industrial Revolution, but there are new factors: US financial and military hegemony provided the conditions for increasing international economic integration, while US overseas investment stimulated growth, particularly in the countries devastated by war and Fascism. High demand for industrial products was fed first by post-war reconstruction, then by rearmament and the Cold War. By the sixties, mass consumer demand – itself a result of neo-Keynesian strategies of class cooperation – was becoming a major factor in allowing expansion to continue. The ever greater concentration of capital in the old industry regions led to a constant demand for labour in that period. Labour supply did not grow as fast as the stock of the means of production, indicating that growth always involved technical progress and rationalisation of production, but was nevertheless crucial.[1] Without 'flexible labour markets', expansion would rapidly have been bogged down by sectoral bottlenecks, as well as by wage inflation (see Kindleberger 1967; Glyn and Harrison 1980). Labour for industry came from a variety of sources: absorption of unemployment following the Great Depression and/or the collapse of the war economy, population displaced by the war (particularly in the West German case), transfers from the agricultural sector, increasing participation of women in the labour force, high birth rates (although this applied only to a few countries), and international labour migration (see United Nations Economic Commission for Europe 1979).

36

For the purpose of the present discussion, it may be noted that internal labour sources proved inadequate to fuel economic expansion in all important industrial countries. This applied to North America, Australia and Japan, too, but I will confine myself to Western Europe here. In all cases, migrant labour played a significant part in the post-war boom.

Again, this was nothing new: Irish workers had been central to the British Industrial Revolution, and foreign workers had played an important role in Germany, France and Switzerland before World War I. What was new was the sheer scale of the movements, and the increasing involvement of the states in their management. I estimate that something like 30 million people entered Western Europe as workers, or as workers' dependants in the post-war period. Not all stayed on: the present population of migrant origin may conservatively be put at around 16 million (see Castles *et al.* 1984). Migrants fell into various categories including returning colonists, refugees, and highly skilled specialists moving temporarily. But by far the largest groups were migrant workers coming from colonies or former colonies to work in the 'motherland', and workers coming from the European periphery (Ireland, Finland, the Mediterranean area). Colonial migrants came to France, The Netherlands and Britain, while workers from the European periphery came to all expanding Western European countries.

In recognition of the importance of 'flexible labour markets', the states of the countries concerned took measures to regulate migratory flows, and set up legal and administrative frameworks to control migrant workers. Most Western European countries experimented at one time or another with direct state recruitment overseas (e.g. the British European Voluntary Worker scheme, the Belgian Contingentensysteem, the French Office National d'Immigration). However, such systems were often dropped, as it was found that spontaneous migration met the needs of employers well, with the labour market functioning effectively to assign workers to the areas where they were needed. This applied, for instance, to Commonwealth migration to Britain, or North African migration to France. Indeed, in some cases there was a trend to tolerate clandestine (undocumented) labour migration, with the illegal workers being forced into extremely exploitative jobs, and lacking any protection. (This applies particularly to Iberian migration to France and to Mexican migration to the USA, but to all Western European countries to some extent.)

Migrant labour was valuable to capital for several reasons: first it provided additional labour, allowing expansion of production at a time when lack of domestic labour would have been a constraint (*quantitative function*). Secondly, it provided a particular type of labour: workers who entered the labour market at the lowest levels due to lack of education, vocational training, language proficiency – or who were forced to work at such levels due to discrimination. Such labour was useful to employers who wished to restructure the labour process – it made it possible to deskill sections of the workforce while yet offering upward mobility to at least some local workers (*qualitative function*). Thirdly, migration had a macroeconomic effect, for it helped to brake upward wage drift, which would have resulted from a tight labour market (*regulative function*).

The *qualitative function* of migrant labour is particularly significant for understanding the position that populations of migrant origin were later to take on in Western European societies; it arose in three ways: in the case of colonial migrants entering societies with racist cultures (Britain, France), racial discrimination assigned them to inferior socio-economic positions; in the case of undocumented workers, it was lack of any legal status in the country which forced them into extremely exploitative work and housing situations: in the case of workers recruited through state recruitment systems ('guestworkers'), a network of discriminatory laws and regulations gave migrants no chance to compete as free and equal economic subjects. To this extent, the post-war migrant labour systems were in the tradition of the use of 'unfree labour' which has always been significant in the history of capitalism: e.g. the accumulation of capital for the British Industrial Revolution through slavery in the American plantations, contract 'coolie' labour in the Caribbean and Africa, the migrant labour system in southern Africa, slave labour in the Nazi war economy. However, the migrant labour systems in Western Europe have had their own peculiarities, and have varied from country to country. It would be an oversimplification to regard migrants simply as 'unfree' labour, for there is a broad range of situations, and a great complexity of legal arrangements, laid down by national law, bilateral treaties and multilateral agreements.

When the expansive long wave ended at the beginning of the seventies, governments which had utilised 'guestwork systems' to regulate their labour markets stopped recruitment and expected migrant workers to leave. In fact, although migrant labour forces declined, the foreign populations of virtually all Western European countries went on growing through family reunification in the late seventies and became stabilised in the early eighties. The systems of institutionalised discrimination developed to control temporary 'guestworkers' now became major constraints on the social positions of what had become permanent settler populations. Deprived of civil and political rights, often without a clear entitlement to residence, the settlers were marginalised and pushed into the status of new ethnic minorities, identifiable through appearance, nationality, language, culture, life-style and socio-economic position.

Table 2.1 *Foreign resident population of Germany by selected nationalities*

Nationality	1982 Absolute	Percentage[b]	1983 Absolute	Percentage[b]	1984 Absolute	Percentage[b]	1985[a] Absolute	Percentage[b]
European Community (excluding Italy, Greece, Spain and Portugal)	313,774	6.7	309,728	6.8	310,307	7.1	312,564	7.2
Greece	300,824	6.4	292,349	6.4	287,099	6.6	281,330	6.4
Italy	601,621	12.9	564,960	12.5	545,111	12.5	533,800	12.2
Yugoslavia	631,692	13.5	612,798	13.5	600,314	13.8	592,380	13.6
Morocco	42,590	0.9	44,192	1.0	45,137	1.0	47,467	1.1
Portugal	106,005	2.3	99,529	2.2	82,991	1.9	77,472	1.8
Spain	173,526	3.7	165,998	3.7	158,843	3.6	153,805	3.5
Turkey	1,580,671	33.9	1,552,328	34.2	1,425,798	32.7	1,400,414	32.1
Tunisia	25,189	0.5	25,269	0.6	23,644	0.5	23,322	0.5
Others	891,025	19.1	867,712	19.1	884,404	20.3	943,357	21.6
Total	4,666,917	–	4,534,863	–	4,363,648	–	4,365,911	–

Note: [a] Figures are for 30 September up to 1984, for 31 December 1985.
[b] Percentage of total foreign resident population.
Source: Beauftragte der Bundesregierung für Ausländerfragen, *Daten und Fakten zur Ausländersituation*, Bonn, 1986

State policies towards these new minorities range from more or less voluntary repatriation, through attempts to assimilation, to recognition of the emergence of multicultural societies (Castles *et al.* 1984). It has been suggested that measures concerning ethnic minorities play a key part in neo-conservative strategies of crisis management (e.g. Centre for Contemporary Cultural Studies 1982).

In this chapter I will concentrate on the most developed of the Western European 'guestworkers systems' – that used in Germany from 1956 to 1973 – and its aftermath. At the end of 1985, Germany had a foreign population of 4.4 million – a slight decline from the 1982 peak of 4.7 million (Beauftragte der Bundesregierung für Ausländerfragen 1986). 2.9 million of them had been resident over eight years and many had actually been born in Germany (children born of foreign parents do not easily become German citizens). About one third of foreign residents are Turks (see Table 2.1). Nonetheless, politicians of all the major parties (except the Green party) continued to assert that 'West Germany is not a country of immigration'. This means maintaining the legal framework set up to recruit 'guestworkers'. The centre–right coalition which came to power in 1982 defined the 'foreigner problem' as a major political issue. Chancellor Kohl and the Minister of the Interior Zimmermann announced plans to cut the foreign population by at least a million by the end of the eighties, through strict immigration control and encouragement of repatriation. I will argue that the collapse of Helmut Schmidt's centre–left coalition in 1982 marked the failure of Keynesian strategies of class co-operation in restoring the conditions of capital accumulation. In its search for new ways of regulating accumulation and securing political legitimacy, the centre–right government has given prominence to the 'foreigner problem', as a way of securing mass support for policies which threaten working-class living standards and welfare.

What is the 'foreigner problem' and why is it central to neo-conservative ideology? What contradictions are involved in strategies of repatriation and restriction of civil rights in a parliamentary democracy? What has been the impact of the policies of the centre–right coalition? Adequate answers to these questions would require an historical analysis of the changing structure of the state and its role in regulating capital accumulation. This cannot be attempted here. I can merely point to the major phases of the development of the economy and state in Germany, and relate these to the situation of migrants.

The social market economy (1948–67)

The nascent Federal Republic enjoyed favourable conditions for capital accumulation: the Cold War provided a political climate for capitalist restoration under Adenauer's conservative leadership, large labour reserves and a labour movement weakened by Fascism and war kept wages down and profits up, internal and external (US) capital was available for investment, high demand was guaranteed by export markets.

Despite the collapse of the war economy, the three Western zones which formed the Federal Republic in 1948 had a powerful industrial base. The three Western allies did nothing to break the power of the industrial barons (Krupp, Thyssen, Siemens, Flick) and of the great banks, which had controlled and integrated the economy since the 'founding years' of the nineteenth century. The CDU announced a policy of 'ordered liberalism' designed to create a 'social market economy'. The 'market' component of the slogan meant leaving accumulation to private framework: favourable fiscal and monetary conditions, and legal regulation of class conflicts. The 'social component' referred to the provision of a safety net for people not yet absorbed by the labour process, as well as for those whose conditions of life had been disrupted by economic change.

The availability of plentiful labour was vital to the 'economic miracle' of the fifties and sixties. The reserve army created by the collapse of the Nazi war economy was supplemented by westward migration of millions of Germans from lost Eastern territories and later from the German Democratic Republic. As these reserves were absorbed, unions became more confident in their calls for higher wages and shorter hours. By the mid-fifties, employers were calling for recruitment of foreign workers. German industry had a tradition of large-scale use of migrants, both in the 'founding years' and in the form of forced labour in the Nazi war economy. These unsavoury experiences made unions wary of employers' intentions, but they consented, subject to guarantees on wages and conditions (Dohse 1981). The state took on the task of recruitment and control of the 'guestworkers', initially using regulations passed by the Nazis in 1938.

The first bilateral recruitment agreement was made with Italy in 1955, and was followed by others with Spain and Greece (1960), Turkey (1961 and 1964), Morocco (1963), Portugal (1964), Tunisia (1965) and Yugoslavia (1968). The German Federal Labour Office, Bundesanstalt für Arbeit (BFA), set up recruitment offices in Mediterranean countries. Employers requiring foreign labour had to apply to the BFA and pay a fee. The BFA then selected workers, testing occupational skills, carrying out medical examinations and screening police records. The workers were brought in groups to Germany, where employers had to provide initial accommodation, generally in wooden huts on the worksite. The 'guestworkers' had contracts binding them to a specific job for a year. But even after that, a change of employer required permission from the BFA.

Migrant labour was seen as a short-term economic necessity, to be dealt with at the administrative level. Parliament did not debate the issue until 1965, by which time there were over one million foreign workers in the country. The 'Foreigners Law' (*Ausländergesetz*) of 1965 did little to improve the situation of migrants. It did not give them any right to residence, stating that 'a residence permit may be granted, if it does not harm the interests of the Federal Republic of Germany'. This key phrase is so vague and elastic that it gives the special foreigners police (*Ausländerpolizei*) enormous bureaucratic power over the lives of migrants. Foreign residents are denied the basic rights of freedom of assembly, of association, of movement and of choice of occupation. However long a foreigner lives in Germany, he or she is denied the right to vote, even at the local level. Together with nationality laws which make naturalisation extremely hard to obtain, and labour laws giving preference to Germans and (since 1968) to European Community citizens, the Foreigners Law gives migrants a position of continual insecurity and lack of rights.

The 'guestworkers' were not expected to stay. Family reunification was not envisaged, and no provision was made for housing or other social facilities for migrants. The state followed a short-term labour market policy in response to employers' demands, taking no account of possible long-term consequences for society.

The social-democratic corporate block (1967–73)

Germany entered its first recession in 1966. Wages had grown faster than profits in the early sixties, leading to a decline in investments. The CDU formula of 'ordered liberalism' did not fit the new realities of labour shortage, stronger unions and growing international competition. A 'Grand Coalition' of the major parties passed emergency measures, which paved the way for a social democratic government (in coalition with the small FDP) from 1969. The SPD's aim was to link capital, unions and state in a corporate block, working together for economic and social modernisation. This neo-Keynesian line was expressed in the Stability Law of 1967, which defined the four aims of economic policy (known popularly as 'the magic square'): stable prices, a high level of employment, foreign trade balance and continual economic growth. Consultation between the 'social partners' was institutionalised, while new labour and social legislation guaranteed a high level of social security for the working class. Full employment was seen as the norm, with earnings-related benefits designed to maintain living standards for those temporarily unemployed or ill. The poor-law type *Sozialhilfe* (supplementary benefit) was maintained for the small minority that could not be integrated into the system of wage labour.

During the 1966–8 recession, the number of migrant workers had fallen substantially (from 1.3 million to 900,000), showing the success of the guestworker system in exporting unemployment. Now a new wave of rationalisation started, with increased use of conveyor-line, shift- and piece-work. The aim was expansion and cost-reduction through increased Taylorisation of the labour process and deskilling of the labour force. To provide labour for this strategy, the state stepped up recruitment of migrants to an unprecedented level: the foreign workforce leapt from 900,000 in 1968 to 2.6 million in 1973. Most of the new recruits came from Turkey, and there was increasing emphasis on women workers. Female labour (both German and migrant) played an important part in expansion and rationalisation. But the increased recruitment of women migrant workers encouraged family reunification, with wife and husband both coming as workers, and then establishing their family in Germany. By the early seventies it was becoming clear that many 'guestworkers' were not just temporary residents. Needs for, among other things, housing and schooling emerged. But like its predecessor, the SPD–FDP government was following short-term labour market policies, with no consideration of long-term social consequences (Dohse 1981). The guestworker system seemed beneficial to the unions at this point: the entry of migrants at the bottom of the labour market eased upward mobility for German workers (especially skilled men).

Social-democratic crisis management (1974–82)

But as the world economy moved into crisis in the mid-seventies, the SPD's recipe for growth ran into increasing difficulties. The four aims of the 'magic square' were clearly becoming irreconcilable, and there was no way of avoiding class struggle on the question of who was to foot the bill for restructuring. Export of capital- and labour-intensive workplaces, automation in factories and offices meant long-term structural unemployment while the state's fiscal situation became too strained to finance high living standards for the victims of the crisis. The emphasis of social-democratic policy shifted from growth and welfare to crisis management – a change symbolised by the replacement of Willy Brandt as Chancellor by Helmut Schmidt in 1974.

The impact of new conditions on migrant workers made itself felt quickly: late in 1973, further recruitment of non-European Community workers was suddenly stopped by the German government. The labour market authorities appeared to think that the rotation built into the guestworker system would cause a rapid decline in the foreign labour force and population. Many workers did leave, but the size of the foreign population stabilised through entry of dependants. As the families came, foreign workers moved out of employers' hostels and sought housing in inner-city areas. The already severe housing shortage was aggravated, while, at the same time, the declining income of the local authorities hindered measures of urban renewal. As in other European countries, migrants were at the end of the queue for housing, schools and medical facilities. There was a trend towards partial ethnic segregation, as better-off German workers moved to the suburbs, leaving the inner cities to the migrants, together with the aged, the unemployed, and other under-privileged groups.

Despite the intentions of successive governments, the guestworkers were turning into settlers, and this process went hand-in-hand with the growing urban crisis. Insecurity, lack of civil rights and weak socio-economic position were factors which interacted to marginalise the migrants and to turn them into ethnic minorities. As the living standards and the prospects of the indigenous working class declined, a 'common sense' link between the migrant presence and urban stress and unemployment arose. The foreigners came to be seen as the cause of the problems, and racism (known as 'hostility towards foreigners' – *Ausländerfeindlichkeit*) escalated. The 'foreigner problem' became part of the popular discourse.

The SPD had no clear alternative to offer. Through the latter part of the seventies, the state set up a series of commissions to enquire into various aspects of the situation of migrants: housing, schooling, social needs and the like (see Castles *et al.* 1984; 77–80). Nearly all started from the premise that 'Germany is not a country of immigration', and tried to maintain the myth that most 'guestworkers' would leave. The only exception – the Kühn Report of 1979 – was officially ignored. Various piecemeal measures were taken to cope with specific problems, but the SPD refused to come to terms with the reality of settlement. That would have meant admitting the failure of past policies, and telling the people the apparently unpopular truth, that Germany was on the way to becoming a multi-ethnic society. That, in turn, would have meant repealing the Foreigners Law, and introducing legislation to secure political participation and equal economic and social opportunity for immigrants.

The SPD's inability to grasp the trend towards permanent settlement, and to act accordingly, was, in my view, a significant cause of the growth of racism. In a situation of economic crisis, the most dangerous competitors for workers are those, whose lack of security and civil rights compels them to accept inferior conditions. Maintaining the fiction of temporary migration and the corresponding legal and administrative framework was tantamount to accepting a permanent and deepening split in the working class. Every fifth manual worker in Germany is a foreigner, and therefore excluded from political participation. Yet the SPD is a 'people's party' and not a class party; it was afraid of taking a stand on an issue which might initially cause loss of votes.

The right–centre coalition (since 1982)

By the early eighties, it was apparent that Keynesian strategies, based on the common interest of the 'social partners' in full employment, financial stability and growth, could not cope with the crisis. Capital can only revive accumulation by increasing the size of the surplus population, and by squeezing the living standards of those still in employment. The problem is how to create the economic conditions for a new phase of *accumulation*, and yet maintain political *legitimacy* and social peace. During the long wave of growth, legitimacy was to a large extent based on the economic success of the system: it delivered the goods, in the form of jobs, rising wages and welfare, for large sections of the population. If economic growth can no longer provide legitimacy, it must be sought elsewhere, for instance in the reassertion of national identity, in military greatness, or in battles against the 'enemy within' (Centre for Contemporary Cultural Studies 1982: 23). Reagan and Thatcher have shown the way, but also demonstrated how such policies can destroy the consensus necessary for parliamentary rule. The strength of the German economy delayed the crisis, allowing the state to cushion the impact of restructuring to a greater extent. Neo-conservatism in Germany is not simply replicating monetarism, but is looking for a specific mode of redefinition of the relationship between the state, economy and society. In an important article, Esser and Hirsch characterised the situation as follows:

> It must be assumed that the establishment of a conservative government is the beginning of a further transformation of the system of domination. The crisis of Keynesian–Fordian capitalism necessitates an altered strategy of accumulation based on the changing conditions of world market competition. This will be accompanied by a restructuring of the political apparatus, of the prevailing political discourses and of the modes of societal organisation and division of interests. The culmination of this process could be the construction of a new 'historical block', i.e. an historically new mode of capitalist regulation, linking the

altered strategy of accumulation with a correspondingly transformed structure of hegemony. Our hypothesis is that the conservative party formation now in power does not yet represent
this new 'post-Keynesian' mode of regulation, but rather is
smoothing out the terrain for the coming battles.

(Esser and Hirsch 1984; 51, my translation)

The economic basis of future capital accumulation is to be the new
high-technology industries, based on electronics, new communication
techniques, robotics and bio-engineering. To participate in this trend,
German capital must shift from its previous areas of strength in met-
allurgy, and mechanical and electrical engineering into the new sectors. It
must become transnational and participate in the new international
division of labour. This implies a restructuring of the bourgeoisie and its
political representatives. The old-style barons of heavy industry (so
important in the Third Reich and afterwards) are losing ground, or, like
Friedrich Flick,[2] metamorphosing into financial capitalists. The new
dynamism, both economic and political, comes from the internationally
orientated high-technology sector, with emphasis on innovative medium-
sized enterprises.

The working class is being split and atomised. On the one hand there
are various groups of highly trained blue- and white-collar workers in
production, distribution, services and administration. Their jobs and
living standards appear secure (but nobody knows for how long).
Members of these core groups of the working class tend to see their
interest not so much in cohesiveness with each other, but rather in
identification with their work and employers, and with technological
rationality. On the other hand there are groups temporarily or permanently excluded from the labour process of the dynamic sectors – due to
age, poor health, lack of qualifications, or simply because they have
worked in declining industries or declining areas. This periphery of the
working class includes increasing numbers of young people never
admitted to the formal sector of the labour market. The growing informal
sector produces insecure and exploitative jobs for some marginalised
workers. This 'core–periphery phenomenon' is overlaid by (but not
identical with) the segmentation of the working class according to gender
and ethnic group. Although large numbers of foreign workers have been
marginalised, many remain within the core sector of production and the
services. Migrants have high rates of unemployment, and foreign school-
leavers find it particularly hard to get training and secure employment,
but it would be wrong to conclude that foreign workers have become
superfluous for German capital.

This trend towards the atomisation of the working class poses a threat to the unions, both in terms of membership, and with regard to defining aims. Some German unions have tended to become defenders of the jobs of the male, German, skilled core workers, leaving others out in the cold. German labour law gives workers' representatives an important role in helping to decide who gets sacked first in the event of redundancies. Many employers have followed the strategy of using dismissals of foreign workers to cushion Germans from the effects of declining employment. Unions and work councils appear to have gone along with this policy in many cases – indeed it could hardly have been carried out without their co-operation (Budzinski 1979: 61, Kühne 1982). On the other hand, the strikes in the metal and printing industries in 1984 represented attempts to cut hours and thus share the work available among more people. Such strategies are probably more significant in the fight against splits in the class, and therefore against racism, than any number of educational campaigns to change public opinion.

What is the role of the state in the emerging mode of accumulation? The party propaganda of CDU, CSU and FDP calls for 'less state' and more private initiative. This refers to cuts in social expenditure, and refusal of subsidies to 'lame duck' enterprises, which are no longer profitable. The aim is the partial demolition of earnings-related social security systems and their replacement by private insurance networks for the better-off. Basic state provision on a low level is to be maintained for marginalised workers, no longer likely to be reintegrated into core areas of the labour process. The reassertion of the importance of the family is linked with this aim: the CDU wants to impose greater social security responsibilities on this traditional unit. But the space for cuts in social expenditure is always limited by fears of causing social unrest and losing electoral support – pensioners are after all a major reservoir of votes for conservative parties. However, there is not to be 'less state' with regard to the public order role of government. Strengthening administrative control and police forces is not only a central part of conservative law-and-order philosophies. A strong state is also vital for regulating class conflicts in a period when organised labour cannot be bought off by economic concessions. Stricter control of migrants and minorities is part of this pattern.

The electoral success of the CDU is not the result of a sudden change in public opinion but rather of an 'authoritarian–populist discourse' (Esser and Hirsch 1984: 61) which has been growing in appeal since the mid-seventies, in view of the SPD's inability to contain the crises. The core of this ideology is the denial of the significance of class conflict (or indeed of the existence of social classes) and emphasis on the traditional conservative themes of individual achievement and national identity. The 'new social question', formulated by CDU ideologist Geissler in 1976, is the struggle of individuals against entrenched interest groups (especially the unions), which distort the distribution of power and income and prevent able people from succeeding (Geissler 1976). The current version is the picture of 'possessors of jobs' defending their privileges against the rest of society. The authoritarian–populist discourse embraces vague concepts of anti-bureaucratism and even anti-statism, linking them with a belief in natural inequality and the importance of family and ethnic ties. Such themes enable the CDU–CSU to put forward policies necessary for regulating capital accumulation as a 'spiritual-moral turnabout' (*geistig-moralische Wende*).

Here it is possible to perceive the appeal of the 'foreigner question' as a theme in authoritarian–populist discourse. Extreme-right parties like the NPD have been campaigning against foreign workers since the sixties. But such views found little support as long as migrants were seen as temporary 'guestworkers' necessary for economic growth and not competing with Germans for jobs and housing. As pointed out above, this changed in the seventies through two simultaneous processes: the shift from economic growth to stagnation, and the settlement of migrant families in the inner cities. Now migrants were perceived as competitors for scarce resources, and it was only a small step to portray them as the cause of unemployment and urban crisis. The failure of the SPD to face up to the reality of settlement and to take appropriate measures opened up the field for the right. The decline of class politics blocked perception of migrant workers as an underprivileged fraction of the working class. Instead they were defined by the media and politicians as ethnic minorities with alien cultures, which threatened to swamp German society.

There are obvious parallels to the emergence of what has been called the 'new racism' (Barker 1981) in Britain. The theme gained in strength in Germany towards the end of the seventies, for three reasons. One was the 'discovery' of the second generation: young foreigners born or brought up in Germany, who were crowding into inner-city schools and beginning to enter the labour market. The failure of schools to provide them with qualifications, and of the labour market to absorb them, raised fears of future unrest and street crime. The media put over the idea of a 'social time bomb'. The second was the growing ethnic segregation of the inner cities, which was popularly regarded as a trend towards ghettos, giving rise to inter-ethnic conflict and swamping German culture. The third was the increase in entries of refugees from Third World countries like Afghanistan, Eritrea, Sri Lanka and Iran. The tabloid press portrayed them as phonies, flocking in to take jobs and sponge on social security, and threatening Germans with Third World poverty. Neo-nazis mobilised around the issue, with campaigns of violence against refugees. But demagogues within the major parties also led local movements against the siting of refugee hostels.

By the beginning of the eighties, the new racism was becoming respectable. A group of professors published the 'Heidelberg Manifesto' in 1981, warning that German culture, language and national character were being swamped by immigration (Staeck and Karst 1982). The quality press chimed in, with editorials claiming the Turks and other non-Europeans could not be integrated into German society (see Castles *et al.* 1984: for details, see ch. 7). The language of the CDU became increasingly nationalistic: 'The role of the German Federal Republic as a national unitary state and as part of a divided nation does not permit the commencement of an irreversible development to a multi-ethnic state' said a CDU resolution in the Bundestag in November 1981. Alfred Dregger, leader of the CDU–CSU parliamentary group warned of a coming alien influx, due to Turkey's Treaty of Association with the European Community, which provided for free movement of labour from 1986. Dregger warned that disregarding of the 'natural and justified feelings of our fellow citizens' would pave the way for the extreme right. A CDU leaflet for the state elections in Hesse in 1982 bore the title 'Dealing with the Foreigner Problem', and declared that the CDU would reduce the foreign population by a million within the next five years. By the time Helmut Kohl became Chancellor of a coalition of CDU, CSU and FDP in the autumn of 1982, the stage seemed set for a policy of mass repatriation.

Policies towards foreign residents since 1982

Indeed, in his inaugural address, Kohl announced that a new policy towards foreigners was a major priority of his government. Lip service was still paid to integration, but the emphasis was on stopping immigration, drastically reducing family reunification and encouraging repatriation. Kohl emphasised that repatriation was to be voluntary and 'humane', but the government's aim was to cut the foreign population by a million before the end of the decade.

The Minister of the Interior, Zimmermann, set up a commission linking federal, state and local government to draft new policies. This was doubly significant, first because Zimmermann, one of the Bavarian CSU ministers, was about the most right-wing member of the government, secondly because the shift in responsibility from the Ministry of Labour to the Ministry of the Interior symbolised a change in the perception of migrants: they were no longer useful labour, but rather a problem of public order.

The commission reported back a few days before the federal elections of March 1983. Over eighty recommendations were made, in two main areas. The first was a catalogue of measures to tighten up conditions for issuing and renewing residence permits. Foreigners were only to be permitted to stay if they were in employment, or entitled to unemployment benefit (which is paid for one year at the most). Long-term unemployment or application for social security benefits (*Sozialhilfe*) was to be a cause for deportation. A further condition for granting residence permits was proof of 'adequate' housing. Conviction for a criminal offence was to be an automatic reason for deportation. This included offences against specific regulations concerning foreigners, such as failure to renew permits on time, or taking up work without permission. Foreigners active in organisations regarded as extremist by the Minister of the Interior were to be deported. Another recommendation was that children under sixteen should also have to apply for residence permits (children born in Germany would have to apply before reaching the age of three months). It was also proposed that foreigners should be obliged to carry a passport or identity card at all times – failure to produce it would be a cause for deportation.

The second area concerned restrictions on further immigration. The maximum age of entry for dependent children was to be dropped from fifteen to five. This was said to be in the interest of integration, as it would allow foreign children to get German schooling. Restrictions on entry of foreign spouses were also proposed. Ideas ranged from an absolute prohibition of entry (unless the partner in Germany obtained naturalisation), to a waiting period of up to five years, or even to annual quotas of foreign wives and husbands. Further proposals aimed at restricting entries of political refugees and undocumented workers (Bundesminster des Innern 1983).

It was generally expected that a new and highly restrictive Foreigners Law would be on the statute books by the end of 1984. The basic principle was the expulsion of those foreigners unable to conform to German expectations concerning work, life-style and political behaviour, in order to allow those remaining to be assimilated. There was a clear expectation that it would be mainly Europeans who would be acceptable, and that many Turks and other non-Europeans would have to go. The essence of the approach was to make regulations much more concrete and binding than they had been in the 1965 Foreigners Law. Dohse and Groth suggest that the wide latitude given to the police and administrative authorities at that time has been seen as an effective form of control, but this had gradually been undermined through court verdicts to the advantage of foreign residents. The new law was to give the bureaucracy clear and specific instruments of control over migrants (Dohse and Groth 1983).

The commission made no specific recommendations on repatriation, as this was already the subject of a specific parliamentary bill (which had in fact been drafted by the previous government). The law to encourage foreigners to return home (*Gesetz zur Förderung der Rückkehrbereitschaft von Ausländern*) was passed by the Bundestag in November 1983. Its main stipulation was that migrant workers from non-European Community countries, who became unemployed through plant closures between 30 October 1983 and 30 June 1984, were offered premiums of DM 10,500 plus DM 1,500 per dependent child if they left the country immediately and finally. Workers who had been working on short time for at least six months were also eligible. Other clauses aimed to speed up repayment of employees' pension insurance contribution and were applicable to all non-EC workers leaving the country. The scope of the main provisions were extremely restricted, both in duration and in terms of who was eligible. In all, only 16,833 workers (14,459 of whom were Turks) applied for premiums. About 140,000 foreigners (120,000 Turks) applied for refunds of pension contributions (SOPEMI 1984: 36). The latter figure in no way implies that those concerned left Germany because of the law – any migrant leaving can claim back contributions, the law merely speeded up procedures.

This is hardly the policy of mass repatriation that CDU–CSU politicians led the public to expect. The foreign population dropped from 4.6 million in 1982 to 4.3 million in 1984, but that was probably due more to economic conditions and to fluctuations in the migratory process than to government action. In 1986 the total foreign population was still just under 4.4 million, indicating a stabilisation. The real impact of this law was ideological: it led people to think that the government was doing something about the 'foreigner problem', as well as giving the impression that foreigners were being offered a humane alternative, and not just being pushed out.

More significant is the failure of the Minister of the Interior to come up with the expected new Foreigners Law. Various preliminary drafts were leaked in 1983 and early 1984. They encountered a storm of opposition from migrant groups, trade unions and sections of the major Churches, as well as the Green Party and the SPD. The proposals were rejected as infringements of civil liberties, violations of Germany's *Grundgesetz* (constitution), and likely to cause impoverishment and social unrest. The Churches saw the measures to cut family reunification as an attack on the family. In the autumn of 1984, the Bundestag debated the issue, and Zimmermann announced that there would be no legislation for the time being.

Why has the conservative government retreated from its stated intentions concerning migrants? One reason is that the 'foreigner problem' seems less acute than a few years ago, and mobilisation of public opinion by the right is running out of steam. New entries of foreigners have dropped, the rate of return has increased, and the process of family reunification is more or less complete. Deterrent measures such as visa requirements and the establishment of internment camps have kept out potential refugees. The number of persons seeking asylum declined from a peak of 107,818 persons in 1980 to 19,737 in 1983. However, the trend then became reversed, with 73,832 persons seeking asylum in 1985 (Beauftragfte der Bundesregierung für Ausländerfragen 1986). By 1986 refugees were again a major issue, which influenced attitudes to all migrants. But behind these immediate factors lie deeper contradictions. The very limited scope of repatriation measures reflects the concern of employers that they might lose an important section of their core labour force (Miles 1986). Moreover, reserves of unemployed migrants maintain the flexibility of the labour market, which has always been a significant aim of German capital. Illegal or semi-legal employment in the informal sector is officially frowned upon, but is often highly beneficial to capital in the core areas, providing cheap services and sub-contractors.[3] This type of work depends heavily on foreign workers, especially of the second generation.

Extreme policies towards foreign residents also affect the political legitimacy of the state. Mass repatriation and increased discrimination would infringe international and bilateral agreements, harming Germany's foreign policy profile. Foreign Minister Genscher (FDP) has frequently had to smooth the ruffled feathers of friendly foreign powers, after overzealous pronouncements by Zimmermann. At home, such policies may be seen as contradicting the principle of the rule of law in a bourgeois-democratic state. The exclusion of 7 per cent of the population from the political process is an anachronism, and a long-term threat to political legitimacy and social peace. Discriminatory measures which violate the *Grundgesetz* also endanger the unity of the forces behind the neo-conservative coalition. When both the Catholic and the Protestant bishops declare publicly that the policies of a Christian-Democrat government are a threat to the family, then alarm bells start ringing.

Zimmermann is popularly known as the 'Minister of Announcements' (*Ankündigungsminister*) because he has had to retreat from most of his loudly proclaimed policies, not only concerning migrants, but also with regard to environmental issues and public order. The neo-conservative government has had more than its fair share of scandals and affairs. It is possible that Kohl's bumbling *bonhomie* conceals not a cool and ruthless interior, but genuine muddle-headedness. But it would be wrong to be complacent about the coalition's failure to introduce a new and more repressive Foreigners Law. After all, the old one is bad enough, and perhaps the CDU–CSU has achieved its objective after all. The discourse on the 'foreigner problem' has continued the process of marginalisation of migrants in Germany, isolating them from other workers, and imposing an ethnic minority situation upon them. The popular concept of an 'enemy within' has been established, helping to stabilise conservative rule and to generate pressure for more policing and stronger administrative control.[4]

The state of Germany has constructed ethnic minorities in a dual sense: first by bringing in migrant workers in response to employers' demands in the growth phase, secondly by defining them as a 'foreigner problem' in the crisis. Yet the migratory process is young compared with France, Britain or other capitalist countries. The current system of bureaucratic marginalisation is unlikely to remain stable for long. The trend will be either towards the increased repression advocated by Zimmermann and other conservatives, or towards strategies designed to encourage and co-opt ethnic elites, as in Britain. Having helped to construct the 'foreigner problem', the state is still far from solving it.

Notes

* This chapter refers to the position in West Germany before unification. Unless otherwise indicated, 'Germany' should be taken to mean the 'Federal Republic'.
1 The stock of the means of production in the capitalist countries grew by 6 per cent annually from 1950 to 1970, while employment grew by 1 per cent per year on average (Glyn and Harrison 1980). Economists have long debated whether accelerated rationalisation and introduction of new technology could have made labour migration unnecessary. In fact decisions on forms of production were made by capital on short- to medium-term profit calculations (and without consideration of social or political consequences for the community). Labour migration appeared useful to large sectors of capital, and helped to provide the profits needed for future investment (see Castles and Kosack 1985; ch. 9, for a discussion of the issues involved). When new technology or the export of labour-intensive labour processes to low-wage off-shore production areas appeared more profitable, this was done – a major reason for the curtailment of labour recruitment in the seventies.
2 The 'Flick Affair' – the *cause célèbre* of the Kohl era – demonstrates the thinness of the line between bourgeois urbanity and gangsterism. The Flick family enriched itself through the Nazi war economy, owning heavy industrial and armaments plants. After 1948, the Flicks helped recreate the German military machine. But in the eighties Flick decided to sell off his industrial assets, take his profits and invest them in US-based transnationals. He made bribes of several million DM to CDU, FDP and SPD politicians to obtain tax

exemptions, saving himself up to 1,000 million DM. The affair ended (due to the persistence of the Green Party) with an FDP Minister of Economics forced out of office, and leading politicians charged with corruption.

3 The most sensational success in German post-war publishing history was the book *Ganz unten*, by the investigative journalist Günther Walraff, which sold over a million copies in just a few months. Walraff disguised himself as an illegal Turkish worker and was employed without documents by 'slave-dealers' (labour-only sub-contractors) to work for some of the best-known companies, such as the Thyssen steelworks in Duisburg (Walraff 1986). The book led to the arrest of the slave-dealers, and to a public outcry for control of such practices. However, as always, it is the illegal workers who are the losers: stricter controls will simply lead to their deportation.

4 The end of the Cold War, the collapse of the Soviet Union and the re-unification of Germany led to dramatic changes in immigration patterns and policies. In the late 1980s there were rapid increases in the number of asylum seekers, with the total reaching 194,000 in 1990. Many came from non-European countries, but the majority were Eastern European: Poles, Romanians and citizens of the Soviet Union. This movement was hard to separate from that of temporary undocumented workers, especially from Poland, and of gypsies from Romania. There was also an influx of 'ethnic Germans' from Eastern Europe, with 397,000 entering in 1990. Many citizens of the GDR moved to the FRG – a movement which became internal migration after re-unification. Altogether over one million immigrants per year entered the FRG in 1989 and 1990. The result was a new debate on the immigration and considerable pressure on earlier groups, which came to a head with the violent racist outbursts of late 1991. Germany finally passed a new Foreigners Law in 1990. It was considerably milder than the earlier proposals of Zimmermann (who had lost office by then), with provisions to make it easier for children born to immigrant parents in Germany to obtain citizenship. But the new law still clings to the myth of temporary immigration and cannot be seen as a durable solution to the problems of minorities.

3

Deindustrialisation and racial minorities in the Great Lakes region, USA

Introduction

The world economy is going through a profound transition. Manufacturing companies are reorganising their activities in the face of stagnant demand, excess capacity and stiff international competition; and that economic reorganisation has brought severe dislocation to industrial communities in many nations. Particularly traumatic has been the crisis and reorganisation in the world's metal-bending industries: auto, steel and machine tools. In those industries employment tends to be highly concentrated in one or two regions in each producing country. So when the crisis hit auto and complementary metal-bending industries in the 1970s, job loss was abrupt, it occurred in large production units, and it had sharp regional impact.

There is reason to believe that racial minorities and women have suffered most from the great slump in the world's metal-bending industries. Minorities are more concentrated in the kinds of jobs, in the kinds of factories, in the kinds of neighbourhoods that are at the epicentre of today's industrial earthquake. And although men outnumber women in manufacturing, one must not overlook the possibility that women have suffered more from the crisis in the manufacturing sector. The number of households headed by a woman continues to rise, and even in households consisting of two adults, the woman's earnings are usually a necessity. Today, more than ever, women cannot afford to lose their jobs. This is especially true of minority women, who are disproportionately represented among the ranks of women who are single heads of household (Sidel 1986).

Minorities are less protected against economic adversity now since global economic crisis has enabled conservative political coalitions to combat shrinking profit rates by contracting the social regulation and welfare programmes fought for and won by civil rights and feminist groups in the 1960s and early 1970s. Even more troubling, the very reasons that indicate that racial minorities and women may have suffered most from the current economic crisis also suggest they may benefit least from the reorganisation of production now under full steam. The better paying manufacturing jobs in the factories of the future are not likely to match up well with the skills minorities and women now possess, and the factories themselves are not likely to be built in the areas where most minorities now live.

Our aim in this chapter is to investigate the impact of deindustrialisation and the reorganisation of production on racial minorities who live and work in the Great Lakes region, the industrial heartland of the United States.

Deindustrialisation and racial minorities

Great Britain and the United States number among the nations which have experienced contracting manufacturing industries and persistent unemployment since the late 1960s. There are scholars in both countries who argue that these trends indicate a process of national deindustrialisation. British political economists have used the deindustrialisation concept to designate the declining ability of British manufacturers to earn enough foreign currency through exports to pay for the materials and capital equipment they must import to keep their industries growing (Blackaby 1979). In the United States, analysts have extended the term to cover other sources of harm to a nation's industries besides declining international competitiveness. Bluestone and Harrison (1982: ch. 1), for example, have also placed under the deindustrialisation mantle

(1)   various forms of business disinvestment in net productive capacity ranging from corporations that milk the coffers of new acquisitions to running down plant and equipment, and outright plant closure;
(2)   the reallocation of profits from productive to speculative or merger activity; and
(3)   unproductive transfer of capital between economic sectors, regions, or nations.

When Bluestone and Harrison investigated Dun and Bradstreet data on plant openings, closings and relocations, they uncovered extraordinary capital mobility within and between regions in the United States. For example, 39 per cent of the jobs listed by Dun and Bradstreet in 1969 had disappeared by 1976 (Bluestone and Harrison 1982: 29). Readily in evidence, too, was the powerful role conglomerates play in the US economy. For example, when the authors surveyed a list of new manufacturing plants owned by the nation's 500 largest corporations, two out of three turned out to be not really new at all; instead, they were plants big companies had acquired from other owners (Bluestone and Harrison, 1982: 40–1). US business investment abroad has also outpaced the rate of investment at home. Between 1950 and 1980, for example, direct foreign investment grew sixteenfold while domestic investment increased eightfold. Overseas profits are now one-third or more of the total profits of the biggest 100 multinationals, and nearly one-third of all US imports actually come from overseas subsidiaries of American companies (Bluestone and Harrison 1982: 42–4).

Deindustrialisation – via runaway shops, plant closings, conglomeration, or investment in other regions or nations – has had a harsh impact on many workers and the communities in which they live. Based upon the analysis of Dun and Bradstreet data, Bluestone and Harrison estimated that various kinds of disinvestment caused between 32 and 38 million jobs to disappear in the United States during the 1970s. In a more recent follow-up investigation, which covered manufacturing plants with 100 or more employees between 1978 and 1982, Candee Harris (1984) discovered that, on average, 900,000 jobs were lost through plant closings each year. And in a special Bureau of Labor Statistics household survey about job loss between January 1979 and January 1984, Flaim and Sehgal (1985) found that plant closings or relocations were responsible for about half the 5.1 million jobs lost by workers who had been at their jobs three years or more. Besides the immediate loss of employment, the human consequences of deindustrialisation often include long-term unemployment, loss of family income, decline in occupational status, loss of health insurance and pension rights, deterioration in physical and mental health, family violence, lost tax revenue and shrinking social services.

There is reason to believe that deindustrialisation shrinks employment opportunities most for minorities. People of colour, particularly black men, are more likely than whites to work in industries experiencing long-term employment decline: primary metals, auto apparel and timber. For that reason, it has been argued that black men are more likely than white men to lose their jobs due to the restructuring of the economy (Bluestone, Harrison and Gorham 1984). Findings from a 1980 study of plant shutdowns by the Illinois Advisory Committee to the US Commission on Civil Rights (1981) support this conclusion. According to Gregory Squires (1981), author of the government report: 'Minorities accounted for 20 per cent of total employment in Illinois companies that closed between 1975 and 1978, compared with only 14 per cent of the statewide labor force.'

Overall company employment often drops when businesses move to new plants, but in Illinois the employment drop was more severe for minorities. According to Squires (1981); 'Among companies relocating from major Illinois cities to suburban rings, minority employment declined 24 per cent and white employment declined 9 per cent. For companies relocating from Illinois to the Sun Belt, minority employment dropped 26 per cent and white employment dropped 17 per cent.' This suggests that dislocated blacks have a harder time finding new jobs than do whites, and that conclusion is supported by a US Bureau of Labor Statistics (BLS) study of workers dislocated from their jobs between 1979 and 1984. The BLS found that 42 per cent of black workers found new jobs after lay-offs in comparison to 63 per cent of whites (Flaim and Sehgal, 1985). It stands to reason, too, that young blacks, newly entering the labour market, are less likely to find their traditional sources of employment although there may be gender differences since young black women may be experiencing employment gains in service industries which are less subject to international competition.

Findings and arguments like these have sparked a debate about industrial policy in the United States. Analysts disagree about the direction US manufacturing is actually taking, about the severity of the impact of employment change on minorities and women, and about the kinds of policy responses that should be forthcoming.

It is not our aim to try and evaluate these contending technical and policy positions here. With deindustrialisation, as with all aspect of social life, *context* becomes important because actions and events always occur in particular settings (Wolin 1972: 44–5). And the insight to be had from analysing nationally aggregated trend data can be limited. For example, the nation is a limited context for understanding the forces promoting deindustrialisation since is it also a profound transformation in the world economy that is putting US manufacturing industries through hard times. Nor does that nation necessarily provide the best context for understanding the impact deindustrialisation is having on employment and the consequences job loss brings for people and the places in which they live. Deindustrialisation may or may not rack up a big economic score on an aggregate national balance sheet; but disinvestment is certainly having a dramatic impact on certain industries and communities (see, for example, Markusen 1985; Hill and Indergaard 1987).

Considerations like these led us to undertake a study of deindustrialisation in the Great Lakes region, the industrial heartland of the United States. Our research objectives in this chapter are to assess the magnitude of industrial job loss and the way declining manufacturing employment has been distributed among social groups in the region. But before we begin that assessment we must explain how we have defined the Great Lakes region and why we selected this area for investigation.

The Great Lakes

> ... a region has no more objective existence than an event; we divide it at will ... the region will be what we make of it by the questions we choose to put to it.   (Veyne 1984: 35)

We chose the Great Lakes, in the first instance, because the crescent of land that bounds the lakes is the traditional heartland of North American industry. Our past work suggests that the states and cities which front this massive waterway are bound together by an interlinked chain of metal-bending industries in crisis and transition (Hill and Negrey 1985).

Three arguments suggest why we think it is defensible to treat the Great Lakes states as a region and as an object of investigation. The first argument is *ecological*. The Great Lakes states share a natural ecosystem – a fragile web of water and air, minerals and sediments, fish, birds, insects, and countless other species of flora and fauna. And the hazards now posed to this ecosystem by toxic pollutants and the diversion of water to outlying, more parched regions implicate all Great Lakes states in a shared fate (Pierson 1984; Washington 1985).

The second argument is *economic*. The bridge from ecology to economy is often short and fairly straight, and so it is with the Great Lakes. One crossing is through the soil, for beneath this industrial crescent lie limestone, coal and iron ore for the production of steel – the structural fabric of an industrial society. A second pathway is along the St Lawrence Seaway which links Great Lakes states to one another, to the Atlantic Ocean and to Europe. Completed in 1959, the seaway was a massive undertaking. Bodies of water were connected, passages dug down as deep as 27 feet, locks built to raise and lower vessels by the height of sixty-storey buildings – all to allow ships to journey the 2,343 miles from Duluth on the Minnesota side of Lake Superior to other industrial entrepôts along the Great Lakes, then into Canada, along the St Lawrence River, and finally into the Atlantic Ocean (Bailey 1984).

The Great Lakes and the seaway system allow cargo ships to move iron ore mined in northern Minnesota to steel mills along Lake Michigan and Lake Erie; to move coal from the eastern fields of Pennsylvania to power plants in industrial metropolises like Buffalo, Cleveland, Detroit and Milwaukee; and to move grain from Chicago docks to domestic and overseas markets. Just how critical a role the seaway plays in linking the economies of the Great Lakes states to one another and to international markets is suggested by the amount of cargo carried on the seaway each month: it is greater than the tonnage transported on all of Michigan's highways each year (Bailey 1984).

The third argument is *political*. Facing common ecological and economic problems, public officials in the Great Lakes are co-operating more and constructing a firmer regional political identity. The regional impact of industrial decline, the consistent effort by the Reagan administration to shift the federal government's domestic responsibilities back to the states, and the threat that water diversion could damage the Great Lakes ecosystem led to the formation of the Council of Great Lakes Governors in June 1983 (Herbers 1983). Sometimes this fledgling regional alliance brings together governors from six states, as in the Council's summit conference on co-operative economic growth (Council of Great Lakes Governors 1983); at other times all eight of the states that border the Great Lakes have joined forces, as in the Great Lakes charter agreement to fight water diversions (Pierson 1985).

In any case, the Council of Great Lakes Governors has engaged in a number of cooperative steps, including

(1) putting together a charter, organisational goals, task forces and priorities;
(2) drafting a long-term regional economic blueprint;
(3) mounting a co-ordinated strategy for dealing with Washington;
(4) developing a regional natural resource policy; and
(5) promoting the image of a unified region through public relations and by designating the region as a common market (Council of Great Lakes Governors 1983: 19–22).

Regional definitions shift with the problem at hand. The bureau of the census, for example, does not group the Great Lakes states into one regional category; rather the bureau spreads them across the 'Middle Atlantic', 'East North Central', and 'West North Central' regional census categories. But we think our ecological and political arguments justify grouping the eight states bordering the Great Lakes into one object of investigation. From west to east the states composing the Great Lakes region are: Minnesota, Wisconsin, Illinois, Indiana, Michigan, Ohio, Pennsylvania and New York (see Map 3.1).

States are politically defined administrative units, so they often encompass multiple and diverse local economies. We do not agree with all that Jane Jacobs has to say, but we think she is right when she argues that cities play a critical role in creating the wealth of nations (Jacobs 1984). We also think that states establish ties to one another and to the rest of the

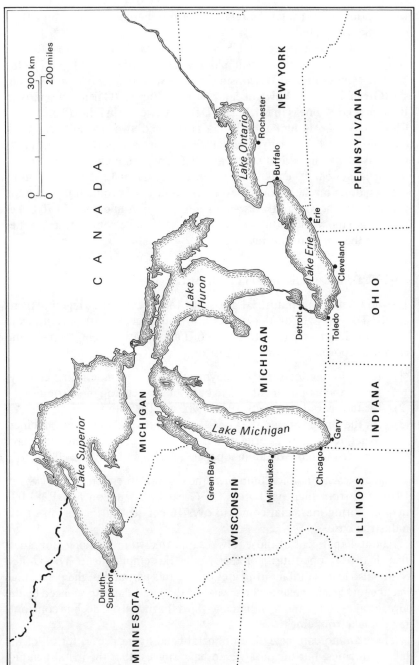

Map 3.1 The Great Lakes region, Great Lakes states and lakefront cities

world primarily through the relations of production and exchange their own cities promote.[1]

If you run a pen along the US shore of the Great Lakes, west to east, you will eventually cross eleven major lakefront cities (see Map 3.1). One borders Minnesota and Wisconsin (Duluth-Superior), two are in Wisconsin (Green Bay and Milwaukee), one is in Illinois (Chicago), one is in Indiana (Gary), one is in Michigan (Detroit), two are in Ohio (Toledo and Cleveland), one is in Pennsylvania (Erie) and two are in New York (Buffalo and Rochester). These lakefront cities are ports and entrepôts interlinked by the seaway into a still mighty, though shaken, urban-industrial system. The lakefront cities are the Great Lakes states' industrial windows on the world. They are the centres of production and trade which mesh the Great Lakes states into a region and the Great Lakes region into the world industrial economy. These lakefront industrial cities are also the object of our investigation.

Deindustrialisation in the Great Lakes

Just how severe an industrial crisis has the Great Lakes region experienced? To shed light on this question, we put together a time series from data provided in various US Bureau of Labor Statistics employment and earnings reports. This time series is for

(1) total non-agricultural employment, total manufacturing employment, and employment in five basic metal-bending industries;[2]
(2) for the years 1960, 1970, 1979, 1982 and 1985; and
(3) for the United States, the Great Lakes states and the lakefront cities. What follows is a brief summary of research findings we have reported in more detail in a paper (see Hill and Negrey 1987).

The biggest economic slump since the Great Depression hit the USA in 1979, and from then until 1985 the Great Lakes region lost 1,371,000 manufacturing jobs; that comes to over 16 per cent of the region's total industrial base.

About 46 per cent of those jobs disappeared from the lakefront cities; they lost over one-fourth of their industrial employment. The United States also lost manufacturing jobs during this period, but the percentage decline for the nation as a whole was less than half that experienced by the Great Lakes states and less than one-third the industrial decline confronting the lakefront cities.

There are no complete data on metal-bending industries for all of the lakefront cities, but the data we do have suggest that the metal-bending industries carried the brunt of the slump in manufacturing. Particularly hard hit were primary metals (-34.9 per cent) and fabricated metals (-14.3 per cent), but the overall percentage decline in metal-bending jobs outpaced the drop in all of manufacturing by 5.2 per cent in the Great Lakes and by 2.5 per cent in the nation as whole between 1979 and 1985.

But has not growth in other sectors of the economy, like high technology and services, compensated for the precipitous decline in manufacturing? The trends in total non-agricultural employment suggest the answer is yes, for the United States, and no, for the Great Lakes region. US manufacturing employment declined 7 per cent (1.6 million jobs) between 1979 and 1985, but total non-agricultural employment actually grew by 8.8 per cent (7.8 million jobs); so growth in other sectors offset manufacturing decline. Not so for the Great Lakes states; there, employment growth in other sectors was insufficient to counterbalance industrial decline. All told, Great Lakes employment hardly changed at all between 1979 and 1985, and growth in other economic sectors did not come close to compensating for the slump in manufacturing experienced by the lakefront cities – they lost half a million jobs during the period.[3]

The data also show a sharp decline in the Great Lakes share of national employment – not just total employment, but also jobs in manufacturing and, more ominously for the region, jobs in metal-bending, too. In 1960, Great Lakes manufacturing accounted for 48 per cent of US industrial work, and the Great Lakes generated 42 per cent of all jobs in the nation. By 1985, the Great Lakes' share of manufacturing had declined 12 percentage points, and the region accounted for less than one-third of the nation's total employment. A declining regional share is apparent for every metal-bending industry, too. These trends indicate that much of the manufacturing decline in the Great Lakes comes from corporate flight to other regions of the USA.

What do we conclude from these findings? Deindustrialisation in the Great Lakes has been palpable since the Great Slump began in 1979;[4] metal-bending industries have been hit the hardest; and, unlike the nation as a whole, job loss in the Great Lakes has not been counterbalanced by job growth in other sectors. To the contrary, we need just the reverse sort of logic to make sense out of the calamity that seems to have befallen the lakefront cities. There, as metal-bending jobs disappeared, other jobs left, too.

Deindustrialisation and racial minorities in the Great Lakes

Just how severely have racial minorities been afflicted by the industrial crisis besetting the Great Lakes region? The US Equal Employment

Table 3.1 *Percentage change in employment by occupation (durable goods manufacturing: USA, Great Lakes states and selected lakefront cities, 1979–84)*

	USA	States	cities[a]
Total	− 18.5	− 27.8	− 34.0
White collar	4.2	− 9.7	− 13.8
Officials and managers	− 7.8	− 18.9	− 24.2
Professionals	20.1	1.1	− 7.5
Technicians	1.9	− 11.0	− 18.7
Sales workers	7.1	2.6	24.9
Pink collar			
Office and clerical workers	− 13.5	− 26.9	− 31.2
Craftworkers	− 23.3	− 29.4	− 36.1
Production workers	− 29.7	− 36.0	− 45.3
Operatives	− 28.3	− 35.1	− 44.4
Labourers	− 34.5	− 39.5	− 48.9
Service workers	− 24.4	− 32.5	− 28.8

[a] The selected lakefront cities include Milwaukee, Wisconsin; Chicago, Illinois; Detroit, Michigan; Cleveland, Ohio; and Buffalo, New York.
Sources: US Equal Employment Opportunity Commission, *1979 Report: Minorities and Women in Private Industry*, Washington, DC: Government Printing Office, 1981; US Equal Employment Opportunity Commission, (printout of 1984 data)

Opportunity Commission (EEOC) provides the best data available on this issue.[5]

Unfortunately we cannot match EEOC employment data exactly to the Bureau of Labor Statistics data reviewed in the preceding section. The most recent available EEOC data are for 1984; EEOC data cover larger firms only; durable goods manufacturing is the closest classification we can get to metal-bending; and while data are available for all eight of the Great Lakes states, they are available for only five of the eleven lakefront cities. Even so, we can put together a very informative profile on how employment changes in durable goods manufacturing between 1979 and 1984 variously affected (1) white-, pink- and blue-collar workers; (2) blacks, Hispanics and whites;[6] (3) men and women – in the United States, in the Great Lakes states and in five lakefront cities. The data organised in Tables 3.1 through 3.3 move from general to more specific categories. Employment changes in durable goods manufacturing are first presented separately by occupation, race and gender. Then we cross-classify race and gender, and then race, gender and occupation – all in an effort to pinpoint the subgroups of the labour force most affected by job loss in the manufacturing industries.

Occupation

Of all the job categories surveyed in Table 3.1, production workers (operatives and labourers) were hardest hit by the slump in heavy industry. Between 1979 and 1984, production job losses ranged from − 29.7 per cent in the USA to − 45.3 per cent in the lakefront cities. Pink-collar (office and clerical) and service workers also experienced consistent job losses, although at a lower rate than production workers. White-collar workers suffered fewer job losses than other occupational groups, and some white-collar categories, including professional and sales workers, actually added employment while the rest of the manufacturing labour force was sharply contracting. Evidently, during economic slump periods large companies cut back their production facilities more severely than their largely white-collar, regional and central headquarters' operations.

Race

Table 3.2 divides the manufacturing labour force into race and ethnic categories. As can readily be seen, black workers suffered considerably

Table 3.2 *Percentage change in employment by race and gender (durable goods manufacturing: USA, Great Lakes states and selected lakefront cities, 1979–84)*

	USA	States	Cities[a]
Total	− 18.5	− 27.8	− 34.0
Race			
White	− 18.5	− 27.1	− 32.2
Black	− 26.7	− 36.1	− 43.2
Hispanic	− 15.0	− 28.8	− 36.0
Gender			
Male	− 20.9	− 29.0	− 35.2
Female	− 11.8	− 24.1	− 29.9
Race and gender			
White male	− 20.4	− 28.0	− 33.2
White female	− 13.0	− 23.8	− 28.4
Black male	− 31.4	− 38.6	− 45.2
Black female	− 15.9	− 29.4	− 37.6
Hispanic male	− 20.0	− 32.2	− 38.2
Hispanic female	− 3.8	− 20.2	− 30.4

[a] The selected lakefront cities include Milwaukee, Wisconsin; Chicago, Illinois; Detroit, Michigan; Cleveland, Ohio; and Buffalo, New York.
Sources: US Equal Employment Opportunity Commission, *1979 Report: Minorities and Women in Private Industry*, Washington, DC: Government Printing Office, 1981; US Equal Employment Opportunity Commission (printout of 1984 data).

higher rates of industrial job loss than whites, and they did so at every geographical level: for the USA as a whole (-26.7 per cent for black compared to -18.5 for whites), in the Great Lakes region (-36.1 per cent for blacks compared to -27.1 per cent for whites) and in the lakefront cities (-43.2 per cent for blacks compared to -32.2 per cent for whites).

Hispanic workers consistently experienced lower rates of job loss than blacks, but the employment experience of Hispanics in comparison to whites is less uniform. At the national level, Hispanic workers had a lower rate of job loss than whites (-15 per cent compared to -18.5 per cent). In the Great Lakes region, Hispanics and whites lost industrial jobs at about the same rate (-28.8 per cent and -27.1 per cent, respectively). In the lakefront cities, Hispanic workers experienced a bigger percentage job decline than whites (-36 per cent and -32.2 per cent, respectively). These findings – that Hispanic workers suffered lower rates of industrial job loss than whites in the USA and higher rates than whites in the lakefront cities – probably reflect the migration of northern industrial capital to low-wage, right-to-work states in the south-west. Most Hispanics of Mexican heritage live in the south-western United States, and Mexican-Americans are disproportionately employed in low-wage, non-union jobs.

Gender

Contrary to our expectations, between 1979 and 1984, women workers in durable goods manufacturing suffered considerably lower rates of job loss than did men. This finding is particularly distinct at the national level where the percentage job loss among women (-11.8 per cent) was just over half that experienced by men (-20.9 per cent); a similar, though less pronounced disparity is also evident in the Great Lakes states and lakefront cities.

The distribution of employment losses among men and women in durable goods manufacturing is linked to the kinds of jobs that contracted *and* the kinds of jobs that expanded during the economic slump. Since most women in the manufacturing sector work in clerical and office jobs, lower job loss rates among women as compared to men is partly explained by lower job loss rates among pink-collar as compared to blue-collar workers (see Table 3.1). But that is not the whole story.

Non-union, low-wage, part-time and temporary employment grew during the economic crisis even while unionised, full-time, high-wage industrial jobs sharply declined. Gender differences in job loss reflect this trend.[7] Of the 7.3 million jobs added to the US workforce between January 1980 and March 1986, an amazing 84.3 per cent went to women

(Serrin 1986). The proportion of the labour force working part-time since 1980 has increased and women are 57 per cent of part-time workers (Serrin 1986). Most part-time jobs filled by women are in retail trade and miscellaneous services, but there is evidence that part-time positions also have grown in durable goods industries.[8] Office automation also encourages part-time work, so some of the decline in office and clerical work may be offset by increasing part-time work in that job sector.

Race and gender

When race and gender categories are combined, it is black men who consistently experience the highest rates of job loss followed by Hispanic men and black women. Nearly a third of all black men working in durable goods manufacturing in the United States lost their jobs between 1979 and 1984. Black male production workers also suffered the greatest rate of job loss in the region (− 43.3 per cent) and in the nation as a whole (− 37.2 per cent).

Place

The EEOC data, like the findings from the Bureau of Labor Statistics reviewed above, indicate uneven distribution of industrial job losses across the nation, the Great Lakes region and the lakefront cities. With stunning regularity the worst job losses and inequities are concentrated in the lakefront cities. Table 3.1 indicates that between 1979 and 1984, jobs in durable goods manufacturing shrunk by 18.5 per cent in the USA, by 27.8 per cent in the Great Lakes states and by 34 per cent in the five lakefront cities. The decline in production jobs was even more pronounced. As profiled in Table 3.3, between 1979 and 1984, 29.7 per cent of the nation's durable goods production jobs disappeared, that figure rose to − 36 per cent in the Great Lakes states, and to − 45.3 per cent in the five lakefront cities.

Why have blacks suffered most from the industrial crisis besetting the Great Lakes region? We think the answer is largely given in one word: segregation. Black workers tend to be concentrated in older industrial plants and those are the ones most frequently closed; and black city dwellers tend to be concentrated in older urban neighbourhoods and that is where plants and production jobs are disappearing the fastest. To make this argument conclusive, we would have to examine several examples of industries, states and cities. We cannot go into that much detail here, but we can discuss the case we know best: the auto industry in Detroit and Michigan – the epicentre of the Great Lakes industrial earthquake.

Table 3.3 *Percentage change in employment among production workers[a]
by race and gender (durable goods manufacturing: USA, Great Lakes
states and selected lakefront cities, 1979–84)*

	USA	States	Cities[b]
Total	− 29.7	− 36.0	− 45.3
White male	− 32.0	− 38.7	− 45.5
White female	− 26.8	− 33.4	− 43.0
Black male	− 37.2	− 43.3	− 49.5
Black female	− 24.7	− 36.5	− 46.1
Hispanic male	− 28.6	− 39.0	− 43.8
Hispanic female	− 14.4	− 27.0	− 37.2

[a] Production workers include operatives and labourers
[b] The selected lakefront cities include, among others, Milwaukee, Wisconsin; Chicago,
Illinois; Buffalo, New York
Sources: US Equal Employment Opportunity Commission, *1979 Report: Minorities and
Women in Private Industry*, Washington, DC: Government Printing Office 1981; US Equal
Employment Opportunity Commission (printout of 1984 data).

Black employment in the auto factories began in 1916, but until the eve
of the Second World War black auto workers were largely confined to
foundry work or the lowest paying maintenance positions. Blacks and
women joined the assembly lines during the Second World War, and by
the late 1940s the number of black production workers at Ford and
Chrysler was sizeable. But as blacks entered production jobs, the
company and the union reacted with dual seniority lists, dual assignment
of jobs and other caste-like divisions of the labour force (Denby 1968;
Hill 1969). And even today, when blacks account for 25 per cent of the
labour force at Chrysler, 15 per cent at Ford, and 14 per cent at General
Motors, they are still struggling against a racially biased evaluation
system administered by whites who want to preserve skilled craft jobs for
themselves.[9]

As blacks migrated to Detroit during the post-war period, inner-city
auto plants were engulfed by black neighbourhoods. White workers
sought employment in the suburbs while the inner-city auto operations
became increasingly black. By the mid-1960s, some downtown Chrysler
plants had a majority of black hourly employees. On the second shift at
Chrysler the ratio was as high as 85 per cent (Northrup 1968). By 1979,
Chrysler had twenty-one production facilities in the Detroit metropolitan
area, fifteen of those were in the central city. One-third of Chrysler's
entire blue-collar workforce and one-tenth of its white-collar employees
were black, and 50 per cent of Chrysler's black employees resided in
central Detroit. The Chrysler payroll to black workers alone amounted to

$800 million – an estimated 1 per cent of total black income in the United States (Northeast–Midwest Institute 1979: 11–13).

Between 1960 and 1980, racial segregation in the Detroit region hardly changed. The index of dissimilarity, a good measure of residential segregation, indicates the proportion of blacks that would have to move to achieve a distribution of blacks and whites among neighbourhoods that corresponds to their percentage in the metropolitan population. In 1960 the index registered 87 per cent, in 1980 it was 86 per cent. During those two decades, the central city went from under 40 per cent to over 60 per cent black while the suburbs stayed 94 per cent white (Darden 1985: 12–13). The Motor City was choked off from surrounding suburbs by a white noose. And it was in the surrounding suburbs that the auto companies built their new plants.

Car factories are built next to railroad lines, in open space, but not far from an available labour force. Once built, an auto plant attracts metal-bending supply industries, then residential subdivision. So, as the auto industry expanded, the Motor City sprawled, further and further out. Detroit's first mass production facilities were located on the near eastside of the city, the industrial and residential expansion to the north-west followed. Ford later built the Rouge plant to the south-west, and around it grew one of the world's largest manufacturing complexes. After the Second World War, the Big Three auto companies constructed some twenty new plants in the Detroit region, all in the suburbs (Jacobs 1981).

Little wonder, then, that when the crisis hit the auto industry in the 1970s, it hit minority workers and inner city minority neighbourhoods in Detroit the hardest.[10] In Tables 3.4 through 3.6, we repeat our earlier analysis of industrial job loss by occupation, gender and race, but now with data from Michigan and Detroit. These tables reveal the same pattern of job loss as the tables reviewed above, only the tendencies are accentuated. For example:

(1)   Over one-half of industrial production workers in Detroit lost their jobs between 1979 and 1984, and job loss reached 59 per cent among operatives in the Motor City (see Table 3.4);

(2)   The employment inequalities facing minorities are more pronounced in Michigan and Detroit than in the Great Lakes region as a whole (See Table 3.5);

(3)   Contrary to findings for the USA and the Great Lakes region, men and women lost about the same percentage of jobs in Michigan and in Detroit (see Table 3.5);

(4)   The contrast between the industrial employment experience of Hispanics in Detroit and Hispanics elsewhere in the nation is striking;

Table 3.4 *Percentage change in employment by occupation (durable goods manufacturing: USA, Michigan and Detroit, 1979–84)*

	USA	Michigan	Detroit[a]
Total	−18.5	−30.7	−39.0
White collar	4.2	−14.7	−20.3
Officials and managers	−7.8	−25.6	−31.3
Professionals	20.1	0.1	−6.8
Technicians	1.9	−15.9	−25.2
Sales workers	7.1	−12.5	−9.5
Pink collar			
Office and clerical workers	−13.5	−32.4	−36.3
Craftworkers	−23.3	−28.9	−39.8
Production workers	−29.7	−37.5	−50.4
Operatives	−28.3	−36.7	−49.2
Labourers	−34.5	−41.5	−59.2
Service workers	−24.4	−32.5	−28.8

[a] Standard Metropolitan Statistical Area
Sources: US Equal Employment Opportunity Commission, *1979 Report: Minorities and Women in Private Industry*, Washington, DC: Government Printing Office, 1981; US Equal Employment Opportunity Commission (printout of 1984 data)

Table 3.5 *Percentage change in employment by race and gender (durable goods manufacturing: USA, Michigan and Detroit, 1979–84)*

	USA	Michigan	Detroit[a]
Total	−18.5	−30.7	−39.0
Race			
White	−18.5	−29.1	−36.4
Black	−26.7	−39.1	−48.0
Hispanic	−15.0	−33.1	−48.9
Gender			
Male	−20.9	−30.8	−39.3
Female	−11.8	−30.5	−37.7
Race and gender			
White male	−20.4	−29.0	−36.8
White female	−13.0	−29.2	−34.2
Black male	−31.4	−40.0	−48.2
Black female	−15.9	−36.0	−47.0
Hispanic male	−20.0	−33.5	−50.0
Hispanic female	−3.8	−31.9	−44.5

[a] Standard Metropolitan Statistical Area
Sources: US Equal Employment Opportunity Commission, *1979 Report: Minorities and Women in Private Industry*, Washington, DC: Government Printing Office, 1981; US Equal Employment Opportunity Commission (printout of 1984 data)

Table 3.6 *Percentage change in employment among production workers[a] by race and gender (durable goods manufacturing: USA, Michigan and Detroit, 1979–84)*

	USA	Michigan	Detroit[b]
Total	− 29.7	− 37.5	− 50.4
White male	− 32.0	− 35.3	− 48.8
White female	− 26.8	− 37.8	− 50.0
Black male	− 37.2	− 43.5	− 52.1
Black female	− 24.7	− 40.8	− 54.5
Hispanic male	− 28.6	− 37.6	− 57.5
Hispanic female	− 14.4	− 37.0	− 54.8

[a] Production workers include operatives and labourers.
[b] Standard Metropolitan Statistical Area
Sources: US Equal Employment Opportunity Commission, *1979 Report: Minorities and Women in Private Industry*, Washington, DC: Government Printing Office, 1981; US equal Employment Opportunity Commission (printout of 1984 data)

44.5 per cent of Hispanic women workers in Detroit's manufacturing industries lost their jobs compared to only 3.8 per cent nationwide (see Table 3.5);

(5)　Hispanic males had the highest job loss rate among Detroit's production workers, but race and gender differences pale in comparison to the devastating job loss experienced by all production workers alike in the Motor City (see Table 3.6).

Reorganisation of production, minorities and public policy

By almost any measure, blacks are now poorer than before the deep recession of 1979–82. Between 1960 and 1975, the proportions of blacks in poverty fell from 55 to 31 per cent. But after 1979, an additional two million blacks fell below the poverty line. Today, 34 per cent of the black community is in poverty and nearly half of all black children are poor. In 1984, the poverty rate for black female-headed households was 51.7 per cent (Sidel 1986: 3). Black infant mortality is twice as high as white; in some central cities, like Detroit, it is even higher than in some Third World countries. And the proportion of black youth going to college has actually declined from about one-third to 1976 to slightly more than one-fourth in 1983 (Shulman 1984).

According to the deindustrialisation argument, the most important cause of rising black poverty is shrinking employment opportunities for black men. In 1930, four-fifths of black men were employed; by 1983, only one-half had jobs. In 1984, 37 per cent of black men aged sixteen to twenty-four were employed, while 63 per cent of white men in that age category had jobs. A rise in labour force participation by black women in the 1970s was insufficient to offset the loss in black male income (*Dollars and Sense* 1986: 6).

What sorts of strategies are corporations and governments pursuing in response to the industrial crisis and with what consequence for racial minorities in the Great Lakes region? Federal policies have exacerbated the detrimental impact of deindustrialisation on racial minorities. Blacks bore the brunt of the Reagan administration's fight against inflation – during the last steep recession black unemployment reached 18.6 per cent compared to 9.7 per cent for whites. National economic recovery, beginning in mid-1982, has not fundamentally altered this picture. In the past, black unemployment rose faster than white in recessions but dropped faster in recoveries. This time black unemployment has responded more slowly to renewed national economic growth. Today, blacks are two-and-a-half times more likely to be unemployed than whites (*Dollars and Sense* 1986: 6).

Federal budget cuts have caused public sector lay-offs and that disproportionately affects racial minorities, who work for the government in higher proportions than whites. Programmes that might assist black workers in finding jobs, like employment and training efforts, were cut in half between 1981 and 1986. Civil rights enforcement agencies have been hamstrung and affirmative action policies largely been abandoned. The number of cases of labour market discrimination brought by the Equal Employment Opportunity Commission and the Department of Justice has dropped 50 per cent since 1980 (Shulman 1984).

A conservative national administration has devolved government responsibilities and contracted federal assistance, forcing troubled states to rely more upon themselves. White House policy makers argue that cuts in federal civil rights expenditures and other government activities, when paired with state and local financial incentives for the private sector, serve to stimulate economic growth and create more jobs. The special beneficiaries of this growth strategy, the national administration argues, are minority communities with high unemployment rates. Yet a 1982 study on *Business Incentives and Minority Employment*, conducted by the Wisconsin Advisory Committee to the US Civil Rights Commission, concluded that supply-side measures to generate economic growth – tax cuts, deregulation and other business incentives – actually victimise rather than benefit minorities and women.

The Civil Rights Advisory Committee compared employment patterns in South Carolina, a state offering many business incentives, and Wisconsin, a state with a deteriorating industrial economy. As it turned out, minorities were under-represented in businesses moving to or created in South Carolina. Minorities were under-represented in businesses relocating from the city of Milwaukee to the suburban ring. And Wisconsin's industrial revenue bond programme, a supply-side policy to encourage business investment, discriminated against minorities and women. Racial minorities and women were under-represented in 75 per cent of a sample of Milwaukee firms receiving Industrial Revenue Bond financing, despite state prohibitions against discrimination.

If, however, a national industrial policy is to emerge in the United States, it will most likely grow out of the new legislation, new agencies, and new programmes states and localities have been putting forward to reroute their economies in directions they hope will ensure their economic future (Schweke and Webb 1984). We can draw upon Michigan once again to illustrate the industrial policy path many Great Lakes states are following today.

Michigan's economic development officials argue that the state's best hope for the economic future continues to be founded upon durable goods manufacturing. Still in place are sizeable clusters of manufacturing and labour skills, industrial infrastructure, networks of suppliers and complementary industries, and universities strong in industrial technology. But what is required is a reorganisation of the state's metal-bending economy from standardised mass production to a more flexible, targeted system of production.

Michigan's long-term strategy is to shift the state's economy to a higher valued position in the international division of labour by specialising in the 'factory of the future' (State of Michigan 1984). In the auto industry, for example, this means replacing the conventional production of cars and parts with computer- and robot-assisted manufacturing; it means precision engineering and incorporating new materials technology – graphite, ceramics and plastics – into the production process. In the steel industry it means replacing basic steel production with custom cast, speciality steel and applying advanced manufacturing techniques – continuous casting, computerised controls, automated inspection – to the organisation of work.

General Motors' new Saturn project is an excellent example of what movement toward flexible system production is all about. General Motors has recently bought into robotics, machine vision, artificial intelligence, information processing and advanced micro-electronics companies, and the company is going all out to become the leading creator of the factory of the future. And Saturn is designed to bring these new ventures together in a new corporate subsidiary charged with making a new car with new methods to boost the company's share of the small car market. Saturn will have a computer for a heart; robots will perform most tasks; work stations will be linked by computer-guided vehicles; and fancy software of all sorts will guide the design, engineering, production and distribution of the vehicle.

But Saturn's mission is to increase productivity and corporate profits vastly by producing as many cars as now with less than half the workers and plant space. So, the flexible system model applied to most of manufacturing also forecasts a big decline in industrial employment and a society where the most visible social divisions may lie between those workers who manage to become attached to a big corporation and those left on the other side of the corporate divide.

Michigan's economic policy analysts are pretty straightforward about the social implications of their industrial development strategy. This is what they have to say about it:

> To prosper, Michigan's economy must change. Change can create new opportunities for many people and places, but it can also disrupt them. The transition to a more technology intensive, high skill manufacturing economy that creates a job for a recent community college graduate with computer programming skills may also end up laying off middle-aged unskilled steel workers somewhere down the line. Such a transition may contribute to the prosperity of Ann Arbor, Troy and Grand Rapids while deepening the economic despair in Detroit, Flint, and Jackson. Transitions can be both painful and uneven.
>
> (State of Michigan 1984: 103)

This quote is from a state document entitled *The Path to Prosperity*, but the road it forecasts for Michigan's black labour force is rocky, indeed. Black workers are unlikely to get their share of the new jobs, and black communities are unlikely to get their share of the new production complexes coming out of the corporate-initiated and state-supported industrial transition.

As compared to whites, middle-aged blacks are more likely to be unskilled metal-bending workers and, therefore, more likely to be displaced. In 1982, one-third of black adults in the Michigan labour force were unemployed (Gregory 1985: 49). Black youths are less likely to have computer programming skills and, therefore, less likely to find entry level work. In 1982, two-thirds of the black teenagers in the Michigan labour force were unemployed. In 1976, blacks held 50 per cent of all entry level auto industry jobs in Detroit; today it is 35 per cent (Bailey 1985; Gregory 1985).

Ann Arbor, Troy and Grand Rapids are likely growth centres in

Michigan, but 80 per cent of Michigan's 1.2 million black residents live in metropolitan Detroit and Flint – areas state policy makers think may encounter 'deepening economic despair'. New employment policies are critically needed, including job training, but the most serious mismatch is not between skills and jobs, but between jobs and places. Between 1973 and 1982, for example, metropolitan Detroit lost 108,000 jobs, but the area's labour force grew by 105,100 (State of Michigan 1984: 108). This is the structural basis for 'deepening economic despair'. Since the supply of jobs is now so desperately inadequate, new job creating policies which complement advanced technology strategies must have priority. Most resources need to be put behind work sharing, community-based economic development schemes, and alternative use strategies for abandoned or underutilised plants. The problems of uneven development can only be addressed by targeting places as well as industries and that means regional political co-operation and more state planning. Our findings suggest there are some hard political challenges ahead for those who value racial justice in America.

Notes

Research reported in this chapter was supported in part by financial assistance from Urban Affairs Programs at Michigan State University.

1 About one-third of the US population resides in states that border the Great Lakes, and this area produces more than 40 per cent of the nation's commodity transactions. The Great Lakes region generates more in retail sales than all European nations except France, and its income approximates that of the United Kingdom (Council of Great Lakes Governors 1983).

2 The five metal-bending industries, as listed in the *Standard Industrial Classification Manual* (Office of Management and Budget 1972) are Primary metals (SIC 33), Fabricated metals (SIC 34), Machinery, except electrical (SIC 35), Electrical and electronic equipment (SIC 36) and Transportation equipment (SIC 37).

3 By comparing 1979 and 1985 are we not masking the 'Reagan Recovery' beginning in the middle of the period? True, total US manufacturing declined sharply between 1979 and 1982, then turned slowly upward after that. The Great Lakes slumped much more severely early on but failed to generate new manufacturing employment and remained stagnant right on through the end of the period. The lakefront cities went further and faster, suggesting they played locomotive to the slumping states.

4 Note, however, that Great Lakes manufacturing was declining even before the slump of 1979. Great Lakes industries grew before the 1960s, but even then at a sluggish pace relative to the rest of the country. Great Lakes industries started spiralling downward in the 1970s and then took a deep plunge at the end of the decade.

5 As part of its mandate under Title VII of the US Civil Rights Act of 1964, the Equal Employment Opportunity Commission requires annual employer reports on the social make-up of the workforce in private firms with 100 or more employees. These data are published by sex of worker under nine occupational categories for each of four minority groups: Black, Hispanic, Asian American/Pacific Islander, and American Indian/Alaskan native. And according to the US Department of Labor, '... the EEOC's survey data are the only source of comprehensive (annual) employment statistics for minorities and women in private industry, by occupational categories, for the United States, and for States, Standard Metropolitan Statistical Areas (SMSAs) and smaller geographical areas such as counties' (US Department of labor 1983: 72). The data reported here are drawn from United States Equal Employment Opportunity Commission (1979, 1984).

6 The numbers of Asian Americans/Pacific Islanders and American Indians/ Alaskan natives were too few in the Great Lakes region to allow for reliable comparisons.

7 While the EEOC definition of employees excludes temporary and casual workers hired for a specified period of time or for the duration of a specified job, regular part-time and full-time employees are included.

8 According to *Business Week* (1 April 1985), to cite two examples, Ford Motor Company has begun hiring part-time workers at its Rawsonville plant and General Motors is doing so at its Packard Electric Division in Warren, Ohio.

9 Interview with the Rev. James Kennedy, President of Pro-Minority Action Coalition at AC Spark Plug in Flint, Michigan, as reported in Chauncey Bailey, 'Black Workers and the Auto Industry – An Uncertain Future,' *Detroit News*, 9 June 1985.

10 By the late 1970s, over half the families in the metropolitan Detroit area relied on paycheques from two family members, usually the husband and the wife. In one of every five families with children, a woman was the sole parent and head of household; within the city limits of Detroit, women were the sole parent in 45 per cent of all families with children (Babson *et al.* 1984: 218).

4

Black workers, recession and economic restructuring in the West Midlands

This chapter falls naturally into two sections. The first is largely descriptive, attempting to summarise some of the main features of economic restructuring in the West Midlands, with particular reference to the position of black workers. The second part is theoretical, comprising a critical overview of some approaches that might offer a full or partial account of the phenomena earlier described. It is suggested that the problem – which could be seen as one of incipient ghettoisation – has two aspects. The first is to account for processes of apparent labour market exclusion; the second is to explain why this has been accompanied by growing ethnic concentration. To understand what Stephen Castles (1984) has called 'new ethnic minorities' we need new lines of thought. As powerful as migrant labour theory has been in the past, it can hardly be applied unchanged to communities that are neither labouring nor migrating.[1]

Economic restructuring in the West Midlands

The area delineated by the label 'West Midlands' is the West Midlands County (WMC) which is an administrative region that has existed since 1974. It comprises the so-called 'Black Country' (Dudley, Wolverhampton, Smethwick, Walsall, West Bromwich, Stourbridge and Oldbury), Birmingham (including Solihull and Sutton Coldfield) and Coventry. Despite the quite separate and distinguishing histories of each city or major town within the county, they have more in common than is true for the West Midlands region as a whole, which includes the four surrounding counties. The most distinctive and critical feature of the WMC is its heavy dependence on manufacturing and in particular the metal manufacturing industries. Within the county, however, there is functional specialisation and interdependence with basic processes (e.g. foundries for metal

77

castings) being concentrated in the Black Country and finished manufac-
tures in Birmingham and Coventry, notably vehicles, machine tools and
other engineering products (Batley 1984).

The concentration on engineering and vehicle production increased
after the depression of the early 1930s and was given a further boost by
military demands in World War II. Almost two-thirds of Coventry's
labour force was dependent on these sectors in the mid-1950s together
with nearly a third in the case of Birmingham (Batley 1984: 14). Post-war
attempts at controlling uneven development through regional policy were
not sensitive to this vulnerability, preferring to focus on areas suffering
declines in heavy manufacturing and mining.

The inter-war years brought the full participation of the West Midlands
in the wider processes of combination and agglomeration that resulted
from the recession of the 1930s and the restructuring which followed from
it. First, through a process of horizontal integration, larger firms emerged
which were further strengthened by vertical integration in the post-war
years. By the early 1970s these processes were well entrenched and the
West Midlands became less a haven for small firms enmeshed in a stable
web of interdependence and more one area of operations for multinational corporations directed from London, Paris, Detroit or elsewhere.
The restructuring of the late 1970s and the early 1980s has to be seen in
this light. However, the earlier dependence on a few main industrial
sectors remains. In 1981, 40 per cent of employees in the WMC worked in
manufacturing and two-thirds of these were in motor vehicles, metal
goods, metal manufacturing and mechanical engineering.

The changes brought about by restructuring and by the recession have
been startling and dramatic. Nearly a quarter of a million manufacturing
jobs have been lost since 1979, and from a region of the country with the
highest wages and lowest unemployment, WMC now comes eighth out of
ten regions in income terms and has the highest level of long-term
unemployment in England and Wales. The West Midlands region as a
whole was second only to the South-East in 1976 in terms of GDP per
head, but by 1981 it had become the poorest region in England in this
measure. Changes in unemployment rates from the mid-1970s can be seen
in Figs. 4.1 and 4.2. These suggest a major turning point around 1980.
Until that time WMC fared a little worse in trade cycle lows and a little
better at peaks than the national average. Since 1980 this relationship has
been broken. Similarly, women's unemployment was within a percentage
point of men's until 1980. From that time, it has risen at a far slower rate
than men's and is now a little more than half the male rate.

It is a mistake to see this collapse in employment as arising solely from
the metal manufacturing and engineering industries. This has been highly

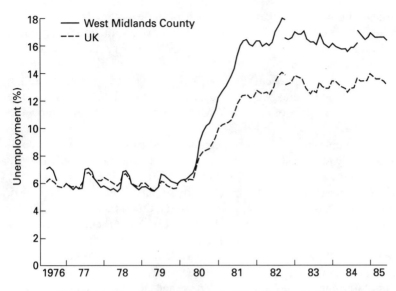

Figure 4.1 Unemployment rates in West Midlands County and the UK (Source: West Midlands Districts Joint Planning and Transportation Data Team)

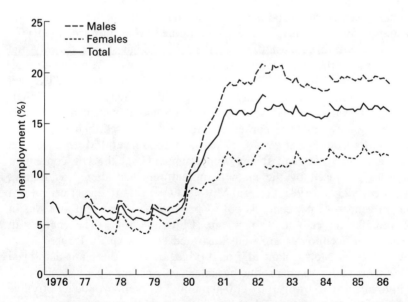

Figure 4.2 Unemployment rates in the West Midlands County (Source: West Midlands Districts Joint Planning and Transportation Data Team)

significant numerically because of the size of these sectors, but others have declined at the same rate. Falls in employment of about a quarter – equal to manufacturing – were recorded in the food industry, in textiles and in construction between 1979 and 1982. Falls were even recorded in the service sector (– 6.9 per cent) and in distribution (– 16.0 per cent), and in both cases these declines were half as large as in the UK as a whole. The overall result in terms of current WMC unemployment rates is shown in Table 4.1.

Falls in employment have not been confined to small, inefficient companies unable to cope with the pressures of recession. In fact, as Table 4.2 shows, in terms of redundancies announced from May 1979 until May 1985 at plants in the WMC, multinationals have fully held their own. These 'top ten' in terms of announced redundancies contributed 49 per cent of those in the region as a whole (142,146). All of them are within the top fifteen manufacturing companies in the West Midlands, and only four have their headquarters in the county (while four are in London and two overseas). Chief amongst them have been the car and vehicle manufacturers. Although it is not possible to be exact, declines in employment in car and vehicle assembly and in component companies appear to have contributed more than 50 per cent of redundancies in the West Midlands County over this period.

It is important to be clear that vehicle manufacturers are leading the way in restructuring production, rather than in responding to declining demand. Overall vehicle sales have continued on an upward trend. For example, sales in August 1985 are the second highest ever for any one month and in the first twenty days of August they were 21 per cent up on the same period in 1984 (*The Sunday Times*, 25 August 1985). The two major changes that have occurred are, first, the increasing internationalisation of production and, second, the adoption of advanced manufacturing technology. In 1984, market leaders Ford increased their proportion of imports from 54 per cent to 57 per cent and General Motors from 53 per cent to 58 per cent. It has been estimated that the UK content of vehicles produced by the main manufacturers has altered as follows between 1973 and 1983: General Motors 89 per cent to 26 per cent; Ford 86 per cent to 43 per cent; Talbot 97 per cent to 35 per cent and Austin Rover 100 per cent to 92 per cent (EDU 1985: 33). The changes in production technology are well illustrated by the Austin Rover Group (ARG) at its Metro plant at Longbridge. In 1979 the plant employed 15,000 manual workers producing sixteen cars per man per year. By 1985 employment had dropped to 11,000 manual workers producing fifty-five cars per man per year (EDU 1985: 20). This is the same or better than productivity per man in other European plants producing small cars. The

Table 4.1 *Unemployment in the West Midlands County, June 1985*

Travel to work area[a]	Male		Female		Total		Change on last month	Change on last year
	Absolute	%	Absolute	%	Absolute	%		
Birmingham	85,210	19.1	33,593	11.2	118,803	15.9	−1,391	1,177
Coventry and Hinckley	25,022	17.2	11,751	12.4	36,773	15.3	−476	−76
Dudley and Sandwell	32,316	19.2	13,367	13.1	45,683	16.9	−455	170
Walsall	18,761	20.7	7,287	12.4	26,048	17.4	−528	657
Wolverhampton	18,105	21.5	7,087	13.3	25,192	18.3	−204	448
West Midlands County	153,771	19.3	59,312	11.6	213,083	16.3	−2,209	2,173
UK	2,196,838	15.7	981,744	9.6	3,178,582	13.1	−62,365	148,859

Note: [a] Unemployment statistics for areas within the county are collected on the basis of 'Travel To Work Areas' (TTWAs) which do not necessarily correspond with district boundaries. Hence, the total for the West Midlands County is not equal to the sum of the constituent TTWAs.
Note that from September 1984 the travel to work area boundaries have been redefined. For futher information see the September 1984 issue of 'Unemployment Briefing'.
Source: Figures provided by the Department of Employment.

Table 4.2 *Main contributors to redundancies in the West Midlands County, May 1979 to May 1985*

British Leyland	27,948
Lucas	9,895
GKN	8,410
British Sound Reproducers	6,444
Cadbury–Schweppes	4,200
Dunlop	3,968
Tube Investments	2,520
Talbot	2,340
Massey Ferguson	2,005
British Steel Corporation	1,700
	69,430

Source: West Midlands Enterprise Board, 'Unemployment Briefing'

tendency within the industry as a whole is to standardise and externalise components increasingly and to use UK plants for assembly rather than manufacture. The implications for future employment are severe; even now 60,000 jobs are dependent on ARG alone.

Race and restructuring in the West Midlands County

The evidence has been mounting for some time that ethnic minorities, with their origins in recent waves of migrant labour, are deeply affected both by recession and by restructuring. From a position of high levels of employment in the early years, they are now being forced disproportionately into the ranks of the workless. With continuing high rates of labour market participation and age profiles skewed towards the young, they are likely to be major victims of recession and restructuring wherever it occurs (Fig. 4.3).[2] What is less well appreciated is that there is a strong spatial dimension to current processes of economic change and that the areas of cities most vulnerable to decline are precisely those where minorities were initially forced to congregate and where more recently they have sought to consolidate their communities. The overall position for the West Midlands County in terms of unemployment rates in 1984 is shown in Fig. 4.4 for major ethnic minority groupings. It shows that exceptionally high rates of unemployment are found for Afro-Caribbean and Asian workers in the WMC, mirroring – but at a much higher level – the poorer chances of employment that have followed from the decline in economic activity for all workers. There is a strong areal effect in this decline. In some wards of the cities and towns that comprise the WMC, the unemployment rates have reached the levels of labour market

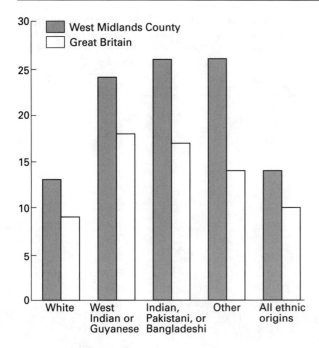

Figure 4.3 Percentage unemployment rates for persons aged sixteen or over by ethnic origin, June 1984 (Source: *The Employment Gazette*, June 1984)

Table 4.3 *Rank order correlations between ward level unemployment rates (1985) and population proportions in households headed by NCWP (= New Commonwealth with Pakistan) migrants (1981) in the West Midlands County*

Metropolitan Districts	Rank order correlation	Significance	Wards (N)
Birmingham	+0.711	p < 0.01	39
Coventry	+0.682	p < 0.01	18
Sandwell	+0.589	p < 0.01	24
Wolverhampton	+0.717	p < 0.01	20
Walsall	+0.645	p < 0.01	20

Source: 1981 Census (SAS): WMCC (EDU)/DE unemployment statistics (unpublished)

Table 4.4 *Unemployment rates and percentage change in unemployment rates for the West Midlands County by concentration of minorities, 1981–5*

Metropolitan Districts	Concentration of ethnic minorities[a]		
	High	Low	All
Birmingham			
1981	21.5	12.5	15.2
1985	29.2	16.7	20.3
1981–5	+35.6	+32.0	+33.5
Coventry			
1981	18.8	13.4	15.2
1985	24.2	15.4	18.3
1981–5	+28.6	+14.8	+20.4
Sandwell			
1981	18.4	13.9	15.2
1985	24.1	17.5	19.3
1981–5	+30.5	+25.8	+27.3
Walsall			
1981	17.8	11.9	13.3
1985	23.3	14.0	17.5
1981–5	+31.2	+17.3	+21.6
Wolverhampton			
1981	17.6	14.2	16.1
1985	22.4	15.4	19.3
1981–5	+27.2	+8.4	+19.9
WMC[b]			
1981	19.6	12.9	15.1
1985	25.9	16.0	19.2
1981–5	+32.1	+24.4	+27.6

Note: [a] 'High refers to wards with 10 per cent or more of the population in a household headed by someone of black migrant (from the New Commonwealth with Pakistan) origin; 'low' refers to wards with less than 10 per cent.
[b] WMC excludes Dudley and Solihull.

Source: 1981 Census: WMC unemployment statistics by ward (unpublished)

collapse. In June 1985, for example, the unemployment rate for all workers in the Sparkbrook ward of Birmingham was over 42 per cent, while for Aston it was 39 per cent and Nechells 38 per cent. Rates in excess of 30 per cent are found in some wards in all the constituent Metropolitan Districts of WMC, with the exception of Dudley and Solihull.

Moreover, there is a close correlation between minority concentrations and unemployment rates. Table 4.3 shows that in the five main Metropolitan Districts of the West Midlands County there is a highly significant relationship between unemployment levels and the proportions of ethnic minorities in the wards that comprise them.[3] This is remarkably consistent across the county. What is even less well appreciated is that as restructuring has gathered pace, the relationship has become more pronounced. This can be shown in Table 4.4 which indicates unemployment rates in the main Metropolitan Districts (MDs) and the percentage rise in unemployment over the four years 1981–5. Thus there was a 28 per cent rise in unemployment in the five main MDs over the past four years from 15.1 per cent to 19.2 per cent. Table 4.4 also divides each MD into areas of 'high' and 'low' concentration of minorities.

This distinction is arbitrary, but on balance a figure of 10 per cent or above living in households headed by a black (NCWP) migrant was chosen as the dividing line. Thirty-two per cent of the workforce or just under one million live in wards with a 'high' concentration of minorities on this definition, ranging from 56 per cent in Wolverhampton to 23 per cent in Walsall. Two points are immediately obvious. First, the unemployment rate is substantially higher in 'high' concentration wards for WMC as a whole and for all five MDs. Second, the overall rate of decline in employment prospects, characterised by a rise in unemployment of nearly 28 per cent since 1981, masks a major difference between 'high' and 'low' minority areas. This is particularly striking in Wolverhampton where the rise in unemployment has been marginally less severe, and it is least obvious in Birmingham where the overall decline has been most marked. However, this relationship is not linear since Coventry has declined less rapidly overall, but 'high' concentration areas have been burdened with rising unemployment at twice the rate experienced by those wards with smaller minority proportions. It is clear, however, that not only are the inner area wards where minorities are concentrated more likely to experience unemployment, they are also declining faster in employment terms than elsewhere in the county. Thus the unemployed in the 'high' concentration areas constituted 42.1 per cent of the total unemployed in 1981 and 43.5 per cent only four years later. In fact, as far as *rates* of unemployment are concerned, the earlier figures almost certainly underestimate the position for 'high' concentration areas, since they are based on denominators derived from the 1981 census. We know that between 1971 and 1981, the population loss in 'inner-city' areas was far higher than for the outer city. For example, population in the 'Core Area' of Birmingham fell by 18.6 per cent between 1971 and 1981, compared with a fall of 3.6 per cent for the rest of the city (Birmingham

ICP 1985: 41). If the differential has been sustained, as is true for the labour force as for the population as a whole, and is roughly the same for all MDs, then a best guess might be that 'high' concentration areas actually showed unemployment rates of 28–9 per cent, rather than 26 per cent in 1985. This means that the differential rates of decline are even more marked than the earlier figures suggest.

The salience of the foregoing would be lessened if ethnic minority populations were moving out of the inner areas of original settlement to live in the outer city, suburbs or beyond where employment prospects are brighter and where most of the limited economic growth has occurred. There is no evidence that this has taken place; on the contrary, the picture throughout Europe, including Britain, is one of selective out-migration (Drewe 1981; Eversley and Bonnerjea 1980). The familiar pattern of white flight and black persistence leads to core areas of cities coming to contain higher proportions of blacks, even though levels of absolute concentration may remain more or less the same. Thus in 1971, the worst seventeen wards in Birmingham in terms of urban deprivation contained 34 per cent of the city's total population but 78 per cent of the city's black population. By 1981, the overall population in these wards had fallen by 17 per cent, but their racial composition had altered from 20 per cent black to 49 per cent black. The proportion of minorities in the city living in these wards had remained about the same at nearly four out of five (census 1981).[4]

In explaining why black workers find themselves in such desperate straits in the West Midlands County, there are two major tasks. First, we have to know *why* they are disproportionately affected. This is not as obvious as it might at first appear. After all migrant labour generally is incorporated because of the advantages of cost and docility that it supposedly offers over indigenous labour. On that basis would it not be the last, rather than the first to be removed in times of recession and market pressure? Secondly, there is the puzzle of why black labour remains concentrated in areas of decline. Given the history of recent geographical mobility, why is there not greater evidence of black labour following white labour to the suburbs, small towns or rural areas? I will call these questions, respectively, the problem of exclusion and the problem of concentration.

Accounting for exclusion

The reversal in the fortunes of the West Midlands County has been so sudden and severe that it is no surprise to find a lively debate as to its cause or causes. It is equally unsurprising to discover that local debates reflect national preoccupations and that these themselves follow well worn grooves etched by the pens of countless platoons of economists. Devotees of micro-economics see the malaise in terms of restrictions on individual firms. A lack of small firms, or too little diversity or constraints arising from local planning decisions, all attract support. Fothergill and Gudgin (1982), for example, in one of the most discussed contributions, ascribe much of the demise to nothing more startling or subtle than a shortage of space for industrial expansion. The implausibility of this view in accounting for the current crisis and its locational consequences has led others towards exploring the particular structural features of the region. The so-called 'shift-share' perspective has the benefit of opening up the debate to embrace questions of restructuring because it focusses attention on deindutrialisation and, in particular, the reliance of the WMC on those aspects of metal manufacture which have been subject to international-isation and technological change (Blackaby 1979). A concentration on the economic history of the *region*, however, has the disadvantage of attribut-ing economic decline to the vagaries of chance, although a variant of regional thinking in the case of the WMC focusses on the negative impact of post-war regional policy. More persuasive is a view that attributes job loss in part to the production decisions of multi-location companies (Massey and Meegan 1982).

Detailed consideration of these perspectives is beyond the scope and purpose of this chapter. What is clear, however, is that they have rarely paid attention to the incorporation of secondary labour or its exclusion as spatial shifts occur in the production process. But it cannot be said that traditional approaches to the study of 'race' have provided greater insight. While it may have been true that ideologies of racism generated out of a colonial encounter have been critical in structuring the position of ethnic minorities in British society and in shaping their subsequent experiences, the recent processes of exclusion cannot be explained in this way. This is one of the central arguments in Wilson's controversial study of blacks in the US economy (1978). When he writes that 'it would be difficult to argue that the plight of the black underclass is solely a consequence of racial oppression' the argument is framed in terms of class divisions amongst American blacks (1978: 151). In Britain there is no such division, since the black middle class is largely absent, but the argument is equally valid since it is impossible to account for recent processes of exclusion without reference to restructuring and the evolution of new processes of accumulation. There is no evidence that the dramatic deterioration in the labour market position of British blacks is simply the result of increasing black subjugation. On the contrary, there has been some growth in equal opportunity legislation, analogous to but less significant than that which occurred in the US after 1964.

It is then to the political economy of production that we have to turn for a more adequate account. Unfortunately this research has yet to be undertaken in the UK but previous work suggests two possible lines of investigation. The first is that considerable body of literature relating to labour market segmentation. The second is the rapidly developing body of ideas on the spatial organisation of production. Of course, these two lines of thinking are not always distinct, but the observed phenomenon of labour exclusion could be the result of changes in the production process, or of shifts in its location. To express this in other language: if racial minorities are to be seen as 'fractions' of the working class, is the separation that is implied dependent on splits in the labour market consequent upon changes in the labour process or upon divisions in production as the result of spatial reorganisation? (See Miles 1982.) Should we look for changes in the 'social structure of accumulation' or in the 'geography of production'? (See Gordon *et al.* 1982; Massey 1984.) Before dismissing this distinction as artification, because both may occur, it is important to consider the political implications of each, which are quite opposite. Both are processes rather than absolute states. If the former dominates, then, as Gordon and his co-authors suggest, we may have an explanation of labour quiescence (1982). If the latter, the prediction would be a healing of fractures between black and white as they face a common dilemma.[5]

The argument in the New International Division of Labour thesis is that restrictions on the valorising of labour in Western capitalist countries, together with the 'new' availability of labour power in the Third World in a usable (i.e. proletarian) form, and production processes and forms of communication that diminish the problem of dislocated production, have made possible massive capital migration and externalisation of production (Fröbel *et al.* 1980; Ernst 1980 and 1981). One of the major problems with this well-known and important thesis is that it is largely oblivious to divisions within internal labour markets. As Cohen and Henderson have noted:

> For those concerned with issues that arise from an international division of labour, there is a major task of theoretical labour ahead of them, a task which involves the full incorporation of race and gender categories into their analysis. (Cohen and Henderson 1982: 28)

As account which sought to explain differential impacts on sectors of local labour markets through this approach would have to show either that, notwithstanding the mobilisation of racism and its effects, comparative rates of labour valorisation were such as to lessen attractions of incorporated black labour, or that what were once sufficient attractions to guarantee high levels of utilisation had changed so that later generations of blacks were no more attractive or even less attractive, than their white peers.

The debate over labour market segmentation has taken many forms.[6] Perhaps the most developed and sophisticated version is that which takes an historical perspective in which segmentation is seen as a phase following a previous period of increasing homogenisation (Gordon *et al.* 1982). Labour segmentation is understood as a strategy by corporations to overcome the success of union power:

> Increasingly after 1930s, females and black males composed a growing proportion of the U.S. labour force. This growing heterogeneity afforded many employers an opportunity to play upon race and sex divisions within their workforces and to enhance their relative bargaining power over workers in their establishments. (Gordon *et al.* 1982: 238)

But even if this thesis holds for the UK, it is clearly more relevant for migrant labour *inclusion* rather than *exclusion*. We have to look to the *failure* of labour market segmentation (at least on racial lines) rather than its success. The argument for the US is that the pact with the primary sector failed to guarantee quiescence after 1970. The result has been shifts in production accompanied by an aggressive anti-union stance. Alternatively the argument could be that labour market segmentation failed not so much because of a disinclination on the part of the primary sector to accept its rewards but because black workers themselves have become unionised and therefore have come to resist their continued exploitation (Massey 1984: 42).[7] Shifts of production, the incorporation of new technology and the use of part-time female labour are then explicable in terms of the deracialisation of the workforce. Processes of exclusion, far from being the result of discrimination, are evidence of its decline. Falling levels of discrimination, possibly assisted by equal opportunity legislation, undermine the returns to capital of labour market segmentation on racial lines and lead to the adoption of alternative strategies.

Both the NIDL thesis and various forms of labour segmentation theory turn on the question of labour power and the terms for its utilisation. It is by no means clear, however, whether actual shifts in production from the WMC can properly be seen in this light. For example, the best economic account to appear so far – while not denying the salience of labour cost and control strategies – also identifies diversification as a major factor (Flynn and Taylor 1984). Diversification, of course, need not lead to areal decline. In the West Midlands, however, diversification did not occur through new company starts but through the acquisition of companies outside the West Midlands. Thus TI, for example, moved rapidly out of capital goods, following steel nationalisation in 1967, and into consumer goods because these had much higher added-values. The companies they acquired were not in the West Midlands. Similarly GKN, the largest engineering group in Britain, rapidly diversified in the late 1960s and early 1970s, building up a capability in more sophisticated engineering products but also concentrating on distribution and industrial services. The company acquired or collaborated with firms in Belgium, Holland, France and North America as a result of their policy changes which led to a rundown in the low technology manufacturing side of the enterprise, such as the fastener business in which it used to be dominant. The increase in transnational production did not occur therefore solely because of an attempt to control costs within the same industry; it came from diversification into new products and new services in new markets. Partly this was to avoid protectionism, partly to appease nationalistic tastes and partly to keep abreast of increasingly international markets. The emergence of Japanese motor manufacturers as transnational corporations is further evidence of the same motives. Thus a very significant reason for the decline in the economy of the WMC comes not from manipulations of labour power but from mergers, acquisitions and other means of concentrating capital. As Flynn and Taylor write:

> As the West Midlands was specialised in the industrial sectors which the 'prime movers' were attempting to shift away from, acquisition had, by definition, to take place outside the conurbation or region. (1984: 134)

The implication of this argument is that the impact on labour will be undifferentiated, affecting all within the area, rather than some sectors more than others. The effect on black labour will only be greater because of its concentration in areas from which locational shifts are occurring.

Accounting for concentration

A great deal of the energies of those interested in social space in cities has been expended on accounting for *segregation* (Peach et al. 1981; Woods 1979). Largely as a counter to earlier assimilationist belief, social geographers have demonstrated the salience of ethnicity in accounting for the distribution of minorities in European and North American cities. One of the key debates that this has given rise to is that between 'constraint' and 'choice' perspectives, in which the key issue is whether observed patterns of spatial distribution suggest community preferences or the result of opportunities limited by structural factors. There are three problems with this literature. First, the most common measure used to estimate segregation, the index of dissimilarity, is a measure of the spatial distribution of a specified group in a given area. It is not the same thing as *concentration*, which is the proportion of a given group occupying a given area. Segregation may be low, or it may be falling, within – say – streets. Concentration may, however, be rising. It matters less in Birmingham, for example, that there are areas which are largely occupied by Mirpuris and much more that most Afro-Caribbeans live in the four wards of the city with the greatest social deprivation. Second, the argument between constraint and choice models is largely factitious. The reality of all choices is that they are made under conditions of constraint. It is true that class factors alone cannot account for the distribution of minorities in cities, any more than can ethnicity on its own account for the low levels of out-migration from the inner urban areas. Finally, the debate has been largely ahistorical. What is perhaps more interesting than patterns of segregation, or even of concentration, is why, given local labour market collapse, there has been so little evidence of internal out-migration.

It is quite apparent that theories of discrimination and racism have a role to play in accounting for patterns of persistence of urban communities. If housing allocations are racially structured, or if mortgage lending policies are patterned by racist practice, then this is bound to have areal effects. It seems unlikely, however, that this would itself account for continuing concentrations. The counterposing of discrimination and ethnicity is as false in accounting for continuity of communities as it is for their initial development.

Processes of discrimination, racial attacks and exclusion from the social relations of production through unemployment appear to strengthen bonds of resistance and to underpin the defence of urban space. Processes of decline and restructuring bring about a new specialisation of urban space that is 'resisted by neighbourhoods that do not want to disappear, by regional cultures that want to cluster together, and by people who, previously uprooted, want to create new roots' (Castells 1983: 314–15). This is an important theoretical point. Is it the case that urban communities composed of one or two major ethnic groupings, being in conditions of increasing poverty and worklessness, become *more* rather than less entrenched? Castells sees this process as linked to restructuring itself:

> The world's rootless economy and the local cooperative community are two faces of the same process, heading towards a decisive confrontation. (Castells 1983: 315)

If that is so then the contradiction between economic rootlessness and community cohesion is most extreme with ethnic communities in British industrial cities and is fully exemplified in the urban disorders in Brixton and Toxteth in 1981 and in Handsworth in 1985.

Conclusion

The first part of this chapter attempts to show that the West Midlands County has experienced an unprecedented change in its economic base since the mid-1970s. It has shed labour at a massive rate, and large transnational corporations have figured very prominently in this process. The change has been led by the metal manufacturing and processing industries, but it is not due to them alone. Processes of inner urban decline, experienced in almost all older industrial cities, appear to have been compounded by this rapid industrial change. Almost all categories of manual workers have suffered in this process but none more so than the post-war migrant labourers and their offspring. It is not entirely clear whether this is because of their concentration in *sectors* of decline or because they are disproportionately concentrated in *areas* of decline. If the former, then there may be a link between migrant incorporation and exclusion, perhaps through the labour process itself or through the cost calculus at the point of production. Questions are then posed about the defensive actions of black and white workers, which may have affected the benefits to capital of labour segmentation (at least on racial grounds). In the West Midlands case some doubt is thrown on these propositions but they are not rejected. The economic processes appear to be complicated, however, involving changes to capital itself, as well as to the relations of production. What is argued is that propositions concerning discrimination as the motor of exclusion are untenable.

A second theme, although less developed, concerns the concentration of ethnic minorities in areas of urban decline. It is argued that this is more important than ethnic segregation because the latter tells us very little about ghettoisation. This is because it matters more that blacks are in ghettos rather than that the ghettos are black, which in any case they are not. Although discrimination approaches are important here they do not tell the whole story. Even in the absence of racism, ethnic communities would probably exist, partly as a result of the 'spatial division of labour' and partly because of the communalising effects of a common experience. Curiously, this may mean that approaches to research emphasising political economy and 'ethnicity' are compatible. Concentration may not be the result of 'choice' or 'constraint', or even of constrained choice, but of choice through constraint. That is inner urban communities may gain ethnic coherence because of labour market exclusion.

Notes

1 What is being sought here is an extension, not a rejection, of migrant labour theory (Castles and Kosack 1985; Miles 1982).
2 However, neither skill levels nor the age profile account for more than a small proportion of the difference between black and white unemployment rates. Racism is normally regarded as the major factor, but it is part of the argument in this chapter that we must also look to the social relations of production for an explanation.
3 The nature of the data here necessitates an inference that could be criticised as an ecological fallacy. It *could* be the case that unemployment rates and the minority presence are unrelated, but this would conflict with direct evidence on black unemployment.
4 There are a number of data problems here, mainly due to the changing of ward level boundaries between censuses but also because of alterations in the census questions from which race and ethnicity data are derived. However, there is no evidence that dispersal is growing; rather the pattern for Birmingham of high levels of concentration of minorities with rapidly rising overall proportions appears to be true in all major cities of the UK where blacks have settled.
5 Incorporating 'space' into our analyses may help explain why both appear to happen together. For example, north/south splits have become much more pronounced in the UK since 1979, but inner urban disturbances appear to involve both black and white young people (cf. Urry 1981; Harris 1983).
6 The literature contains its own segmentation between adherents of the Piore approach in which technology is stressed, and more Marxian variants (Berger and Piore 1980).
7 Forms of resistance may vary and should not be thought of as only industrial. The unrest and riots in Brixton, Toxteth and Handsworth all contained an element which could be seen as a defence of territory and in which the police, for example, were seen as agents of an external power.

5

Jobs for the girls: the production of women's outerwear in the UK

Introduction

It has become a part of conventional wisdom to state that the UK clothing industry is in decline and that the major cause of declining production and employment is the penetration of the domestic market by imports from low-wage countries. But if the balance of comparative advantage enjoyed by producers in the low-wage countries is so great we need to ask why do the multiples who control 70 per cent of British retailing in clothing continue to source any of their range in the UK?

There is certainly plenty of evidence to show that confronted by declining profitability and the controlling influence exerted by the highly centralised buying power of the big retailers the UK clothing industry has undergone a massive restructuring. This has been accompanied by equally massive job losses in the registered sector of work since 1979. Rationalisation and technological job displacement in medium and large firms has been juxtaposed by an officially unrecognised expansion of domestic subcontracting, particularly in areas of high unemployment and ethnic minority residential concentration.

The outcome of this restructuring is a dualist form of industrial organisation which is much more clearly differentiated in terms of product market and capital/labour ratios than anything we have witnessed since World War II when factory production became more profitable than production based in the home. This increasingly two-tier industry is headed by a far slimmer band of firms looking to increased mechanisation to meet the more stable portion of demand and in some cases supplementing ranges with off-shore processed goods. This tier is linked to a much larger and unofficially expanding band of small and medium sized firms who operate in a largely precarious subcontractual position to manufacturers (with and without their own production facilities), and to

94

wholesalers. The latter off-load their stock holding risks onto these smaller firms. In turn the subcontractor survives at the expense of his workforce through the intensification of work, the extension of the working day and the under-reward and often casualisation of the labour force. There is good evidence to suggest that firms operating under such conditions compete on price and speed with Third World producers.

I want to comment on these developments in two main ways; first, to suggest that at a theoretical level a dynamic dualist model is most appropriate in analysing both industrial structure and the complex of class, gender and ethnic relations which support it; secondly, from a policy perspective we need to consider the wisdom of current local authority intervention in the clothing industries.

'Dualism' or the best of both worlds

In 1980, the English translation of Fröbel, Heinrichs and Kreye's *The New International Division of Labour* was published. Focussing on the production strategies of West German textile and garment firms the authors argue that confronted by a falling rate of profit at home (due principally to the cost and strength of indigenous labour) such firms began to apply the Babbage Principle of an increased division of labour, allowing the substitution of skilled by less skilled (cheaper) labour power, on a global basis. From the early 1970s onwards West German firms began relocating an increasing share of their labour intensive assembly stages of production to low-wage developing countries and to centrally planned economies of Eastern Europe. The authors argue that, given the constantly changing nature of the product in the clothing industry, further mechanisation of the production process is deemed too risky, thus the continuing search for cheap labour or methods of cheapening labour on a global basis as the preferred strategy of firms in combatting a falling rate of profit.

The basic thesis of *The New International Division of Labour* has been criticised for its tendency to identify the search for cheap labour (and the extraction of absolute surplus value) as capital's prime means of restoring the rate of profit, rather than identifying relative surplus value or increasing the productiveness of labour (principally through technical innovation) as the general basis of capital accumulation (Duffield, 1981 and Jenkins 1984).

In his critique Jenkins argues that when it is recognised that relative surplus value is the general basis of accumulation in the capitalist mode of production, relocation can be seen as a specific response which arises in circumstances when there are major obstacles to increasing relative surplus value. Thus it occurs primarily in industries (such as clothing and electronics) where economic and technological considerations make increased mechanisation difficult with existing technologies (1984: 43). Jenkins goes on to argue that such relocation may be temporarily limited to the extent that once the obstacles to technological innovation are overcome such production may be redomesticated.

A rather different formulation is possible if one does not regard these strategies as mutually exclusive but as interdependent in so far as technical innovation has always been related as much to labour supply side factors as it has to the technical possibilities within an industry. Furthermore a dualist industrial structure of primary and secondary firms linked by a complex web of internal and international subcontracting allows firms in the primary sector to reap the benefits of 'both worlds' of capital accumulation. Following Piore (1979 and 1980) it is posited that much demand in the clothing industry can be effectively separated into stable and unstable portions with the larger, primary sector firms using increasingly capital intensive techniques at home and relocation of much assembly work off-shore to meet predictable demand, while the smaller, secondary sector firm caters for the unpredictable portion of demand. These two sectors are linked by a complex web of subcontracting which reduces the rigidities found in the primary sector due to the inflexibility of factory based production, labour legislation and trade union organisation.

Thus while the primary sector firms have a range of strategies available to them in their pursuit of profitability, based on technological innovation and the allocation of factors of production to their most efficient use at home and abroad through an international division of labour, the secondary sector firm has little scope for independent action. The prime means of maintaining profitability amongst secondary sector firms is the extraction of surplus through the intensification and casualisation of work within the realms of the underground economy. The following section outlines more precisely the form this restructuring has taken in the UK.

The decline and restructuring of the UK clothing industry

In the immediate post war-period the UK clothing industry was buoyant and factory based production had become more profitable than that based in sweatshops or in the home. Taylorised production methods were introduced for standardised goods such as men's tailored outerwear, shirts and underwear. The new production methods alongside piece work and bonus payment systems considerably raised labour productivity in these sectors. In contrast the production of fashionwear, particularly women's unstructured outerwear underwent less change in location and production methods.

As late as 1962 Hong Kong was the only significant exporter of clothing among the developing countries (Keesing and Wolf 1980: 13). This export trade was largely controlled by British overseas trading companies who were joined during this period by buyers from US and European retailing outlets. But all this was to change over the next decade as many developing counties chose clothing to spearhead their export-led growth. Given their longer lead times they could only successfully compete in those standardised product categories subject to lower levels of seasonality and unpredictability in demand. Despite an increasingly protectionist stance by the developed countries and significantly higher levels of labour productivity, domestic manufacturers in these product categories were faced with 'automating, relocating or evaporating'. Firms such as Burton's went down the first route in as many stages of production as was technically feasible before virtually abandoning manufacturing altogether for the more profitable retailing option, while Tootals relocated most of their shirt production off-shore.

Between 1975 and 1979 the UK and Italy were the only countries in the European Community to increase their output in clothing production. However, since 1979 the UK index of production has steadily declined from 110.7 to 90.4 in 1983 (*British Business*, 10 August 1984: 598). By 1983 imports had captured over 40 per cent of the market in some sectors with men's and boys' tailored outerwear, weatherproof outerwear and men's shirts being the worst affected sectors and women's unstructured clothing the least affected (see Table 5.1). Exports either failed to grow at a compensatory rate or actually declined so that a crude trade deficit of £250.7 million in 1978 had become a deficit of £736 million in 1983 (*ibid.*: 600). The most significant feature of import penetration over the period in question is that the main area of growth was from within the EC itself (33 per cent in value of all clothing imports). The notion of decline due to cheap imports does not hold in the case of most EC produced clothing as it is neither cheap to buy nor cheap to produce. Britain has in fact the lowest clothing industry wages in the EC and the lowest non-salary wage costs (for instance employers' national insurance contribution). Labour productivity is the final factor affecting unit labour costs, and productivity remains as high in Britain as in other major European clothing producers such as France and Germany.

However small the increases in productivity in the industry it results in job loss. An EC report published in 1981 on the prospects of the clothing industry calculates that for every 1 per cent increase in productivity in the European clothing industry 15,000 jobs a year are lost (CEC 1981: 15). A

Table 5.1 *Output, import penetration and employment by sector of the clothing industry in the UK*

	1978	1979	1980	1981	1982	1983	1st quarter 1984
Weatherproof outerwear – output		110.5	100.0	83.5	85.7	88.4	79.7
Import penetration		32.1	32.0	41.3	39.9	33.5	
Employment		15.2	13.3	11.9	11.8	12.6	
Men's and boys' tailored outerwear – output	127.4	122.9	100.0	88.8	82.6	81.9	83.8
Import penetration		27.3	27.5	31.6	33.8	43.4	
Employment		58.8	42.3	35.6	33.5	35.8	
Women's and girls' tailored outerwear – output	107.6	122.7	100.0	90.0	83.7	77.7	78.8
Import penetration		23.9	24.1	29.3	29.5	33.5	
Employment		35.6	28.3	26.0	25.7	22.2	
Work clothes, overalls – output	102.4	106.6	100.0	88.5	85.9	99.9	103.4
Men's and boys' shirts, underwear etc. – output	102.1	105.0	100.0	92.2	104.4	106.2	98.1
Import penetration		32.8	35.7	37.2	35.7	32.8	
Employment		39.1	34.1	31.7	34.9		
Women's and girls' light outerwear and lingerie – output	100.8	108.0	100.0	94.3	94.6	93.2	93.3
Import penetration		19.0	18.8	23.0	22.6	22.6	
Employment		93.9	81.5	76.9	74.4	77.9	

Source: Business Monitor Census of Production 1980 = 100, and Department of Employment Gazette

number of studies have concluded that changes in productivity per employee are more important in reducing employment in clothing than the effects of import penetration (See Keesing and Wolf 1980: 36 for a guide, and Cable 1982 for an alternative analysis of existing data). The trade versus productivity debate over job loss is very much ongoing and very differing conclusions can be drawn depending on the data set used. Some of the uncertainties surrounding this debate are highlighted in the following extract from the Commission report cited above: 'This loss of jobs is mainly the result of the stagnation or even drop in Community production, coupled with the increase in productivity. Increased productivity itself is the result of both a reduction in manpower, owing to the disappearance of firms which are too weak and of the necessary rationalisation measures. However the relative importance of each of these causes and the direct or indirect influences of the penetration of imports cannot be determined because there are no direct statistics' (CEC 1981: 15). The reference to the disappearance of the weak firms resulting in a measurable

Table 5.2 *Import penetration ratios in the UK*

	1970	1971	1972	1973	1974	1975	1976	1977	1978	1979[a]	1980	1981	1982
Weatherproof outerwear	13	16	20	27	22	21	15	24	27		33	37	42
Men's and boys' tailored outerwear	8	10	13	20	22	25	28	27	30		35	38	42
Women's and girls' tailored outerwear	8	10	19	13	13	16	23	22	24		28	32	36
Overalls and men's shirts, underwear	22	27	28	31	37	36	41	37	35		39	38	41
Dresses, lingerie, infants' wear	7	8	10	12	13	13	17	15	17		19	22	24
Hats, caps and millinery	22	18	16	21	24	22	23	30	30		21	22	24
Other dress industries	12	13	12	13	17	22	31	28	26		27	28	34

Note: [a] Figures for 1979 are notr available
Source: Business Monitor Census of Production 1980 = 100, and Department of Employment Gazette

Table 5.3 *Men and women employed in the various sectors of the UK clothing industry, 1978–82*

	1978		1979		1980		1981		1982	
	M	F	M	F	M	F	M	F	M	F
Men's and boys' tailored outerwear	14,891	53,281	13,991	50,875	11,451	42,872	9,197	31,970	7,133	27,612
	68,172		64,866		54,323		41,167		34,745	
Women's and girls' tailored outerwear	7,210	23,968	7,425	23,272	6,228	21,191	4,774	14,646	3,939	12,671
	31,178		30,697		27,419		19,420		16,610	
Dresses, lingerie, infants' wear	9,120	58,187	11,455	69,889	10,636	65,588	9,802	58,709	9,585	56,757
	67,307		81,344		76,224		68,511		66,342	

Source: Clothing and Allied Products Industry Training Board *Annual Report & Accounts 1982–3*, Appendix E

improvement in productivity implicitly raises but fails to make the point that import penetration and productivity improvements are related. In 1953, 92 per cent of global production in clothing and 67 per cent of employment was concentrated in the developed countries of the world. In 1980, 75 per cent of global production was still concentrated in the DCs, but employment had slumped to 39 per cent in those same countries. Thus the combined effects of adverse trade balances and productivity improvements is a massive loss of registered jobs. In 1973 there were 331,000 registered workers in the clothing industry, in 1982 there were 202,300, a 39 per cent cut in nine years. In the traditional centre of women's outerwear production, London, employment declined even more steeply so that by 1983 the workforce was only a third of its 1973 size.

Set against this overwhelming evidence of decline in production and employment there is the claim by some commentators that the upper limit of import penetration has been reached and that the conditions now exist for a return to home sourcing or even that such a move is underway. These claims rest on the general premise that the balance of comparative advantage has tipped back to the industrialised countries for one or more of the following reasons: rising wages in the developing countries, high interest rates globally, increased transportation and insurance costs, reluctance of retailers to order forward and hold stocks, increased unpredictability in consumer demand, tighter quality specifications – all factors necessitating shorter supply lines. Others have pointed to the availability of a largely female ethnic minority workforce (trapped in declining inner city areas), whose powerlessness ensures the cheapness and flexibility of their labour power (Hoel 1982), as an additional factor in promoting home sourcing. What is significant here is that the impact of new labour saving and productivity boosting technology is not mentioned as a significant factor in improving a developing country's comparative advantage because this is largely based on labour costs.

We need to examine, therefore, what evidence exists to support the notion that any or all of the above factors are promoting a return to home sourcing. First, it needs to be re-emphasised that there is no official evidence to support these claims, quite the reverse – with continued declining production, exports and jobs and increased import production and penetration. Secondly, analysis by sector is vital as we have seen in the differing levels of import penetration with women's outerwear being the least affected. As this sector is the focus of my research, I obtained information on sourcing policies from the major retailers, including the largest mail order firm in the UK (but excluding C&A). All of them source at least 60 per cent of their women's outerwear orders in the UK. In three cases the retailer had increased overseas sourcing within the last five years, in four cases overseas sourcing had decreased in the last five years, and for the retailer with the largest market share in this sector the percentage had remained the same. In terms of market share of each of these firms, the divergent trends probably offset each other, though it is very difficult to be more precise than this. Finally, there is the fact that official statistics take no account of the contribution of the underground economy in production and employment terms. Much has been written and debated about the expansion of the underground economy, particularly within the last five years. What does need to be emphasised in the case of the clothing industry is that unrecorded production and employment has always been a feature of the industry in the UK, what needs verifying is whether the contribution of unrecorded production and employment has increased relative to what is recorded. We do know that in certain areas of the country such as the West Midlands a relatively new clothing industry has grown up, generating a large number of unregistered jobs in sweatshops and in the workers' own homes. Nevertheless, my own research indicates that this growth has in fact been at the expense of unregistered work in London, where payment, however meagre, is currently slightly better than in the West Midlands. Finally, in cities such as London, Birmingham, Manchester and Leicester one can safely double the number of officially registered workers in order to obtain a realistic estimate of workforce size. This unregistered workforce plays a vital part in the restructured UK industry.

The main features of this restructured industry are as follows: bankruptcies and closures have been the characteristic feature of the post-1979 period with continued restructuring into major textile and clothing groups. The vertically integrated textile giants (Courtaulds, Tootals, Coats Paton and Viyella Vantona) have been in a far stronger position to withstand the adverse trading conditions during this period than many of the smaller independent manufacturers. For the textile multinationals, strategies to maintain profitability have included rationalisation through the sale or closure of less profitable manufacturing plant and the tighter grouping of those which remain. New overseas production units and outward processing have been paralleled by rapid investment in new office and manufacturing equipment as strategies to maximise profitability.

For the independent manufacturer a close link as supplier to at least one of the big chain retailers has proved an important lifeline. Both groups have largely evacuated the commodity garment sector based on price. It has long been assumed that the latter has been irrevocably lost to imports, but my own investigations show that this is not the case. The traditional, small firm sector produces a wide range of cheap clothing as well as the high fashion, high risk orders. The relationship between the so-called 'modern' and 'traditional' sectors is very mixed as the following examples will illustrate.

Firm A has an output of, for example, 25,000 dresses, skirts, separates a week, output has steadily increased over the last five years. 85 per cent of output is produced by subcontractors in the UK, 10 per cent is 'outward processed' in six factories abroad, and 5 per cent of the output is produced in the firm's own manufacturing plants. Design is centralised as is most cutting. The most up-to-date knitting and embroidery machines are used in the firm's own plant to ensure the distinctive look is maintained in the finished product.

Firm B has an output of 25,000 dozen garments per week all of which it produces internally in its own twenty factories using the most up-to-date manufacturing equipment available. The firm's emphasis on technical innovation is motivated by a single factor according to the financial director; the need to respond rapidly to changes in fashion. This statement flies in the face of conventional wisdom which holds that it is rapid changes in fashion which mitigate against investment in new technology.

Firm C is part of one of the largest independent clothing groups in the UK, it has recently undertaken an extensive modernisation programme installing advanced equipment with government aid. Firm C subcontracts a high proportion of its own brand name range to firms that cut, make and trim, while using its own high capacity plant to manufacture for Britain's largest retailer of women's wear.

Viewed within the context of our theoretical formulation, Firms A and C reap the benefits of 'both worlds' of technical change and subcontracting, while Firm B has chosen technical innovation as the prime means of maximising profitability. The following sections very briefly outline what each entails and its implications for the level and character of employment in the clothing industry.

Increasing labour productivity

> At last the critical point was reached. The basis of the old method sheer brutality in the exploitation of the workpeople, accompanied more or less by a systematic division of labour, no longer sufficed for the extending markets and for the still more rapidly extending competition of the capitalists. The decisively revolutionary machine ... is the sewing machine
>
> (Marx, *Capital*, I: 443)

Major leaps in productivity are normally only achievable through technical innovation, yet, since the sewing machine was introduced in Britain in 1851 little has changed for the majority of firms within an industry with one of the lowest capital/labour ratios in manufacturing as a whole. The principal methods of increasing labour productivity are work reorganisation, payment systems and varying levels of technical change. In the first instance the Babbage Principle has been applied in so far as an increase in the division of labour allows for the substitution of skilled labour by less skilled labour. As a managerial strategy the principle as developed by Frederick Taylor has been applied throughout the large and the majority of medium-sized firms in the industry in the post-war period and involves the reorganisation of work methods so that skilled work is broken down into a number of simple operations allowing skilled labour to be replaced by what is classified as semi- or unskilled (cheaper) labour. The remaining areas of skilled work such as design and cutting ('men's' jobs commanding higher rates of pay) are rapidly being mechanised.

But this type of work organisation applies mainly to those larger and medium-sized firms located outside the big cities (and London in particular), producing higher volume, more standardised garments for the big chain retailers. The situation in the small, inner-city firms largely remains unchanged at the assembly stage, with one worker sewing a complete garment, 'making through'. It is suggested that the retention of this arrangement in small firms allows for flexibility when a firm is usually involved in the production of a number of different lines at the same time.

Increases in the productivity of labour are also achieved by a system of payment by results for assembly workers. Earnings are linked to measured time standards which are calculated in the following way: the task is broken down into elements, a stopwatch is used to obtain times for each element (for instance, pick up work, match pieces and sew seam), usable cycle times for each element are averaged, operators' performance is rated against a 'normal' pace, bundle time and allowances are added. The standard allowable time (SAM) for a given unit of work is then calculated and piece rates fixed. In small firms, where the practice is making through on a garment, the calculation of piece rates may be far more arbitrary.

Finally, the type of productivity leap necessary to ward off international competition bypasses much of the industry because firms are unwilling or unable to invest in the range of automated equipment now available on the market. Until very recently the incorporation of minor production aids to the general sewing machine constituted the scope of such innovation for many firms in Britain whose labour costs remain sufficiently low to act as a deterrent to investment in new machinery. Also it is erroneously assumed that it is only the larger firms producing more standardised goods on longer runs that would benefit from investment in the new technology. A recent study of the impact of microelectronics on the clothing industry has indicated that digital computer and micro-processor based innovation on the pre-assembly stage of production, e.g. pattern-making, grading and marker-making and cutting have raised capital intensity to 100 times that of the assembly stage (Hoffman and Rush 1983). Thus, it is the assembly stage constituting 80 per cent of labour costs and 30–40 per cent of total costs, and it is the reduction of time spent handling as opposed to sewing the material, which is the principal focus for further automation. The nature of the material being handled, that is its limpness, has proved an obstacle to complete mechanisation. Nevertheless, semi-automatic and automatic, computer-controlled sewing machine and spreading devices are already in use.

What these innovations mean in practice is summed up by H. Joseph Gerber, President, Gerber Scientific Inc.; 'For many operations we can already take the human skills acquired over time by those directly involved in producing garments and translate them into instruction sets which direct a computer controlled machine to perform the same function as a skilled operator. The skill is thus memorised, transferrable and can be replicated indefinitely' (*Bobbin*, February 1983: 90). In short, computer-controlled machines are deskilling and labour-displacing.

Let us look more closely at the implications of their use, first in pre-assembly. Computer-aided design (CAD) in pattern-making is now used by about sixty firms in the UK. Cockburn has examined its application in some detail (1985). She suggests (a) that the kind of firm most likely to benefit from CAD is one where rather few garments of each style are produced and (b) that women have become operators in an area of work designated 'male' prior to computerisation. Her research also shows that in the related pre-assembly task of cutting (unlike pattern-making), investment in automated machines requires large numbers of garments of each style to be economic.

The implications of new technology for clothing workers are therefore not encouraging, at best some new jobs for women in firms where new orders outstrip productivity improvements, at worst, deskilling and technological job displacement. But for most firms investment in new technology is not yet viewed as the primary means of maintaining profitability as long as labour can be obtained cheaply either at home or abroad through the complex web of subcontracting.

Subcontracting and the search for cheap labour

The whole question of 'imports' is far more complex than it first appears, once we recognise that the clothing industry constitutes a web of international production and subcontracting of which UK firms are very much a part. As retailers and wholesalers began in the 1960s to source in the low-wage countries, some manufacturers followed suit lest they be bypassed altogether by the manufacturers. This overseas connection takes three main forms. First, direct investment in production facilities. Nearly all the vertically integrated textile firms, such as Tootals and Coats Paton, and some of the large independent manufacturers, have overseas production facilities. Much of this production is destined for overseas markets but some manufacturers are producing abroad solely for the UK market. The advantages of siting production for the home market in low-wage countries are obvious, particularly if production is located in one of the numerous Free Trade Zones. For instance, in December 1982 machinists in one Philippines-based subsidiary of a British clothing firm were earning approximately £7 for a 40-hour week after deductions (*Kasama* 1983).

The second way in which manufacturers may be involved in overseas production is simply to source part of their range abroad. This has become common practice with brand name, colour co-ordinated ranges.

The third way in which British manufacturers may be involved in overseas production is through 'Outward Processing' (OP). Unfortunately there is no official statistical information on OP in the British case, but most commentators are agreed that, largely due to union resistance, it plays a smaller role in the UK industry than in other Community countries, such as Germany and The Netherlands, or in the US. 'Outward Processing' refers to the dispatch of cloth abroad for making up and the subsequent reimportation of the assembled garment. The rationale for the strategy is simple: as the assembly stage of garment production constitutes 80 per cent of labour costs, subcontracting this stage of production to low-wage sites results in considerable savings on the wage bill (see Fröbel, Heinrichs and Kreye 1981, for an extensive analysis of OP in the German situation).

In many countries OP is a strategy which bypasses the Multi-Fibre Agreement (MFA) and similar restraint levels. For instance, in the US under tariff item 807 producers using OP pay duty only on the value added to the garment abroad. Most European countries have arrangements whereby additional quotas are set aside for outward processed goods. The position in the UK is different in that apart from those countries with which the EC has a preferential trading agreement, OP goods are counted against UK quotas or restraint levels. However, my own enquiries show a vigorous use of OP amongst British manufacturers, particularly in those countries bordering on the Mediterranean which have a preferential trading agreement with the EC. This agreement allows garments made up in those countries from fabric woven or knitted either in the EC or in the exporting country to enter the EC duty-free. British manufacturers also shift their OP to developing countries whose quotas are expanded in MFA renegotiations. One UK manufacturer now has its coats made up in Paraguay but finished in the UK; such coats quite legitimately carry a 'Made in UK' label. Such practices are deemed 'unfair' by those manufacturers who continue to carry out all the production process domestically.

To reiterate, trade unions in the UK remain opposed to OP. The TUC argues: 'It would have serious implications for employment in the most labour intensive sectors of the industry and would be especially damaging for the employment of women and to a number of regions which already experience high unemployment' (NUTGW 1979: 281–2). The clothing union itself argues that OP is simply the direct export of manufacturing jobs, a position which is amply supported by the study of Fröbel *et al.* already cited.

Nevertheless, the European Commission officially encourages the use of OP arguing that it allows part of the industry to be retained within the Community, while achieving 'greater competitiveness through the device of cost equalisation' (CEC 1981: 51). But the attractions of OP diminish if domestic manufacturers have access to low-pay ghettos within the Community itself, and there is good evidence to suggest that firms operating within the so-called 'traditional' sector in the UK compete on price and speed with Third World producers.

It was argued earlier that if demand is separated into stable and unstable portions, the larger 'modern' sector firms use increasingly capital intensive techniques and OP to cater for the predictable portion of demand, while the small firm, 'traditional' sector caters for the unpredictable portion of demand. The two sectors are linked by a complex of sub-contracting which reduces the rigidities found in the modern sector due to the inflexibility of factory based production, labour legislation and trade union organisation.

While there is no official evidence to suggest that the small firm sector has grown overall since 1979 we know that in certain conurbations which have become areas of high unemployment the sector has grown rapidly, for instance in the West Midlands. We are suggesting, therefore, that this growth has been encouraged by recessionary conditions, not in spite of them.

The continuing viability of the sector is linked to a number of factors: paradoxically, the first is the slower growth in demand overall for clothing coupled with increasing unpredictability in consumer behaviour. Another factor is the necessity for flexibility in a sector which survives through the production of unstandardised garments to meet 'discretionary' demand. Finally, the sector will remain viable as long as a cheap and malleable workforce is available, and as long as minimum wage agreements and protective labour legislation are ignored by employers and enforcement agencies (due to grossly inadequate staffing).

If retailers and manufacturers source abroad they must expect long lead times, they must anticipate demand well in advance, and in turn they must be prepared to have a build up in stocks at certain periods of the year. At a time when interest rates have been high and demand unpredictable, retailers and manufacturers have sought to minimise their risks by sourcing very close to 'home' and in line with demand. Under these circumstances they will turn to contractors who can accommodate stringent demands of flexibility in production and speed of delivery. It is exactly this role that the small inner city workshop with its retinue of homeworkers has come to play.

The viability of the sector rests on the payment of very low wages for long hours and in many cases the evasion of statutory employment practices such as the payment of National Insurance contributions. Even though wages throughout the industry are very low compared to the national manufacturing average, workers in this sector have taken a pay cut since 1979 (Anthias 1983). The West Midlands Low Pay Unit carried out a limited survey of small clothing firms in the areas and found in 1984 average hourly pay of £1.08 (statutory minimum £1.50), 73 per cent of the workforce were working forty hours a week or more, all were on piece rate, 64 per cent had fewer than twenty days annual holiday, and only 8 per cent were members of a union (Low Pay Unit 1984). If a garment is assembled in the home, the same study suggests that the worker will receive as little as 15 pence a garment for simple work. If, as is usually suggested, imported goods must be at least 20 per cent cheaper than domestically produced goods for retailers and manufacturers to source abroad, then we have here one very simple factor in explaining expansion of domestic production in this sector.

The National Union of Garment Workers in Britain admits that if such firms were to abide by Health and Safety regulations, were to pay the minimum agreed wages within the industry, were to pay for overtime, holidays and indirect labour costs, then they would go out of business. If a firm does not complete an order in the time and at the price agreed, it will lose any future orders from that manufacturer.

Since the early 1970s this sector has become dominated by ethnic minority entrepreneurs and labour. The entrepreneurs, predominantly male, opt for the small business route out of manual labour or, more recently out of unemployment. This type of entrepreneurial activity provides an escape route for some at least from the discrimination they have encountered in British labour markets. Many have had no previous experience in the clothing industry, others have had long years of experience as employees themselves working under the same exacting conditions that they now expect their employees to endure without complaint.

Ethnic minority women often constitute an ethnically homogeneous labour force in such firms, many of them constrained from finding better paid work because of language difficulties, cultural restrictions or pure racial discrimination. The entrepreneur can use patriarchal attitudes and practices to discipline and control such a workforce often combined with an assertion of 'ethnic' loyalty and honour (see Anthias 1983 and Hoel 1982).

The very lowest rung in the clothing industry is occupied by homeworkers who serve a buffer function for contractors with an erratic flow of work. If there is a rush order or a full book they will receive work, if there is not, they receive nothing. Their rates of pay are exceedingly low; nevertheless, a Low Pay Unit study found that the supplement to the family budget provided by homeworkers' earnings was essential to keep many families from falling below the poverty line (Bisset and Harding 1981). The vast majority of homeworkers are women confined to the home because of domestic responsibilities, particularly the care of pre-school children. Most fail to recognise the hidden costs involved in homeworking which include the purchase or hire of their own machine and running costs. Most homeworking is 'off the book' and a completely precarious occupation.

What price fashion?

As we can see, the traditional sector plays a crucial role in the restructured UK industry, some might argue for its very survival. In addition, it generates employment in depressed inner-city areas for a group of workers who are doubly disadvantaged in finding alternative work. But are we prepared to see the conditions characteristic of nineteenth-century sweated trades surviving and expanding in the traditional centres of capitalist production?

The British government has recently 'waged a campaign' to enforce standards through its inspectorate, but as no new inspectors have been appointed it remains an open question as to how effective such a campaign can be. A number of recent Labour controlled local authority policy documents have suggested ways in which production and employment practices might be improved. Most of these measures hang on the carrot principle, that only 'good practice' firms will be rewarded with local authority aid in the form of access to shared bureau facilities, marketing advice, training in management skills, and access to productivity enhancing new technology such as computer-aided design. The rationale is that if efficiency is improved in the sector so, too, must employment practices. Such a rationale would obviously require a high level of policing if the benefits were to be passed on to the workers rather than merely finding their way into the pockets of the entrepreneurs. But at the end of the day such authorities are faced with the Equal Opportunities paradox, and with the reality of continuing racism and racial discrimination.

Part II

The city and the underclass

CERI PEACH

6

Urban concentration and segregation in Europe since 1945*

One of the major and unforeseen developments of post-1945 European history has been the immigration of non-Europeans into Western Europe. While North America has long been thought of as a continent of immigration, Europe was considered a continent of emigration. Thus, although the sources of immigration into the USA shifted spectacularly from Europe to Latin America and to Asia in the 1970s and the 1980s, the people of the United States seemed psychologically and politically geared to accepting 15 million immigrants. In Western Europe a similar number of international migrants added to a population larger in aggregate than that of the USA has produced political trauma. Many European countries have refused to come to terms, politically, with demographic facts.

The heart of the matter is not the total of 15 million immigrants, but the 6 million or so who are non-European. When one writes about international migration in Europe, the assumption is that the material refers to Turks in Germany, North Africans in France, Asians and West Indians in Britain. These groups do indeed lie at the core of this chapter, but to put their situation into context, the international migration of workers and their families must be seen as one of the two major international movements to have affected Europe since 1945.

The first movement was the forced return migration of European metropolitan populations from territories in which they had settled. Germans were forced out of Eastern Europe, French out of North Africa, Portuguese out of Angola and Mozambique, British out of India, Dutch out of Indonesia. Although all of the countries of Western Europe, with the exception of Switzerland and Luxembourg, were affected by the movement of expatriates, the German Federal Republic was affected to the greatest extent. The federal census of 1961 showed just under 9 million persons living in West Germany had been displaced from territories

113

occupied by Poland and the USSR. In addition, just over 3 million of the total population of 56 million had moved to the West from East Germany (Statistisches Bundesamt 1966: 22–3). Between 1968 and 1983 over 600,000 *Volksdeutsche Aussiedler* had been repatriated to the Federal Republic from Poland (Statistisches Bundesamt 1984: 84).

In France, the number of expatriates was smaller, about 1 million (Guillon 1974: 645), but the movement of *pieds noirs* from Algeria to France was compressed into a very short time-span after Algerian independence in July 1962. The Dutch received a return migration of about 250,000 citizens from Indonesia between 1948 and 1958 (van Amersfoort 1974: 86–7). British expatriate population numbered perhaps 250,000 in the 1970s. Between 65,000 and 107,000 persons in the 1971 census were thought to have been British born under the Raj in India (Peach and Winchester 1974: 391). In fact, nearly 300,000 of the 1.5 million persons living in Britain in 1981 and born in the New Commonwealth were white (OPCS, Labour Force Survey 1983). A second group, numbering 153,000 in 1981 (HMSO 1983: 2), consists of Australians and New Zealanders, most of them thought to be young people who came to Britain as part of a rite of passage.

The returned expatriate population has merged into the background of the metropolitan countries. The returnees remain important in France and Germany as right-wing political forces, but they have been socially absorbed. The non-European immigrant populations, on the other hand, have been economically integrated into the European economies but not socially assimilated into their societies.

Intra-European, international migration has long been a feature of European migration. The movements were generally between adjacent countries, such as the Irish to Britain, Belgians to France and so on, but with occasional longer distance migrations, such as Poles to France. The post-1945 movements, however, have been characterised by a dramatic extension of the migration fields outside European cultures and ethnicities. From the late 1950s and early 1960s the migration field of the industrialised European countries expanded not only within Europe but beyond it into the Maghreb, into Sub-Saharan Africa, into Asia Minor, into the Caribbean and into south Asia. Within the main immigration countries, there was a kind of sectoral division of the world. France extended its field to the south and south-west into Spain, Portugal, the Maghreb and the Sub-Saharan ex-French colonies; Italy was shared with Germany and Switzerland. Germany extended her field southward and south-eastward into Yugoslavia, Greece and Turkey. Britain drew in its immigrant population from its overseas ex-colonies and was largely cut off from the Mediterranean world (see Map 6.1).

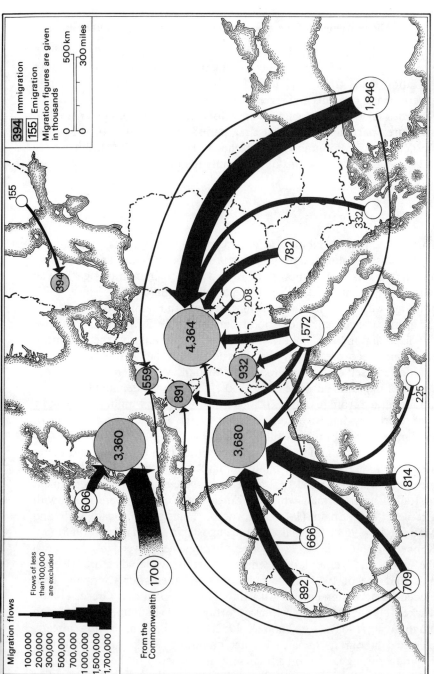

Map 6.1 Major migration flows to selected European countries in the early 1980s (Sources: UK Census 1981; and OECD SOPEMI, 1985, Paris 1986, 41)

The figures represent the number of migrants leaving or living in selected countries in the early 1980s (UK 1981; France 1982; Belgium 1983; Germany, Netherlands, Sweden, Switzerland 1984)

The movement of the new working class into metropolitan areas

Very broadly, the international immigration into Europe can be divided into the period of very rapid but fluctuating growth and extending migration fields from 1945 to 1973/4 and the period of freeze, reflux, governmental controls and increasing family reunion in the metropolitan countries since the economic collapse, following the 1973/4 oil crisis. The literature, particularly on the first period, is extensive (Castles and Kosack, 1985; Böhning 1972; Kennedy-Brenner 1979; Mühlgassner 1984). Given the limitations of space only the main features are reported here.

1945–1973

There were in 1983 about 15 million foreign immigrants living in the industrialised countries of north-west Europe. France and Germany dominated this distribution with over 4 million immigrants each. The numbers present in 1983 had remained roughly stable since 1973, although with some fluctuations in the ethnic and family composition of the groups concerned. The period from 1945 to 1973 witnessed a massive but irregular increase in the number of immigrants as the European economies recovered from the devastation of the war. The recovery manifested itself earliest in France and Britain, with Germany acting as a source of migrants until the early 1950s. The German demand for foreign labour surged from just over 100,000 in 1958 to over 1 million in 1966; by 1968 Germany had overtaken France as the largest concentration of foreign labour in Europe (Mühlgassner 1984: 73).

France set up a national immigration office (ONI) in 1945 and thereafter concluded a series of bilaterial agreements with different governments. Between 1945 and 1951 agreements were made for the recruitment of Italian and German workers. Further agreements were made with Greece (1954), Spain (1961), Morocco, Tunisia, Portugal, Mali and Mauritania (1963), Senegal (1964), Yugoslavia and Turkey (1965) (see Kennedy-Brenner 1979: 22–3). These arrangements were in addition to the supply of Algerian labour which was freely available before Algerian independence in 1962 and which continued thereafter. Germany concluded bilateral agreements with Italy (1955), Spain and Greece (1960), Turkey (1961), Morocco (1963), Portugal (1964), Tunisa (1965) and Yugoslavia (1968) (see Thomas 1982: 181). Britain, having already recruited labour in Jamaica for her munitions works during the war, began recruiting labour on a small scale in Barbados in the early 1950s to work for London Transport, British Rail and in the hospital service. She also had some small-scale Italian labour to work in the coal mines and in the Bedfordshire brick industry. In summary, France had started recruiting non-European labour in Algeria immediately after the war; Britain began attracting labour from the West Indies in the early 1950s, and Germany began attracting non-European labour from the early 1960s.

In the early 1950s, although one cannot speak with great accuracy, the number of non-Europeans in Europe was probably less than 350,000. Judging from Castles and Kosack's figures, France had less than 200,000 at that time, largely Algerians (Castles and Kosack 1985: 33); Britain had less than 50,000 (Peach 1982: 23) and Germany a negligible number. By the early 1960s there were probably about 1 million non-Europeans in Europe. France, again judging by Castles and Kosack's figures, had about 300,000 (Castles and Kosack 1985: 33); Britain had about 500,000 (Peach 1982: 23), The Netherlands perhaps 250,000 (Amersfoort 1974: 87). A decade later, there were probably about 4 million non-Europeans. France had 1.4 million and Germany 1.1 million (Mühlgassner 1984: 72), Britain about 1.2 million (Peach 1982: 23) and the Netherlands about 0.3 million. By the early 1980s the number had risen to about 6 million. France had 1.67 million and Germany 1.66 million (Mühlgassner 1984: 72), Britain had 2.2 million (Peach 1982: 23), and there were perhaps a further 0.4 million in the Benelux countries.

1974–1984

Between 1974 and 1981 the overall numbers of foreigners living in Europe stabilised. Generally speaking, the number of foreign workers declined, but the number of dependants increased. This is well illustrated by Mühlgassner's (1984: 72) figures for Germany and France. Between 1974 and 1981 the total number of foreign workers in Germany decreased from 2,416,000 to 2,096,000 and in France from 1,813,000 to 1,600,000. On the other hand, the foreign population increased during this period from 4,127,000 in Germany to 4,630,000 and in France from 4,043,000 to 4,148,000. In other words, Germany lost 300,000 workers but gained 500,000 more foreigners; in France the changes were less dramatic. The German figures were dominated by the Turks whose share of the foreign population increased from one quarter to one third. The French figures were dominated by North Africans (35.3 per cent) and by the Portuguese (21.4 per cent in 1981). In Britain, the West Indian population showed a very slight decrease during the decade of 1971 to 1981, but the Asian population continued to grow.

With the greater stability of total figures, political pressure is shifting from immigration to natural increase and citizenship as sources of controversy. However, the pressure for family reunion will remain substantial. In Germany, for example, although the number of women per 1,000 men had increased from 638 in 1974 to 738, it is still some way from unity. The Turkish ratio had risen from 554 to 719 but was still below the average for all foreigners (Statistisches Bundesamt 1984: 17). In France in the census of 1982 the ratio of women for 1,000 male foreigners was 856 compared with 786 in 1968 (Lebon 1984: 4). The increase in family reunion would be expected to have a profound effect on the housing requirements and therefore the distribution of the immigrant groups in the urban fabric.

Segregation in European cities

Germany

The foreign-born population for Germany has risen from 686,000 in 1961 to 1,807,000 in 1967, 4,127,000 in 1974 and 4,535,000 in 1983. It is in Germany that the greatest governmental worries about segregation have been expressed and also where the strongest action has been taken to prevent the overdevelopment of concentrations. Action has taken place at three levels: at national level there was the *Anwerbstop*, or halt of immigration recruitment of November 1973. At the local level, municipalities which had over 12 per cent of their populations from abroad have the power to prevent additional foreigners from settling in their administrative areas. This *Zuzugsperre* was available from April 1975 and was used by the Kreuzberg and Wedding districts of Berlin to prevent further immigrant settlement. Because of legal challenges, the instrument has not been used since 1978. The third level of control has been to designate some of the areas of dense immigrant settlement as urban renewal project areas; urban renewal means immigrant removal (Holzner 1982; Hoffmeyer-Zlotnik 1980). This has had the effect in West Berlin of lowering the Turkish indices of dissimilarity (IDs); but in Ludwigshafen, the fact that the reductions in the German population were greater than those in the foreign population led to local increases in segregation (Gans 1984: 97). (The 'Index of Dissimilarity', ID, ranges from a value of 0, zero segregation, to 100, total segregation. It may be interpreted as the percentage of an ethnic group which would have to shift its area of residence in order to replicate exactly the group with which it is being compared.)

The general consensus in the geographical literature, however, is that at the borough, ward, or tract level, very high concentrations do not exist, but that at a very detailed scale, high concentrations can be pinpointed. The foreign-born constituted 7.4 per cent of the German population in

1983. Because of the concentration of job opportunities, immigrants have been concentrated in large cities and now constitute more than 12 per cent of the population of Munich, Frankfurt, Stuttgart, West Berlin, Cologne, Düsseldorf, Duisburg and Nuremberg (O'Loughlin and Glebe 1984a: 273). In many of the major cities, foreigners composed 30 per cent of the population of certain districts (the Altstadt and the Wiesenviertel of Munich; the Etzelstrasse area of Cologne; Schorndorf in Bochum; Kreuzberg in Berlin and Stadtbezirk in Ludwigshafen). Overwhelmingly, the immigrants are concentrated into the inner areas of cities. There are, however, punctiform patterns of high concentration where workers' barracks have been erected on outlying building sites (Jones 1983: 125), although Hottes and Mayer (1977) indicated that this type of housing accounted for only a small minority. In contrast to the situation elsewhere in Europe, concentrations also exist in old village cores and outlying villages (Geiger 1975; Gans 1984; 83).

The highest percentage of foreigners found in a block in Kreuzberg in 1973 was 61 per cent (Hoffmeyer-Zlotnik 1980: 50). In a later study of Kreuzberg, Holzner concluded that there were only three blocks where Turks formed over 50 per cent of the population, seven where they formed 40 to 50 per cent and thirteen where they formed 30 to 40 per cent (Holzner 1982: 67). Jones (1983: 123) shows that over extensive areas of inner Nuremberg the foreign population exceeded 20 per cent of the total in 1980 (at district level), rising occasionally to over 30 to 40 per cent. However, only 13.6 per cent of the foreign population were living in areas where they formed over 40 per cent of the population (Jones 1983: 128). Successive reductions of scale increase the degree of observed segregation and O'Loughlin and Glebe's (1984a) studies at the level of *Stadtteile* (ward about 12,300), *Stimmbezirke* (voting districts of about 1,500 people), blocks and blocksides (block frontages) indicate a doubling of the indices of segregation between the largest and the smallest units (see tables 2 and 7 in O'Loughlin and Glebe 1984a).

There are, however, some conceptual problems with reducing the scale too far. It is not clear from this study how many people reside, on average, in each blockside. Peach (1981) has indicated that measures of segregation increase not only as areal scale is reduced, but as group size diminishes and that for purely statistical reasons it is possible to achieve very high levels of segregation when very small groups are measured over very fine areal frames. When the number of areal units begins to converge with the number of individuals in an ethnic group, randomness will produce high readings.

Holzner (1982), having specifically considered the question of whether Turkish ghettos were forming, concluded that in Berlin's case the situation was exaggerated and that nothing like the North American black ghetto existed. Generally speaking his conclusion seems to conform with that of other geographers, although there is a degree of caution in the recent work of O'Loughlin and Glebe and of Gans (1984). This slight ambivalence of view by O'Loughlin and Glebe derives from two different approaches in their work. The first is that the small-scale statistics show a very high degree of ethnic concentration at the level of individual buildings (O'Loughlin and Glebe 1984a: 279) and that IDs computed at the blockside scale give some very high values – in the 70s. The second is that through their analysis of small-scale migration data they can demonstrate both a purposive regrouping of migrants into ethnic areas, while at the same time they can detect a high turnover of Germans and also a net loss of Germans in areas of high ethnic concentration. This, they think, may possibly indicate the beginning of racial transition, ethnic succession and tipping point type development (O'Loughlin and Glebe 1984b: 20–1). They also show significant increases in the level of segregation in Duisburg from 1970 to 1980, although not in Düsseldorf. Gans (1984: 99) also shows the development of separate housing markets for Germans and foreigners, and he shows that despite the beginnings of movement by foreigners to better class areas in Ludwigshafen, the general trend is for slow polarisation of the two populations.

One issue which emerges from the recent literature on the German situation is that the Turks do not seem to be as segregated as their position in social distance terms would suggest; on many of the measures the Greeks appear to be more highly segregated. O'Loughlin and Glebe (1984a: 276–7) ascribe this phenomenon to Greek self-segregation. This would accord with earlier findings of high levels of Greek segregation in Australia (Peach 1974) and of Greek Cypriots in London (Peach, Winchester and Woods 1975). O'Loughlin and Glebe (1984a: 279), however, use the fact of the mismatch between expected and observed degrees of segregation in the case of the Turks to call into question the use of segregation scores as measures of social isolation.

France

In the census of 1982, the foreign population of France was 3,680,000 or 6.8 per cent of the population (cf. the figure of the Ministry of Interior, which was 4.2 million). This was about the same percentage as in 1931. In 1954, foreigners formed 4.1 per cent; in 1962, 4.7 per cent; in 1968, 5.3 per cent and in 1975, 6.6 per cent (Algerian Muslims are included in these figures; see Lebon, 1984: 3).

While, in some ways, the pattern of immigrant settlement in French cities shows clear parallels with the situation elsewhere in Europe, in other respects there are unique features. The general features are that run-down inner city areas have traditionally shown a high concentration of immigrants. The unique features are the existence of *bidonvilles* – shanty towns – although their significance has diminished substantially since legislation in 1964. Anne Jones reports, for example (1980: 37), that by July 1975, thirty-four of the forty original *bidonvilles* in Marseilles had been removed. Often, however, the *bidonville* inhabitants were placed in *cités de transit* which were only marginally better in amenities and which showed tendencies of permanence despite their name (White 1984: 133). The effects of clearance policies and also attempts to restrict immigrants, in some cases, to 15 per cent of the state subsidised apartments (Jones 1984), together with the construction of these new *grands ensembles* in the suburbs at some considerable distance from the centre, has produced a degree of ethnic dispersion.

Kennedy-Brenner reports the pioneering work done on the housing of foreigners by J.-P. Butaud in 1970 in which he concluded that nationality was the most important single determinant of housing condition. He found that there was a considerable difference in the quality of housing between Italians, Spaniards and Yugoslavs on one hand and Portuguese, North and black Africans on the other. However, a further disparity existed between the Portuguese, who were less exposed to racism and North and black Africans (Kennedy-Brenner 1979: 64). Butaud concluded that region and length of stay in France was a secondary rather than primary determinant of housing conditions, the length of stay being inextricably linked to a whole complex of economic processes concerning the type of permit, which in turn conditioned intentions with regard to the degree of permanence of immigration, which in its turn determined the transfer of savings to families left behind (Kennedy-Brenner 1979: 64).

Housing type varied considerably between national groups. Kennedy-Brenner (1979: 63) indicates that in 1968, Italians and Spaniards were living principally in rented unfurnished apartments, including HLMs; Yugoslavs were evenly distributed between furnished and unfurnished accommodation. The Portuguese, while living principally in furnished accommodation, were proportionally almost as numerous as the Italians in individual housing and represented the highest proportions in makeshift housing and shanty towns. Maghrebians were found principally in furnished hotels while a high proportion of Africans were living in hostel accommodation (Kennedy-Brenner 1979: 62).

There are too few studies of segregation in French cities to make worthwhile generalisations. Detailed statistics seem elusive and may seem to lack credibility. However, it appears that indices of dissimilarity for

Paris are very low (Ogden 1977) and anomalous, while those for Marseille are not only higher, but display the types of pattern that assumed social distance scales would lead us to expect. In 1975, Ogden showed for Paris (Ogden 1977: 32) that at the *arrondissement* level the Portuguese, who were of low status, recent arrival and had, at one time, notable concentrations in *bidonvilles*, had an IS of 8.17, while the Luxembourgers stood at 30.23 and the Algerians at 24.87. (The 'Index of Segregation', IS, measures the clustering of one group relative to the total population. It ranges from 0, indicating no segregation, to 100, indicating total segregation.)

Anne Jones (1980: 320–1) showed for Marseille in 1975 at the *arrondissement* scale (*c.* 57,000 residents) that the Portuguese were the most segregated group (IS 52.88), closely followed by the Algerians (51.10), while the Spaniards (29.55) and the Italians (20.65) were much lower. Most importantly, Jones's indirect standardisation demonstrates that economic class 'explains' only a quarter of the high segregation levels of the Portuguese and Algerians, but over a third of the lower index levels of the Spaniards, and nearly half of the segregation levels of the Italians (Jones 1980: 409) (see Tables 6.1 and 6.2).

Figures for the 1975 census produced by Brettell (1981: 8) for Paris show the highest concentration of foreigners to be 22.3 per cent in *arrondissement* 2 and 20.5 in *arrondissement* 3. Brettell's figures may not be totally reliable (the figure for Algerians in the 16th is clearly incorrect). However, on this basis the IDs would certainly be low. White, though, can point to studies showing extreme social segregation of Islamic West Africans in Lyon (White 1984: 122). Simon's work (1979: 186–9) shows high concentrations of Tunisians in the decaying central *arrondissements* of Marseille and Lyon. The 1st, 2nd and 3rd *arrondissements* of Marseille between the Port and the St Charles Station, contained 50.8 per cent of the Tunisian population of that city in 1970. Lyon showed a similar

Table 6.1 *Ethnic segregation in Marseilles by 'arrondissement', 1968–75*

	French	EEC	Italian	Spanish	Algerian	Portuguese
French	–	9.30	10.47	19.26	44.50	n/a
EEC	14.17	–	34.34	26.49	49.61	n/a
Italian	19.67	5.15	–	21.95	43.40	n/a
Spanish	30.63	29.78	31.30	–	30.57	n/a
Algerian	51.49	50.20	51.99	49.48	–	n/a
Portuguese	51.87	51.58	52.57	52.01	65.03	–

Above diagonal, 1968; below diagonal, 1975
Arrondisement population: average of 55,590 in 1968; average of 57,000 in 1975
Source: Jones 1980: 320

Table 6.2 *Indices of segregation derived from indirect standardisation Marseilles, 1962–75*

	Index of segregation		
	Indirect standardisation	Observed	Percentage segregation due to socio-economic status
1968			
Algerian	17.42	56.94	30.59
1975			
Algerian	13.18	51.10	25.79
Italian	9.4	20.65	45.52
Spanish	10.17	29.55	34.41
Portuguese	13.0	52.88	24.58

Source: Jones 1980: 409

concentration in the old quarters (3rd, 7th and 8th) *arrondissement* on the left bank of the Rhone. Thus, paradoxically, there are substantial proportions of immigrant groups in restricted areas where they do not form outstandingly high percentages of the population. In Paris, at least, there are low IDs.

Most interestingly of all, Simon publishes a map of the distribution of Tunisians according to religion which, despite his comments, seems to suggest a significant degree of segregation of Jews from Muslims outside the central areas (Simon 1979: 195). Elsewhere in his work (1979: 92–101), he demonstrates the internal segregation of Maghrebians. Similarly the work of Salah (1973: 71–2) showed how chain migration led to the reconstitution of Algerian village communities in parts of the north, but such concentrations can be found at a very small scale.

One problem in the French literature remains unresolved. According to Kennedy-Brenner's research, the Portuguese suffered particularly poor housing conditions and had some notable concentration in *bidonvilles*. However, according to Brettell who was attempting a comparative study of Portuguese ethnic areas in Toronto and Paris, 'in Paris, I found no little Portugal' (Brettell 1981: 1). Brettell's view was that Toronto was horizontally segregated while Paris was vertically segregated. The Portuguese acting as servants or concièrges occupied poor apartments, but achieved an even distribution in the city of Paris.

Great Britain

In Britain, the geographical analysis of immigrant minority groups has been long established (Peach 1965, 1966, 1968, 1975b; Jones 1978). Since the late 1960s the literature has burgeoned with important contributions from Lee (1977) and Jones (1978). The net movement of West Indians to Britain in the period 1955–74 has been shown to be very closely correlated with fluctuations in unemployment in Great Britain (r = −0.65) (Peach 1978–9). The net migration from India and Pakistan shows a similar but weaker relationship. Robinson (1980) found an inverse correlation (r = −0.52) between unemployment and net immigration from India for the period 1959–74 and a weaker relationship, (r = −0.49) for net movement to Britain from Pakistan for the same period. The abandonment by the British government of the counting of departing migrants after 1974 prevents the extension of this investigation. However, the correlations themselves may be suspect because of temporal auto-correlation. Despite the loss of return figures since 1974, it seems that there has been a net outflow of West Indians since that time and a continued new inflow of south Asians. Between the censuses of 1971 and 1981, the West Indian-born population in Britain decreased from 304,070 to 296,913. The Indian figures increased from 321,995 to 389,823 and the combined Pakistan/Bangladesh population from 139,935 to 235,321 (HMSO 1983: 164).

The total population of Asian or West Indian origin in Great Britain has shown a very substantial increase since 1945. In 1951 it was less than 50,000; by 1961 it was probably less than 500,000 (or less than 1 per cent of the population); by 1971 there were probably between 1.25 and 1.5 million (i.e. between 2.3 and 2.8 per cent of the population); by 1980 the figure was probably 2.2 million or about 4.1 per cent of the population (Peach 1982: 23–4). By 1984, the figure was probably 2.4 million or 4.5 per cent of the population (OPCS Monitor 1985: 3). The uncertainty in the precise figure is due, in part, to the lack of an ethnic question in the British census and to the increasing proportion of the ethnic population born in Britain. Since 1979, however, the OPCS has conducted labour force surveys on a sample basis, which have included direct questions on ethnicity. In 1984, over half of the West Indian population (281,000 out of 529,000) had been born in the UK; 41 per cent of the Pakistani population (151,000 out of 371,000), 36 per cent of the Indian population (290,000 out of 807,000) and 32 per cent of the Bangladeshi population (30,000 out of 93,000) had been born in the UK (OPCS 1985: 11). The Irish remain, however, probably the largest single ethnic group with just under one million persons (949,371) in households headed by someone born in the Irish Republic (Census 1981, HMSO 1983: 114).

Great Britain presents the classic case of the black immigrant population as a replacement of population. Analysis of 1961 census data revealed a pattern which has not changed in essence since that time. West Indians, Indians and Pakistanis were concentrated in regions, which despite their demand for labour were failing to attract, or were being abandoned by, the white population. Coloured immigrants avoided areas of high unemployment, but, on the other hand, were relatively restricted in their penetration of areas which were attractive to whites. The immigrants were particularly concentrated in the conurbations which were losing population and had been doing so since before 1951. This pattern has continued to the 1981 census. Regressing the absolute numbers of the ethnic population of West Indians given by the NDHS (National Dwelling and Housing Survey) in 1978/9 against the absolute increase or decrease in population by county for the period 1971–81 yielded a very high inverse correlation coefficient ($r = -0.934$ for the forty-six pairs of observations). In other words, West Indians are very concentrated in areas that had experienced growth. Regressing the ethnic Asian population with the same set of absolute population change figures produced almost as high an inverse correlation, $r = -0.891$ (Peach 1982: 31).

Given that the black population is locked into an allocative system that is concentrating them in areas which the white population is abandoning, it seems inevitable that an increasing degree of polarisation of blacks and whites should be expected. The parallels with the US situation, where the white population is decentralising while the black population continues to centralise, are strong. Not only is the immigrant or immigrant-descended population concentrated in the conurbations, but they are concentrated in the inner areas where the greatest absolute and proportional decreases have taken place (Winchester 1975; Woods 1979; Shah 1980). Inner London, for example, lost 535,000 residents between 1971 and 1981 (18 per cent of the 1971 total) while outer London boroughs lost 221,000 or 5 per cent of their population. If one correlates absolute increase or decrease in population between 1971 and 1981 for each borough with the ethnic West Indian population given by the NDHS survey, there is a marked inverse relationship ($r = -0.714$). In other words, the higher the loss of population, the higher the number of West Indians. Certainly, some of the boroughs with the highest West Indian numbers (Lambeth, Hackney, Haringey, Lewisham and Wandsworth) have some of the largest losses in total population. However, not all boroughs with large West Indian concentration have large decreases in total population (Brent, for example). Nor does the correlation between absolute population loss and concentration of ethnic minorities hold for the combined south Asian groups. Only 25 per cent of this combined group was in the inner boroughs compared with 69 per cent of West Indians. This reflects, perhaps, the later arrival of the Indians and Pakistanis and also the greater importance of Heathrow airport as the port of entry and source of employment when compared with the railway termini for the West Indians (Peach 1982: 33–5).

Given that the black population is concentrated in regions, cities and parts of cities which have for a considerable period of time been losing population, it seemed inevitable that the degree of concentration and of segregation of these groups would increase between 1961 and 1981. This was certainly the prediction of a book which I published in 1968, which forecast ghettos for the 1980s (Peach 1968: 100). The macro-scale statistics suggest that the degree of segregation measured by ID has remained rather stable. Thus, the evidence does not seem to bear out these predictions so far.

Borough-level statistics, disaggregated by birthplace groups, are available for Greater London for 1981 and IDs directly comparable with earlier work by Woods (1976) have been calculated (Table 6.3) The borough level units are rather coarse: there are thirty-three boroughs in London with an average population in 1981 of about 200,000. Woods's equation for converting borough (B) level segregation to ward level (W) (wards are about 9,000 persons) for 1971 data was $W = 12.75 + 0.86 B$, and for converting wards to enumeration districts was $ED = 16.04 + 1.09 W$. In real terms, West Indians had an IS of 37.7 at the borough level in 1971, an IS of 49.1 at ward level and an IS of 64.5 at ED level in 1971.

These figures show that, with the exception of the south Asian population (India, Pakistan, Bangladesh, Sri Lanka) which increased its IS from 22.5 in 1971 to 30.28 in 1981, there has been relatively little change in the degree of segegation. Because this table has been produced to make a comparison with Woods's earlier analysis, Woods's birthplace categories have been used. However, these categories are rather unsatisfactory in several cases. For example, Woods combined the Maltese and Cypriot populations which are distinct from one another, and the south Asian category conceals the very sharp differences that exist between the Bangladeshis and the other Asian groups.

Data from the 1981 census, despite the coarse areal scale, show that disaggregation of the south Asian birthplace groups increases the degree of segregation which they individually display. Bangladeshis stand out as displaying very high levels of separation, being more segegated from the Pakistanis (with whom they shared a nationality in the 1971 census) and Indians than they are from the population as a whole. The Bangladeshis show an extraordinary concentration with 20 per cent of the total population enumerated in Britain located in the one London borough of Tower Hamlets. The Cypriot population also shows very high levels of segregation, almost as high as that of the Bangladeshis. This is particularly significant because the Cypriot population is largely Greek and white, and is not a population that is subjected to any notable discrimina-

Table 6.3 *Greater London: IDs for 1971 and 1981 (borough level)*

	Total population	Ireland (Republic)	Malta and Cyprus	South Asia	West Indies	New Commonwealth
Total population	–	20.6[a]	41.2[a]	22.5[a]	37.7[a]	25.1[a]
Ireland (Republic)	22.28[a]	–	36.4[a]	22.9	28.7	15.5
Malta and Cyprus	40.74[a]	37.9	–	47.9	36.9	37.9
South Asia	30.28[a]	28.44	48.88	–	40.0	34.3
West Indies	38.39[a]	29.93	37.49	38.94	–	29.0
New Commonwealth	25.30[a]	17.29	34.63	20.22	21.38	–

Notes: [a] Index of Segregation rather than ID
1971 above diagonal (*Source:* Woods 1976)
1981 below diagonal (*Source:* author's calculations from census for Greater London)

Table 6.4 *Greater London (boroughs): segregation levels of selected birthplace groups 1981*

	Total	Ireland	West Indies	India	Pakistan	Bangladesh	Cyprus
Total	–	21.66	36.53	30.75	35.09	50.15	44.14
Ireland		–	29.94	30.37	34.95	46.73	42.48
West Indies			–	42.72	39.32	51.37	39.92
India				–	24.28	59.59	56.23
Pakistan					–	59.33	57.91
Bangladesh						–	53.08
Cyprus							–

Source: Calculation based on birthplace figures for Greater London boroughs, 1981 Census

tion in Britain (a major contrast with the position of the Bangladeshis). The population does include a Turkish Cypriot element of unknown size (but probably about 10 per cent of the total); so if these two groups are disaggregated, as were the south Asian populations, the resulting level of segregation might well be even higher.

The Turkish Cypriots do (from sociological evidence produced by Oakley) overlap the Greek Cypriots. As a check, the small London Turkish population (7,955) was measured against the Cypriot population. This produced the lowest Cypriot ID with any of the groups measured (29.93) – a much lower degree of segregation than the Turks show against the total population (38.00). The Cypriot levels of segregation seem to be the product of voluntaristic self-segregation rather than the result of externally imposed constraints. Although Greek Cypriots would be likely to be a lot closer to the British population on Bogardus type social distance scales, than, say the Pakistanis, they are significantly more spatially segregated. This finding might help to explain O'Loughlin and Glebe's puzzlement about the higher degree of segregation of Greeks than Turks in Düsseldorf (1984a: 279) when the Turks were regarded by the German population as more socially distant than the Greeks. In studies of immigrants in Sydney, Australia, in the early 1970s, the Greeks were found to be the most segregated and in-marrying of all groups (Peach 1974). The solution may lie in the attitude of the Greeks rather than in the attitude of the British or the Germans.

The only published work available so far on British 1981 data at the enumeration district level is that by D. J. Evans (1984) on Wolverhampton. Unfortunately, only the aggregated New Commonwealth population data were available to him rather than the individual birthplace groups. However, on this basis he published a series of IDs at ED level for the four censuses 1961–81. There are a number of problems which may make

Evans's series of IDs less comparable than they seem. Apart from the fact that the 1966 census was a 10 per cent sample rather than a 100 per cent coverage (together with the corresponding change of areal scale at the ED level), the New Commonwealth population definition varies from census to census. In 1961 and 1966, the birthplace is taken; in 1971 the population is that born in the New Commonwealth or with both parents born in New Commonwealth countries, while the 1981 data are for those in households headed by a person born in the New Commonwealth rather than for the birthplace groups alone. Definitional shifts are probably less important than the problems of aggregating West Indians, Indians, Pakistanis and Bangladeshis together. Evans's maps show that there are significant differences between the West Indians and Asians.

Taking the figures at their face value, they show a diminution of segregation over time, and their values accord well with findings from other cities for comparable dates and scales. Although it is not possible to establish the true micro-level scale of segregation without fully disaggregated birthplace data, if the relationship established by Woods (1976) for the different scales on 1971 holds true for 1981, it seems that West Indian ED levels of segregation will remain around the mid-60s, with similar levels for Pakistanis in London, but with Bangladeshis showing levels in the high 70s. Small area data (largely from electorate rolls) for northern industrial cities with high Asian concentrations suggest that high levels of segregation, in the 70s, exist at ED or smaller levels in these cities (Peach *et al.*, 1974; Jones and McEvoy 1978; Robinson 1979).

To summarise, the British situation differs considerably from that in most European countries as far as the ethnic composition of its immigrant groups is concerned; only the Netherlands has an equally prominent Caribbean population; the French Antillean population in metropolitan France numbered only about 160,000 in 1975 (Butcher and Ogden 1984: 52–5). Unlike France and Germany, where the settlement of immigrant groups at a regional level seems positively correlated with rates of population growth, in Britain, the correlation for West Indians and Asians is negative. There are comparisons to be made between the British and German immigrant trend surfaces. In Germany, the surface is highest in the south and lowest in the north (O'Loughlin 1984) and the same is true in Britain. Similarly, just as the earliest migrants to Germany (such as the Italians) were concentrated near the initial southern entry points and the later migrants (such as the Turks) had a more northerly distribution, so the earlier Afro-Caribbean migrants to Britain had a more southerly centre of gravity than the later Asian arrivals.

In many ways, Britain approximates more closely to the American model of settlement than do other European countries, though this is not to say that Britain conforms closely to the US model. The levels of segregation of its most highly segregated groups approach those of American blacks. Curiously, British blacks have Hispanic levels of segregation, and Asians achieve levels most corresponding to those of American blacks. Despite the fact that the public housing sector is larger in Britain than in the US, there is evidence of ethnic polarisation in British housing estates reminiscent of that in some US project housing. The dynamics of suburban growth and inner-city decline coinciding with black central city polarisation and white peripheral growth is common not only to the British and US situations, but to other European countries.

Comparison with the US

The pattern which emerges from these studies of segregation in European cities is that although immigrant groups are often concentrated in the inner-city areas of population decrease and poor housing conditions, it is only at the very localised level that they constitute majorities of the population. If very fine areal meshes are adopted for measurement, Indexes of Segregation in the 70s may be reached, but, for the most part the readings are in the 30s, 40s, 50s, and 60s, much like the situation of European immigrants in US cities in the first half of the century.

The 'ghetto' is a term which is used very loosely in a journalistic fashion. Holzner (1982), for example, goes into considerable detail to refute it in West Berlin, but applies it cavalierly to the British situation (Holzner 1982: 65). For some it is the situation where a high proportion of a group is found in a single area, even if they do not constitute a majority of the population (Tiger Bay in Cardiff was thought in the later 1940s to be an example of such a 'coloured quarter'). To others, a ghetto is an area where all of the population is of a given group, even if not all of that group lives in that area. A recent paper has devoted some consideration to the problem of measuring segregation (Peach 1981); but as a brief working definition, a ghetto is an area in which a very high majority of the population is of a particular group and in which a high percentage of group members live in such concentrations.

European ethnic areas in US cities were very rarely, if ever, ghettos. Philpott's statistics for ethnic concentrations in Chicago demonstrate this point clearly. Not only were the percentages which Europeans formed of local populations small – but generally only small proportions of the ethnic populations lived in such areas (Philpott 1978: 141). On the other hand, the black ghetto in American cities was totally different in kind and in ethnicity. The large majority of American blacks lived and live in areas in which they form a substantial majority of the population (Duncan and Duncan 1957: Taeuber and Taeuber 1965). European ethnic areas in American cities were never as intense as the black ghettos: the black ghetto is not just a voluntaristic temporary phenomenon.

Thus, if our comparison of the European segregation model with that of the American model rests on comparison with Europeans in American cities, similarities can be found. If our comparison is between the black American ghetto and ethnic areas, comparisons are much fewer. Some northern British cities have high ID for Asian groups; the Bangladeshis and the Cypriots are highly segregated in London. Yet, the high indices of the Cypriots that are found in Britain, seem to be more voluntaristic than imposed. European countries seem capable of producing degrees of social distance between their native populations and their immigrants at least as high as those that exist in the US but without the concomitant spatial segregation.

There are, however, three circumstances which make it difficult to speak of a 'European' situation with regard to immigrant settlement. First, the ethnic mix differs considerably between the main countries so that they do not confront similar component mixtures. Germany is dominated by Turks and by population drawn from south-eastern and southern Europe; France is dominated by North Africans and Portuguese and by populations drawn from the south and south-west; the British situation is dominated by immigrants from Ireland and from its former colonial empire. The smaller European countries have intermediate positions: The Netherlands is perhaps most like Britain, Belgium and Luxembourg are like France, and Switzerland and Austria like Germany. Even here, however, the scale and historic specificity of the situation do not allow too many direct comparisons.

Secondly, the attitudes and reasons for immigration differ considerably between the countries. Britain became a country of immigration by default. Immigration took the British by surprise. Her immigrants are, for the very large part, British citizens. France actively sought population both to boost its demographic position and to increase its workforce. It wished, however, to distinguish between the two roles. The Europeans were regarded as assimilable and the North Africans not. Germany, Austria, The Netherlands, Belgium and Switzerland wanted workers but not settlers. The degree of intended permanence, the degree of turnover of the foreign-born populations and the degree of family reunification differed significantly between the different countries.

Thirdly, not only did the ethnic mix vary from country to country and the housing needs of the different ethnic groups in different countries vary according to the degree of intended permanence and with the degree of family reunification, but the type and availability of housing varied considerably between the countries. Britain is dominated by single-family houses, has a substantial degree (56 per cent) of owner-occupation and of council housing (31 per cent) and a small, shrinking amount (11 per cent) of private rented property. The French system is dominated by rentals of apartments (producing vertical segregation) and of massive peripheral *cités ouvriers*, relatively unpenetrated by immigrants. France had the distinctive elements of *bidonvilles* (now largely eliminated), *hôtels meublés* and *hôtels garnis*, as well as the *cités de transit*. Germany has apartment houses, some workers' barracks, but little by way of subsidised housing available to immigrants.

In all of the countries, however, certain regularities occur. Immigrants show notable concentrations in inner city arcs around the urban cores and in industrial areas. They are concentrated in areas which the local population is abandoning. In Germany these are characterised by the 'three As': *Ausländer, Arbeitslose, Alte* (the foreigners, the unemployed and the old). Some of the areas of densest settlement have been subject to clearance through urban renewal, partly in order to disperse immigrants. Typically, however, immigrants rarely form majorities over large administrative areas. The highest percentage in a Brussels commune in 1970 was 33.5 out of a total population of 55,055 in St Gilles; in Paris in 1975, the highest concentration was 22.3 per cent out of 26,225 in Deuxième; in Berlin in the late 1970s, the highest concentration seems to have been less than 20 per cent in Kreuzberg; the highest percentage that people born overseas formed of a London borough in 1981 was 37.2 in Brent's population of 248,092. If the dependants of those born overseas were included, higher concentrations could be shown. In Brent, for example, 53.8 per cent of the population was living in households headed by a person born outside the UK. For the most part, however, immigrants do not achieve the substantial areas of majority presence such as those formed by blacks in the United States. Immigrants can, nevertheless, achieve high concentrations in limited areas and some groups manifest high IS and IDs when measured over a fine areal scale.

The picture with respect to the relationship between spatial segregation and social distance is blurred. In studies such as De Lannoy's in Brussels, there is a strong relationship for most groups. The Turks are highly segregated, as are the North Africans; the Spanish and Italians hold a middle position, and the French, Dutch, British and Germans show generally low degrees of segregation from the Belgian population and from each other. Only the high degree of American segregation was unexpected on the social distance scale. In Lucerne, Good's (1984) analysis of a much more restricted number of nationalities produced a fairly close approximation of the expected social distance scale. The Germans show low IDs with the Swiss, the Italians rather higher, the Spaniards higher still, and the Yugoslavs highest of all. One surprising finding in Good's work is the low degree of segregation of the Spaniards, Italians and Yugoslavs from each other, indicating, perhaps, that pressures of Swiss society are more important than internal desires for self-segregation in explaining immigrant segregation. In Britain high degrees of segregation have been recorded for Asian groups, particularly in industrial cities in the north of England. West Indian levels are lower than the political temperature, particularly between young blacks and the British police, and the rash of inner city riots in 1980, 1981 and 1985 would lead one to expect. In the Netherlands, the low degree of segregation of the Surinamese population, so far as it has been successfully measured, is surprising in terms of expected social distance and media comment. The situation in France is more difficult to comment on in the absence of large numbers of observations of IDs. From what is available, however, the degree of North African and Portuguese segregation is much lower in Paris than one might expect, although for certain sub-Saharan groups very high degrees of encapsulation do occur. In Marseille, segregation accords more closely with expectations. In Germany, the degree of Turkish segregation measured by IDs seems much lower than expected, and there is some evidence in Berlin that the *Zuzugsperre* of 1975 may have spread out the Turkish population more and reduced its ID. The IS fell for the Turks from 49.4 in 1973 to 38.0 in 1979 (White 1984: 129). Thus, in the European situation, there is not the clear-cut ranking of ethnicities which seems to characterise the American cities over both place and time.

The political consensus seems to be that non-European immigrant workers were economically necessary but socially undesirable. Economically they were integrated into the sectors of the economies which had the greatest difficulty in attracting native labour; socially they were allocated some of the least attractive housing in areas of cities which were often decaying. In the popular consciousness, effect was often identified as cause. It is a short step from recognising that immigrants are living in decaying parts of cities to arguing that parts of cities are decaying because immigrants are living in them. Fears of a black American ghetto-type situation developed. Britain experienced in 1980, 1981 and 1985 a stunning series of riots in which race and ethnicity were prominent elements; all of this was reminiscent of the USA in the 1960s. The political view has become that it is not simply poor conditions which are important, but the spatial concentration of those conditions. Social geography has become a hot political issue.

The Marxist view of immigrant concentrations is that they are merely the reflection of the capitalistic allocative system. Immigrants are given the worst jobs and get the worst housing; the worst housing is geographically concentrated, therefore the immigrant groups are themselves geographically concentrated. Ethnic consciousness is seen as false consciousness, and attempts at using ethnicity as an academic category are represented as attempts to divide the working class solidarity that might otherwise exist.

The main difficulty of the Marxist proposition is that it allows nothing for ethnicity: it assumes that the economic position of the immigrant groups is the main explanation of ethnic concentrations. Economic considerations, however, are only one part of the equation, the desire to settle or to return home, religion, language, family size and structure, the whole complex of what we term ethnic identity is another, and it seems, larger part. The problem for social geographers is this: if the poor are segregated from the rich and if immigrants are poorer than the native populations, to what extent are they segregated because they are poor rather than because they are ethnically different?

The view which seems to emerge from my scrutiny of the empirical evidence in the European literature is that economic class explains little of ethnic segregation. Working class immigrants, it is true, live in working class areas; upper class immigrants such as the Americans in Brussels or the Japanese in Düsseldorf live in upper class areas, but neither the working class immigrants, nor all of the upper class immigrants are randomly distributed throughout their respective class areas. Peach, Winchester and Woods showed that economic class explained only 17 per cent of West Indian ward level segregation in London in 1971, and that it explained 9 per cent of Indian and 22 per cent of Irish segregation (1975: 405). In Amsterdam, Amersfoort and Cortie (1973) reported that class standardisation of data affected Surinamese segregation hardly at all. Similarly, O'Loughlin and Glebe (1984) indicate that class does not contribute much to the explanation of immigrant concentrations in Duisburg and Düsseldorf. In Brussels, De Lannoy (1975) has shown that upper class Americans are highly segregated and not dispersed among the upper class. Anne Jones has shown that economic causes explain only a small amount of segregation for the most segregated groups, the Portuguese and Algerians. However, perhaps the most persuasive evidence is that in most European cities (Swiss cities perhaps excepted), working class immigrants are segregated from each other. In other words, the ethnic component in the segegation of working class immigrant groups (and to some extent of upper class groups like the Americans and Japanese) was not 'explained' by their class positions.

Ethnicity was a stronger element than economic class in explaining segregation.

If class explains relatively little of immigrant concentrations, the next question is: to what extent are concentrations voluntary and to what extent are they enforced? The answer to this question is paradoxical. In both Germany and France there is evidence that the initial destinations of sponsored immigrants are often dispersed, but that secondary and subsequent moves by immigrants may be to achieve regrouping. Peter de Riz shows this for the immigrant groups which he studied in the Frankfurt area, and O'Loughlin and Glebe (1984) demonstrate the marked preference of Turkish migrants for relocating in areas of existing Turkish concentrations. Robinson (1979) shows for Blackburn how offers of suburban council housing are rejected by the Islamic population in favour of remaining close to the mosque and to the ethnic communal centre. Flett has shown for Manchester how coloured immigrants specified a preference for housing in the conurbation centre while whites showed a preference for suburban housing (Flett 1977). Anne Jones has shown how Algerian immigrants in Marseille rejected subsidised HLM working class housing in favour of *bidonville* accommodation (Jones 1984: 35–6). Evidence from London in 1981 indicated that Cypriots remained one of the most highly segregated of immigrant groups, despite the fact that they did not face the racial discrimination confronting West Indians and Asians. Thus, there seems to be substantial evidence that the positive virtues of association play a major part in the formation of ethnic concentrations. There is, on the other hand, considerable evidence of immigrant exclusion from certain areas and the concentration of immigrants into the worst available housing. Work in London by Parker and Dugmore (1977/8) and Peach and Shah (1980) demonstrate this, and numerous other studies could be cited. Gans (1984: 92) also indicates substantial differences in the degree of social rehousing of German and foreign families in urban renewal areas in Ludwigshafen.

If external factors of constraint were dominant in the explanation of the causation of ethnic residential segregation, immigrants would be segregated as a whole from the host community. In other words, there would be immigrant areas in cities in which the mixture of immigrants would be random. Instead, there is clear evidence of substantial internal sorting of immigrant groups. Similarly, the evidence by O'Loughlin and Glebe on entropy levels of new immigrants and established immigrants supports this pattern of purposeful ethnic grouping (O'Loughlin and Glebe 1984b: 21). The situation in Europe, as in the USA and in Australia, is that immigrant groups are segregated not only from the host populations but from each other. Not only is this the case, but Lichtenberger has produced evidence of increasing life-style segregation (Lichtenberger 1984: 231–2). Ethnic segregation, in other words, is just one aspect of a much larger pattern of urban differentiation which is affecting European cities.

Note

* This chapter refers to the position in West Germany before unification. Unless otherwise indicated, 'Germany' should be taken to mean the Federal Republic.

7

Urban disadvantage and racial minorities in the UK

Definition of the problem area

In order to avoid repetition of much that is described elsewhere in this volume, it is necessary to define what questions this chapter tries to answer, and to indicate its starting point. Perhaps it is best to state first what topics the chapter will *not* attempt to cover: it is not about the distribution of racial minorities within the United Kingdom; not about the changes in the degree of concentration in certain areas, or the concomitant movements of dispersal from previous concentrations; it is not about the position in which ethnic minorities find themselves in the urban labour and housing markets. Instead, this chapter starts from the proposition that in the last two decades, areas of severe disadvantage have been identified in most of the large, old, cores of British conurbations, and that ethnicity clearly shows up as an integral part of the analysis of the extent, nature and causes of these disadvantages. The questions we shall have to face here are these: how far does ethnicity itself constitute a causal element of this disadvantage? Is a high proportion of people living in ethnic minority households an explanation of disadvantage? Is it a necessary and sufficient condition of disadvantage? If only a proportion of all members of ethnic minority groups can be shown to be living in inner urban areas, what determines the process of selection? If there are large areas where no ethnic minorities exist, but the state of deprivation nevertheless prevails, can we identify whether urban areas without ethnic minorities are in some way different from those which do have this element strongly in evidence?

To posit these questions is a necessary part of the analysis: to answer them adequately would require different research from that on which this chapter is based. Nevertheless, we must keep them in mind so that we can present existing research findings in a form which points the way to future investigation. Stating the problems in this way makes it necessary to define what a 'deprived inner-city area' is in terms of national comparisons and also to state clearly what we believe the causes of the 'inner area syndrome' to be. First, however, we should define 'ethnicity', or 'ethnic minorities'. In order not to add to the already far too numerous definitions used, we shall here employ the device adopted by the 1981 census of population: ethnic minorities are those people who were recorded as living in households where the head was born in one of the New Commonwealth countries, or Pakistan (NCWP). That this is inadequate is accepted, but no alternative definition has been widely adopted. If 'ethnicity' is mentioned, it means simply the state of belonging to such a household. This excludes some people, who are technically part of an ethnic minority, but who lived in other households or are descendants of former immigrants whom we no longer treat as being part of an ethnically distinct group in society (e.g. Jews, Gypsies, Americans who are of Indian or African descent). To try to give reasons for including or excluding one or other group is to venture out on to the thin ice of racial definitions – this will not be done here, partly because it makes our analysis unnecessarily contentious, and partly because the information is simply not available. A question dealing with ethnicity was asked in the 1991 census; the results are not yet known, but warnings have already been given that accuracy is not likely to be high, especially in the main areas with which we are here concerned: the disadvantaged inner cities.

The ethnic minorities this chapter analyses are those 2.161 million persons who in 1981 lived in households where the head was born in an NCWP country. This excludes 1.239 million persons born somewhere else outside the UK; it excludes NCWP households in Scotland and Northern Ireland (where they were not counted in this way); it includes phenotypically white persons living in NCWP households, and it excludes a large and unknown number of people who belong to ethnic minorities but who were living in households where the head was born in the UK. This includes, of course, second-generation immigrant-descended households.

Areas of deprivation

The definition of a deprived area used in this chapter is essentially that developed for an exercise undertaken as part of the ESRC's major research project on the inner cities (Hausner and Robson 1986). This was a statistical analysis based entirely on 1981 census of population data, designed to describe urban disadvantage in terms of policy problem areas, and to rank order parts of cities (defined usually in terms of groups of wards), identified by the Department of the Environment and the local authorities for their own policy and resource allocation priority purposes (Begg and Eversley 1986). The underlying assumption of this exercise was that it is not possible to say, without using quite unscientific value judgements, by how much the most disadvantaged areas fell below the national average, in the sense of being able to devise a financial weighting factor for their share of grants, or by how much the better-off areas should be penalised. It was, however, possible to undertake a computation which would serve as a basis for rank-ordering areas. The essential calculation for this was the number of standard deviations by which each area differed from the national mean. These observations (in this particular exercise seventy-two census-based variables based on ratios derived from a much larger number of 'cells') were then made comparable by a method known as z-scoring, and combined into subject groups of 'advantage' and 'disadvantage', to arrive eventually at composite scores for each area, and group scores for seven subject areas of 'disadvantage', and five of 'advantage'. There is in this procedure, of course, an element of arbitrariness, as in all such analyses; first, in choosing certain characteristics as having policy significance; and secondly, in the way the group indicators are implicitly weighted. The authors of the exercise did not follow Department of the Environment practice in weighting the group scores by a simple process of multiplying each observation by an arbitrary weight, but nevertheless in scoring, for instance, ten variables to arrive at a housing and household composition indicator, there was an underlying tendency to stress some policy areas more than others.

There is also an element of selectivity in using only census indicators: for instance, such highly important variables as the state of health of the local population had to be omitted, except in terms of a single census variable: economically inactive men reported as 'long-term sick'. There is nothing about comparative mortality; nothing about the incidence of various forms of social pathology as measured by social services records; nothing about crime; only very restricted information about educational standards. Still less can census variables throw light on environmental quality (except in the narrowest sense of housing conditions); they tell us nothing about recreational and leisure amenities and participation rates; nothing about the quality of landscape, air and water. Still more seriously, there is nothing about incomes, or reliance on social security and other benefits in kind and in cash. There is very little about social structure except in terms of class or socio-economic group.

On the other hand, what is certainly present is a certain amount of multi-collinearity – and this is inevitable both within the policy groups and between them. If it had been possible to include some or all of the other variables just mentioned, the degree of overlap, or (statistical) auto-correlation would have been greater still, as was ascertained in test-runs for certain selected areas for which data could be collected in 1981. The authors are fairly confident, however, that the results do represent a 'robust' picture of relative disadvantage.

Allowing then for some in-built selectivity, as well as the importance of the subjective judgements shown by the compilers in grouping census variables, the national, regional and local picture built up from the seventy-two variables relates to those subject areas of disadvantage which are most commonly taken into account by central and local government when deciding on priorities, total resource allocations, or special administrative arrangements to cope with the problems perceived. The variables used here are, at the same time, more complex than those used by the Department of the Environment when identifying urban priority areas, and much simpler than the formulae used in assessing rate support grants (Bennett 1982). The fact is that no one system is universally acceptable: it may be branded as being too simplistic, or too complex. The most usual charge is that a particular locality, which does not score particularly highly on deprivation, has been unfairly treated: it considers itself worse off than some other local authority, and provides a system all of its own to prove the point. Few local authorities accept the need for a national system of social indicators which can be used generally for the distribution of resources whether for local government services, health or any other policy area, and political scientists doubt whether such decisions can ever be made rationally (City of Liverpool 1986; Carley 1981).

In undertaking the final rank-ordering of areas by the degree of relative advantage, the authors found that it was not enough to use one simple measure of combined scores. One had to take into account such additional measures of comparative advantage or disadvantage as the degree of contrast between core, periphery and adjoining fringe areas (what is called the 'gradient' of disadvantage – essentially a measure of social polarisation); the absolute size of the areas of deprivation; the relative size of the deprived area within the sub-regional context (conurbations, metropolitan county, or 'travel to work area'). One also had to take into account the question whether the poor score was mainly due to the presence of negative factors (high unemployment, high proportion of tenants in privately rented furnished property, heads of households in social classes IV and V), or, on the other hand, the absence of positive factors, which were not necessarily simply a mirror image of the negative factors. (Thus, a positive factor would be the proportion of adult males and females with completed tertiary education, or the percentage of persons in the growing service industries who were in the professional and

Table 7.1 *Ranking of most deprived areas of the UK in 1981*

| Area | Basis for ranking[a] | | | |
	Favourable minus adverse	Favourable	Adverse	Population (in thousands)
Glasgow old core	1	= 1	2	181
Glasgow peripheral	2	= 1	10	170
Birmingham old core	3	5	1	235
Hull core	4	3	4	51
Derby core	5	4	12	54
Manchester/Salford old core	6	17	5	289
Liverpool old core	7	14	8	250
Nottingham core	8	22	3	70
Teesside core	9	6	18	236
Other West Midlands cores	10	8	17	388
Other Strathclyde cores	11	7	24	74
Other Greater Manchester cores	12	12	14	292
Leicester core	13	23	10	121
Merseyside peripheral	14	11	21	51
West Yorkshire cores	15	19	15	343
London Docklands	16	25	9	437
Plymouth core	17	15	23	34
Other Tyne and Wear	18	10	9	276
Sheffield core	19	18	22	228
Newcastle/Gateshead old core	20	20	25	215
Other Merseyside cores	21	21	26	336
Other South Yorkshire cores	22	9	–	132
Stoke core	23	13	–	48
Hull outer area	24	16	–	216
Hackney and Islington	25	–	7	337
Kensington and Chelsea, Haringey and Westminster[b]	26	–	13	209
Lambeth[b]	27	–	6	156

Note: [a] Lowest ranking is most deprived
       [b] Parts of these boroughs only
Source: Begg and Eversley 1986

managerial categories.) Having rank-ordered all the areas examined in six different arrays, it was possible to obtain a combined rank-order score which the authors believe represents as objective a picture of disadvantage as one can derive from the census variables alone. As this would take too much space, we do not in this chapter show all the different rankings, but reproduce instead, in Table 7.1, only the outcome of the first part of the exercise, where the combined score was arrived at by deducting the favourable from the adverse scores; the favourable scores alone, and the adverse scores alone. The table also shows the populations included in each area. It is these measures which we shall discuss in relation to the incidence of ethnicity, rather than some of the more complex measures which are essentially designed as a device for arriving at policy priorities.

Out of the twenty-seven identified inner-city areas, a number do not have a substantial ethnic minority presence in the 1981 census. (In fact, twelve have such minorities, fifteen do not.) These twenty-seven areas account for a population of under 5.5 million, out of 33 million in the English and Welsh and southwestern Scottish urban areas studied. Disadvantaged areas *without* a significant presence of ethnic minorities account for 2.27 million of the 5.5 million population listed in this table, or more than 40 per cent. We can, therefore, make our first obvious assertion: ethnic minorities are not a *necessary* condition for the presence of deprivation. This observation would have been strengthened had we included in our survey the whole of urban Northern Ireland, and the cores of the remaining Scottish cities – Edinburgh, Dundee and Aberdeen. The deprived population would then have been more than 6 million, and the areas containing ethnic minorities would have formed little more than a third of the total.

On the other hand there were in 1981 several important concentrations of ethnic minorities outside the major metropolitan areas and other conurbations: taking as our guidelines the list of local authority districts for which separate statistics are issued in respect of such categories as births by mother's origin, we find that there are two areas considered important enough to warrant detailed analysis as well as time series: Slough in Berkshire and Luton in Bedfordshire (OPCS 1986). A total of twenty districts outside metropolitan counties were considered important enough for a mention of births in one year; of these the largest is Leicester, which is included in the areas analysed for the inner-cities exercise. Of the remaining districts, several are included because of the presence of United States army personnel, not New Commonwealth and Pakistan immigrants, notably in Cambridgeshire, Oxfordshire and Suffolk.

Taking the statistics of the 1981 census of the whole of England and Wales, we find 2.161 million people in NCWP-headed households, or 4.5 per cent of the population (see Table 7.2). Of these, 73.5 per cent were resident in Greater London, the metropolitan counties of West Yorkshire, Greater Manchester, and the West Midlands, and in the East Midlands (i.e. effectively Leicester, Derby and Nottingham); and a further 2.3 per cent lived in the other metropolitan counties analysed in the inner areas report. (Others were included because they lived in 'fringe' areas, i.e. districts immediately adjoining the metropolitan counties or

Table 7.2 *Birthplace of household head, England, Wales and selected counties, 1981*

	All birthplaces	Caribbean	India	Pakistan	Total NCWP
England and Wales					
All persons	47,806,003	544,236	657,563	285,558	2,161,057
Born inside UK	44,680,520	272,804	253,341	113,704	875,172
Born outside UK	3,125,483	271,432	404,222	171,854	1,285,885
West Yorkshire metropolitan county					
All persons	2,000,305	18,720	34,715	50,556	118,372
Born inside UK	1,879,082	10,328	15,062	20,382	50,942
Born outside UK	121,223	8,392	19,653	30,174	67,430
East Midlands region					
All persons	3,738,253	28,442	62,069	11,906	140,991
Born inside UK	3,548,804	15,214	21,395	5,092	53,876
Born outside UK	189,449	13,228	40,674	6,814	87,115
Greater London					
All persons	6,492,642	306,792	223,664	52,192	945,148
Born inside UK	5,322,649	146,730	68,594	19,162	350,421
Born outside UK	1,169,993	160,062	155,070	33,030	594,727
West Midlands metropolitan county					
All persons	2,604,414	77,393	120,577	54,819	285,350
Born inside UK	2,349,825	41,172	52,846	21,663	126,599
Born outside UK	254,589	36,221	67,731	33,156	158,751
Greater Manchester metropolitan county					
All persons	2,552,650	20,288	29,612	25,572	100,045
Born inside UK	2,404,570	10,841	11,785	10,100	40,924
Born outside UK	148,080	9,447	17,827	15,472	59,121

Table 7.2 (cont.)

	All birthplaces	Caribbean	India	Pakistan	Total NCWP
South Yorkshire, Merseyside and Tyne and Wear					
metropolitan counties					
All persons	3,893,410	10,283	11,580	11,806	50,796
Born inside UK	3,797,779	5,716	5,350	4,958	22,817
Born outside UK	95,631	4,567	6,230	6,848	27,979

Source: Census 1981 National Report, Appendix A, Table 11

other large urban districts.) Altogether, about 80 per cent of the NCWP population in the UK in 1981 was included in the analysis of all the inner areas, which is in itself a rough measure of concentration. The other 20 per cent of all persons in NCWP households lived in districts which were not subject to the 'area deprivation' analysis, i.e. mostly smaller towns.

Thus we have some confidence that the statements we make about persons in NCWP-headed households in the 1981 census relate to the great majority of those living in the UK at that time (in effect, they were almost entirely absent from Scotland and Northern Ireland, and only 25,000, or little more than 1 per cent, were present in Wales).

This confidence, however, in the representativeness of the four-fifths of NCWP population included in the analysis is eroded when we consider the internal migration of the ethnic minorities. If we admit that we should really have considered those living in Luton and Slough, then we are implying that they are like those in Lambeth or Bradford – i.e. we suspect that they are disadvantaged minorities. When we consider whether Luton might not be the next city on the list for the development of the 'inner areas' syndrome, what we are mainly saying is that its ethnic minorities exhibit the same symptoms as those in the existing inner area concentrations. However, those whom we do not consider (because they live outside the main concentrations) are not just a minority within a minority, they are almost certainly different. It is precisely those who are better-off, better educated, and secure, who will be found in the many areas where the immigrant-descended populations form less than the national average or are virtually an invisible minority.

Those outside the main areas of concentration include a higher proportion of professional and managerial workers, more of the self-employed (e.g. in retailing and the catering trades), and the skilled manual workers. They will include fewer one-parent families, have lower proportions of unemployed workers, but higher proportions of owner-occupiers, and there will be more car-owners among them. No estimate will be made here of the numbers and proportions involved: given the fact that the census only asked the socio-economic questions of a 10 per cent sample of households, and that in the majority even of English local government districts we are dealing with only a few hundred households of ethnic minority origin, it would be dangerous to make too detailed a comparison of social structure. Overall, it must be true that the position of the minorities in areas where there are only a few of them is economically and socially better than it is in areas of concentration. This does not allow us to draw any conclusions as to their position within the local structure, whether there is more or less discrimination against them, whether they are as well-off as the average of the people of the area as a whole, and questions of that kind. All we conclude is that they are likely to be different from those in the inner areas in many important respects.

Origin and nature of urban deprivation in 1981

Industrial composition and immigration

We have established that the great majority of persons in households headed by someone born in the New Commonwealth and Pakistan, in 1981, lived in those metropolitan districts, and a few other large urban areas, which were also identified, nationally, as containing the largest concentrations of deprived households. This statement in itself does not prove that the majority of members of NCWP households are deprived, nor that the presence of such households is a principal cause of an urban area being labelled as disadvantaged. We have already established that it is not necessary for an area to contain a sizeable ethnic minority to exhibit the symptoms of widespread deprivation: in fact Strathclyde, Merseyside and Northern Ireland, the three poorest major urban areas in the UK, contain practically no NCWP-descended populations.

This statement itself gives us one clue to the causal mechanisms involved: the areas which already had the worst unemployment in the 1950s and early 1960s, when the majority of the NCWP population arrived, did not attract the immigrants. They had no shortage of labour in public transport, the health services, in construction, or in manufacturing industry. Iron and steel, coal-mining, ship-building, the older types of heavy engineering, and the cotton textile industries all suffered almost continuous decline after the initial post-war boom. None of the areas which were predominantly dependent on these industries had substantial immigrant populations in 1981 (except the old cotton towns of Blackburn and Preston, though even these were, by that time, more heavily dependent on engineering than on cotton). The large waves of immigrants after World War II had been drawn into other types of heavy engineering, much of it subsidiary to the automotive industries, including the foundry trades, into the woollen and worsted industry which was still flourishing when cotton languished (Bradford), into the garment and hosiery trades of the East Midlands, motor car assembly, electrical engineering and other consumer goods industries where manual assembly was the norm. In addition, there were the public services of the Midlands and the South-East, where there were not sufficient members of the indigenous workforce to take the lower-paid jobs, those involving unsocial hours, or dirt and danger. There were other parts of the British Isles which were economically stable or showing growth, but which managed to attract migrants from within the UK so that ethnic minorities never gained much of a foothold. Other areas had, in 1945, a sizeable agricultural labour force so that the growing public services as well as modern manufacturing plants were able to recruit staff from the declining rural sector. In two of the regions where there are now fewest NCWP households, the South-West and East Anglia, both these factors applied. Sizeable ethnic minorities exist only in Bristol, Swindon and Gloucester, but even in these cities the proportion was only at or below the average for England. So we establish three conditions for the presence of ethnic minorities at above average concentrations: that the area should be economically flourishing before 1965, that the vacant jobs should be predominantly in low-pay industries, and that it should not be attractive to British-born migrants. (Note that the last condition does not apply to Greater London and the rest of the South-East.)

This hypothesis of initial distribution is quite consistent with the presence of immigrants from NCWP countries in medicine (whether the well-paid doctors or the badly paid nurses), in self-employed retail trades and in catering (whether as owners, managers, or low-paid workers) all over the British Isles. In addition, certain skills were universally in short supply throughout the UK, and groups like Sikh carpenters were distributed in many localities before the economic decline began.

These industrial and occupational classifications help us not only to explain the distribution of the immigrant-descended population, but also their economic position in 1981. By that time, many of the industries which had flourished until 1965 had also declined substantially: the remainder of the textile manufacturing and garment trades; electrical and mechanical engineering assembly, heavy engineering including the foundry trades, the automotive industries (Begg, Moore and Rhodes 1986). Secondly, the halt to the expansion of the health service and social services, the decline of public transport, especially railway and bus services, where immigrants had occupied the lowest grade occupations – all these help to account for higher unemployment of adults amongst the immigrants. This is not, of course, a sufficiently general explanation, and there are many exceptions to the rule. Contrary to widespread belief, the number of persons employed in these 'non-growth' services did not actually decline, certainly not before the 1981 census, except in public transport. However, in areas where the services mentioned had attracted immigrants of young working age in the 1950s and 1960s, a problem would automatically arise if the children of these immigrants entered the labour market just at the moment when this type of employment was no longer increasing. If then young people were in any way disadvantaged, either by reason of inappropriate education and training, or owing to discrimination against them in the labour market, or even generally because of the very high ratio of new entrants to the labour market compared with leavers, the employment chances of the young, whatever their ethnic origin, would be lower than they had been twenty years earlier, and the children of immigrants would bear the brunt of the change.

There is another change in the labour market in general which also has to be considered when looking at the economic position of ethnic minorities. The change from declining manufacturing industries to the growing service industries also marked a reduction of full-time jobs for men and an increase in part-time employment (usually for women) (Begg, Moore and Rhodes 1986). This change had particularly severe effects in the large urban areas, where manufacturing declined fastest and services grew in line with national trends. The ethnic minorities reflect this general experience rather accurately in most areas and occupations, though not all ethnic groups were equally affected (e.g. some of the Asian populations had objections to married women taking up work outside the home, which is reflected both in economic activity rates and in local unemployment rates).

It seems, then, that the present position of the ethnic minorities within the inner cities is quite largely a matter of their involuntary involvement in the underlying changes in the fortunes of British industries. At the time of their arrival, most of them had little choice but to enter some of the lowest-skilled and worst-paid jobs, and indeed it was precisely these for which they were recruited by employers like London Transport and British Rail. There were some exceptions to that rule, like the carpenters we have already mentioned, who had good jobs in the construction industries in the 1960s, the more highly trained East African Asians, who also often had some capital, and those from all parts of the world with medical or legal qualifications. The great majority, however, were in the two lowest skill groups. It is, of course, precisely these which have the highest unemployment rates now. This is again exemplified by looking at some of the inner areas where there is the strongest association of unemployment, low-skill populations and ethnic minorities.

This can be most easily demonstrated by looking at disadvantaged areas within a general region of prosperity, such as London and the South-East. In 1981 the national unemployment rate was 11.6 per cent for men, and 7.7 per cent for women (census definitions). In Greater London, these rates were 9.7 per cent and 6.7 per cent for men and women, respectively. But within that metropolitan area, the heaviest concentrations occurred in the inner boroughs (see Table 7.3). Most of these boroughs formed part of the identified areas of greatest deprivation in

Table 7.3 *Unemployment ratios for men and women in selected London boroughs, 1981*
(Percentage of usually resident population with head of household born in NCWP and percentage of population in households with head in social classes IV and V)

| Borough | Out of employment | | NCWP | Social classes |
	Men	Women		IV and V
City of London	8.2	3.7	3.8	9.1
Camden	12.2	6.3	10.1	14.4
Hackney	16.1	8.0	27.5	22.3
Hammersmith and Fulham	12.1	6.2	14.8	16.9
Haringey	11.1	5.9	29.4	17.1
Islington	14.1	6.8	16.5	21.7
Kensington and Chelsea	10.4	6.3	8.9	12.5
Lambeth	13.7	7.0	23.0	19.5
Lewisham	11.4	5.1	15.0	17.9
Newham	13.3	6.2	26.5	24.9
Southwark	14.4	6.0	16.2 ·	22.6
Tower Hamlets	17.4	6.9	19.8	27.8
Wandsworth	10.8	5.4	18.4	16.0
Westminster	10.8	6.1	11.5	16.7
Brent	10.1	6.0	33.0	16.6
Ealing	8.7	5.1	25.0	17.3
Hounslow	7.4	4.1	16.9	15.5

Sources: For unemployment ratios and NCWP-headed households – *OPCS County Monitors*
For SC percentages – *Key Statistics for Local Authorities in Great Britain 1981*, Table 4, p. 30

London in 1981, and between them they (and their counterparts in the metropolitan counties) account for most of the territory of partnership areas which received the largest amounts of central government aid during the 1980s. However, as Table 7.3 also shows, they are not identical with the boroughs with the highest proportions of NCWP residents, nor does unemployment reflect social class structure with complete accuracy. For the inner-city deprivation scoring exercise, we went below borough level to groups of wards. This was necessary because so many boroughs which had large proportions of deprived households were rather mixed in their composition: Kensington and Chelsea, Westminster, Camden, Haringey, and Brent, Ealing and Hounslow in outer London. That is why we undertook the analysis in grouped wards. Even then, however, the identity of unemployment, ethnicity and adverse social class structure was not complete. Thus, if we take Hackney, arguably the most deprived of inner London boroughs, only one of the five wards with the largest unemployment rates also figured in the top five of the largest ethnic component. Nobody doubts that there is an association – but even without using the more sophisticated but misleading correlation and regression tests which figure so largely in the literature, we know that on the most elementary test (rank-order correlation) the association is only a partial one.

It seems, therefore, rather important to stress the differential experience of NCWP populations, according to their origins, their places of initial settlement, their educational and training experience, the industries in which they were originally employed, and other matters, rather than label them 'deprived ethnic minorities' without further qualification. We shall return to the difficulties which stand in the way of this further analysis at the end of this chapter.

The same applies when we test for other obvious signs of deprivation – like housing conditions, the presence of one-parent families, or lack of a car in a household. Sometimes there is a strong association, sometimes it seems rather weak. The tests of association break down completely if we examine owner-occupation (and we did, in our inner-city analysis, use owner-occupier ratios as one of the significant variables of advantage). Some of the greatest poverty (and the worst overcrowding) occurs in ethnic minority households in owner-occupation, just as in the district of Knowsley in Merseyside some of the worst social and economic conditions occur in fit, purpose-built public sector housing. So we would need to differentiate between different ethnic groups, as well as distinguishing owner-occupied housing by size and location, in order to find out why tenure by itself cannot be used as a good guide to the extent of deprivation.

We would need, in fact, to tabulate minority groups by origin, by area of residence, and ultimately by social class, by educational attainment, and other characteristics which might bring us, in the end, to rather tautological statements. Unemployment is highest amongst males of West Indian or Guyanese descent, lowest amongst 'others' (African, Arab, Chinese, 'mixed'), intermediate amongst those of Asian origin (see Table 7.4). Subdividing the Asians, unemployment is highest amongst Bangladeshis, lowest amongst Pakistanis. Then we rank order by area, and we find that within each ethnic group, the ordering corresponds to unemployment ratios for area of residence. There were a large number of smaller settlements where there were small concentrations of NCWP households, (arbitrarily defined as having 50 per cent more than the national percentage of such households), but with well below average male unemployment rates, like Aylesbury, Crawley or High Wycombe. As it happens, the observer can come up with a ready explanation in each of these cases why these places should combine relatively large immigrant

Table 7.4 *Economic status of the population of working age in the UK, by sex and ethnic origin, 1984*

	Males					Females				
	Ethnic origin					Ethnic origin				
	White	West Indian or Guyanese	Indian/ Pakistani/ Bangladeshi	Other[a]	All males[b]	White	West Indian or Guyanese	Indian/ Pakistani/ Bangladeshi	Other[a]	All females[b]
Economically active (percentages)										
In employment										
Employees – full-time	65.3	50.7	47.9	44.1	64.4	31.3	44.7	22.9	28.9	31.3
– part-time	1.9	1.4	1.5	2.1	1.9	23.9	13.0	8.3	13.5	23.3
– all[c]	67.3	52.2	49.5	46.5	66.4	55.2	57.7	31.2	42.3	54.5
Self-employed	10.8	6.2	16.2	10.2	10.9	3.7	1.1	4.7	3.6	3.6
All in employment[d]	78.2	58.4	65.8	56.9	77.4	59.0	58.7	35.8	45.9	58.2
Out of employment	9.8	24.2	16.3	12.1	10.1	6.8	11.7	9.5	11.6	7.0
On government scheme	0.2	2.1	0.4	0.1	0.2	0.1	0.2	0.1	0.2	0.1
All economically active	88.2	84.7	82.6	69.2	87.7	66.0	70.6	45.5	57.7	65.4

Table 7.4 (cont.)

	Males					Females				
	White	Ethnic origin				White	Ethnic origin			
		West Indian or Guyanese	Indian/ Pakistani/ Bangladeshi	Other[a]	All males[b]		West Indian or Guyanese	Indian/ Pakistani/ Bangladeshi	Other[a]	All females[b]
Economically inactive (percentages)										
Long-term sick or disabled	3.8	2.3	3.7	1.8	3.8	2.7	3.0	1.7	1.4	2.7
Looking after home	0.3	0.6	0.1	0.4	0.3	21.7	13.7	41.1	23.8	22.1
Full-time student	3.5	5.8	9.7	23.5	3.9	3.4	8.2	6.8	11.2	3.7
Retired	1.7	–	0.9	0.5	1.6	0.6	0.2	0.4	0.2	0.5
Other inactive	2.5	6.5	3.0	4.7	2.6	5.6	4.3	4.5	5.7	5.6
All economically inactive	11.8	15.3	17.4	30.8	12.3	34.0	29.4	54.5	42.3	34.6
Total of working age[e] (=100%) (thousands)	16,281	178	409	212	17,327	14,763	198	349	175	15,716

Note: [a] Includes African, Arab, Chinese, other stated, and mixed.
[b] Includes ethnic origin not stated.
[c] Includes hours of work not stated.
[d] Includes employment status not stated.
[e] Males aged sixteen to sixty-four, females aged sixteen to fifty-nine.

Source: Social Trends 16, p. 64
Labour Force Survey, 1984, Department of Employment

populations with low unemployment, but this would replace statistical analysis with anecdotal evidence. It seems better to accept that the manipulation of the statistical data will not yield a clear picture.

There are, as it were, a number of hierarchies, which are clearly in some sort of relationship to each other, but not to such an extent that we can establish causality. It is highly unlikely that a forty-five year old university graduate of East-African Asian origin in Wiltshire will be unemployed. It is highly probable that a twenty year old son of Caribbean parents without education beyond school-leaving age, living in Brixton, will be without a job.

But then this can also be said of the indigenous population – the same hierarchy obtains, albeit at a much lower level: in 1984, 9.8 per cent of white males were unemployed, but 24.2 per cent of West Indian or Guyanese males. So what needs explaining is not only the extent of the overall difference, but also the difference between localities, and how these two interact with each other. How far, by 1984, had the process of segregation gone? How likely was it that those with certain characteristics had moved to areas where there was work, leaving behind those who could not make the choice, and did this selection process differentially favour the white population? It seems very probable, but how can we prove it if we cannot refine our groupings further than the census (or for that matter the Labour Force Survey with its limitations to areal break-down) permits?

To sum up the state of our questions so far: The difficulty we find ourselves in is that because there are concentrations of NCWP-descended populations in areas of high unemployment, poor housing, low car-ownership, and (in some cases) high proportions of rented property, with relatively large percentages of households lacking amenities and living at high densities, we necessarily assume a causal connection. This, however, is no different from any demonstration (such as the one the Newcastle-on-Tyne planners undertook twenty-five years ago) that in the poorest areas – like Byker – there was a strong association between poverty in all its forms and poor housing. They could not conclude from these associations that bad housing causes unemployment, or vice versa; that unemployment caused ill-health, or the other way round. We do not know in what sequence people fall into the cycle of deprivation, or indeed are born into it, where poverty, one-parent households, unemployment, poor health, overcrowding, poor educational attainment all play a role (Rutter and Madge 1976).

The area deprivation scores and their relation to ethnicity

Is ethnicity a factor in its own right?

We next examine, in more detail, the role of ethnicity in the scores of deprivation within our total inner area system. The methodological question which had to be asked at the outset was this: is ethnicity itself a quantifiable factor in arriving at such a score? The Department of the Environment's different urban aid programmes and indeed, all governmental schemes from the Educational Priority Areas programme of the 1960s onwards automatically assumed that it was. It does, however, need more justification than mere precedent.

It could be argued that it would be enough to add up factors, such as employment, housing, tenure and car-ownership, both on the negative and the positive side, without counting ethnic origin separately. We rejected this approach, however, because we felt that the weight of the evidence showed ethnicity itself to have a quasi-independent role in establishing that an area was disadvantaged. One is aware that this is, in some ways, a circular argument. We know, nationally, that NCWP populations are more likely to be unemployed, live in overcrowded conditions, lack higher educational qualifications, and so on. If, therefore, the presence of large numbers of such individuals and households means, prima facie, that the district (or the ward or census tract) is more likely to be disadvantaged, the ethnicity ratio alone may not be needed to establish the fact of deprivation, or be a reason for including such an area in our analysis. To add this ratio itself may, therefore, seem unnecessary or even misleading. But circularity is not the only logical issue involved.

We need to add for the purpose of our analysis a number of other, often unquantifiable, factors which we know to be present, and for which ethnicity may well stand proxy. First there is prejudice – discrimination and disadvantage in the labour market and in the housing market. Therefore, all other things being equal, people of NCWP origin will have greater difficulty in getting jobs, achieving promotion (and with it, status and income), in securing private or public sector tenures or property in desirable areas; and this exacerbates any existing social or economic disadvantage.

Secondly, there will be difficulties in attracting to areas of ethnic minority concentrations sufficient teachers of the right calibre to overcome the handicaps of the children (hence the original Educational Priority Area concept long since eroded in practice). The same is arguably true of qualified social workers who will prefer to work in salubrious areas with a predominantly white population, of health service workers, including doctors, and so on. Whether or not this propensity is in part or wholly outweighed by the opposite tendency, for voluntary movements to swoop on black neighbourhoods, (as they have always done in the USA and began to do, in London, in the Notting Hill district in the 1960s, and in Sparkbrook in Birmingham, and later in East London), is not something we can discuss here – it seems unlikely at the very least that they would meet the shortfall of the statutory provision, and in the long run their well-meaning but untrained assistance may turn out to have been counter-productive.

Next, a large ethnic minority is of crucial importance in determining private (and public) investment in the infrastructure, and in the provision of current services. This argument was central to our whole chain of causality in the inner-city context (Begg and Eversley 1986: Introduction). The reasoning turns on the role of perceived purchasing power in determining levels of investment. Predominantly black areas in the USA were identified many decades ago as abounding in abandoned property (i.e. houses of which the landlords could not be traced, because they wanted to avoid being forced to invest in refurbishment of unfit housing, even with public subsidies). Neither individual investors nor multiple businesses would build new stores, existing store owners would close down and move to suburban hypermarkets. Doctors and dentists would not establish surgeries. Similar conditions exist in the UK, though they do not figure prominently in the research literature. Even if in the UK there is some attempt to steer practitioners to areas which are poorly provided, the current statistics show that this policy never wholly succeeded: ethnic minority areas are medically understaffed. At the most, they will have minimal 'lock up' surgeries, rarely properly equipped health centres, which require public and private investment. It may be that specialists like Halal butchers, or purveyors of West Indian vegetables, or saris, will congregate round Muslim, Caribbean or Indian concentrations, but that hardly amounts to a flourishing retail trade. Employers in search of a labour force in growth industries (especially offices, high-tech enterprises, quaternary services of all kinds) will not settle in an ethnic minority area if they can help it: despite the relative success of black women in clerical jobs, and the widespread recruitment of Asian youngsters in financial service industries, all the indications are that such growth firms will go to white suburbs, new towns, growth points within or just beyond the green belts, and hope to recruit from the children of families in new owner-occupied properties (Eversley 1990a). The public sector acts on the same principles. Local authorities and public corporations are not likely to invest in new libraries, swimming pools and other sports facilities, or leisure centres when they suspect low usage – citing, perhaps, low literacy amongst adults, prejudices against girls participating in sports amongst some Asian communities, or high unemployment rates and general poverty, making it too risky to install facilities which require entrance fees, personal equipment, a high standard of nutrition, and appropriate motivation. If this is thought to be the type of argument advanced by authorities of one political persuasion, it can be shown that their opponents also fail to invest in such facilities, but on the grounds that they would be culturally irrelevant. The outcome is the same – no investment in deprived areas. Just how much of this sort of prejudice is in some way 'justified' (i.e. based on sound accountancy principles) is not the issue: non-investment in such services provides a self-fulfilling prophecy.

What sequence and combinations of private and public decisions make an area appear run-down, neglected and undesirable cannot here be discussed: the subject has been amply aired in the literature of the inner city. The three major inner area studies commissioned by the Department of the Environment and published fifteen years ago (Department of the Environment 1976 and 1977), of which two dealt with ethnic minority concentrations (Birmingham and Lambeth) and one did not (the one on Liverpool), showed unanimity about the need to invest in the environment in order to make places green and airy, the need to remove debris and to put on coats of paint. These studies did in fact recognise that more had to be done than planting a few trees; but they always started with some rather naive plan to make the locality attractive to prospective investors. The idea was that a little seed-money spent by central and local government to hide the scars of neglect would result in the arrival of much larger amounts of private money; this is also the theory underlying the operations of the present urban development corporations. The precedent, in fact, had been set by the Hunt Committee Report on the Intermediate Areas, published in 1969 (Hunt 1969). The spiral of declining investment has continued in most of the areas identified fifteen years ago, the only exceptions being two kinds of localities: those which attracted private investment through gentrification, i.e. the replacement of disadvantaged populations by middle-class newcomers, and in urban development corporation areas. Where gentrification took place, there was not only the improvement of the micro-environment of private dwellings, but the process attracted publicans, restaurateurs, boutique owners, high-class artisans and all the other bees that come swarming round the honeypot once the magic stage has been reached where there is a clear margin of spending power, especially on personal services and the more expensive ranges of consumer goods.

Ethnicity in the deprivation scoring system

As we shall see, counting the ethnicity factor separately affected the rank-ordering of areas of deprivation, but not significantly: the top twenty-seven areas in the national deprivation league would have remained more or less the same, with only Leicester becoming a marginal case if ethnicity is taken out. Leicester was in any case halfway down our deprivation league table. No other area in the country would have qualified for inclusion in the table of maximum deprivation even including the ethnicity score. Some of the southern concentrations of ethnic minorities, like Luton and Slough, well away from the main centres of metropolitan poverty, might be eligible if we took only a small group of wards within the districts, and they had not, by 1981, developed a typical inner-city syndrome. These smaller towns, on the other hand, being islands of relative poverty in a sea of considerable affluence, would have been excluded by our sub-regional scoring system, where the presence of employment opportunities, higher purchasing power and good educational facilities in the wider area would cancel out the disadvantage of small concentration. If this sounds callous, we need to remember that social policy pivots on two foundations: the individual in a disadvantaged situation and area concentrations. If the number of individuals who are clearly in need of help is small relative to the total population, conventional wisdom has it that the state relies on statutory individual and household benefits and services to give the required help; and that there is a threshold (never clearly defined) of area disadvantage where other types of measures have to be used. This (to some extent artificial) division has for long been debated; we remember the change of policy twenty-five years ago when government help (special status) was withdrawn from isolated employment exchange areas where the tally exceeded the then dangerous level of 4 per cent registered unemployment.

In Table 7.5 we reproduce the overall results for six types of area which we identified and which between them covered about two-thirds of the total population of England and Wales and southern Scotland (omitting predominantly rural counties and districts unless they immediately adjoined an urban agglomeration and were subsumed under the heading of 'fringe' districts). If we look at the column headed 'Ethnic' amongst the adverse factors (there was no corresponding column under the favourable indicators), we see that positive scores (i.e. a high degree of presence of the factor as measured by standard deviations above the national mean) existed only in the metropolitan cores, and 'other old cores' (meaning inner cities which were not part of a partnership area or other clearly identifiable conurbation centres). The first figure, 3.0, indicates the total

score derived from the four ethnic 'cells' we used – NCWP-born population, children under fifteen in NCWP-headed households, persons from
45 to retirement age not born in the UK (an indication that there was a
long-established NCWP population if the score was high); and all persons
in households where the head was born in the NCWP. The second line
(0.76 in the case of the metropolitan core) indicates the arithmetic average
of the four separate scores, which was our way of reducing the bias shown
by allocating a certain number of cells to each type of indicator.

The result shown in Table 7.5 shows ethnicity in the metropolitan core
areas to account for 3.0 out of a total disadvantage score of 40.7, and for
2.5 out of the total disadvantage score of 23.8 for the 'other old cores'.
None of the other four types of area have positive ethnicity scores – i.e.
their NCWP populations are below the national mean. In computing the
overall situation for each type of area, we averaged the scores under
each heading. The relative positions remain the same. Ethnicity contri-
butes the second smallest component to the total disadvantage score
(0.76) for the metropolitan cores and the third smallest for other old
cores. For our final scores (last three columns of Table 7.5), we divided
the total adverse and favourable scores by the number of items we
counted under each heading. In the case of the adverse indicators, the
total negative score of 40.7 was divided by forty-seven indicators, giving
a mean of 0.87. If we had taken out the four ethnic scores, the adverse
total would have been 37.7, and the mean score 0.8 – no difference in the
order of magnitude or the relative position of these areas to the others in
the table. We cite these details because it needs to be demonstrated that
ethnicity, in itself, did not change the general map of deprivation in
British inner-city areas.

If we now turn to individual areas, the same is true: the general
position does not change if we choose to disregard the ethnic factor,
except in some cases in respect of the exact position of an area in the
league table of deprivation. Thus, for instance, inner Birmingham has, on
our extended list of local factors, a total adverse score of 60.4, and an
average of 1.28 (see Table 7.6). If we take out the very high ethnicity
component (14.8), the total score is reduced to 45. (The reader should
remember that these figures do not indicate absolute ratios of NCWP
populations, but the relative score of the area compared to the national
mean.) This would still leave inner Birmingham, in that rank-ordering,
ahead of inner Manchester (minus ethnicity), inner Liverpool (with
hardly any ethnic component) and well ahead of inner Leicester minus
the ethnic factors. There are other apparent local anomalies elsewhere or,
rather, obvious outward appearances are shown to be false when examined by a system of rigorous testing. Thus, for instance a composite area
we identified as 'Brent and Ealing Special Area' in outer London, has a

Table 7.5 *Overview of adverse and favourable indicators for six types of area in the UK, 1981*

	Adverse indicators							Favourable indicators					Adverse total	Favourable total	Favourable minus adverse
	Demo-graphic	Hous-ing	Ethnic	Economic activity	Class	Family	Other	Hous-ing	Economic activity	Educa-tion	Family	Other			
Metropolitan Inner	3.80	8.50	3.00	6.60	8.50	4.40	5.80	-3.50	0.20	-6.40	-2.50	-3.00	40.70	-15.30	-1.48
	0.42	0.85	0.76	0.94	1.07	1.10	1.16	-0.87	0.02	-0.81	-1.26	-1.00	0.87	-0.61	
Other old cores	2.80	5.00	2.50	4.20	4.80	2.10	2.40	-1.60	-1.70	-4.60	-1.40	-2.20	23.80	-11.40	-0.97
	0.31	0.50	0.62	0.60	0.61	0.52	0.48	-0.40	-0.21	-0.57	-0.69	-0.74	0.51	-0.46	
Heart of old industrial urban	0.80	-1.00	-1.00	-3.00	-3.00	-0.50	-0.60	0.20	0.70	1.00	0.20	-0.30	-8.30	1.80	0.25
	0.09	-0.10	-0.25	-0.43	-0.37	-0.12	-0.12	0.05	0.09	0.12	0.11	-0.10	-0.18	0.07	
Heart of agglomerations	-1.70	-4.20	-1.30	-2.50	-4.80	-1.70	-0.80	1.20	1.70	4.30	1.00	1.10	-17.00	9.40	0.74
	-0.19	-0.42	-0.33	-0.36	-0.60	-0.43	-0.16	0.30	0.22	0.54	0.52	0.37	-0.36	0.38	
Peripheral estates	-5.90	-2.40	-1.70	12.10	12.00	4.30	4.10	-2.80	-5.90	-12.60	-2.50	-3.30	22.60	-27.30	-1.57
	-0.65	-0.24	-0.42	1.73	1.50	1.06	0.82	-0.71	-0.74	-1.58	-1.24	-1.11	0.48	-1.09	
Fringe areas	-1.70	-4.80	-1.90	-4.80	-5.40	-2.70	-3.80	2.40	0.50	5.10	1.80	2.70	-25.20	12.50	1.04
	-0.19	-0.48	-0.47	-0.69	-0.67	-0.66	-0.77	0.60	0.07	0.63	0.88	0.91	-0.54	0.50	

Source: Begg and Eversley 1986

high adverse score, making it comparable with other deprived areas in northern England at 29.1; but if we take out the ethnic component (12.3), the total adverse score is under 14, making Brent and Ealing comparable with Cardiff (no significant ethnic component), rather than with inner West Yorkshire (which has an ethnic component, though not as important as Brent and Ealing).

Without entering into the details of all the eighty-eight area groupings studied, it is enough to state that our methodology turns out to be robust as regards ethnicity: that is to say, to remove this single factor from the scoring system does not affect the overall position, and if we use the sum of adverse and favourable factors, as in the last three columns, there is no detectable change in the rank-order sequence of disadvantage. We reproduce in Table 7.6 the detailed scores only for the twenty-seven most disadvantaged areas in Great Britain. This shows why we retained the ethnic group in our scoring system: because it enables us to see, when looking at the extent and composition of disadvantage and advantage in each locality, to what extent the total score includes an ethnic element, and with what other disadvantages (or absence of advantages) ethnicity is associated in each area.

The overall view derived from this exercise is the disappointingly obvious one: that ethnicity cannot of itself help to describe an area as being highly deprived, and the absence of an ethnic factor does not give a deprived area an advantage over others. Nor does it look, from these figures, as if areas which are disadvantaged, but have no ethnic component, were very different from those which do have this element. A careful look at all individual areas confirmed some long-held prejudices: since, for instance, we counted one-parent families as one of the components of the adverse 'family' score, it is not surprising that this adds some weight to the presence of NCWP (mostly West Indian) households in the area. However, the group of 'peripheral estates' (which includes only an Asian element, in Leicester, on the ethnic minority side) has an equally high adverse family score. Again, since we counted owner-occupation as a plus, the Brent and Ealing favourable score is increased because that is the most common form of tenure amongst the Asian community in Southall in particular. Thus we can use the method of analysis to make more precise statements about the nature of deprivation and help to meet the objective of the exercise: to identify areas for policy intervention.

If much of this seems obvious, it still needed to be shown on a reasonably neutral scoring indicator system. One comparative conclusion is perhaps worth adding: that we have demonstrated that ethnic minorities are not a necessary component of disadvantage; in contrast to North American studies which invariably point to the presence of a major black

Table 7.6 Group scores for the twenty-seven most deprived authorities (totals and means) in the UK

	Adverse indicators							Favourable indicators							
	Demo-graphic	Hous-ing	Ethnic	Economic activity	Class	Family	Other	Hous-ing	Economic activity	Educa-tion	Family	Other	Adverse total	Favour-able total	Favourable minus adverse
Glasgow old core	2.00	16.50	−0.50	14.60	14.20	4.00	6.60	−10.90	−3.90	−15.70	−3.50	−4.40	57.40	−38.40	−2.87
	0.23	1.65	−0.53	2.08	1.77	1.01	1.65	−2.73	−0.49	−1.97	−1.73	−1.47	1.34	−1.54	
Glasgow peripheral	−9.60	6.90	−0.60	16.70	15.50	5.60	7.00	−8.40	−5.20	−16.20	−3.60	−4.90	41.50	−38.40	−2.50
	−1.07	0.69	−0.61	2.39	1.94	1.40	1.75	−2.11	−0.65	−2.02	−1.81	−1.63	0.97	−1.53	
Birmingham old core	−2.50	5.30	14.80	13.60	17.80	5.70	5.70	−1.20	−8.20	−10.40	−3.10	−4.20	60.40	−27.10	−2.37
	−0.28	0.53	3.71	1.94	2.22	1.42	1.15	−0.30	−1.03	−1.30	−1.52	−1.41	1.28	1.08	
Hull core	6.50	19.50	−2.00	9.30	10.50	5.20	3.00	−6.30	−6.90	−9.40	−2.50	−3.70	52.00	−28.80	−2.26
	0.72	1.95	−0.51	1.33	1.31	1.30	0.61	−1.56	−0.87	−1.17	−1.26	−1.24	1.11	−1.15	
Derby core	4.30	10.20	6.40	2.60	11.60	1.80	2.20	−2.50	−9.30	−9.90	−2.20	−4.50	39.10	−28.30	−1.97
	0.48	1.02	1.59	0.37	1.45	0.45	0.44	−0.62	−1.16	−1.24	−1.09	−1.50	0.83	−1.13	
Manchester/Salford old core	4.80	8.70	1.80	8.50	10.30	7.10	6.60	−3.00	−3.40	−6.30	−3.10	−3.00	47.70	−18.80	−1.77
	0.53	0.87	0.45	1.21	1.28	1.77	1.32	−0.76	−0.43	−0.79	−1.52	−0.90	1.02	−0.75	
Liverpool old core	2.00	7.20	−1.70	13.10	13.40	2.90	6.30	−2.20	−1.20	−9.90	−2.80	−4.00	43.20	−20.10	−1.73
	0.23	0.72	−0.42	1.87	1.67	0.73	1.26	−0.54	−0.15	−1.23	−1.42	−1.34	0.92	−0.81	
Nottingham core	7.80	8.80	5.40	7.00	9.70	8.60	5.20	−2.60	−2.60	−3.60	−3.40	−2.20	52.60	−14.50	−1.70
	0.88	0.88	1.34	1.00	1.21	2.14	1.04	−0.65	−0.33	−0.45	−1.69	−0.74	1.12	−0.58	
Teesside core	−2.10	1.20	−1.70	12.80	9.50	3.90	2.30	−1.30	−8.00	−11.40	−2.30	−3.10	26.10	−26.10	−1.60
	−0.23	0.12	−0.42	1.83	1.19	0.98	0.47	−0.33	−1.00	−1.42	−1.13	−1.05	0.55	−1.04	
Other West Midlands cores	−0.40	1.80	5.10	8.40	9.20	1.50	2.00	−1.70	−9.20	−9.80	−1.60	−3.00	27.60	−25.30	−1.60
	−0.05	0.18	1.28	1.20	1.15	0.38	0.40	−0.43	−1.14	−1.23	−0.80	−1.00	0.59	−1.01	

Table 7.6 (cont.)

	Adverse indicators							Favourable indicators					Adverse total	Favourable total	Favourable minus adverse
	Demographic	Housing	Ethnic	Economic activity	Class	Family	Other	Housing	Economic activity	Education	Family	Other			
Other Strathclyde cores	-6.40	0.70	-0.60	11.90	10.20	2.80	4.10	-5.30	-3.50	-11.70	-2.00	-3.10	22.70	-25.50	-1.55
	-0.71	0.07	-0.61	1.69	1.28	0.71	1.02	-1.33	-0.43	-1.46	-0.98	-1.02	0.53	-1.02	
Other Greater Manchester cores	2.70	6.40	1.70	5.50	10.50	2.90	3.20	-2.20	-6.80	-8.20	-1.40	-2.30	33.00	-21.00	-1.54
	0.30	0.64	0.42	0.78	1.31	0.74	0.64	-0.55	-0.86	-1.03	-0.68	-0.78	0.70	-0.84	
Leicester core	2.00	8.90	12.40	3.60	9.50	1.90	3.10	-2.10	-3.10	-4.00	-1.30	-3.10	41.50	-13.60	-1.43
	0.23	0.89	3.09	0.52	1.18	0.48	0.63	-0.52	-0.39	-0.50	-0.65	-1.03	0.88	-0.55	
Merseyside peripheral (Knowsley)	-14.60	-9.80	-2.50	21.80	20.20	3.30	5.20	-0.70	-4.30	-11.30	-2.30	-2.90	23.70	-21.50	-1.36
	-1.62	-0.98	-0.62	3.11	2.53	0.84	1.05	-0.16	-0.54	-1.41	-1.16	-0.96	0.50	-0.86	
West Yorkshire cores	5.70	3.70	4.00	4.40	7.20	3.40	3.50	-1.70	-4.40	-5.80	-1.80	-2.80	32.00	-16.60	-1.34
	0.64	0.37	0.99	0.63	0.90	0.86	0.71	-0.42	-0.55	-0.73	-0.91	-0.95	0.68	-0.66	
London Docklands	3.90	10.40	4.20	1.40	10.80	5.00	6.60	-4.70	7.10	-6.60	-2.90	-3.10	42.30	-10.20	-1.31
	0.43	1.04	1.05	0.20	1.34	1.25	1.32	-1.18	0.89	-0.83	-1.43	-1.03	0.90	-0.41	
Plymouth core	8.10	9.40	-2.10	5.20	-0.50	1.20	1.60	-3.30	0.80	-11.30	-1.90	-4.00	22.80	-19.70	-1.27
	0.90	0.94	-0.52	0.74	-0.07	0.29	0.32	-0.82	0.10	-1.41	-0.93	-1.35	0.49	-0.79	
Other Tyne and Wear	-0.10	0.10	-2.50	8.90	5.00	1.10	4.50	-2.30	-5.60	-10.00	-1.70	-3.00	16.90	-22.60	-1.27
	-0.01	0.01	-0.63	1.27	0.63	0.26	0.89	-0.58	-0.70	-1.25	-0.84	-1.00	0.36	-0.90	
Sheffield core	5.70	4.70	-0.10	2.30	5.70	0.80	3.90	-1.70	-4.40	-7.00	-1.20	-3.40	23.10	-17.70	-1.20
	0.64	0.47	-0.03	0.32	0.72	0.21	0.78	-0.44	-0.55	-0.87	-0.58	-1.14	0.49	-0.71	

	Adverse indicators							Favourable indicators							
	Demo-graphic	Hous-ing	Ethnic	Economic activity	Class	Family	Other	Hous-ing	Economic activity	Educa-tion	Family	Other	Adverse total	Favour-able total	Favourable minus adverse
Newcastle/Gateshead old core	5.20	−1.40	−2.00	7.20	4.30	1.30	7.00	−2.40	−2.40	−7.70	−1.60	−2.00	21.60	−16.10	
	0.58	−0.14	−0.50	1.03	0.53	0.33	1.40	−0.61	−0.30	−0.96	−0.81	−0.67	0.46	−0.64	−1.10
Other Merseyside cores	−0.80	2.00	−2.30	9.80	7.10	1.80	3.90	0.40	−3.30	−8.40	−1.80	−2.30	21.40	−15.40	
	−0.09	0.20	−0.57	1.40	0.88	0.44	0.78	0.09	−0.41	−1.05	−0.89	−0.77	0.46	−0.62	−1.07
Other South Yorkshire cores	−1.80	−0.60	−1.80	3.20	3.90	−0.30	2.40	−1.30	−9.60	−9.00	−0.90	−2.60	5.20	−23.30	
	−0.20	−0.06	−0.44	0.46	0.49	−0.07	0.49	−0.31	−1.20	−1.12	−0.43	−0.88	0.11	−0.93	−1.04
Stoke core	0.50	6.10	−1.00	2.60	−1.30	0.04	−0.20	−1.60	−6.30	−9.20	−0.60	−3.20	6.70	−20.80	
	0.06	0.61	−0.25	0.37	−0.17	0.01	−0.04	−0.39	−0.79	−1.15	−0.29	−1.06	0.14	−0.83	−0.98
Hull outer area	−0.50	0.50	−2.50	2.70	3.20	−0.30	0.80	−1.10	−7.50	−6.90	−0.60	−2.90	3.80	−1.90	
	−0.06	0.05	−0.62	0.38	0.40	−0.07	0.15	−0.29	−0.93	−0.86	−0.27	−0.97	0.08	−0.76	−0.84
Hackney and Islington	3.30	11.90	6.90	1.00	4.90	7.40	9.70	−4.30	10.90	1.30	−3.00	−1.40	45.00	3.50	
	0.36	1.19	1.72	0.14	0.61	1.86	1.95	−1.08	1.36	0.16	−1.48	−0.47	0.96	0.14	−0.82
Kensington and Chelsea, Haringey, Westminster	0.80	9.70	10.20	−0.40	4.20	6.00	6.40	−4.00	9.10	1.60	−2.40	−1.30	36.80	3.00	
	0.09	0.97	2.55	−0.06	0.52	1.50	1.27	−1.01	1.14	0.20	−1.22	−0.43	0.78	0.12	−0.66
Lambeth	5.10	8.70	8.20	1.40	4.50	10.30	8.40	−3.60	15.00	2.80	−3.60	−0.90	46.60	9.70	
	0.57	0.87	2.04	0.20	0.56	2.56	1.68	−0.90	1.87	0.36	−1.82	−0.30	0.99	0.39	−0.60

Source: Begg and Eversley 1986

or Hispanic element in the urban population as an essential part of the deprived structure. Similarly, in the former Federal Republic of Germany, urban disadvantaged populations are predominantly foreign (or guest) workers or their descendants.

There remains the reverse question: are there urban areas with large ethnic minorities which score favourably on our analytical scheme? Apart from Luton and Slough, which we did not score separately, only one area stands out as having a favourable overall balance, despite a strong ethnic component, and that is inner Bristol. The ethnic component is larger there than that for Manchester and Salford, but with a total favourable score of 0.56 it just outweighs the adverse score of 0.53. We showed elsewhere in our study that Bristol is, in fact, an example of a large urban area which has successfully weathered the storms of the last twenty years, and though we have evidence, as elsewhere, that the ethnic minority, such as it is, is relatively disadvantaged, this observation still relates to a level of prosperity which takes inner Bristol, alone amongst the large inner-city areas, into the group with a positive overall score. (It should be pointed out that this rosy view of Bristol based on our comparative analysis is not shared by the local research team which investigated Bristol as part of the ESRC exercise. (Boddy, Lovering and Bassett 1986).)

In Nottingham, the adverse score was very small for the inner city, despite the presence of a sizeable ethnic element; its overall score is pulled down by the absence of favourable factors. The group labelled 'other Inner London' (i.e. inner London less the Lambeth, Hackney/Islington and Docklands Special Areas, and minus the composite Kensington and Chelsea, Westminster and Haringey aggregation) also has a considerable ethnic element, but has a positive overall score because the area has so many in-built advantages, especially as regards employment opportunities, that the relatively large contribution of ethnicity to the total disadvantage score does not make itself felt. In other words, if the ethnic minorities are located in areas which are otherwise prosperous (in the London case, this refers to boroughs like Wandsworth, Camden, Lewisham, and Hammersmith and Fulham), then, without being able to state that the ethnic minorities are noticeably better off than in centres of absolute decline, we can at least confirm that the presence of large NCWP minorities does not automatically stigmatise an area.

Our main conclusion from this study was that the association between ethnicity and disadvantage existed, but was too weak, and its causalities too intractable, to warrant further exploration. It is of course possible, given our method of investigation, to give precise expression, whether through rank correlation co-efficients, or through multiple regression analysis, to the degree of association. (We did this successfully, for instance, when showing the association between the rate of population decline and the degree of deprivation.) In the following section it is explained why such manipulations are thought to be fraught with danger, and why they would be unlikely to shed any light on the central questions still at issue.

Conclusions

There are two possible responses to the impasse we seem to reach when trying to express the relationship between ethnicity and disadvantage. One is to produce ever more refined techniques to measure association; to introduce more and more variables; to investigate ever smaller areal units. In addition, there are now well-tried techniques for longitudinal studies of individuals. We have recently seen some very interesting examples of the efficacy of public user samples in the longitudinal studies carried out on survivors of the 1971 census, comparing their position in the base year and in 1981; these proved particularly useful in connection with the changes in the position of the NCWP population (Fox and Grundy 1985; Hamnett, Randolph and Evans 1985). Admirable as these devices are, they still do not help us to understand the relationship between individuals, households and the community in which they live, let alone the wider urban context with its changing economic fortunes. The other approach is to put away the computers and to take a closer look at the underlying reasons for our apparent inability to make closely reasoned statements supported by evidence, before we embark on the next round of statistical analysis, perhaps on the basis of the 1991 census.

The first method has severe disadvantages – a fact long since recognised, but not apparently to such an extent as to stop the flood of new areal analyses, urban typologies and sub-regional nomenclatures. From a purely practical, policy-oriented point of view, these attempts have to be treated with great scepticism because they rapidly become out of date. Secondly, we have known for nearly fifteen years that census questions would not enable us to make precise statements about ethnicity even if the response rate was high and the answers reliable. Thirdly, given the demonstrable inter-area differences, any national sample procedure used to make statements about individuals or ethnic minority households would need to be qualified by reference to the area of residence, a qualification which cannot be made using Public User Samples or surveys like the General Household Survey or the Labour Force Survey. Fourthly, the more sophisticated statistical statements become, the less is the chance that their validity can be tested in relation to a perceived reality (Eversley 1978).

So we turn to the other approach: to ask ourselves if there is something in our whole methodology which somehow precludes us from coming up with useful answers? Demographers are quite used to this kind of self-questioning: having wrestled, ever since Malthus, with the problem of differential fertility, that is, in practice, finding out why some individuals/groups/nations control their fertility earlier or more severely than others. Having seen all their explanatory hypotheses vanish as soon as they were empirically tested, they have learned to ask different questions, which, as it happens, do not depend for their answers on multiple regression techniques. Given the amount of research into the social and economic conditions of the ethnic minorities in Britain in the last twenty-five years, and in the USA for much longer than that, why can we not be more precise in our statements? Having worked for a number of years on the unemployment problems of the Roman Catholic minority in Northern Ireland (a much more easily identifiable group than the various ethnic minorities in Britain, though the difficulties of using census data are similar), one can give a fairly categorical answer: if one says anything very precise about the characteristics of any particular group in society, it is bound to be wrong for a large fraction of that population; if one makes statements that are demonstrably true of the whole group, then they become almost meaningless because of the countless exceptions, cautions and special conditions with which one has to hedge about the general statement (see Eversley 1990b).

Research into the problem of ethnic minorities in Britain suffers from precisely this disadvantage. We can show that this is so by looking at the history of an earlier immigrant group. It is not the custom, in the UK, to denote Jews descended from immigrants from eastern Europe in the late nineteenth century as a racial minority; this nomenclature was outlawed in the aftermath of the war against fascism. Those who arrived fifty years later were dubbed 'enemy aliens' after 1939, but not 'an alien race'. Yet, one hundred years ago the new arrivals spoke no English, had a different religion, apparently possessed few skills which were in immediate demand in later Victorian Britain (such as the building trades), and they tended to settle in closely packed run-down areas in East London. They could have given rise to a literature similar to that about the Asian immigrants who now occupy the streets long since abandoned by the Jews. The central European arrivals of the more recent past also spoke little English, adhered to a different religion, but did possess a range of marketable skills. In fact, though both groups encountered hostility, some persecution, discrimination in housing and the labour market, and in society generally, they never gave rise to any large literature about the 'Jewish problem'. Their numbers were significant. They had, at first, high fertility.

They were clearly visible. Within a generation, however, if we look at the Russian and Polish Jewish immigrants, and in less time than that in the case of the Germans and Austrians, they have all but disappeared from the chronicles of the poor (where Charles Booth had put them prominently). They have been absorbed, assimilated, integrated – the exact term is irrelevant. Similar phenomena are well known from the much larger North American literature on immigrants. The black population of the USA (who were not immigrants at all, but descendants of slaves who arrived with their masters, the Founding Fathers), whose language and religion were no different from that of the white population, who had in theory access to the same educational opportunities as the majority, and who were not prevented from moving to any areas where they could get work, these people remained, and have remained, a major problem throughout American history. The much later 'Hispanic' arrivals (who are, on present indications, likely to outnumber the black population before the end of the century) were seen as problems from the moment of their arrival, have language difficulties, experience discrimination, often make little progress in the American educational system and occupy the worst housing in the big cities.

Despite our knowledge of the history of the Jews in Britain, of the Poles who arrived in the UK with their families after World War II, and the displaced persons who followed them; despite the huge American literature on the blacks, Hispanics and other groups of immigrants, we still get many examples of the refusal to face the fact that, in the UK, 'ethnic minorities' were not a homogeneous group. We enumerate people by place of birth and households by the place of birth of the head, or births by birthplace of mother (and father); we even note differential unemployment rates – but we do not ask other questions which might help to throw a little light on these very startling differences.

If we talk about Jews at all, we appear to assume that all that needs to be said about them is that some adhere to a different religion from the majority of British people. Sometimes we refer to Sephardic Jews, who came to Britain much earlier, grew exceedingly wealthy, and today form part of the elite of British society, and to Ashkenazy Jews – as if the latter were as easily identifiable a tribe. Yet the Ashkenazy range from the Rothschilds who arrived 180 years ago, through the East European Jews who came eighty years later (mostly artisans and small traders), to the professional and managerial cadres who were permitted to emigrate in the 1930s from German-speaking Europe. The fact that these groups (and many sub-groups within them) had totally different experiences of assimilation, intermarriage, social mobility and degrees of discrimination seems to be a matter for specialised monographs of Jewish history.

What has all this to do with the recent NCWP immigrants? It happens to illustrate how we avoid, if we are wise, making statements which could brand us as racists. Some are not so careful. When, early in 1986, the Church of England published its important study, *Faith in the City*, with its compassionate approach to the plight of the ethnic minorities, the then Chief Rabbi of the Jews in Britain, Sir Immanuel (now Lord) Jacobovits, published an article in *The Times* in which he said, in effect, that there must be something inadequate about these deprived immigrants in the inner cities who could not break out of the cycle of disadvantage. He recounted, with pride, the history of his own people who had, entirely by their own efforts, and against great odds, succeeded in achieving prosperity, learning and social status in the hostile urban environment. This is not the place to criticise the Chief Rabbi's historical errors, because the only point of this episode is to show that there is a widely held view (to which the Chief Rabbi, from his privileged position, could give full utterance) that those immigrants (or their descendants) who do not succeed are either of inferior intelligence, or lazy, or dishonest, or have other undesirable personal characteristics. If anyone, however, points to differences in experiences within the ethnic minority groups and attempts to explain possible reasons for the disparities, such statements are immediately greeted with abuse. The history of the reception accorded to B. F. Skinner's ideas (or research findings) shows what happens. It is not permitted to hold such views, let alone utter them. Therefore, there is no point in researching the origins of differences in social and economic development, because should the outcome be a confirmation of any of the starting hypotheses about interracial differences, the results could not be published. Those British politicians, journalists and academics who have stated that they believe part of the plight of the NCWP population at least to be attributable to their personal characteristics (Anthony Flew and Woodrow Wyatt, for example) have been ostracised and dismissed as fascists and racists for even raising the question.

If we look at the country of birth tables in the 1981 census, we find that 6.3 per cent of the population of Great Britain at that time were born outside the UK. Of these, the New Commonwealth accounted for less than 40 per cent. Add Pakistan, and the figure becomes 45 per cent. Take away the Mediterranean New Commonwealth (generally regarded as being ethnically white people), and we are back to 41 per cent – or little more than 2.5 per cent of the British population. (Let us assume for the purposes of this argument that those who live in NCWP-headed households form similar proportions of the population, in their various subdivisions – this is not strictly true, but the illustrative point is not affected.) Within the remaining group (those born in Asia, Africa and the

Caribbean), there are further sub-divisions which everybody knows about, but nobody discusses. About 10 per cent of the NCWP immigrants are East-African Asians – a group which was politically important when it first arrived in the UK, but which figures hardly at all in the detailed analysis of the sub-groups of the immigrant-descended population.

The conspiracy of silence on inter-group differences is the main explanation for our inability to make statements about the ethnic minorities in the inner-city context. We cannot put into one category Pakistani-born shopkeepers in affluent suburbs and young males of Caribbean origin in Brixton, or large Bangladeshi families in Tower Hamlets and Newham. The groups mentioned have nothing in common, other than the fact that their skins are not white, that they speak in a way that the rest of us sometimes find hard to understand, that their customs are different from those of the white educated middle class which undertakes the investigation of the minorities. We look at unemployment figures for youngsters of Caribbean origin and note without comment the fact that this differs considerably between boys and girls, that gender makes much less difference in the case of Asians, that is almost non-existent for the 'other' group and that the whites have figures similar to those of the Asians. We respond by supposing that this had something to do with differential economic activity rates, or family cultures, or make some other evasive contention. Alternatively, we attribute differential experience of minorities to differential amounts of prejudice on the part of the host population, prejudices which, of course, by their nature must be totally irrational and cannot possibly correspond to any past experience. This applies, whether the police search black youths for drugs and ensure in this way that a higher proportion of these people have criminal records, or examiners fail black students and thus ensure that they have no educational qualifications, or employers have the audacity to demand such educational qualifications and thus ensure the perpetuation of black unemployment.

This lack of differentiation, with its implication for the failure to target policies, can best be demonstrated by looking at contemporary US work. In particular, the *Report of the Secretary's Task Force on Black and Minority Health* (US Department of Health and Human Services 1985–6) demonstrates the importance of distinguishing at all times between different minorities. In a sense they are all disadvantaged, but their health experience (morbidity and mortality) can be shown to vary greatly, and in some respects some of the groups are healthier than white people. Whether the differences arise because of their diet, their willingness to seek and accept medical help, or because of their environment, whether they are due to alcohol abuse or to living conditions, need not be discussed here. At any rate, the report (in eight large volumes) makes it abundantly clear that even in such a relatively narrow field as mortality from specified cancers, one needs to take into account a whole range of social, economic and environmental circumstances to explain why experience differs as much as it does.

Such a report makes it impossible to generalise about 'the blacks', or even 'the Hispanics', or 'the Asians'. The specific recommendations of the task force make it abundantly clear that no blanket prescriptions would work: ethnicity *is* a factor, but this has no constant weight, and it does not operate in only one direction.

The conclusion which arises from our statistical exercise is that places in the United Kingdom differ according to their economic health, past, present and future, and this accounts for differences in unemployment, housing and other indicators of well-being or otherwise. This differential in past experience and future prospects arises not only between regions and sub-regions, but between inner cities and peripheries, between peripheries and rural fringe areas. The NCWP-descended population fits into that pattern. Overall, they are worse off than the indigenous population. Within the regional, sub-regional and local pattern, they mirror, but at an enhanced level, the differences that exist for the population as a whole.

For that whole population, internal migration exacerbates the problem. Those who are young, fit, well educated and perhaps have some starting capital are forming married-couple households and are moving from the urban agglomerations to the growth areas beyond. Those of the NCWP populations who can be similarly characterised take part in the move. For example, in all the new towns of the London ring, the Asian element in particular is much higher than in the adjoining county districts. Banking and other financial services, the accountancy profession and similar industry groups requiring a high degree of numeracy, have a particular predilection for young Asian entrants, and apparently they are not denied promotion.

For the inner areas, this selective out-migration means that the statistics of deprivation become more marked even if the population remaining were not itself suffering further impoverishment; simply by removing the best-situated, whilst reducing total numbers, we increase the proportion of the deprived. Council house tenants who can do so buy their dwellings, and five years later move away. Council house tenants who are ineligible because of age, poverty, unemployment, ill-health, or family circumstances, stay behind, claim housing benefit, and they have helped to transform the 28 per cent of households still in council property into a serious, and it seems permanent, concentration of the disadvantaged.

The NCWP households are a special case of this general process. Since more of them are poor, uneducated and have family structure problems, they are even more tightly trapped than their white counterparts. This applies even though the percentage of NCWP households in owner-occupation is now much higher, and only certain sub-groups in some areas are still predominantly council tenants. So the proportion of ethnic minorities as a part of the deprived urban minority grows, at least *pari passu*, but probably faster.

Britain is now, as much as ever, a country of two nations, or perhaps three or four. The divisions do not run exactly along the same lines as they did in the days of Disraeli. The intricate pattern of settlement prevents too fine a classification of areas. The division into an arbitrary, limited number of sub-groups necessarily hides the continuum. There is a spectrum from absolute advantage to absolute disadvantage. Places, households, individuals' occupations all lie somewhere along the spectrum, and so do the ethnic sub-divisions. They overlap in every respect, and make clear statements impossible. The analysis of the 1981 census, however, shows that ethnic minorities are disadvantaged. It does not show that for an area to be economically disadvantaged it must have a substantial ethnic minority component. What we need to look at, then, are not the statistics of past censuses and surveys, but the mechanisms operating in society which ensure that those who are now part of the disadvantaged minority stay mostly where they are. If these mechanisms continue to operate, we shall end of up with true ghettos – something we have not yet got in Britain.

For the situation as it exists overall, we can blame government and its institutions. For our inability to analyse disadvantage in ethnic terms, we must blame ourselves, as social scientists. Caught in our own code of linguistic ethics, we prevent ourselves from going beneath the superficial level of analysis. We have to stop pretending that all human beings are alike. We can only demand that they should be treated equally, have the same rights and obligations, that they should not be discriminated against on any grounds at all, that much bigger efforts should be made to enlarge the opportunities of those who are now at the bottom of the heap.

For this purpose, new policies have to be devised. This, however, is impossible as long as we pretend that there is an identifiable group known as the NCWP ethnic minority. There is not. What is unacceptable is not that too little research has been done, but that by a system of academic censorship we are prevented from undertaking investigations of a qualitative kind, in case it should turn out that the deprived inner-city populations are in some less obvious way than mere ethnicity, or lack of skills, or their state of health, different from those who move to the suburbs and beyond. Many observers believe that a large part of the effort, such as it has been, to give assistance to the inner areas, has been wasted. There may be all sorts of malpractices behind this fact. But it could also be that we simply do not know enough about the inner-city populations to devise an effective package of measures. Our inability to link ethnicity and inner-city deprivation in a meaningful way is only an outward sign of this serious defect in our armoury of knowledge.

8

Racial minorities in the London labour and housing markets: a longitudinal analysis, 1971–81

Introduction: race, recession and the riots

During the first half of the 1980s Britain was in the grip of a deep recession of a severity unknown since the 1930s. Although the recession has also affected most other advanced Western capitalist economies to varying degrees, its impact was particularly severe in Britain because of the deflationary monetary policies pursued by successive Conservative governments. In an attempt to reduce the level of inflation, the exchange rate was kept artificially high and government expenditure on housing, health and education was tightly controlled. While inflation fell considerably, the costs of government policy were severe. Manufacturing employment fell by 30 per cent between 1979 and 1985, and the number of unemployed almost tripled to stand at over 13 per cent of the economically active population even on conservative official statistics. Britain also became a net importer of manufactured goods for the first time since official statistics on the subject were collected a century ago (Martin and Rowthorne 1985).

The deindustrialisation of Britain is not solely, however, a product of these six years. Although it has increased dramatically over this period, the decline in manufacturing employment has been well established since the mid-1960s (Singh 1977; Blackaby 1979; Thirwall 1982). The last twenty years have also witnessed a marked relative increase in the importance of non-manufacturing and 'service' employment. This restructuring process has had its greatest impact on the older inner-city areas where manufacturing industry was traditionally concentrated (Massey and Meegan 1982; Danson, Lever and Malcolm 1980; Anderson *et al.* 1983; Martin and Rowthorne 1985; Fothergill and Gudgin 1983). It is in precisely these areas that the great majority of the black minorities from the New Commonwealth are concentrated (OPCS 1982).

Given the generally disadvantaged position of racial minorities in the British labour and housing markets (Smith 1977 and 1984) and the concentration of such minorities in metropolitan areas, it might be expected that the collapse of metropolitan employment will have hit the minorities particularly badly. As Cross (1983) has argued:

> The great processes of technological change that initiated the demand for less skilled labour have now guaranteed its redundancy as production shifts out of the large conurbations to the small towns, suburbs and overseas. There are twin transformations at work as industrial processes dictate a newly segmented labour force and then leave it high and dry on the gray sands of the inner city. (p. 6)

The 1980s have certainly been marked by the growth of very high levels of unemployment in the inner cities and some peripheral council estates. The level of male unemployment had reached over 30 per cent in many inner-city areas by 1981 (Hamnett 1983), and black minorities have been particularly badly hit. The level of unemployment among black males under nineteen years of age in the Brixton area of London in 1981 was estimated at 55 per cent, and it is significant that the 1980s have been marked by the outbreak of disturbances in a number of inner-city areas. Although the causes of these disorders frequently involve repressive policing and cannot be reduced to variations in economic and social conditions alone (Rex 1982; Peach 1986), it is clear that high unemployment and poor housing are important predisposing factors. In his report on the Brixton disorders of 1981, Lord Scarman (1981) stated: 'There can be no doubt that unemployment was a major factor in the complex pattern of conditions which lies at the root of the disorders in Brixton and elsewhere' (p. 205). More generally, Scarman argued that although

> some of the disturbances occurred in areas which, by most yardsticks, could not be described as severely deprived ... most of the disturbances occurred in inner city areas which share many of the features of Brixton: a high ethnic minority population, high unemployment, a declining economic base, a decaying physical environment, bad housing, lack of amenities, social problems including family breakdown, a high rate of crime and heavy policing ... the striking feature is not the differences but the similarities between Brixton and the majority of areas which were the focus of later trouble (Scarman 1981, pp. 29–30)

There is considerable evidence to show that racial minorities in Britain were initially concentrated in the less skilled and lower paid parts of the labour market and, partly as a result of their limited purchasing power and partly as a result of direct or indirect discrimination, that many of them were also initially concentrated in the poorest sections of the inner-city, privately rented and owner-occupied housing markets (Rex and Moore 1967) where access was easiest. Less is known, however, of the changing position of these minorities over time. The key question we therefore wish to analyse empirically in this chapter is how different racial minorities have fared over time in the labour and housing market. Has their position relative to the indigenous white population improved, worsened or remained stable over the years? The focus of our analysis is on the changing position of minorities within the London labour and housing markets over the intercensal decade 1971–81, and it forms part of a larger study of labour and housing market restructuring in London over this period. The first part of the chapter examines the changing position of racial minorities within the London labour market and the second their changing position within the housing market. First, however, it is necessary to say a little more about the nature of immigration to Britain and the changing structure of the metropolitan labour market over the last twenty-five years.

Immigration and the changing structure of the London labour market

It is now well established that immigration into Britain from the New Commonwealth countries during the 'long boom' of the 1950s and early 1960s was closely related to the demand for labour, especially in the low-skilled sectors of the labour market in both manufacturing and services (Peach 1968; Lee 1977). In an era of negligible unemployment, the indigenous workforce had become increasingly reluctant to fill this demand. These jobs were concentrated in London and the other large cities, and it was to the metropolitan centres that the majority of New Commonwealth immigrants moved. As table 8.1 shows, they are still overwhelmingly concentrated in the cities.

Since the 1960s, however, major changes have occurred in the structure of metropolitan labour markets. With the ending of the long boom and the rapid decline of inner-city manufacturing industry many manufacturing jobs have been lost, both skilled and unskilled. But while deindustrialisation and decentralisation of production have been largely responsible for the overall decline in the number of jobs located in metropolitan centres, there has been a marked shift in the composition of the labour market as a result of the expansion of employment in the service sector. This is particularly true in London, where the city's role as a centre of

Table 8.1 *Population resident in the British metropolitan counties by ethnic group, 1984* (in thousands)

	Greater London	Percentage of GB	Metropolitan counties	Percentage of GB	Great Britain
			Area of residence		
White	5,497	11	15,758	31	50,895
West Indian	309	58	430	81	529
Indian	318	39	556	69	807
Pakistani	43	12	248	67	371
Bangladeshi	60	65	78	85	93
Chinese	37	34	56	51	109
African	71	65	85	78	109
Mixed	84	41	134	65	205
Other	62	45	81	59	138
Not stated	155	19	332	40	829
Total	6,637	12	17,758	33	54,084

Note: Metropolitan counties: Greater London, Merseyside, Greater Manchester, West Midlands, Tyne and Wear, West Yorkshire and South Yorkshire
Source: Labour Force Survey, 1984

national and international corporate capital and finance has been reinforced and strengthened.

As a result, at least until the start of the current recession, London experienced a rapid growth in the number of highly paid managerial and professional jobs, particularly in the financial and business services sector. But at the same time, lower-grade clerical employment has tended to decentralise into the suburbs and beyond, as well as being subject to increasing levels of part-time working and feminisation (Knight *et al.* 1977; GLC 1983). In addition, with the deskilling of some labour processes in manufacturing, the growth of tourism and personal service sector employment, and the growing tendency towards feminisation and part-time working in the retailing sector, there has also been an increase in the number and proportion of low-paid and low-skilled manual service jobs (GLC 1985). Coupled with the growth in the numbers of unemployed and those who derive an income in marginal forms of employment or are dependent on supplementary benefit and job creation initiatives, the decline in skilled manufacturing employment and the growth of both high status managerial and professional jobs and low-skill, clerical and manual service sector employment has led to the emergence of an increasingly polarised labour market in London (Lovett and Ham 1983). Similar tendencies have also been documented in other major metropolitan areas (Sassen-Koob 1984).

This tendency towards the bifurcation of employment opportunities which has accompanied deindustrialisation and the increasing shift to non-manufacturing employment has been characterised by a complex process of labour market segmentation. The various ethnic minorities have tended to occupy distinctive positions within this structure, partly as a result of their differential pattern of recruitment into the British labour market over the last thirty years. In general, New Commonwealth immigration has played an important role in low productivity or labour intensive segments of the labour market during a period of generally rising wages. Initially this meant employment in either the lower paid public sector or in those sectors of manufacturing where productivity improvements were gained by substituting a cheaper, less demanding immigrant workforce for the indigenous one.

The first wave of immigrants to respond to this demand were West Indians, drawn into both low-wage public sector employment, such as transport and ancillary occupations in the National Health Service, and into manufacturing. Demand for such labour was particularly acute in London, due to both the concentration of such jobs in the capital and the buoyant nature of the economy which had caused labour supply problems in these low-wage segments. As table 8.2 shows, from the mid-1950s to the mid-1960s, this group formed the dominant source of black immigration into Britain. But West Indian migration peaked in the mid-1960s and today constitutes only a small proportion of total New Commonwealth immigration into Britain.

Table 8.2 *Residents born in the New Commonwealth by year of entry and county of birth, Great Britain, 1984* (in thousands)

	Year of entry						
	Pre-1955	1955–64	1965–74	1975–84	Not stated	Total	Percentage white
Caribbean	18	146	52	8	18	242	5
Indian	61	87	148	64	23	382	18
Pakistani	5	41	72	63	9	189	2
Bangladeshi	0	5	10	20	2	38	0
East African	6	16	113	49	9	192	13
Rest of Africa	7	9	22	30	7	75	31
Far East	10	23	44	38	3	118	36
Other New Commonwealth	41	52	49	16	7	163	75
Total New Commonwealth	147	379	509	288	77	1439	21

Source: Labour Force Survey, 1984

The main consequence of this migration history is that West Indians represent the longest established section of the black community in Britain. As a result, a much higher proportion of the West Indian community are second-generation British born than is case with other, more recently arrived, minority groups. It is amongst these second-generation West Indians that unemployment and poor job prospects have been particularly acute. It can thus be argued that West Indians are strongly represented in at least two secondary labour market segments: the established and ageing West Indians still associated with the low-wage, public service sector, and the second generation which, to all intents and purposes, represents a pool of surplus labour feeding the general secondary labour market.

As West Indian immigration was beginning to tail off in the mid-1960s, the next wave of migrants from the Indian sub-continent and Africa began to arrive. Despite the numbers of immigrants from Africa, this stream was overwhelmingly Asian in character, and well over half of this latter group were in fact East Africans of Asian origin (OPCS 1985). There were considerable differences between these two streams of immigrants. While many of the Indian and Pakistani immigrants were attracted to Britain to fill low-wage jobs in the declining textiles and engineering sectors in the Midlands and the north of England, many East African Asians have moved to London and into retailing, service and other white-collar occupations. This reflects their previous background in commerce and business. In many respects, the East African Asians represent distinctive primary labour market elements within the black community. Finally, the most recent group to arrive has been a small but growing community from Bangladesh who have almost exclusively moved into the small-scale manufacturing and clothing sectors, again concentrated in London.

Thus the Asian community itself is characterised by a wide variety of quite distinctive labour market situations. And second-generation Asians have only recently moved on to the labour market in any numbers. Many may well fare much better than second-generation immigrants of West Indian origin, partly as a result of the common practice for children to find employment in family businesses. This may not be the case, however, for those whose parents moved into the low-skill manufacturing sector. These British Asians are more likely to face the same constraints on job opportunity that other black youths face.

This brief review of the main trends of black immigration into Britain over the past thirty years illustrates that New Commonwealth ethnic minorities have occupied a considerable variety of labour market positions, particularly in the secondary labour markets. We might expect that the impact of labour market restructuring will have been far from uniform across these various segments. It is to the consideration of the impact of this restructuring on the main New Commonwealth ethnic groups that we now turn.

The data source

The data used in the following analysis is derived from the Office of Population, Census and Surveys (OPCS) Longitudinal Study (or LS) which consists of information on a 1 per cent sample of all *individuals* enumerated in the 1971 census of population in England and Wales. This sample of some 500,000 individuals was followed through to the 1981 census, and the two sets of census records of the surviving and trace LS members (LSMs) resident in England and Wales have been linked together. The LS, therefore, includes all the data from the 1971 and 1981 census records for those individuals and the households of which they were a part on the two census dates. To compensate for those original LSMs who died or emigrated since 1971, OPCS have added a 1 per cent sample of all new births and immigrants into England and Wales between 1971 and 1981. This analysis concentrates on the great majority of LSMs who were present in both years and whose census records were success-fully traced and matched. It should, therefore, be borne in mind that the analysis does not compare cross-sections of the total sample population at two points in time. Instead, we are following longitudinal changes in the characteristics of the surviving part of the original sample enumerated in 1971.

The LS is particularly useful for research on the changing position of racial minorities in Britain because – although the 1971 census included a question on ethnic origin as well as on country of birth – the 1981 census only asked about country of birth and therefore made it impossible to identify the growing number of British-born blacks unless they lived in a household headed by a person born in the New Commonwealth. The LS allows the ethnic origin of all continuing LSMs to be derived from their 1971 census record. This is a major advantage over conventional census analysis, but while this analysis includes both persons born in the New Commonwealth and British-born blacks, we have not differentiated between the two groups because of the relatively small number involved.

The sample has also been limited to include only those LSMs of UK, West Indian or Asian New Commonwealth and Pakistani ethnic origin who lived in London in *either* 1971 *or* 1981 or in *both* years. Of a total sample of 57,278 continuing LSMs 53,728 (or 93.8 per cent) were of UK ethnic origin, 1,977 (or 3.5 per cent) were of West Indian origin and 1,573 (or 2.7 per cent) were of Asian or Pakistani origin. These figures compare closely to the proportions enumerated in London in the 1971 census. Given the sensitivity of questions on ethnic origin and the linkage of computer records, it cannot be stressed too strongly that the records are linked anonymously by computer within OPCS and that the data available to researchers is in the form of aggregate numbers and tables shorn of identifiers. There is no way in which individual census records can be identified or used, and the data source is completely confidential. In the analysis which follows we shall look first at the position of racial minorities in the London labour market in 1971 before turning to the changes between 1971 and 1981.

Racial minorities in the London labour market in 1971

The evidence from the 1971 LS clearly reveals the concentration of New Commonwealth immigrants and British-born blacks in manufacturing industry. As Table 8.3 shows, 29 per cent of economically active and employed white LSMs were employed in energy, utilities and manufacturing (EUM), 31 per cent in construction, distribution and transport (CDT) and 40 per cent in services (S). The proportion of West Indians (40 per cent) and Asians (51 per cent) employed in manufacturing was considerably higher and their representation in the other two sectors was correspondingly lower. Whereas manufacturing employed a smaller proportion of whites than any other sector, it employed the largest proportion of West Indian and Asian workers. The level of ethnic unemployment was also approximately double the white rate.

When these figures are disaggregated by sex as well as ethnic origin (Table 8.4), they show that whereas white males were evenly distributed by industrial sector, West Indian and Asian males were disproportion-

Table 8.3 *Industrial sector of economically active and employed by ethnic origin in England and Wales, 1971* (in percentages)

	UK	West Indian	Asian	Total
Energy, utilities and manufacturing	29.1	39.1	51.0	30.0
Construction, distribution and transport	31.3	27.3	23.7	31.0
Services	39.1	33.1	25.3	39.0
Total number	28,864	786	814	30,464
Unemployment rate	3.6	7.0	6.6	3.8

Source: OPCS, Longitudinal sample

Table 8.4 *Industry sector by ethnic origin and sex in England and Wales, 1971*

	UK		West Indian		Asian		Total	
	M	F	M	F	M	F	M	F
Energy, utilities and manufacturing	32.4	24.8	42.4	38.0	53.2	44.0	33.1	25.4
Construction, distribution and transport	36.0	24.6	38.7	15.1	27.1	14.5	35.8	24.2
Services	31.6	50.6	18.9	46.9	19.6	41.5	31.1	50.5
Total number	15,638	11,068	413	326	580	200	16,631	11,594

Source: OPCS, Longitudinal sample

ately concentrated in manufacturing and underrepresented in services. And whereas females in all ethnic groups were overrepresented in services, both West Indian and Asian women were also strongly concentrated in manufacturing. These figures are consistent with the view that the ethnic minorities have fulfilled the function of a substitute labour force in the manufacturing sector and were disproportionately concentrated in manufacturing in 1971.

Analysis of the occupational characteristics of the ethnic groups in 1971 (Table 8.5) shows the highly uneven distribution of occupational status. For the purposes of this analysis we have adopted a four-way classification of census socio-economic categories which aims to reflect the dual divisions of the labour market into manual and non-manual and primary and secondary segments. A description of the composition of these categories is appended at the end of this chapter. Whereas some 56 per cent of white LSMs were in non-manual occupations, only 24 per cent of those of West Indian origin and 35 per cent of those of Asian/Pakistani origin were in these occupations. Where those of Pakistani origin alone

Table 8.5 *Occupational status by ethnic origin in England and Wales, 1971*

	UK	West Indian	Asian	Total
Primary non-manual	23.3	11.6	17.3	22.9
Secondary non-manual	32.9	12.9	17.7	31.9
Primary manual	23.1	27.5	23.6	23.2
Secondary manual	20.7	48.0	41.4	22.0
Total number	26,885	765	790	28,400

Note: See appendix for the composition of the four occupation categories
Source: OPCS, Longitudinal sample

Table 8.6 *Occupational status of males by ethnic origin in England and Wales, 1971*

	UK	West Indian	Asian	Total
Primary non-manual	28.4	5.3	17.5	27.4
Secondary non-manual	19.1	8.1	16.2	18.7
Primary manual	35.0	43.3	27.3	35.0
Secondary manual	17.5	43.3	39.0	18.9
Total number	15,725	432	587	16,744

Source: OPCS, Longitudinal sample

were concerned, the figure fell to 22 per cent. Although the proportions in the primary or skilled manual group amongst the West Indians was slightly higher than in the white population, the proportion of both the West Indians (48 per cent) and the Asians (41 per cent) in the secondary manual sector was more than double that of the white population (21 per cent). These figures clearly reveal the concentration of minority groups, particularly the West Indians, in the less skilled manual occupations in 1971.

These are aggregate figures, however. When they are disaggregated by sex, they reveal the usual marked differences in occupational structure. There are also striking differences between the different racial groups by sex, as Tables 8.6 and 8.7 indicate. While women in general were under-represented in both the primary non-manual and the primary manual sectors, they were heavily overrepresented in both the secondary sectors and particularly the secondary non-manual sector. But whereas white women were heavily overrepresented in the secondary non-manual sector (52 per cent), both West Indian (54 per cent) and Asian (48 per cent) women workers were strongly concentrated in the secondary manual

Table 8.7 *Occupational status of females by ethnic origin in England and Wales, 1971*

	UK	West Indian	Asian	Total
Primary non-manual	16.2	19.8	16.7	16.3
Secondary non-manual	52.3	19.2	22.2	50.9
Primary manual	6.3	6.9	12.8	6.4
Secondary manual	25.2	54.0	48.3	26.4
Total number	11,160	333	203	11,696

Source: OPCS, Longitudinal sample

sectors. These figures indicate that black women tended to fare worse than women in general in the London labour market in 1971. Table 8.6 also clearly reveals the marked concentration of West Indian males in the two manual sectors.

Tables 8.2–7 treat industrial and occupational structure separately. When the two are brought together in Tables 8.8–10, it is clear that the London labour market in 1971 was segmented by race and gender as well as by industry and occupation. Whereas white males were particularly concentrated in primary non-manual service employment and primary manual manufacturing and CDT employment, West Indian and Asian males tended to be disproportionately concentrated in primary and secondary manual manufacturing and CDT segments. Asian and West Indian females tended to be disproportionately concentrated in secondary manual jobs in manufacturing and services, whereas white females tended to be disproportionately concentrated in the secondary non-manual sector. But as the small cell numbers in the minority groups may be subject to considerable sample error, the figures must be interpreted with caution.

Changes in industrial and occupational structure, 1971–81

Over the ten years from 1971 to 1981 the industrial structure of the London labour market changed considerably. As a GLC research report pointed out:

> Between 1971 and 1981 London has lost nearly 400,000 manufacturing jobs, representing nearly four-fifths of all jobs lost. The number of persons employed in manufacturing in 1981 was only 60 per cent of the 1971 figure in Greater London as a whole, and just 50 per cent in Inner London ... Over a quarter of all London's jobs were in manufacturing in 1971, but less than one fifth in 1981 ... During the same period of time the percentage share of the service industries (which also include distribution, catering, local and national government) rose from 53 to 62 per cent, but it did not increase in absolute terms to make up for the loss of manufacturing jobs. (Hodgeson 1984: 55)

What has been the impact of this decline in manufacturing employment and the growth of employment in the CDT and service sectors on ethnic minorities relative to the white population? As Table 8.11 shows, the distribution of the economically active by industrial sectors in 1981 was very different from that in 1971.

Despite an increase of 5 per cent in the total number of economically

Table 8.8 *Industrial sector by labour market position for economically active and employed white males and females in England and Wales, 1971*

	Males					Percentage	Females				
	Primary non-manual	Secondary non-manual	Primary manual	Secondary manual	Total		Primary non-manual	Secondary non-manual	Primary manual	Secondary manual	Total
Energy, utilities and manufacturing	7.2	4.2	14.6	6.4	5,058	32.4	1.5	10.4	4.2	8.7	2,747
Construction, distribution and transport	7.9	5.9	15.6	6.6	5,636	36.0	2.5	18.3	1.0	2.8	2,719
Services	13.4	9.0	5.0	4.2	4,944	31.6	12.4	23.8	1.1	13.2	5,602
Total number	4,461	2,996	4,490	2,691	15,638	100	1,813	5,822	697	2,736	11,068
Percentage	28.5	19.2	35.1	17.2	100		16.4	52.6	6.3	24.7	100

Source: OPCS, Longitudinal sample

Table 8.9 *Industrial sector by labour market position for economically active and employed West Indian males and females in England and Wales, 1971*

	Males					Percentage	Females				
	Primary non-manual	Secondary non-manual	Primary manual	Secondary manual	Total		Primary non-manual	Secondary non-manual	Primary manual	Secondary manual	Total
Energy, utilities and manufacturing	1.7	1.5	19.1	20.1	175	42.4	-	3.4	5.2	28.5	124
Construction, distribution and transport	1.5	2.7	19.4	15.2	160	38.7	-	9.2	-	5.2	49
Services	2.4	4.1	5.8	6.5	78	18.9	19.0	7.1	1.5	19.3	153
Total number	23	34	183	173	413	100	66	64	23	181	326
Percentage	5.6	8.2	44.3	41.9	100		20.2	19.6	7.1	53.1	100

Source: OPCS, Longitudinal sample

Table 8.10 *Industrial sector by labour market position for economically active and employed Asian males and females in England and Wales, 1971*

	Males						Females				
	Primary non-manual	Secondary non-manual	Primary manual	Secondary manual	Total	Percentage	Primary non-manual	Secondary non-manual	Primary manual	Secondary manual	Total
Energy, utilities and manufacturing	4.0	4.7	17.6	27.1	309	52.3	1.0	2.0	10.5	30.5	88
Construction, distribution and transport	4.7	6.2	8.3	7.9	157	27.1	1.5	6.5	2.0	4.5	29
Services	9.1	5.5	1.7	3.3	114	19.6	14.5	14.0	0.5	12.5	83
Total number	103	95	160	222	580	100	36	45	26	98	200
Percentage	17.7	16.4	27.6	38.3	100		17.0	22.5	13.0	47.5	100

Source: OPCS, Longitudinal sample

Table 8.11 *Changes in the industrial structure of all economically active and employed Longitudinal Survey Members (LSMs) in England and Wales, 1971–81*

	1971	Percentage	1981	Percentage	Absolute	Percentage	Percentage change
Energy, utilities and manufacturing	8,501	30.1	6,568	22.2	−1,933	−22.7	−7.9
Construction, distribution and transport	8,750	31.0	9,302	31.4	+552	+6.3	+0.4
Services	10,974	38.9	13,754	46.4	+2,780	+25.3	+7.5
Total number	28,225	100	29,624	100	+1,399	+5.0	-

Source: OPCS, Longitudinal sample

active and employed LSM's between 1971 and 1981, the number in manufacturing decreased by 23 per cent, whereas the number in construction, distribution and transport rose by 6 per cent and the number in services by 25 per cent. In proportionate terms, manufacturing declined from 30 per cent of economically active and employed LSMs in 1971 to 22 per cent in 1971. Service employment, on the other hand, increased by 7.5 percentage points. But when these figures are disaggregated in Table 8.12, the *absolute* decline in manufacturing employment among ethnic groups is shown to have been proportionately much *less* than it was amongst the white sample. This might well be expected, given the role of immigrations as a substitute low-wage labour supply. In other words, immigrants have maintained a position within a declining manufacturing sector because of their secondary labour market characteristics, while the more skilled, high-wage, white manufacturing workforce has taken the brunt of deskilling and rationalisation. It may also be partially a product of the age structure of the different groups. The higher proportion of older workers in the white population is more likely to have been employed in manufacturing in 1971 but may have subsequently left through retirement. Conversely, the higher proportion of new entrants to the labour market among the ethnic groups may well have served to counteract partially the extent of manufacturing job loss among the existing ethnic labour force. This point is discussed further below.

The relative changes in the industrial composition of the ethnic groups show a rather different picture, however. The percentage point decline in manufacturing employment among the West Indians and Asians was *double* that of the white sample. But this is primarily a product of the much greater increase in numbers of economically active minority workers in the other two industrial sectors. What this appears to indicate is that while the decline in manufacturing has had less impact on those ethnic minority workers already in manufacturing, the remainder of the ethnic minority workforce has experienced a much greater relative shift into other industries. Table 8.12 also indicates a growing divergence within the ethnic employment structure. Whilst the increases in West Indian employment were strongly concentrated in services, the major increase in Asian employment was in construction, distribution and transport. This may reflect the rapid growth in Asian involvement in the distributive trades, both retailing and wholesaling, noted above.

When the changes in employment structure are disaggregated by gender as well as race (Table 8.13), several points stand out. First, the relative shift out of manufacturing was greatest amongst the minority groups, both for males and females. Second, Asian males and females were the only groups to display a marked proportionate increase in the

Table 8.12 *Changes in employment structure by industry for all economically active and employed in England and Wales, 1971–81*

	UK			West Indian			Asian		
	Absolute	Percentage	Percentage change	Absolute	Percentage	Percentage change	Absolute	Percentage	Percentage change
Energy, utilities and manufacturing	−1839	−24	−8	−39	−13	−16	−55	−14	−14
Constructions, distribution and transport	+333	+4	+0.1	+94	+45	0	+125	+67	+10
Services	+2423	+23	+8	+276	+119	+16	+81	+41	+5
Total number	+917	+3	-	+331	+45	-	+151	+20	-

Source: OPCS, Longitudinal sample

Table 8.13 *Percentage point changes in employment structure by industry, and by race and gender in England and Wales, 1971–81*

		Males				Females		
		Energy, utilities and manufacturing	Construction, distribution and transport	Services		Energy, utilities and manufacturing	Construction, distribution and transport	Services
UK males	1981	25.8	36.8	37.4	females	15.5	23.6	60.8
UK males	1971	32.4	36.0	31.6	females	24.8	24.6	50.6
Change	71–81	−6.6	+0.8	+5.8	Change	−9.3	−1.0	+10.2
West Indian males	1981	30.9	38.5	30.6	females	17.1	17.3	65.6
West Indian males	1971	42.4	38.7	18.9	females	38.0	15.1	46.9
Change	71–81	−11.5	−0.2	+11.7	Change	−20.9	+2.2	+18.7
Asian males	1981	38.3	37.1	24.6	females	33.0	24.7	42.3
Asian males	1971	53.3	27.1	19.6	females	44.0	14.5	41.5
Change	71–81	−15.0	+10.0	+5.0	Change	−11.0	+10.2	+0.8

Source: OPCS, Longitudinal sample

CDT category. Third, although the relative shift into services was generally greater among females than males, it was most marked for West Indian women. This group has seen the greatest relative shift in its industrial composition.

The differential components of industrial change, 1971–81

The analyses of industrial change discussed above raise the question of how far the changes are the product of changes in the industrial composition of continuing labour market members, and how far they are the result of differential entries to and exits from the labour market. Both are potentially major sources of change. On the assumption that an individual's *potential* working life is between forty and fifty years, then between a quarter and a fifth of the labour force is replaced every ten years solely as a result of natural turnover. If the industrial characteristics of new entrants differ substantially from those leaving the labour force through retirement or redundancy, this can result in major change in industrial composition. Analysis of the components of change in industrial structure reveals that the large decline in manufacturing employment among those who are economically active and employed in both 1971 and 1981 was partially offset by the surplus of new entrants into manufacturing employment in 1981 over exits from the manufacturing labour force since 1971. This was true of all three groups, and the increases in both the other two sectors were primarily the result of a large surplus of new entries over exits from the labour force rather than internal movements into these sectors from manufacturing. This indicates the important role played by differential rates of retirement and recruitment in labour market change in London during the 1970s among both blacks and whites.

Differential change in occupational structure, 1971–81

We have already seen that the occupational structure of ethnic minorities in 1971 differed considerably from that of the white population. How did it change between 1971 and 1981? Unfortunately the official classification of occupations into socio-economic groups changed somewhat between the censuses. The main effect was that some intermediate and junior white-collar occupations were reclassified into the semi-skilled manual grouping. While the changes were generally marginal and our use of a fourfold occupational classification reduces the impact of most of these changes, they have not been explicitly taken into account in the following analysis.

Table 8.14 *Occupational position by ethnic origin of economically active and employed LSMs in England and Wales, 1971–81* (in percentages)

	UK 1971 1981 Percentage change	West Indian 1971 1981 Percentage change	Asian 1971 1981 Percentage change
Primary non-manual	23.3 30.8 +7.5	11.6 18.5 +6.9	17.3 22.4 +5.1
Secondary non-manual	32.9 30.2 −2.7	12.9 21.0 +7.1	17.7 21.2 +3.5
Primary manual	23.1 20.6 −2.5	27.5 22.8 −4.7	23.6 23.9 +0.3
Secondary manual	20.7 18.4 −2.3	48.0 37.7 −10.3	41.4 32.5 −8.9
Total	100 100 -	100 100 -	100 100 -

Source: OPCS, Longitudinal sample

Table 8.14 shows that the distribution of occupational groups by ethnic origin in 1981 displayed a broadly similar pattern to that for 1971. The minority groups are still underrepresented in non-manual occupations and heavily overrepresented in the secondary manual sector. There were, however, some significant changes. First, all groups showed a significant proportionate growth of primary non-manual occupations at the expense of manual occupations. This proportional increase was, nevertheless, lower for the minority groups. Secondly, proportions in the secondary manual sector fell for all groups, and the shift away from these jobs was particularly marked for the minority groups. But there were compensatory proportionate increases in secondary non-manual occupations for the minority workforce. This latter trend was in clear contrast to the white workforce, which saw the proportion of secondary non-manual workers decline. The proportional shift from secondary manual to secondary non-manual positions was greatest for West Indians.

Thirdly, the links between Asian immigration and manufacturing employment appear to be confirmed in the proportional increase in primary manual Asian workers. Both the other groups saw their proportions of primary manual workers fall. Finally, if movement into primary employment (both non-manual and manual) is taken as a general index of upward socio-economic mobility, then it seems clear that the Asian workforce has fared somewhat better than West Indians in overall terms. Primary employment amongst Asians increased from 41 per cent in 1971 to 46 per cent in 1981, while the increase for West Indians was from 39 to 41 per cent. While both immigrant groups experienced an important, and encouraging shift into primary non-manual occupations in line with the workforce as a whole, there were significant differences in the changes in their labour market composition compared to the white workforce, and in the relative changes between the two immigrant groups.

It should be pointed out, however, that these figures relate to the economically active and employed. When the unemployment figures for 1971 and 1981 are compared, they indicate that unemployment had risen far faster among the ethnic minorities, especially the West Indians. Among economically active whites, unemployment rose from 3.6 to 6.8 per cent. Among Asians it rose from 6.6 to 11.2 per cent and among West Indians it rose from 7.0 to 16.2 per cent. In percentage terms the absolute level of unemployment rose by 99 per cent among whites, by 102 per cent among Asians and by 290 per cent among West Indians. Since 1981, unemployment among the latter community, especially amongst West Indian youth, has undoubtedly increased rapidly and it needs to be borne in mind that the occupational shifts discussed above relate only to economically active and employed blacks – not the growing number of unemployed blacks. In many respects, the growth of black unemployment is more important than marginal improvements in the occupational position of the employed.

When the figures given in Table 8.14 are disaggregated by sex, a more complex picture emerges. Whilst some caution is necessary in interpreting the tables due to the small sample numbers involved for the minority groups, it is nevertheless clear from Tables 8.15 and 8.16 that the impact of economic change on the London workforce over the 1971–81 decade has been far from simple once gender is added into the analysis. For example, it appears that the expansion of primary non-manual workers has been a general trend, but with the significant exception of female Asians. It is possible that there are social factors operating above and beyond the operation of the labour market which have blocked the movement of female Asians into higher-status employment. In fact, the overall numbers of female Asians in the workforce underwent a significant decline, contrary to the general trend for all the other categories. Why this should be is unclear. It is also apparent that while the decline in white secondary non-manual employment has been due to a loss of males, the growth of secondary non-manual jobs amongst the minority groups has had the greatest impact on females and, to a lesser extent, West Indian males. As white females appear to have maintained their position in the secondary non-manual workforce, the net result is that white males have been replaced by blacks in these low-status white collar occupations. In other words, feminisation of the secondary non-manual workforce has also been accompanied by an increase in black employment.

Similarly, while the loss of white primary manual workers was common

Table 8.15 *Changes in occupational position by ethnic origin and sex of economically active and employed LSMs in England and Wales, 1971–81*

| | UK | | | | West Indian | | | | Asian | | | |
| | M | | F | | M | | F | | M | | F | |
	Absolute	Percentage	Absolute	Percentage	Absolute	Percentage	Absolute	Percentage	Absolute	Percentage	Absolute	Percentage
Primary non-manual	+1427	+32	+854	+47	+50	+217	+62	+94	+62	+60	−5	−15
Secondary non-manual	−420	−14	−11	-	+37	+106	+92	+145	+2	+2	−3	−7
Primary manual	−274	−5	−206	−29	+31	+17	+7	+30	+34	+21	−6	−23
Secondary manual	0	0	−424	−15	+15	+8	+27	+15	−25	−11	−44	−45
Total number	+733	+5	+213	+2	+133	+31	+188	+56	+73	+12	−58	−29

Source: OPCS, Longitudinal sample

Table 8.16 *Percentage point changes in occupational position by ethnic origin and sex of economically active and employed LSMs in England and Wales, 1971–81*

	UK M	F	West Indian M	F	Asian M	F
Primary non-manual	+ 7.4	+ 7.3	+ 7.6	+ 5.8	+ 7.5	− 0.3
Secondary non-manual	− 3.4	− 1.0	+ 4.6	+ 10.7	− 1.5	+ 14.2
Primary manual	− 3.2	− 2.0	− 4.7	− 1.1	+ 2.1	− 1.6
Secondary manual	− 0.8	− 4.3	− 7.7	− 14.3	− 8.1	− 12.5

Source: OPCS, Longitudinal sample

to both sexes (and particularly females in relative terms), there were absolute increases of black primary manual workers, and a significant increase in the proportional importance of primary manual work amongst Asian males. This conforms to the notion of a continuing substitution of black males for whites in those skilled occupations which remain in the declining manufacturing sector, with a shift to Asians as the most recent, and by implication most compliant, minority element.

Lastly, the relative decline in secondary manual jobs was concentrated amongst white females and Asian males and females. In contrast, the numbers of white secondary manual males remained static, and both male and female West Indian secondary manual workers actually increased. Whilst the latter trend is compatible with a marginalisation of some West Indians into low-status manual jobs, the other trends are more difficult to explain. It is quite possible that the apparent stability of white males in the secondary manual sector is a reflection of the impact of the deskilling which has accompanied deindustrialisation within the manual workforce. Manufacturing decline may have therefore pushed some white male manual workers into lower skilled employment. But white and Asian female secondary manual workers may simply have been displaced from the active workforce or moved into other industrial sectors. The implication is that deskilled white males may thus have helped to displace females out of the secondary manual workforce.

New immigrants into London from the New Commonwealth

It is clear from the previous analyses that New Commonwealth immigrants in Britain prior to 1971 have experienced considerable changes in their labour market position between 1971 and 1981. The question then arises as to whether these changes are specific to these earlier immigrants

or whether more recent immigrants have also tended to move into different labour market positions from those held by the earlier generation of
immigrants in 1971. We can shed some light on this question by looking at
the labour market characteristics of immigrants who have moved into
London from outside Britain since 1971. As the 1981 census does not
provide information on ethnic origin, we are limited to an analysis using
data based on country of birth, only. The three categories utilised refer to
New Commonwealth immigrants born in the West Indies (West Indian),
India and Pakistan (Asian) and New Commonwealth Africa (African).
While the West Indian and Asian immigrants are largely drawn from
indigenous ethnic groups, the African immigrants are much more diverse,
including ethnic Africans, African Asians and a substantial white component. It is therefore necessary to approach the analysis of the labour
market characteristics of the African category with some caution.

The data in Table 8.17 show that recent immigration to Britain from
the New Commonwealth has been largely Asian in character. Only 112
immigrants between 1971 and 1981 were born in the West Indies, compared to 1,233 born in the Indian sub-continent and 716 born in Africa.
The majority of the latter category will be Africans of Asian origin,
although this analysis does not allow us to identify them as a separate
category. The data also point to significant differences in the labour
market position of these three immigrant groups.

The small number of recent West Indian immigrants were disproportionately concentrated in the service sector, which accounted for
over 50 per cent of those in employment. The much more numerous Asian
and African groups were more widely distributed between the three
industrial sectors. These differences broadly paralleled those between
continuing Asian and West Indian LSMs in 1981 and indicate that new
immigrants may tend to move into the same industrial sectors as earlier
arrivals and their children. It is interesting to note, however, that whereas
the proportion of post-1971 Asian and African immigrants employed in
services is almost identical at around 36 per cent, the proportion of
post-1971 Asian arrivals in manufacturing is higher than the proportion
of Africans, while post-1971 African immigrants showed a greater propensity towards the construction, distribution and transport sector than
did either of the other two groups. If we assume that the majority of
African immigrants are in fact of Asian origin, this confirms the very
different position of these two Asian sub-groups in the British labour
market. Thus, recent Asian immigrants from the Indian sub-continent are
still more likely to enter the British labour force through the manufacturing sector, following the pattern for earlier immigrants from the sub-
continent. But Asians of African origin have shown a greater tendency to

Table 8.17 *Industrial sector by country of birth of economically active and employed immigrants in England and Wales, 1981*

	West Indian	Percentage	Asian	Percentage	African	Percentage	Total	Percentage
Energy, utilities and manufacturing	15	22.4	197	36.3	118	31.4	330	33.5
Construction, distribution and transport	18	26.9	146	26.9	128	34.0	292	29.6
Services	34	50.7	200	36.8	130	35.6	364	36.9
Total number	67	100.0	543	100.0	376	100.0	986	100.0
Unemployed and inactive	45		690		340			
Total number	112		1,233		716			

Source: OPCS, Longitudinal sample

Table 8.18 *Occupational position by country of birth of immigrants in England and Wales, 1981*

	West Indian	Percentage	Asian	Percentage	African	Percentage
Primary non-manual	11	16.4	94	17.3	88	23.4
Secondary non-manual	24	35.8	128	23.6	134	35.6
Primary manual	12	17.9	99	18.2	66	17.6
Secondary manual	67	28.9	222	40.9	88	23.4
Total of economically active	67	100.0	543	100.0	376	100.0
Unemployed and inactive	45		690		340	
Total number	112		1,233		716	

Source: OPCS, Longitudinal sample

move into construction, distribution and transport, and particularly into the wholesaling and retailing segment of this sector.

Where occupational position is concerned, a comparison of Tables 8.18 and 8.16 shows that post-1971 West Indian arrivals tended to be over-represented in non-manual occupations compared with continuing LSMs of West Indian origin. In particular, they were much more likely to have secondary non-manual jobs and much less likely to have secondary manual ones. This may well be a reflection of the markedly different structure of opportunities facing recent immigrants compared to members of the established West Indian community. The decline in overall demand for manual workers as a result of deindustrialisation may well have reduced opportunities for employment in these segments. Recent West Indian immigrants, therefore, appear to have been disproportionately drawn into the secondary non-manual service sector.

This does not appear to be the case for recent immigrants from the Indian sub-continent, however. These were not only more likely to have entered the London labour market in secondary locations in general, but were particularly concentrated in secondary manual occupations. These data appear to confirm that more recently arrived Asian immigrants, particularly those from Bangladesh, may well constitute part of a new low-wage segment within what remains of manufacturing industry in London.

But there are also marked differences between the occupational characteristics of post-1971 Asian and African immigrants: 59 per cent of Africans were in non-manual occupations in 1981 compared to 41 per cent of Asians, and Africans were also much less likely to occupy secondary manual positions than Asians. Again, this undoubtedly reflects the tendency for African Asians to work in retailing, wholesaling and general services, while other Asian immigrants have, as we have seen, greater likelihood to work in manufacturing. It is also noticeable that post-1971 African immigrants had a significantly higher proportion in the primary non-manual segment than the other two groups. This is explicable in terms of the emergence of the East African Asians as an increasingly important entrepreneurial segment within the immigrant community, particularly in catering and distributive trades.

Racial minorities in the London housing market, 1971–81

In those economies where access to the housing market is primarily controlled by price and ability to pay, position in the labour market is generally a major determinant of housing market position. Other things being equal, the more highly skilled and highly paid will generally tend to command the better and usually more expensive housing. In Britain this has increasingly meant owner-occupation (Hamnett 1984; Saunders 1990), although it should be pointed out that the owner-occupied sector is far from homogeneous, and there is a substantial older, smaller, low-quality, low-income owner-occupied sector in the inner areas of many large cities, particularly those in the Midlands and the North, where house prices are considerably lower than in London and the South-East (Karn 1979; Karn, Kemeny and Williams 1985). For those excluded from owner-occupation by virtue of occupation and income, the principal alternative is council housing or a place in the rapidly contracting privately rented sector. *In general*, the incidence of owner-occupation is positively related to occupational class and income, whereas the incidence of council renting is negatively related. We stress 'in general' because although this relationship between occupational class and tenure holds true at the aggregate level for the white population, the relationship is very different where racial minorities are concerned.

It is clear from Table 8.19 that in 1971 a substantially higher proportion of ethnic LSMs lived in owner-occupied households than was the case in the white population. The West Indian figure was 9 points higher and the Asian figure was no less than 20 points higher than the equivalent white figure. Where council renting was concerned, the West Indian figure was 10 points less than the white figure, and only 3 per cent of Asians lived in council housing. Both ethnic groups had a lower proportion living in the unfurnished private rented sector than whites, but they both had a much higher proportion living in the furnished rented sector. It is also clear that

Table 8.19 *Housing tenure by ethnic origin of all economically active and retired LSMs in England and Wales, 1971* (in percentages)

	UK	West Indian	Asian	Total
Owner-occupation	44.7	53.4	65.1	45.5
Council housing	29.2	19.1	3.1	28.3
Unfurnished rented accommodation	20.5	11.0	7.5	19.9
Furnished rented accommodation	5.6	16.4	24.2	6.3
Total number	30,751	809	836	32,396

Source: OPCS, Longitudinal sample

when we control for differences in occupational class (Table 8.20) not only is the level of ethnic owner-occupation high across all occupational classes; it is also highest amongst the less skilled.

A number of reasons can be advanced to explain the differences between ethnic and white patterns of housing tenure in 1971. The private rented sector, particularly the furnished sector, has historically played a major role in accommodating newly formed households and newly arrived migrants into urban areas, and Table 8.19 indicates its importance for New Commonwealth immigrants at this date. Furnished renting is generally expensive and of poor quality, and it therefore tends to function as an interim, short-stay tenure, and most households move out as quickly as possible into better, cheaper and more permanent accommodation. Where the white population is concerned, the more highly skilled and better off have generally moved into owner-occupation, while a higher proportion of the less skilled have tended to go into the council sector. This did not happen in the case of the racial minorities for two reasons. First, access to the council sector was generally controlled by residence qualifications and by time on the waiting list. Both of these factors

Table 8.20 *Owner-occupation, controlled for occupation in England and Wales, 1971*

	UK	West Indian	Asian	Total
Primary non-manual	63.7	51.7	61.2	63.5
Secondary non-manual	47.0	49.0	58.2	47.5
Primary manual	39.6	59.3	65.6	40.8
Secondary manual	30.3	51.7	68.2	32.9
Total number	44.7	53.4	65.1	45.5

Source: OPCS, Longitudinal sample

Table 8.21 *Housing tenure by ethnic origin of economically active and retired LSMs in England and Wales, 1981*

	UK	West Indian	Asian	Total
Owner-occupation	57.7	50.9	83.8	58.2
Council housing	27.0	38.8	10.0	27.0
Unfurnished rented accommodation	11.3	7.5	3.3	10.9
Furnished rented accommodation	3.9	2.7	2.9	3.9
Total number	36,260	1,292	1,072	38,624

Source: OPCS, Longitudinal sample

militated against recent immigrants, and some councils actively discrimi-nated against blacks. In addition, many Asians appear to have a strong antipathy to renting and an equally strong desire to own their own homes wherever possible. As a consequence, many immigrants, unable or unwill-ing to gain access to the council sector and unable or unwilling to buy suburban owner-occupied houses, moved from furnished renting into the low-cost and low-quality, inner-city owner-occupied market.

By 1981 considerable changes had taken place in the structure of ethnic housing tenure. Table 8.21 shows that the proportions of West Indians and Asians in the privately rented sector fell dramatically over the decade. This tendency was particularly marked in the furnished sector. Although there was an increase of 7 points in the proportion of Asians renting from a council, the level of Asian owner-occupation increased by no less than 19 points to 84 per cent. By contrast, the level of owner-occupation decreased slightly amongst West Indians, while the incidence of council renting grew by no less than 20 points. It is clear from these figures that the housing market position of two groups became increasingly divergent between 1971 and 1981. While West Indians were more strongly repre-sented in the council sector in 1971 and less strongly concentrated in owner-occupation than were Asians, these differences had become much sharper by 1981. In the early 1970s concerns were voiced that minority groups were being deliberately excluded from council housing. The current prospect is that West Indians are becoming increasingly concen-trated in the socially residualised and economically marginalised council sector (Hamnett and Randloph 1986). This concentration can be argued to reflect the opening up of the council sector to racial minorities, the generally weak labour market position of West Indians compared to both whites and African Asians and, more arguably, a greater willingness to rent rather than own.

A comparison of the 1981 housing tenure of post-1971 arrivals

Table 8.22 *Percentage point changes in tenure by ethnic origin of LSMs in England and Wales, 1971–81*

	UK	West Indian	Asian	Total
Owner-occupation	+ 13.0	− 2.5	+ 18.7	+ 12.7
Council housing	− 2.2	+ 19.7	+ 6.9	− 1.3
Unfurnished rented accommodation	− 9.2	− 3.5	− 4.2	− 9.0
Furnished rented accommodation	− 1.7	− 13.7	− 21.3	− 2.4

Source: OPCS, Longitudinal sample

(Table 8.22) with continuing LSMs (Table 8.21) reveals a number of interesting features. First, as might be expected, the proportion of privately rented tenants among the post-1971 arrivals is much higher in 1981 than the proportion among continuing LSMs, while the level of owner-occupation is some 20 points lower. This could indicate that the more recent arrivals are simply at an earlier stage in a progression from private renting to owner-occupation. But, on the other hand, the level of council renting among the post-1971 Asian arrivals from Africa is double the 1981 level for continuing LSMs, and the proportion of post-1971 West Indians in the council sector is almost identical to that for continuing West Indian LSMs. This suggests that the council sector has become increasingly open to racial minorities and also that it may now be acting as a short-stay interim tenure for recent immigrants in place of the declining private rented sector. What is known is that blacks are heavily overrepresented in the worst sections of the council stock and under-represented in the most desirable stock (Phillips 1986). Black ownership is also strongly concentrated in the older, poorer and cheaper inner-city areas. Although the rate of black home ownership is higher than the white rate, the type of property is very different, and it would be a major mistake to assume that blacks have achieved a higher housing standard than whites (Karn, Kemeny and Williams 1984). To some extent, many blacks have simply replaced one form of disadvantage by another.

Conclusions

The current phase of industrial restructuring has undoubtedly had major repercussions on the structure of metropolitan employment opportunities. These repercussions have been particularly acute for the black workforce. While there have been considerable changes in the occupational characteristics of London's black workforce from 1971 to 1981, blacks have remained concentrated in occupations associated with the secondary labour market and in declining industries. They have also experienced much greater increases in rates of unemployment than the white workforce as a whole. These two characteristics are, of course, interrelated, and while there was evidence that certain sections of the black workforce had moved into primary positions in the growing service sector, they did so at a lower rate than their white colleagues. The perception of the black workforce as having been increasingly marginalised in comparison to whites, and 'left high and dry' as employment opportunities have dried up in many of the sectors to which they were first attached, is generally a valid one.

But the black workforce is far from homogenous. As we have attempted to show, it is characterised by a considerable degree of segmentation in which ethnic origin, as well as gender, represent crucial structuring elements. These dimensions of segmentation are also compounded by the repercussions of the specific immigration histories of the various ethnic components. These histories played a major role in determining the initial position each group occupied on entering the British labour market. And they have subsequently also exerted a major influence on patterns of ethnic occupational mobility, as well as largely determining the size and timing of the emergence of a second-generation, British-born black workforce. The consequence of the variety of positions blacks occupy in the labour market is that the impact of current employment restructuring has been far from uniform across the black workforce as a whole. In other words, the pattern of changes which the black workforce has experienced has been far more complex than the simple marginalisation thesis would suggest.

For example, there was clear evidence that a process of 'upward occupational mobility' had occurred as some of those of both West Indian and Asian origin had moved into higher-status primary non-manual positions. Asian males appeared to be moving into skilled manual positions, despite the major losses of these jobs. This may be a reflection of a continuing substitution of blacks for whites in manufacturing, a suggestion supported by the lower rates of decline in manufacturing employment amongst both Asians and West Indians. On the other hand, the number of Asians had expanded rapidly in the distributive trades while West Indians were being disproportionately drawn into the expanding service sector and particularly into low status clerical jobs. West Indians were the only group to maintain their absolute employment numbers in the otherwise declining secondary manual sector. And it is amongst West Indians that the impact of unemployment has been most severe. Much of this may be attributable to the fact that second generation West Indians began to enter the labour market in considerable numbers during a period when job opportunities were rapidly disappearing.

It would be wrong, therefore, to assume that the repercussions of labour market restructuring on the black workforce in London have been uniformally felt. On the contrary, the distinctive variety of employment positions occupied by blacks has meant that restructuring has worked its way unevenly through the black workforce, opening doors for some and closing them for others. And these repercussions have not all been negative, although it is quite clear that black workers in general have fared less well then whites. Whatever understanding we may reach concerning the processes which lie behind these tendencies described here must recognise the significance of this variation within the black workforce if the pitfalls of overgeneralisation are to be avoided.

Rather similar conclusions apply to the changing experience of blacks in the London housing market. The pattern of black housing tenure has changed dramatically in the space of ten years as blacks have moved out of the private rented sector into owner-occupation and council renting. The experiences of West Indians and Asians have, however, been very different. While Asians have become increasingly concentrated in owner-occupation, West Indian owner-occupation rates appear to have fallen slightly, and West Indians have become increasingly concentrated in the council sector. While these changes undoubtedly indicate an improvement in black housing conditions, other evidence indicates that many blacks may have simply swapped poor private rented accommodation for inferior owner-occupied and council rented housing. To this extent, the improvement in their housing conditions is likely to have been far less dramatic than the tenure evidence indicates. The growing number of Asian home-owners may have achieved a greater degree of personal control over their housing circumstances, but there is considerable evidence to show that much of the housing is in poor condition, requiring repairs.

Appendix

Derivation of occupational classification

Primary non-manual: Managerial, professional, intermediate non-manual workers and own account farmers (socio-economic groups 1–5, 13).

Secondary non-manual: Junior non-manual workers (socio-economic group 6).

Primary manual: Skilled manual workers and the self-employed (socio-economic groups 8, 9, 12 and 14).

Secondary manual: Service workers, semi-skilled and unskilled manual workers (socio-economic groups 7, 10, 11 and 15).

ROGER WALDINGER

9

Native blacks, new immigrants and the post-industrial transformation of New York

If New York's brush with fiscal insolvency in the mid-1970s signalled the end for America's industrial economy its revival in the 1980s heralded the emergence of the nation's largest centre for world services. For the smokestack cities of the industrial heartland, with their specialised concentrations of industrial capital and labour, there is seemingly no replacement for the run-of-the-mill production activities that are steadily eroding under the twin impacts of technological change and international competition. But in the largest urban agglomerations in the US, Chicago, Los Angeles and, most importantly, New York, manufacturing is rapidly ceding place to a different set of activities centred around information processing and the transaction of business deals.

In the course of this transition from goods to services, the demographic base of America's largest urban places has simultaneously been transformed. The era of the post-industrial transformation has brought the city two distinctive, largely non-white inflows: first, a movement of displaced blacks from the technological backwaters of the agrarian south; and more recently, a wave of newcomers from the labour surplus areas of the developing world, in numbers that rival the great immigrations at the turn of the twentieth century.

Thus the city of services is also an increasingly non-white city; the central question in urban research is consequently the relationship of the city's new population base to its present economic functions. There are two stories of how the new, minority population groups fit into the new urban economy. One story is essentially that they do not. This is the tale of 'two cities', of the 'new urban reality' of elite and of largely minority poor, in which the city's advanced service base has rendered useless those low-skill residents who had earlier been recruited for the inner-city manufacturing jobs now irrevocably gone.[1] The second story is that, far from being useless, the minority populations are the new drawers of water and

205

hewers of wood. The large urban economy, as this story has it, has not only been transformed, it has been polarised. In this version, it is the rich who need the poor, since the latter prove most suitable for providing low-cost services, maintaining the city's underbelly and propping up what remains of the depressed manufacturing sector.[2]

This chapter offers an alternative to these two prevailing views of the urban post-industrial transformation. The prism is that of New York City, where the economic sea-change is most in evidence and the era of a 'majority minority' city, made up almost evenly of native and foreign non-whites, seems close at hand.[3] The argument is twofold: first, that the succession of new for old populations has mediated the impact of the shift from goods to services; and second, that the driving force of change has been an upward shift in the social structure of the remaining white population, creating vacancies into which non-whites have stepped.

Economic and demographic transformations

New York shifted from goods to services earlier than did the rest of the United States. In 1950, proportionally fewer New Yorkers worked in manufacturing than was true for the nation as a whole and thereafter goods production employment swiftly began to decline. Though the 1950s and 1960s were boom times for the local economy, these two decades were a period of steady decline for New York's manufacturing sector, whose erosion slowed only in the late 1960s, when the nation's superheated economic environment kept New York's old and obsolescent plant in demand. However, the fall-off in goods production was more than compensated by two other developments. Most important was the continued build-up of New York's white-collar, corporate complex. Changes in technology brought new jobs in communications (television) and transport (air); a robust economy led to growth in advertising; the merger mania of the 1960s and the expansion of government regulation meant additional work for New York's corporate offices; and the burst of economic growth in the 1960s spurred a build-up of jobs on Wall Street. While expansion of the private white-collar sector took up part of the slack created by the decline of manufacturing in this way, public employment burgeoned in the 1960s, thus further offsetting any losses in the factory job sector.

The apogee of New York's growth was reached in 1969; thereafter the decline was brutal and swift. Nixon's attempt to curb inflation sparked off a minor recession in 1969; for New York City, however, the downswing produced major job losses. While the rest of the nation soon pulled out of the doldrums, jobs continued to seep out of New York. The root problems were twofold. The 1970s marked the passage to a new stage of intensified interregional and international competition in which capital became increasingly footloose and a revolution in permissive technology speeded up the relocation of jobs from high- to lower-cost areas. Under the impact of this change, New York's manufacturing complex – with its antiquated and inefficient infrastructure, outdated plant, and high-cost labour – could no longer stand up. However, the 1970s were also bad times for the once vibrant white-collar sector. Wall Street went from bull market to bear market as falling stock-market prices registered the effects of the weakening US economy and the squeeze on large corporate profits. To cut costs, the securities firms sought to reduce their back office operations, filled mainly with low-level clerical functionaries; this marked the first phase of office automation and it speeded the winnowing-out process. Further job losses occurred when large corporations moved their headquarters to the suburbs – an event of increasing frequency in the 1970s. The weakening of the export sectors brought inevitable decline to the local economy industries: the city's very large wholesaling/retailing complex was particularly hard hit.[4]

Then in 1977 the erosion stopped, and since that time, the city's economy has marched steadily forward. The precise causes of the turnaround are still a matter of debate, but what appears to have happened is that New York's role as a purveyor of advanced services generated a new set of agglomeration economies that first halted and then reversed the city's economic decline. New York is now principally host to activities centred on the processing of information and the transaction of high-level business deals, all of which are increasingly international in scope. The city's pull on these activities is in part due to its size, which both permits extensive specialisation in legal, financial, consulting and other services, and attracts the massive corps of highly trained talent on which an international post-industrial business depends. For a variety of reasons – having to do with the volatility of financial markets, the importance of discretion, the absence of routinisation – many of these actors rely on face-to-face communication and hence are bound together. Gradually, the strength of the export-oriented advance services has spilled over into the local economy industries, which now show renewed vigour. Manufacturing remains the weak reed, however, though even in this sector the pace of decline has slowed a bit.[5]

The job shifts wrought by these changes in New York's economic function can be steadily grasped from Table 9.1. Manufacturing, the single largest employer in 1950 and the employer of one of every three working New Yorkers, had slipped behind finance to fifth place as of 1985. In its place, the service sector now provided the single largest block

Table 9.1 *Employment by sector, New York City, 1950–85* (in thousands)

	1950	1969	1977	1985
Total	3,468.2	3,797.7	3,187.9	3,466.0
Construction	123	105.7	64.2	94.9
Manufacturing	1,038.9	825.8	538.6	425.6
TCU	331.5	323.0	258.2	235.2
Wholesale/Retail	754.8	749.1	620.1	626.9
Wholesale	n/a	309.2	248.0	245.8
Retail	n/a	439.9	372.1	381.1
FIRE	336.2	464.2	414.4	504.8
Services	507.7	779.8	783.2	1,031.4
Government	374.4	547.0	507.8	544.0

Note: TCU = Transportation, Communications, Utilities
FIRE = Finance, Real Estate and Insurance
Source: United States, Bureau of Labor Statistics, *Employment, Hours, and Earnings, States and Areas, 1939–1982*, V II, Bulletin 1312–17; United States, Bureau of Labor Statistics, *Supplement to Employment, Hours, and Earnings, States and Areas, Data for 1980–1984*, Bulletin 1370–19; New York City, Office of Economic Development, *Quarterly Report*, November 1985

of jobs; in comparison to 1950, when only 15 per cent of working New Yorkers made their living in the services, they employed 33 per cent as of 1985.

Thus, New York City's economy has gone from boom to bust to better times. It would be churlish to quarrel with the city's recent success in generating new jobs. Yet, the worry is that New York has undergone demographic changes over the past three decades that have been just as transforming as the economic shifts, and it is not at all clear how the city's new population groups fit into its new economic base.

The demographic transformation of New York can be divided into two phases. Phase I, which began with the end of World War II and lasted up to the end of the 1960s, involved the exodus of the city's white population and the massive immigration of displaced black sharecroppers from the South and of Puerto Ricans uprooted by the island's modernisation. In Phase II, the white exodus continued. What changed was that the black and Puerto Rican inflows halted, to be replaced by a vast influx of newcomers from abroad. The starting point for this latter change was the liberalisation of US immigration laws in 1965: as Table 9.2 shows, New York has since been a mecca for the nation's immigrants, much as it had been in the early twentieth century. Between 1966 and 1979, the city absorbed over one million legal immigrants; the 1980 census recorded 1,670,000 foreign-born New Yorkers, of whom 928,000 had come to New

Table 9.2 *Immigration to the United States and New York City, 1966–79* (in thousands)

Years	United States	New York City	New York City as percentage of US
1966–79	5834.0	1053.6	18.1
1966	323.0	61.2	18.9
1967	362.0	66.0	18.2
1968	454.4	75.4	16.6
1969	358.6	67.9	18.9
1970	373.3	74.6	20.0
1971	370.5	71.4	19.3
1972	384.7	76.0	19.8
1973	400.2	76.6	19.1
1974	394.9	73.2	18.5
1975	386.2	73.6	19.1
1976	500.5	90.7	18.1
1977	462.3	76.6	16.6
1978	601.4	88.0	14.6
1979	460.3	82.4	17.9

Source: US Department of Justice, Immigration and Naturalization Service, *Statistical Yearbook of the Immigration and Naturalization Service*, annual editions

York City after 1965. The new immigration, as can be seen from the data presented in Table 9.3, has mainly brought the Third World to the First World. Despite the city's large population of European immigrants, Latin Americans, Caribbeans and Asians have accounted for the lion's share of the new arrivals.

How well suited are these new New Yorkers to the city's evolving economy? The post-war migrants arrived with low levels of schooling and, in the case of Puerto Ricans, were further handicapped by lack of English-language facility. Yet, because they arrived at an opportune time, they found a place in New York's then thriving economy. But many of those initial entry-level jobs have since been lost. While the skill and educational levels of black and Puerto Rican New Yorkers have also been upgraded in the interim, it is not clear that they have caught up as quickly as employers have lifted their job requirements. The same questions apply to the immigrants. Though some component of the new immigration consists of a 'brain drain', the majority of newcomers arrive with skills of low to middling levels. The proportion of all immigrants to the US reporting prior professional or related experience has fallen steadily since 1971; the data available indicate that the share of professionals among the newcomers to New York is lower still.[6]

Table 9.3 *Immigrants arrived in the United States
between 1965 and 1980 and living in New York
City in 1980*

Dominican Republic	98,420
Jamaica	76,280
China	62,420
Haiti	43,780
Italy	42,000
Trinidad/Tobago	34,300
Colombia	33,200
Ecuador	32,960
USSR	32,640
Guyana	29,420
Greece	26,000
Cuba	23,520
India	20,680
Philippines	18,920
Korea	17,620
Barbados	14,520
Yugoslavia	14,260
Panama	12,120
Poland	10,760
England	10,520
Israel	10,260

Source: 1980 Census of Population (Public Use Microdata
Sample)

Thus, the characteristics of New York's new demographic base seem
compatible with either of the two stories of the urban post-industrial
transformation reviewed in the introduction above. On the one hand, the
low skill and educational levels of the minority populations should make
them poorly matched with the rising job requirements of post-industrial
employers. On the other hand, the very substantial and constant flow of
recent immigrants suggests that the problem is not so much a paucity of
entry-level jobs, as it is the absence of opportunities to move from bottom
to top.

Ethnic succession and employment change: another look

There is, however, another possible interpretation of the fit between New
York's economic functions and its demographic base; this interpretation
begins with Table 9.4. This table presents data from the public use
microdata samples of the 1970 and 1980 censuses of population (the
former is a 1 per-cent sample; the latter a 5 per-cent sample). Though the
decennial censuses are somewhat dated for my purpose, they are unique,

Table 9.4 *Changes in employment for ethnic groups, New York City, 1970–80[a]*

	(1)	(2)	(3)	(4)	(5)	(6)
	Employment			Job change		
	1970	1980	Expected	Actual	Actual–expected	Actual–expected/ 1970 employment %
White native	1,785,200	1,382,980	−155,939	−402,220	−246,281	−13.8
White foreign-born	417,400	315,520	−36,460	−101,880	−65,420	−15.7
Black native	462,700	440,180	−40,417	−22,520	+17,897	+3.9
Black foreign-born	55,500	170,320	−4,848	+114,820	+119,668	+215.6
Asian native	8,000	10,460	−699	+2,460	+3,159	+39.5
Asian foreign-born	31,200	108,740	−2,725	+77,540	+80,265	+257.3
Hispanic native	242,000	232,640	−21,139	−9,360	+11,779	+4.9
Hispanic foreign-born	132,700	205,520	−11,591	+72,820	+84,411	+63.6

Note: [a] Data in this and all following tables for employed New York City residents, aged sixteen and over
Source: 1970 and 1980 Censuses of Population (Public Use Microdata Sample)

and hence indispensable, for the detailed data on ethnic and occupational characteristics that they provide.

Table 9.4 organises the population according to eight synthetic ethnic groups, classified by ethnicity and nativity: white native, white foreign-born, black native, black foreign-born and so on. It shows the number of jobs held by each of these different ethnic groups in New York City in 1970 and 1980. The table also tells us (in column 4) how many jobs each group would have been expected to lose had its losses been proportional to the decline suffered by the overall economy during this period, when employment fell by 8.56 per cent, from 3,191,370 jobs in 1970 to 2,918,183 in 1980. The table then shows how many jobs the group actually lost and what the difference was between expected and actual employment loss.[7]

Here is where we begin to glimpse a different set of dynamics affecting the process of job change in post-industrial New York. The reason is that the biggest job losers over the course of the 1970s, both quantitatively and proportionally, were ... whites! In fact, the job loss for native and foreign-born whites together was almost twice as great as the total job loss for all New Yorkers.

Why so many whites lost jobs during this period is difficult to say – some undoubtedly began to work in the suburbs after moving there (and we know that there was substantial white out-migration to the suburbs during this time); some joined the vast tide of migrants headed to the sunbelt; some simply left the labour force (looking at the job loss for white immigrants, it is worth remembering that the large cohort of European immigrants who arrived between 1900 and 1915 reached retirement age during this period). But the reasons for white job loss are not nearly half as interesting as their possible effects. What should happen after such a large outflow is that it sets in motion a chain of vacancies up and down the job hierarchy. Moreover, ethnic shifts of this magnitude should have greatly altered gatekeeping mechanisms. Keeping blacks or other minorities out of jobs is one thing when there are plenty of whites among whom to choose, but the costs of discrimination rise when there are fewer whites competing for the jobs available. Similarly, there is a high level of arbitrariness in entry-level requirements. It is well documented that most blue-collar employers do most of their skill training on the job floor and that their hiring criteria are mainly designed to screen out 'bad prospects', not unskilled workers. By contrast, office employers often prefer 'pink-collar' workers to obtain their clerical skills prior to employment. But there is ample evidence of considerable variation among otherwise similar office employers with respect to skill requirements and provision of on-the-job training; this suggests that hiring procedures can be altered if changes on the supply side require that new labour force groups be recruited.[8]

Just how recruitment practices changed in response to shifts in the labour supply is a question that, unfortunately, I cannot directly answer. To my knowledge, no one has done the type of fieldwork that would allow us to look inside the white-collar recruitment and training process. But the data available do allow us to trace the changes in employment position over the 1970–80 period for different groups and to account for the various components of their job change.

I have attempted to do this for four ethnic groups: native born whites, native blacks, foreign Hispanics and foreign Asians. The choice of the four was made partially for reasons of expediency, that is, to avoid a blizzard of tables and numbers, but more importantly, because each group's fate has an importance in itself. In both 1970 and 1980 native whites were the dominant and most numerous group in the labour market; hence, any change, not only in their number but in their position, would be of consequence to all others. The progress of native blacks is a question of obvious concern; it is this group, above all, that has been the main focus of affirmative action and equal opportunity programmes over the past two decades. Foreign-born Hispanics are of interest because they have apparently moved into the lower rungs of the city's economy and they exemplify, if any group does, the situation of newcomers that are confined to the bottom stratum of the labour force. Finally Asians have played a distinctive and more specialised economic role than the other groups and seem akin to the earlier European immigrants in their predisposition for small business and entrepreneurship.

Table 9.5 presents the data on job change for native whites. Column 3 shows that native white employment declined by almost one-fourth: that native whites lost employment in every industry but two, professional services and miscellaneous (the latter consisting mainly of entertainment); and that sizeable losses were sustained in the FIRE and business service industries, two key components of the advanced services complex. The following four columns provide an accounting of the components of the job changes of native whites over the 1970–80 period. Some job change should have taken place simply because certain industries grew while others declined; additional job loss can be expected to have ensued because whites withdrew from the local economy in such large numbers; and any white loss or gain in particular industries, discounting industry change or change in group size, would add still another component to overall job change. What the table tells us is that the principal contribution to job change was the decline in the size of the native white labour force (column 4). Whites also lost substantial numbers of jobs due to industry change, but less than would have been expected and less than would have been proportionate to the decline in the total economy

Table 9.5 Components of job change: native whites in New York City, 1970–80

	Employment			Change due to			
	(1) 1970	(2) 1980	(3) Change	(4) Group size	(5) Industry change	(6) (5) Adjusted for (4)	(7) Share
Total	1,785,200	1,382,980	-402,220	-246,281	-135,140	-381,421	-20,799
Construction	57,400	34,620	-22,780	-7,918	-17,095	-25,014	2,233
Manufacturing	304,800	189,620	-115,180	-42,049	-58,976	-101,026	-14,154
Transport	156,400	104,800	-51,600	-21,576	-39,523	-61,100	9,499
Wholesale	99,100	74,200	-24,900	-13,672	-13,514	-27,185	2,285
Retail	245,900	173,480	-72,420	-33,924	-37,527	-71,450	-969
FIRE	209,900	181,200	-28,700	-28,957	997	-27,960	-739
Business services	108,200	98,660	-9,540	-14,927	8,585	-6,345	-3,198
Personal services	43,400	24,440	-18,960	-5,987	-13,100	-19,087	127
Professional services	222,700	236,680	13,980	-30,723	38,450	7,727	6,253
Miscellaneous	33,300	36,120	2,820	-4,594	2,606	-1,987	4,808
Public Sector	304,100	229,160	-74,940	-41,953	-6,043	-47,996	-26,944

Note 1970/80 Index of Dissimilarity: 7.8
Source: See Table 9.4

(column 5). Additional jobs were lost because native whites suffered a net loss in their share of particular industries: adding up column 6 (which measures the effect of industry change adjusted for change in group size) and column 7 produces the net loss of 402,220 jobs.

There is more to be learned from taking a closer look at column 7, which shows the change in native whites' share of particular industries. The greatest losses took place in the public sector and in manufacturing, and these two instances of loss in share highlight the consequences of natives whites' upward shift in social structure. In the first case, total employment in New York's public sector declined during the 1970s under the impact of the city's fiscal crisis. However, jobs were mainly shed through attrition, not lay-offs – which means that the bulk of withdrawals from the public sector were made by senior civil servants who were most likely to have been white. Thus, while municipal employment fell from 285,856 in 1975 to 236,586 in 1979, the white share of employment dropped from 67.5 per cent to 63.2 per cent. Moreover, a second consequence of the fiscal crisis was that the real earnings of municipal employees plummeted, reducing the pool of white labour who had access to better paying jobs. Since municipal hiring resumed in the late 1970s, the trend has been toward a steady increase in percentage non-white hired, with non-whites now comprising a majority of new hires. Similar conditions apply in the case of manufacturing. The severe erosion of New York's production base led to a sharp decline in real wages and a deterioration in working conditions and employment stability – provoking a further reduction in the availability of white labour. Whatever the sources of shift in share, the 1970/1980 index of dissimilarity – which measures the net 1970–80 change in native whites' distribution among the various industries – shows that this group ended the decade in a position very different from where it began.[9]

Table 9.6 presents the data on job change for native blacks. Overall, native black employment declined over the decade; the sharpest fall-offs were registered in personal services, retail, TCU and manufacturing; however, employment also increased in the public sector and in the three advanced services sectors – professional services, business services and FIRE. The main source of job loss was industry change: those industries in which blacks were concentrated in 1970 were also the industries that suffered the greatest erosion over the following ten years. Column 7 is also of interest. It shows that blacks suffered a net loss in share, but that considerable reshuffling in their employment among industries also transpired – most notably, a large increase in public sector jobs.

Table 9.7 shows the pattern for Hispanic foreign-born. This group experienced increases in every industry – including the advanced services.

Table 9.6 *Components of job change: native blacks in New York City, 1970–80*

	Employment			Change due to			
	(1) 1970	(2) 1980	(3) Change	(4) Group size	(5) Industry change	(6) (5) Adjusted for (4)	(7) Share
Total	462,700	440,180	−22,520	17,987	−37,443	−19,545	−2,975
Construction	12,900	8,100	−4,800	499	−3,842	−3,343	−1,457
Manufacturing	59,900	51,920	−7,980	2,316	−11,590	−9,273	1,293
Transport	45,800	32,580	−13,220	1,772	−11,574	−9,802	−3,417
Wholesale	13,500	13,120	−380	522	−1,840	−1,319	939
Retail	51,600	41,660	−9,940	1,996	−7,874	−5,879	−4,061
FIRE	34,100	36,580	2,480	1,319	162	1,480	999
Business services	22,900	25,840	2,940	886	1,817	2,703	237
Personal services	41,100	20,560	−20,540	1,590	−12,406	−10,816	−9,724
Professional services	46,700	56,440	9,740	1,806	−8,063	9,869	−129
Miscellaneous	6,400	4,300	−2,100	248	501	748	−2,848
Public sector	127,800	149,080	21,280	4,943	−2,540	2,403	18,876

Note: 1970/80 Index of Dissimilarity: 10.9
Source: See Table 9.4

Table 9.7 Components of job change: foreign Hispanics in New York City, 1970–80

	Employment			Change due to			
	(1) 1970	(2) 1980	(3) Change	(4) Group size	(5) Industry change	(6) (5) Adjusted for (4)	(7) Share
Total	132,700	205,520	72,820	84,412	−17,909	66,503	6,317
Construction	3,900	4,040	140	2,481	−341	2,140	−2,000
Manufacturing	44,200	70,720	26,520	28,116	−13,164	14,952	11,568
Transport	7,200	10,860	3,660	4,580	−1,393	3,187	473
Wholesale	5,700	8,480	2,780	3,626	−777	2,849	−69
Retail	19,500	29,880	10,380	12,404	−2,976	9,428	952
FIRE	12,300	18,680	6,380	7,824	58	7,883	−1,502
Business services	7,200	13,000	5,800	4,580	5,718	5,151	649
Personal services	8,500	13,340	4,840	5,407	−2,566	2,841	1,999
Professional services	16,000	17,860	1,860	10,178	2,763	12,940	−11,080
Miscellaneous	800	2,560	1,760	509	63	571	1,189
Public sector	7,400	16,100	8,700	4,707	−147	4,560	4,140

Note: 1970/80 Index of Dissimilarity: 5.0
Source: See Table 9.4

The greatest gains, however, came in two industries where native black employment suffered considerable erosion over the same period: manufacturing and retail. Like native blacks, foreign Hispanics began this period in industries that were to perform poorly over the next ten years: hence the net job losses attributable to industry change. But in contrast to blacks, Hispanics replaced whites in the industries from which the latter withdrew: virtually all of the gain in foreign Hispanic employment was due to a change in the group's size. Column 7 is once again a source of considerable interest. Foreign Hispanics gained in their net share of individual industries – but to a very limited extent; only in manufacturing, an industry in which they were already concentrated, did foreign Hispanics make a sizeable increase in share. The end result was that foreign Hispanics ended the decade in much the same industries they began in – as the very low 1970/80 index of dissimilarity shows.

Table 9.8, which contains the data for the foreign-born Asians presents still another picture. As with the Hispanics, Asians gained jobs in every industry; similarly, change in group size was the motor engine of their increase in employment. Though little change transpired in foreign Asians' net share, a look at column 7 points to significant shifts in Asians' share of individual industries. On the one hand, those industries that contain a preponderance of low-level jobs show either a loss in share (retail and personal services) or a very slight gain (manufacturing). On the other hand, substantial gains in share were made in two advanced service sectors – FIRE and professional services. Thus, while change in group size accounted for the bulk of net job changes, Asians also repositioned themselves to a greater extent than any other group – as indicated by the high 1970/80 index of dissimilarity.

Occupational repositioning

Of course, it is one thing to gain access to the growth sectors of the economy; quite another to get employed in those same industries in higher-level jobs. The shift in economic function from goods to services altered the occupational profile of New York's economy, further swelling the white-collar component. The net white-collar gain, from 59 per cent employed in white-collar jobs in 1970 to 62.5 per cent in 1980, was relatively slight because quite sizeable gains in professional and managerial employment were offset by still heavier losses in clerical and sales jobs. Still, the overall increase in white-collar jobs means that some minority and immigrant gain in white-collar employment could be expected simply on the basis of their shift into service industries. Yet the industry shifts analysed above might also be compatible with the 'hewer of wood' story –

Table 9.8 Components of job change: foreign Asians in New York City, 1970–80

	Employment			Change due to			
	(1) 1970	(2) 1980	(3) Change	(4) Group size	(5) Industry change	(6) (5) Adjusted for (4)	(7) Share
Total	31,200	108,740	77,540	80,265	−3,260	77,005	435
Construction	100	1,160	1,060	257	−30	227	833
Manufacturing	7,200	25,920	18,720	18,522	−1,393	17,130	1,590
Transport	800	4,520	3,720	2,058	−202	1,856	1,864
Wholesale	1,400	6,160	4,760	3,602	−191	3,411	1,349
Retail	10,100	27,060	16,960	25,983	−1,541	24,442	−7,482
FIRE	1,200	9,000	7,800	3,087	6	3,093	4,707
Business services	1,400	3,920	2,520	3,602	111	3,713	−1,193
Personal services	2,100	4,340	2,240	5,402	−634	4,769	−2,529
Professional services	3,700	16,680	12,980	9,519	639	10,158	2,823
Miscellaneous	400	580	180	1,029	31	1,060	−880
Public sector	2,800	9,300	6,500	7,203	−56	7,148	−648

Note: 1970/80 Index of Dissimilarity: 12.2
Source: See Table 9.4

namely, that the gains registered by native blacks, foreign Hispanics, and foreign Asians in the advanced service sectors reflected nothing more than their hiring as cleaners, janitors and so on.

Table 9.9 shows the changes in white-collar employment for the total labour force and for the four ethnic groups at issue in this chapter. As column 3 shows, the number of white-collar jobs declined by almost 68,000, but far steeper declines were experienced by native whites. The white-collar job loss for this group was three times the decline for the total economy; it lost jobs in three of the four white-collar categories; only in the managerial category was there a net white gain, and in this instance, native whites obtained just over a third of the new managerial jobs created over the course of the decade. By contrast, native blacks, foreign Asians, and foreign Hispanics made very substantial inroads in every white-collar category, with the exception of sales jobs for native blacks.

To what extent changes in occupational position can be linked to shifts in group size can be grasped by examining columns 4 through 6. Column 4 tells us how many jobs a group would have lost or gained had its employment in an occupation changed proportionate to its total employment; column 5 shows the difference between actual and expected employment; and column 6 shows this difference as a percentage of 1970 employment. One conclusion is that in addition to the replacement demand arising from the disproportionate white decline, native whites created further vacancies by repositioning themselves within the white-collar hierarchy. A second conclusion, however, is that the non-white population became further differentiated in the process of moving into the white-collar jobs left vacant by whites. Foreign Asians were the greatest beneficiaries of succession, both in numbers and in proportion. Though gains in professional employment were less than expected on the basis of total employment growth, the disproportionately large gains in managerial and, especially, sales employment suggest that job growth for Asians was linked to the strength of the Asian-immigrant sub-economy. Although blacks' gains were not as great as Asians', the blacks' increase in the white-collar sector was substantially greater than expected, with the result that by 1980 more than half of all native blacks were employed in white-collar jobs. As noted above, only in sales was there any black loss in employment, suggesting continued aversion of whites to face-to-face contact with blacks in selling jobs and/or competition with immigrants, whose gains in retailing have already been observed. While native blacks and foreign Hispanics further penetrated the white-collar sector, foreign Hispanics lost ground. Net white-collar job gains for this group were slight: because total foreign Hispanic employment increased substantially

Table 9.9 Occupational shifts in New York City 1970–80

	Employment		Change	Expected change	Actual–expected	Actual–expected/ 1970 employment
	1970	1980				
Total employment						
Professional and technical	500,600	533,560	32,960	−43,728	76,688	15.3
Managers	250,100	314,960	64,860	−21,846	86,706	34.6
Sales	226,200	177,920	−48,280	−19,759	−28,521	12.6
Clerical	883,400	765,960	−117,500	−77,166	−40,334	−4.6
White Collar	1,860,300	1,792,340	−67,960	−162,499	94,539	5.1
White native						
Professional and technical	355,000	335,380	−19,620	−79,984	60,364	17.0
Managers	172,100	196,740	24,640	−38,776	63,416	36.8
Sales	159,400	112,880	−46,520	−35,914	−10,606	−6.7
Clerical	562,300	399,020	−163,280	−126,691	−36,598	−6.5
White Collar	1,248,800	1,044,020	−204,780	281,364	76,585	6.1
Black native						
Professional and technical	43,100	56,460	13,360	−2,098	15,458	35.9
Managers	14,100	25,960	11,860	−689	12,546	89.0
Sales	14,900	13,840	−1,060	725	−335	−2.2
Clerical	134,300	146,060	11,760	−6,537	18,297	13.6
White Collar	206,400	242,320	35,920	−10,046	45,966	22.3

Table 9.9 (cont.)

	Employment			Expected change	Actual–expected	Actual–expected/ 1970 employment
	1970	1980	Change			
Hispanic foreign-born						
Professional and technical	11,900	15,780	3,800	6,530	−2,730	−22.9
Managers	5,900	13,980	8,080	3,238	4,842	−82.1
Sales	5,100	7,680	2,580	2,799	−219	−4.3
Clerical	29,800	36,160	6,360	16,353	−9,993	−33.5
White Collar	52,700	72,520	19,820	29,819	−9,099	−1.7
Asian foreign-born						
Professional and technical	7,600	25,400	17,800	18,888	−1,088	−14.3
Managers	3,000	12,400	9,400	7,456	1,944	64.8
Sales	,400	5,180	4,780	994	3,786	946.4
Clerical	4,300	18,340	14,040	10,687	3,353	77.9
White Collar	15,300	61,320	46,020	38,024	7,996	52.3

Source: See Table 9.4

during this period (see Table 9.4), the proportion of this group working in white-collar jobs actually declined between 1970 and 1980.

Conclusion

What place is there for minorities in the post-industrial economies of the nation's cities? In New York, as this chapter has shown, the shift from goods to services has gone hand in glove with a decline in the availability of white workers, creating a replacement demand for non-white workers. Overall, the fall-off in white employment greatly exceeded the shrinkage in the local economy: the simple outflow of whites from the New York economy left vacancies into which non-white workers could step. While the size of the white labour force diminished, it also repositioned itself over the course of the 1970s: shifts in the distribution of whites, out of clerical and sales jobs, and out of public sector jobs, in particular, created further opportunities for non-white succession.

Yet there is more at work than a simple process of succession. Non-whites have been incorporated in New York's post-industrial economy in a way that has yielded a new ethnic division of labour. As evidence, consider the public sector: in 1980, the employer of one-third of all native blacks, it employed only 8.5 per cent of foreign Asians and 7.8 per cent of foreign Hispanics. Or look at a stronghold of immigrant employment – manufacturing – with a third of foreign Hispanics and almost a quarter of foreign Asians, but less than an eighth of native blacks. Focussing on sector emphasises differences in economic role, but the new ethnic division of labour can also be characterised in terms of position. Roughly speaking, whites continue to monopolise the best rewarded positions: they dominate the growth industries and are increasingly concentrated at the top of the white-collar hierarchy. Native blacks and foreign Asians are taking up the middle grounds left by white outflows and repositioning, though for blacks this is mainly in the public sector, while for Asians it is mainly in the private economy. Foreign Hispanics continue to be relegated to low-level positions in the declining segments of the economy: despite large increases in group size, these newcomers have mainly piled up in the traditional menial immigrant concentrations.

The emergence of a new ethnic division of labour also implies competition for jobs; and though these conclusions are provisional, the big losers in this process appear to be native blacks. Compare, for example, Tables 9.5–7. Whereas immigrants gained jobs in every industry, blacks lost jobs in every instance, save advanced services and public employment. Or consider column 7 in Table 9.5. Substantial gains in share occurred only in the public sector – an industry of diminishing attractiveness for whites, but where blacks' political claims gave them significant advantages over the immigrants. By contrast, blacks lost share in construction, where both whites and immigrants gained share, the former in the large-scale, unionised commercial sector, the latter in the small-scale, non-union additions and alterations sector.

Why native blacks might be losing ground to immigrants is a complex process. The details of this question cannot be pursued here, but several possibilities are apparent. Job loss to immigrants might occur if employers were directly substituting immigrants for blacks – a development of some likelihood, but yet with little confirmation in the empirical literature. A more important source of job loss is a type of indirect competition that occurs when immigrant firms that recruit through the immigrant community expand at the expense of native (largely white-owned) firms that heretofore employed blacks. Developments of this type might explain the black losses in manufacturing, retail and construction as well as the fact that blacks lost jobs in sales, an occupation in which both Asian and Hispanic immigrants made very substantial gains. Still another factor working against blacks in competition with immigrants is a shift in the supply curve of black labour. On the one hand, expectations of reward among native blacks probably increased as the group moved into middle-level positions in the economy. On the other hand, real earnings in industries like manufacturing, retail and personal services declined while the simultaneous influx of immigrants lowered the status associated with these jobs.

These conclusions are tentative; hence this chapter can end on the familiar call for further research. But our findings do suggest that research on the post-industrial transformation be redirected. Rather than another study emphasising the mismatch between urban employers and the urban, non-white population, what is needed is a closer look at the interaction between population dynamics and labour demand and more attention to the complex processes by which America's increasingly variegated minority populations adapt to the post-industrial economies in which they live.

Notes

Research for this article is funded, in part, by a grant from the CUNY Research Foundation.

1 See Sternlieb and Hughes 1983, and Kasarda 1983a and 1985.
2 See Harrison 1982 and Sassen-Koob 1984.
3 Calculations from Bureau of Labor Statistics data (1983) show that New York now ranks first among major American cities in its share of private-sector employment in services and next-to-last, after government-dominated Wash-

ington, DC in the share provided by goods production (see *Geographic Profile of Employment and Unemployment*), Table 27. 'Selected metropolitan areas and cities: employed civilians in nonagricultural industries by sex, race. Hispanic origin, and industry, 1983 annual averages'). The 1980 census of population found that 48 percent of New Yorkers were non-white.

4 For further discussion of New York City's economy, with reference to the problems of the industrial regions of the north-eastern USA, see the essays in Sternlieb and Hughes 1976.

5 Important accounts of New York's economic revival, within the context of the changing economic functions of American cities, are Cohen 1981, and Noyelle and Stanback 1984.

6 Details on these demographic changes can be found in Tobier 1984 and 1982.

7 Data from the censuses report employment for New York City residents only; this raises the possibility that the disproportionate decline in white employment represents a shift in residence from city to suburb and not a drop in white share. Commuting is not especially prevalent in the New York City area, especially in comparison to other major US cities, and the proportion of New York City residents who commute out to the suburbs is very low. However, commuters gained almost 50,000 jobs between 1970 and 1980, with the result that the commuter share of employment rose from 18 to 21 per cent. Since the great bulk of this increase was due to the rise in the number of non-white commuters, the job patterns of New York City residents should resemble the job patterns of all workers with jobs located in New York City.

8 See Doeringer and Piore 1971 and Osterman 1983.

9 Data on public employment from McCormick 1984 and Horton 1986.

10

The new immigration and urban ethnicity in the United States

The third New International Division of Labour is associated with a new geography of immigration and urbanisation. The purpose of this chapter is to outline this geography as a preliminary exercise in understanding the relationships between ethnicity and economic restructuring in the United States. Secular changes within US society and the economy, variously termed post-industrial, late imperial, deindustrialised and global or late capitalist, are having an uneven spatial impact. These variations establish the context of the new immigration in terms of varied local industrial mixes, which in turn are sustained or made possible by immigrant labour. Although contemporary immigration is possibly not as great in absolute or relative degrees as that of earlier periods, to particular locations it is of considerable importance. Such places are also often pivotal to the development of the national economy and its articulation with the world economic system. Where these places are and who lives in them are exploratory questions for the study of ethnic minorities and industrial change.

The chapter begins with the current or fourth wave of immigration in historical context. Data on the origins and destinations of the new immigrants are presented for regions, states and metropolitan areas. In the second half of the chapter some observations on the urbanisation and intra-metropolitan location of immigrant ethnic groups are made. The focus is on how developments in the urban economy are affecting the residential bases of ethnic communities. One line of future research will be the emergent connections between production, location and work on the one hand and labour, ethnicity and territory on the other. For a consideration of the wider context of immigration other sources should be referred to (for example, Crewdson 1983, Kritz 1983, Massey 1981 and Reimers 1985).

Table 10.1 *Continental origins of immigrants to the US, 1831–1984*

Period	Total	Europe	Asia	Americas	Others
1831–80	10,038	8,883	230	741	12
		88.5	2.3	7.4	0.1
1881–1920	23,465	20,669	716	1,971	60
		88.1	3.0	8.4	0.3
1921–40	4,636	2,811	128	1,677	20
		60.6	2.8	36.2	0.4
1941–70	6,872	3,070	613	3,068	104
		44.7	8.9	44.6	1.5
1971–84	6,788	1,065	2,691	2,835	173
		15.7	39.6	41.8	2.5

Notes: Years are fiscal years.
The category 'Others' includes Africa, Australia, New Zealand and the Pacific Islands.
Figures are given in thousands, with percentages displayed below.
Source: US Department of Justice 1986b

The fourth wave

It is common to place immigration to the United States in an historical perspective by classifying it into periods. The current influx is either the third wave of immigration or the fourth wave of all major migrations (Muller 1985, Piore 1979, Portes and Bach 1985). During the first New International Division of Labour between the 1840s and 1870s, the United States was a largely agricultural country, gradually industrialising. Immigration was chiefly a colonising movement undertaken by households, and the cycles of the domestic economy tended to respond to fluctuations in labour supply. In the period 1831 to 1880 over 10 million persons migrated to America, almost 90 per cent of them from Europe (Table 10.1). Germany and the United Kingdom were the main sending countries. In comparison with the European–Eastern United States immigration system, the Asian–West Coast system was small and largely agricultural.

The second wave emerged after the economic downturn of the 1870s corresponding to the self-sustaining industrialisation of the country. High immigration responded to low unemployment (Portes and Bach 1985). Between 1881 and 1920 over 20 million immigrants arrived, again almost entirely from Europe. This inflow was dominated by southern and eastern European nationals displaced by collapsing rural employment. By 1920 almost half of all immigrants came from Italy, Hungary and the USSR. In this period there was also a significant counterstream of returnees, almost two-fifths of all entrants in 1911 (Portes and Bach 1985). Even though World War I and immigration legislation culminating in the National Origins Act 1924 curtailed numbers, in the inter-war period British and German immigrants continued to be significant (Table 10.1). The reduction in international immigration was compensated for by a third period, from the 1920s to 1950s. This rural–urban movement included the northwards exodus of southern blacks. In the south-east there were some Caribbean migrant workers, and in the south-west Mexican migration became important in the agricultural economy. This migration was institutionalised by the bracero guest-worker programme negotiated between Mexico and the USA to fill wartime labour shortages.

The current or fourth wave is commonly dated from 1965 when the Immigration and Naturalization Act altered the grounds for admission. The national quota system devised in 1924 was intended to exclude people on racial grounds, but it had been undermined by black and Mexican movement to the cities (Conk 1985). The new system of ceilings and preferences did not initiate a sudden influx of immigrants. The numbers had been rising since a low point in 1944. However, the composition and eventually the numbers did change as a result of the new legislation.

The United States is by far the most important of only five countries which still admit large numbers of persons for legal and permanent settlement (United Nations 1984). In the 1980s over half a million persons were admitted annually, compared with peaks of 135,000 in Canada in 1974/5 and 69,000 in Australia in 1979. Between 1970 and 1984 there were 6,787,711 recorded immigrants, almost as many as in the thirty years previous to 1970 (Table 10.1). The peak year was 1981, when 596,600 persons were legally admitted, but this ranks only twenty-second for all years since 1820 in absolute numbers. Some individual years between 1902 and 1914 received double this amount when the US population was less than half of the present figure. In 1980 only 6.2 per cent of the population of 226 million was foreign-born (US Bureau of the Census 1983). In 1910, when the population was 93 million, 14.8 per cent were foreign-born. In 1980 there were 14,079,906 foreign-born, in 1930, 14,283,255.

The United States is also part of the Americas' undocumented or illegal immigration system, which includes Argentina, Canada and Venezuela as other important destinations. The exact numbers involved are unknown and politically contentious (Crewdson 1983). Houston (1983) tabulates estimates varying from 1 to 12 million illegal immigrants, with a likely figure between 3.5 and 5 million for 1980. While the total stock may be guessed at, the annual number of entrants is uncertain, and there is a considerable number of return or circulating migrants, especially to

Mexico. In 1984 1,246,977 apprehensions of illegal aliens were made, 94 per cent of them being Mexican nationals (US Department of Justice 1986b). These statistics are not representative of the resident illegal undocumented or illegal population.

If one adds the 1.3 million foreign-born persons enumerated in the 1980 census as arriving in the 1970s but not counted by the immigration authorities, together with a possible undercount of 1 million, the total number arriving in the decade would be 6.6 million (Muller 1985). If so, the period 1970–80 would actually exceed the peak decade of 1901–10 in total immigrant population.

A third component has gained importance in recent years, the refugee population. Between 1965 and 1980 some 1.5 million refugees were admitted, mainly from Cuba and Indochina (Massey 1981). Official numbers have declined in the 1980s since the Cuban Mariel exodus of 125,000. In 1984 only 67,750 persons were recognised as refugees, 34.5 per cent from Vietnam, 26.3 per cent from what was then Kampuchea and 10.9 per cent from Laos (US Department of Justice 1986b). Despite the provisions of the Refugee Act 1980 a *de facto* bias against recognising persons fleeing countries friendly to the US as refugees exists. The effects of the war and unrest in South-East Asia are revealed in official figures, while those of Central America are not. A large and unknown number of 'refugees' entered illegally, from El Salvador, Guatemala, Honduras and Haiti. There may be half a million or more such persons, whose presence is subject to political and juridicial controversy. This was highlighted in the recent trials of church-based sanctuary movement activists.

The numbers of unrecorded refugees and undocumented workers is only one limitation of official data sources (Hernandez 1985, Massey and Schnabel 1983). For example, the Immigration and Naturalization Service counts only 82,094 Salvadorans arriving since 1960, yet unofficial estimates suggest that the Salvadoran population of Los Angeles alone is 200,000–300,000 (Anderson 1983, La Brecque 1983). In the 1980s only information for 1984 is complete, and this is used wherever possible. Bearing this in mind we can proceed to analyse the origins of the new immigration.

Origins of current immigration

The United States is unique in so far as it is part of three continental immigration systems, from Asia, Europe and the Americas. In the 1970s over three-quarters of immigrants came from countries defined by the UN as 'less developed' (United Nations 1984). The geography of origins reflects a number of factors, including the uneven development of the

Table 10.2 *National origins of immigrants to the US, 1971–84*

Country	1971–80		1981–4		1971–84	
Mexico	640,294	(14.2)	274,273	(12.0)	914,567	(13.5)
Philippines	354,987	(7.9)	177,405	(7.7)	532,392	(7.8)
Korea	267,638	(6.0)	130,263	(5.7)	397,901	(5.9)
Vietnam	172,820	(3.8)	191,547	(8.3)	364,367	(5.4)
Cuba	264,863	(5.9)	33,744	(1.5)	298,607	(4.4)
China	124,326	(2.8)	134,371	(5.9)	258,697	(3.8)
India	164,134	(3.7)	92,328	(4.0)	256,462	(3.8)
Dominican Republic	148,135	(3.3)	80,936	(3.5)	229,071	(3.4)
Canada	169,939	(3.8)	49,026	(2.1)	218,965	(2.2)
Jamaica	137,577	(3.1)	80,812	(3.5)	218,389	(3.2)
United Kingdom	137,374	(2.9)	60,882	(2.7)	198,256	(2.9)
Italy	129,368	(2.9)	17,859	(0.8)	147,227	(2.2)
Hong Kong	113,467	(2.5)	27,264	(1.2)	140,731	(2.1)
Colombia	77,348	(1.7)	39,498	(1.7)	116,846	(1.7)
Greece	92,369	(2.1)	14,141	(0.6)	106,510	(1.6)
Laos	22,092	(0.5)	82,264	(3.6)	104,356	(1.5)
Germany	74,414	(1.7)	29,840	(1.3)	104,252	(1.5)
Total	4,493,314		2,294,397		6,787,711	

Notes: Figures in parentheses are percentages.
Country is country of last residence.
Years are fiscal years.
China includes Taiwan; between 1982 and 1984 33.9% of all Chinese immigrants came from Taiwan.
Source: Department of Justice 1986b

world's economy, the incidence of civil unrest and the inability of many countries to provide sufficient opportunities for upward social mobility.

The most significant fact about the origins of the fourth wave is the decline of European immigration and the increase in American and then Asian sources (Table 10.1). American immigrants became most numerous between 1960 and 1980 as the European influx lessened. From 1980 onwards Asia was the leading source of legal immigrants, supplying 47.4 per cent of the 1980 total. With the addition of unrecorded immigrants America is probably the largest continental source overall.

Seventeen countries have supplied 100,000 or more immigrants in the period 1971–84 (Table 10.2). Mexico is the largest single source, with 914,567 persons or 13.5 per cent of the total. It was the dominant national origin between 1951 and 1960, too. Whereas Mexico's pre-eminence is not as marked as those of Italy between 1900 and 1920 or Germany between 1860 and 1880, the diversity of sources is as great. Ten countries provide 3 per cent or more of all legal immigration between 1971 and 1984, compared with nine between 1900 and 1920.

Table 10.3 *Composition of the foreign-born population of the US, 1980*

Place of Birth	Total Numbers	Percentage of total foreign-born population
Europe	4,743,500	33.7
Germany	849,384	6.0
Italy	831,922	5.9
United Kingdom	669,149	4.8
America	5,205,914	37.1
Mexico	2,199,221	15.6
West Indies	1,258,363	8.9
Canada	842,859	6.0
Cuba	607,814	4.3
Asia	2,539,777	18.0
Africa	199,723	1.4
Total	14,079,906	100.0

Source: US Buerau of the Census 1983

The Philippines is the second major source, becoming important in the 1960s, while Korean, Chinese and Vietnamese immigration only assumed significance in the 1970s. Movement from these countries appears to be declining. The United Kingdom is an exception. In the late 1980s some new origins emerged, such as Laos and (not shown in the table) Kampuchea, Guyana and Haiti; each of the last three has supplied more than 30,000 migrants since 1980. One important qualification to be made is that national origin is not the same as ethnic origin. Some Vietnamese nationals are of Chinese origin, while perhaps one in three of recent Chinese immigrants are from Taiwan. If Hong Kong immigrants are added to these, then ethnic Chinese are perhaps the third largest group.

Substantial Asian immigration is too recent to alter significantly the balance of the composition of America's foreign-born population (Table 10.3). In 1980 a third of the foreign-born were still European, led by Germany, Italy and the United Kingdom. A slightly larger proportion were American in origin, with Mexicans almost one in six. Since only 6.2 per cent of the US population is foreign-born, no single nation provides more than 1 per cent of the country's population. All groups are smaller than the black population. The significance of immigrants is less national and more metropolitan or local.

The evidence of socio-economic and demographic characteristics suggests that the new influx is more similar to native Americans than previous waves (Keely and Elwell 1981, Kritz 1983, Massey and Schnabel 1983, Wong 1985). There is support for the observation that the fourth wave is bimodal in status. Asians (particularly Indians and Koreans) are generally of higher status and Americans of lower. The class differences within current immigration result in different roles in local metropolitan economies.

The geography of immigrant destinations

The contemporary phase of economic restructuring involves shifts in the geography of economic location. What places attract immigrant labour and what part does it play in local economies? The pattern of regional, state and metropolitan destinations is an overview or framework for deeper considerations of the connections between immigration, ethnicity and industrial change.

The regional differentiation of the country has been frequently described as a distinction between sunbelt and snowbelt. Although this terminology has been questioned and the scale is perhaps inappropriate, it is useful to make some division (Gertler 1986). The south and west are typified by a diversified and expanding economic mix, while the north possesses a specialised economy which is contracting (Keinath 1985). The regional destinations of the new immigrants can be deduced from the intended destinations given upon entry, although these are not necessarily final.

In 1960 the north-east and west accounted for 64 per cent of all resident

Table 10.4 *Intended regional destinations of recent immigrants, 1960–84*

Region	1960 %	1970–9 %	1982–4 %
North-east	37.1	37.5	27.9
New England	8.9	7.2	4.3
Middle Atlantic	28.2	30.3	21.6
North-central	20.3	13.4	12.4
East north-central	17.5	11.2	9.4
West north-central	2.8	2.2	3.0
South	15.6	19.7	21.8
West south-central	8.8	7.4	9.8
East south-central	0.7	0.9	1.1
South Atlantic	6.1	11.3	10.9
West	26.7	28.4	33.8
Mountain	3.4	2.7	3.4
Pacific	23.3	25.7	30.4

Notes: Figures for 1960 are for all registered aliens, for 1970–9 and 1982–4 they are intended destinations.

Years are fiscal years.

Source: US Department of Justice 1980 and 1986b

aliens, but in the subsequent twenty years the north-east has become relatively less attractive (Table 10.4). In contrast the West is now the dominant regional destination, with a third of all arrivals in 1982–4. North-central has also declined and the south has gained, broadly in line with the sunbelt/snowbelt divide. Sub-regional trends may be distinguished and the west-central has increased in significance a little. The south Atlantic and Pacific sub-regions accounted for most of the gains in the south and west.

The intended destinations by state confirm the regional trends. Within the west and south, Montana, Idaho, Arizona, Delaware, Hawaii and West Virginia showed no real gains in their shares of immigrants (Table 10.5). California and New York are the intended destinations of almost four out of every ten immigrants in 1960 as well as in 1982–4. However, New York is declining in importance and California increasing, receiving a quarter of recent immigrants. Since 1970 three-quarters of newcomers went to just ten states, with Washington, Virginia and Oregon emerging as destinations. One might expect that, all things being equal, the most populous states would receive the most arrivals. In fact the ten states listed in Table 10.5 are residence for only 45 per cent of the US population. New York and Hawaii receive three times as many as might be expected, and California and New Jersey double. Only Michigan and Pennsylvania had fewer immigrants in the 1970s than would be predicted from the 1980 population.

The states with the highest proportion of foreign-born residents are California (15.1 per cent), Hawaii (14.2 per cent), New York (13.6 per cent), Florida (10.9 per cent) and New Jersey (10.3 per cent). The six states with less than 1 per cent foreign-born are all in the south (US Bureau of the Census 1983). In comparison with the peak of the second wave, the current foreign-born proportion is between two and five times smaller (US Bureau of the Census 1913). In New York, Rhode Island and Massachusetts, over two in five of the population were born abroad. New England and north-central states have most declined in importance.

California is the destination most chosen by fifteen of the largest immigrant groups, and New York by five (Table 10.6). In general, the Asian nationalities select California first, then a variety of other states including Minnesota by Laotians and Hawaii by Filipinos. The geography of refugees from Indochina is influenced by resettlement programmes which attempted (and partly succeeded) to achieve some dispersal (Reimers 1985). Consequently, military bases are important locations, although recent evidence suggests that there is much relocation, particularly to California and the Gulf Coast. New York is selected by Caribbean basin immigrants, although Central Americans also chose

Table 10.5 *Intended destinations by states of recent immigrants, 1960–84*

	1960			1970–9			1982–4	
California	567,484	(19.2)	California	957,001	(22.1)	California	438,062	(25.8)
New York	553,703	(18.8)	New York	941,816	(21.7)	New York	285,263	(16.8)
Texas	237,514	(8.1)	New Jersey	270,845	(6.3)	Texas	136,339	(8.0)
Illinois	199,405	(6.8)	Texas	270,796	(6.3)	Illinois	86,461	(5.1)
New Jersey	151,437	(5.1)	Florida	268,020	(6.2)	Florida	84,222	(5.0)
Michigan	141,719	(4.8)	Illinois	257,643	(6.0)	New Jersey	80,940	(4.8)
Massachusetts	127,710	(4.3)	Massachusetts	138,716	(3.2)	Massachusetts	37,874	(2.2)
Pennsylvania	126,073	(3.7)	Michigan	101,833	(2.4)	Washington	34,242	(2.0)
Ohio	108,892	(2.8)	Pennsylvania	100,857	(2.3)	Pennsylvania	33,603	(2.0)
Florida	83,577	(2.6)	Hawaii	77,768	(1.8)	Virginia	31,644	(1.9)
Total	2,297,514	(76.2)	Total	3,385,295	(78.3)	Total	1,248,651	(73.6)

Notes: Figures for 1960 are for all registered aliens resident in the USA. For 1970–9 and 1982–4 figures are for intended destinations.
Years are fiscal years.
Source: US Department of Justice 1980 and 1986b

Table 10.6 *Intended destinations of immigrants by national origin, 1982*

Country of Birth	States of intended destination					
Mexico	Texas	20,819 (37.1)	California	19,552 (34.8)	Illinois	4,098 (7.3)
Philippines	California	20,278 (45.0)	Hawaii	4,478 (10.5)	Illinois	2,664 (5.9)
Vietnam	California	30,057 (41.8)	Texas	8,358 (12.0)	Washington	3,825 (5.3)
Laos	California	9,285 (25.4)	Minnesota	3,318 (9.1)	Illinois	3,951 (8.4)
Korea	California	9,229 (29.1)	New York	2,929 (9.2)	Illinois	1,821 (5.7)
China	California	10,406 (38.4)	New York	6,128 (22.6)	Illinois	809 (3.0)
India	California	3,342 (18.3)	New York	3,258 (15.0)	Illinois	2,231 (10.3)
Jamaica	New York	9,664 (51.6)	New Jersey	1,372 (7.3)	Connecticut	1,055 (5.6)
USSR	California	6,839 (44.2)	Illinois	2,495 (16.1)	Pennsylvania	1,033 (6.7)
United Kingdom	California	2,825 (19.4)	New York	1,835 (12.6)	Texas	780 (5.4)
Kampuchea	California	6,320 (47.0)	Washington	902 (6.7)	Texas	654 (4.9)
Canada	California	1,823 (16.9)	Florida	1,130 (10.5)	New York	948 (8.8)
Iran	California	3,969 (38.5)	Texas	680 (6.6)	New York	663 (6.4)
Guyana	New York	7,057 (70.2)	New Jersey	833 (8.3)	Florida	279 (2.8)
Taiwan	California	3,212 (32.5)	New York	1,113 (11.3)	Texas	1,017 (10.3)
Haiti	New York	4,921 (56.1)	Florida	1,198 (13.6)	Massachusetts	782 (8.9)
Colombia	New York	2,493 (29.0)	New Jersey	1,618 (18.8)	Florida	1,324 (15.4)
El Salvador	California	3,241 (45.6)	New York	1,214 (17.1)	New Jersey	452 (6.4)
Germany	California	919 (14.2)	New York	438 (6.8)	Texas	416 (6.4)
Poland	Illinois	1,918 (32.7)	New York	918 (15.6)	New Jersey	724 (12.3)
Thailand	California	1,756 (31.5)	Illinois	374 (6.7)	New York	303 (5.4)

Notes: Figures in parentheses are percentages.
China includes only mainland China.
Figures for the Dominican Republic not available for 1982.
Years are fiscal years.
Source: US Department of Justice 1986a

California. Three of the four European nationalities also stated California as their first destination.

Some national groups are more concentrated by state than others. Over
70 per cent of Guyanans and Dominicans headed for a single state,
compared with the more diversified destinations of Indians, Canadians,
Britons and Germans. Although figures for Dominicans were not given in
1984, in 1979 70.5 per cent of them intended to reside in New York State.

The geography of destinations can best be conceptualised in terms of
five populous states (California, Illinois, New Jersey, New York and
Texas) and a number of more specific destinations originating in various
historical events. These would include the recruiting of Filipino labour in
Hawaii and the Cuban refugee movements to Florida. Furthermore, the
states of destination are largely reflections of the locations of the metropolitan areas of immigration. The next section deals with the urbanisation
of immigrants.

The urbanisation of immigrants and ethnic groups

The acute geographical differentiation of the US economy cannot be
appreciated fully at either regional or state levels, since the processes of
economic location have become sensitive to place as they have become
more indifferent to space in general. The spatial division of labour is
properly metropolitan or intra-metropolitan (Gertler 1986, Storper and
Walker 1984). Metropolitan areas link national and international
economic transactions, so it is not surprising that contemporary immigration is strongly urbanised (Cohen 1981, Friedmann and Wolff 1983).
Among immigrants arriving in 1984, at least 75 per cent of each
national origin group headed for a 'Metropolitan Statistical Area'
(MSA), and in some cases over 95 per cent (US Department of Justice
1986b).

The most urbanised groups are Dominicans, Haitians, Jamaicans and
Russians. The least are Canadians, Germans and Laotians. Not included
in immigration statistics are the small number of contract workers who
labour in south-eastern and south-western agriculture. Of recent Mexican
immigrants 80 per cent stated MSAs as their destinations in 1984.

All immigrant and census-defined ethnic groups are more urbanised
than either the US population in general or the Anglo-American (non-
Latino white), black and American Indian populations (Table 10.7). In
addition much higher proportions of immigrants are resident in urban
areas (Standard Metropolitan Statistical Areas, i.e. SMSAs) in 1980.
More than 95 per cent of Cubans, Puerto Ricans and Chinese reside in
SMSAs.

Table 10.7 *Urbanisation of ethnic groups, 1980*

Group	Numbers	Percentage urban	Percentage SMSA	Percentage central city
Anglo-American[a]	180,602,838	70.5	72.7	33.0
Black[b]	26,091,857	85.3	81.0	71.2
American Indian	1,478,523	54.6	51.9	42.0
Asian	3,550,605	93.2	91.4	51.0
Spanish origin	14,603,683	89.9	87.6	57.4
Mexican	8,678,632	87.7	85.0	54.5
Puerto Rican	2,004,961	97.0	96.8	77.7
Cuban	806,223	98.0	97.7	41.5
Japanese	716,331	91.6	88.9	47.9
Chinese	812,178	97.0	96.1	60.1
Filipino	781,331	92.4	90.9	49.8
Korean	357,393	92.9	92.5	44.3
Asian Indian	387,393	92.2	91.7	42.6
Vietnamese	245,025	95.3	92.7	55.7
Total	226,545,805	73.7	74.7	40.0

Note: [a] White not of Spanish origin
[b] Black not of Spanish origin
Source: US Bureau of the Census 1983

Since at least 1945 there has been a selective rearrangement of urban economies, including a general decentralisation of capital-intensive activities and a general centralisation of labour-intensive activities. The suburbanisation of some white-collar and much blue-collar employment has reduced the opportunity structure of the cities. Table 10.7 shows the proportion of the metropolitan population of ethnic groups which is located in central cities. All groups are more centralised than either the US total population or Anglo-Americans, but less segregated than two domestic minorities, blacks and Puerto Ricans. Immigrants are arriving in central cities at a time when the native population is leaving, resulting in net losses of population. Even so, only 40 to 60 per cent of the metropolitan ethnic populations are resident in central cities. Cubans, for example, are highly urbanised but weakly centralised, reflecting their residence in Miami's suburban districts. Any comparisons between Asian and Latino or Caribbean centralisation are difficult to make, because of the regional differences in patterns of metropolitan municipal fragmentation.

Which metropolitan areas attract immigrants the most, and which are the most ethnically diverse? The largest SMSAs are also those with the largest ethnic populations and often those with the greatest proportions of non-Anglo-Americans too (Table 10.8 and 10.9). Many of those which seem to receive more immigrants than expected by their size are adjacent

Table 10.8 *Intended metropolitan destinations of immigrants, 1984*

MSA	Total numbers	Percentage	Largest groups as percentage of total moving to MSA					
New York (New York and New Jersey)	92,079	16.9	Dominican Republic	16.4	China	6.6	Guyana	6.5
Los Angeles–Long Beach	49,679	9.1	Mexico	18.0	Philippines	10.6	Korea	9.8
San Francisco–Oakland	23,797	4.4	Philippines	20.0	China	14.0	Vietnam	6.8
Chicago	22,380	4.1	Mexico	17.6	India	10.8	Philippines	9.4
Washington DC (Maryland and Virginia)	14,271	2.6	Korea	10.5	Vietnam	7.2	India	6.5
Anaheim–Santa Ana	12,089	2.2	Vietnam	26.1	Mexico	11.9	Korea	8.4
Miami–Hialeah	11,346	2.1	Cuba	38.8	Jamaica	8.6	Colombia	7.3
San Jose	9,539	1.8	Vietnam	17.0	Philippines	15.5	Mexico	9.9
Boston	8,837	1.6	China	8.8	Vietnam	8.3	Haiti	7.6
Newark	8,075	1.5	India	8.4	Jamaica	7.1	Haiti	7.1

Note: MSA is 'Metropolitan Statistical Area' as defined by Office of Management and Budget.
Source: US Department of Justice 1986b

Table 10.9 *Metropolitan areas and ethnic diversity in the US, 1980*

SMSA	Percentage of foreign-born population	Percentage of non-Anglo-American population	Percentage of largest non-Anglo-American groups					
Miami	35.6	53.5	Cuban	25.0	Black	16.7	Puerto Rican	2.8
Los Angeles–Long Beach	22.3	46.7	Mexican	22.0	Black	12.4	Japanese	1.6
New York	21.3	40.0	Black	20.2	Puerto Rican	9.7	Chinese	1.5
San Francisco–Oakland	15.7	33.3	Black	11.9	Mexican	5.7	Chinese	4.4
San Jose	13.6	29.0	Mexican	13.4	Black	3.2	Vietnamese	0.9
Anaheim–Santa Ana–Garden Grove	13.3	21.6	Mexican	11.8	Black	1.2	Japanese	1.1
San Diego	12.7	25.8	Mexican	12.2	Black	5.5	Filipino	2.5
Newark	11.6	29.4	Black	21.0	Puerto Rican	3.1	Cuban	1.2
Ft. Lauderdale–Hollywood	11.1	15.5	Black	10.9	Other Spanish origin	1.5	Puerto Rican	0.9
Chicago	10.5	30.4	Black	19.9	Mexican	5.1	Puerto Rican	1.8
Boston	10.1	9.7	Black	5.6	Puerto Rican	1.0	Chinese	0.8

Note: Table shows SMSAs with over one million inhabitants in 1980 ranked by percentage of foreign-born population
Source: US Bureau of the Census 1983

to larger metropolitan areas. Anaheim–Garden Grove–Santa Ana is contiguous with Los Angeles, and San Jose with San Francisco. In both places there is substantial self-generating urbanisation rather than simply urban decentralisation. They are both leading regions in the high-technology complex of industries, making use of Vietnamese, Filipino and Mexican labour in the assembly plants. Fort Lauderdale–Hollywood is next to Miami, while Newark and Jersey City are across the Hudson from New York. There are, in fact, four 'Standard Consolidated Areas' (SCSA) which were the intended destinations of 39 per cent of all immigrants in 1984. In 1980 these places held an eighth of the American population.

The New York–Newark–Jersey City SCSA is the destination of almost one in five new immigrants. In New York alone 40 per cent of the population are non-Anglo-American. Jersey City has the second highest foreign-born proportion after Miami, 24 per cent, and the third largest non-Anglo-American proportion, 41 per cent. This urban region is the major destination of Caribbean migrants.

The Los Angeles–Anaheim SCSA was the destination of 12.3 per cent of immigrants in 1984, and it now has a non-Anglo-American majority. The two other SCSAs, Miami–Fort Lauderdale and San Francisco–San Jose accounted for 2.7 and 6.2 per cent of new arrivals respectively. Miami has the highest foreign-born percentage of any SMSA and a non-Anglo majority. However, most of the SMSAs with large foreign-born proportions are not among the largest listed in the tables. Thirty-three SMSAs with over one million inhabitants have foreign-born percentages of over ten points, mostly in Texas, California and New York.

At the peak of the second wave of immigration in 1910 these same cities had much larger proportions of foreign-born persons. In New York, for example, 40 per cent were born abroad, in Chicago 36 per cent and in San Francisco 34 per cent (US Bureau of the Census 1913). Only in Los Angeles has the immigrant proportion risen, but only from 20.7 to 22.3 per cent.

The general pattern of metropolitan destinations consists of the largest SMSAs at the top of the immigrant hierarchy which are important destinations for almost all national origin groups (Table 10.10). Yet in all but three of the SMSAs listed in the two tables there was a net out-migration between 1975 and 1980. The exceptions were Anaheim, San Diego and Fort Lauderdale–Hollywood. The new immigrants are partly a replacement population, but not entirely. Below these SMSAs are a number of specific destinations important for historical reasons, such as proximity or specialised employment.

Los Angeles and New York were either the first or second most popular

Table 10.10 *Major metropolitan destinations of immigrant groups, 1984*

Country	Stated destination, 1984 %						Largest ethnic communities, 1980					
Canada	LA	5.4	NY	5.1	FL	2.7	n/a					
China	NY	25.8	SF	14.9	LA	8.2	SF	17.7	NY	16.4	LA	11.6
Colombia	NY	33.9	MI	7.5	BP	5.0	n/a					
Cuba	MI	41.6	JC	5.5	NY	4.7	MI	50.3	NY	9.1	LA	5.8
Dominican Republic	NY	65.2	BP	3.5	JC	2.8	n/a					
El Salvador	LA	25.4	NY	13.7	WA	11.4	n/a					
India	NY	12.6	CH	9.7	LA	4.3	NY	14.4	CH	8.7	LA	4.8
Iran	LA	23.2	WA	6.0	NY	6.0	n/a					
Jamaica	NY	49.1	MI	4.9	NS	3.5	n/a					
Kampuchea	LA	8.6	NY	6.0	AN	4.8	n/a					
Korea	LA	14.7	NY	7.4	WA	4.6	LA	16.9	NY	7.7	CH	6.0
Laos	FR	5.7	MN	4.9	ST	4.2	n/a					
Mexico	LA	15.5	CH	6.9	EP	5.5	LA	18.9	HO	4.3	CH	4.2
Philippines	LA	12.4	HN	8.5	SF	7.3	LA	12.9	SF	12.4	SD	6.0
Taiwan	LA	17.4	NY	9.4	SJ	8.0	n/a					
United Kingdom	NY	9.4	LA	7.0	WA	2.6	n/a					
Vietnam	LA	8.5	AN	8.5	NO	3.8	LA	11.1	HO	7.4	AN	5.3
Black	LA	8.5	n/a				NY	7.1	LA	5.4	CH	3.5

Note: Table shows percentages of each immigrant group stating MSA as intended residence and percentages of 1980 population for ethnic groups (where available), located in individual SMSAs.

Abbreviations: AN Anaheim–Santa Ana–Garden Grove, BP Bergen–Passaic, CH Chicago, EP El Paso, FR Fresno, HN Honolulu, HO Houston, FL Fort Lauderdale–Hollywood, JC Jersey City, LA Los Angeles–Long Beach, MI Miami, MN Minneapolis–St Paul, NO New Orleans, NS Nassau–Suffolk, NY New York, SD San Diego, SF San Francisco, SJ San Jose, ST Stockton, WA Washington, DC

Source: US Department of Justice 1986b, US Bureau of the Census 1983

destinations among fifteen of the seventeen national origin groups listed in Table 10.10. Although more persons stated New York as their destination, more separate ethnic groups selected Los Angeles. The only exceptions to these were Cubans, who moved to Miami and Jersey City, and Laotians who headed for Fresno, California and Minneapolis–St Paul. The most localised groups, including Dominicans, Jamaicans and Colombians, selected New York first. Nationalities which went mainly to Los Angeles tended to be more dispersed throughout the urban hierarchy. Based on this and other evidence presented so far it seems that New York and Los Angeles are different kinds of immigrant cities. New York is the destination of a large number of immigrants from a smaller number of countries, mostly from the Caribbean basin. Los Angeles is the destination of a smaller absolute number of immigrants but from a larger selection of continents and countries, headed by Asia and Central America. In both cases official figures significantly underestimate the actual immigrant and refugee populations.

As a footnote, the least plural of the large cities (one million and over) in the USA is Minneapolis–St Paul, the fifteenth largest SMSA but 95 per cent Anglo-American. Ten SMSAs of over one million were over 95 per cent US born in 1980. They were Atlanta, Baltimore, Cincinnati, Dallas–Fort Worth, Denver–Boulder, Kansas City, Milwaukee, Minneapolis–St Paul, Pittsburgh and St Louis. Why do these large places not attract immigrants? Is it the local economic mix or some other factor? Further research needs to be done on what kinds of industrial locations seem to require or attract immigrant labour, and which do not.

The intra-metropolitan distribution of immigrants

The intra-metropolitan distribution of immigrant and ethnic groups is usually regarded as important for two sets of reasons (Lieberson 1963). First, the degree of residential mixing or segregation of an immigrant group from the host society has been shown to be an indication of their social assimilation. Secondly, the ethnic residential community was an important part of the transition between the immigrants' society and the metropolitan one. Voluntary proximity of clustering helped to retain traditional cultural traits and institutions which, it was thought, prevented forms of social disorganisation (Kim 1981).

Earlier theorists commonly explained these communities in terms of the culture and preferences of the immigrants in the first instance, and the social distance that the host society wished to maintain in the second. However, from a perspective of change in the urban economy it also makes sense to examine residential patterns in terms of production, location and the role of territory in the social reproduction of labour and ethnicity (Scott 1986).

Models of intra-metropolitan residence for earlier waves of immigration have been proposed by several authors. These models focus less on cultural traits and more on the ecological structure of the city itself and how immigrant groups are incorporated into it through their relationship to work (Hershberg *et al.* 1979, Katznelson 1981, Ward 1982, Yancey *et al.* 1976, Yancey *et al.* 1985). They generally distinguish between the first and second waves of immigration. The first entered an early industrial city in which there was little functional differentiation between workplace and residence, which were separated only by walking distance. Consequently the Germans and Irish were not highly segregated. The second wave entered a city differentiated by the revolution in transport and mass industrialisation, creating homogeneous residential areas in a zone in transition, the ecological bases of high segregation. The shift to capital-intensive, standardised manufacture formed a decentralised labour demand which drew the new Europeans into the suburbs, leaving a jobless vacuum for incoming blacks. The synchronic correlations between residential segregation, socio-economic status and social assimilation recorded by Duncan and Lieberson (1959) are therefore contingent upon the nature of the local economy. Whether employment is predominantly labour or capital intensive, centralised or decentralised, has consequences for the residential distribution of ethnic immigrants.

There may be reasons why the conventional upwards-and-outwards mobility of the European ethnic groups is not applicable to the new immigrants. Many authors have recognised qualitative changes in urban economies, variously termed post-industrial, late capitalist, peripheralisation at the core, the new service economy and world city growth (Bluestone and Harrison 1982, Friedmann and Wolff 1983, Ley 1980, Sassen-Koob 1984). The majority of new jobs are in non-production occupations and industries. Some of these jobs are in the weaker, more fluid and less protected parts of the labour market, usually represented by low-wage, unstandardised or intermittent work. They might be jobs in retailing, producer and personal services, subcontracted and downgraded manufacture (Sassen-Koob 1984, Waldinger 1985). In each case they have low entry barriers suitable for immigrant workers. The possession of credentials from the homeland or obtained after arrival permits entry into expanding white-collar occupations, although often in marginal positions (Kim 1981). This employment may facilitate rapid dispersal and apparent spatial assimilation through higher incomes alone. Therefore, in at least two ways the changing urban economy might have some effect on residential communities.

Ethnic communities may be classified by residential form and they can be categorised by their economic foundations. This is what Yancey *et al.* (1985) try to accomplish in an analysis of various sociological and social distance factors. They argue that the structural or ecological bases of black, Jewish and white European ethnicity differ. Black ethnicity is in part the product of residential exclusion without employment stability which results in homogeneous black social networks for all black status groups. In contrast, the white European urban village is the result of secure and stable industrial employment, although as this declines they suggest that those people remaining increasingly interact across divisions of national origin and religion. The third type that they identify is characterised by Jewish ethnicity, distinguished by an early movement out of manufacturing employment into retail trades and professions. Although they have moved out of enclaves, Jews maintain close social ties through secular and religious organisations. These three types can be distinguished by their relationship to work as well as residence. One is excluded from stable employment, another anchored by it and the third freed to seek residence outside enclaves. In each case the sociological nature of ethnicity differs.

To what extent are the classifications and descriptions of earlier eco-logical communities applicable to the current period? A provisional scheme linking community, ethnicity and the locational tendencies of production and business can begin to differentiate between the structural foundations of the new immigrant groups. This typology is not exhaustive but consists of three clearly different communities. It is illustrated with examples drawn mainly from southern California.

The first type of ethnic residential community remains the ghetto or barrio. It is defined by low rates of labour force participation, a lack of local work opportunities and low rates of occupational mobility. Ghettos are commonly areas of high daily labour outflow and reduced retail or commercial functions. There are contrasting ideas as to how the ghetto has been affected by economic restructuring and its locational con-sequences. Taking Los Angeles as an example, the collapse of the auto and related industries has resulted in considerable job loss for the black community (Soja, Morales and Wolff 1983). Trapped in central locations blacks have been poorly placed to take advantage of surburban job growth, while they have not participated in low-wage manufacturing and service employment. Yet black unemployment has been persistently high and above national levels, and socio-economic conditions in some parts of the ghetto appear to have changed little since 1945. Far from displacing black workers, the new immigrants are apparently entering occupations and sectors not traditionally held by blacks (Muller 1985). Rather than direct displacement, it is probable that the privatisation of services, some of which may have once been public, has had a greater impact. Whatever is the case, the connections between urban economic change, the location of opportunities and black ghettoisation are less simple than crude theories of underclass formation.

Some distinction can be made between the contiguous black or Latino residential district and the ghetto or barrio. The contiguous district may include high-status areas, the inhabitants of which enjoy conventional professional relations between secure work and secure residence. Baldwin Hills on the north-western edge of Los Angeles' ghetto is an example, while other areas might look like ghetto overspill.

A second qualification concerns the heterogeneity of such areas. Hernandez (1985) recognises a pan-Latino barrio in Chicago, while in New York the proximity of blacks, Puerto Ricans and Haitians is well known. In Los Angeles the black ghetto is 'eroding' from the inside as recent arrivals from Mexico and Central America either replace of displace residents. In east Los Angeles a recent influx of Asians has begun to transform the traditional barrio. Some authors have warned of the potential formation of an immobilised black and/or lower status Latino underclass, trapped inside ghettoised colonies (Massey 1981). However, the developments mentioned above question the permanence of the conventional ghetto, which may turn out to be simply another distinct and extreme phase in black residential exclusion.

Outside the ghetto, black and Latino suburbanisation has been increasing and there is clear evidence of declining black segregation in all regions (especially the west), and in both cities and suburbs (Logan and Schneider 1984, Taeuber 1983). This movement appears to be more than just an overspill, because the profile of black households selecting urban residence has begun to resemble that of white households (Frey 1985). Figures for Latinos are scarce, but there is some evidence that the dispersal of the 1960s was not maintained in the 1970s (Hwang *et al.* 1985, Van Valey *et al.* 1982). For example, in Los Angeles between 1970 and 1980 black residential segregation as measured by the index of dissimilarity fell by twelve points. Spanish origin segregation rose by ten points, largely due to the influx of foreign-born Mexicans.

The second type of ethnic community is comparable with the ports-of-entry of earlier immigrants. Often they are multinational, and Hernandez (1985) terms them areas of multi-ethnic succession. His examples are north-central Chicago and Brooklyn New York, to which one might add the neighbourhoods west of downtown Los Angeles. These include Pico Union, Temple Beaudry, Echo Park and Silverlake. This area is a major port-of-entry for Central American refugees and immigrants, particularly

Salvadorans, Guatemalans, Hondurans and Nicaraguans, in addition to some Mexicans. An unknown number of residents are refugees without asylum, or undocumented persons.

One means of understanding the formation and maintenance of this community is to recognise the crystallisation of new work opportunities in personal and producer services, downgraded or petty manufacturing and retailing around the emergent international business centre of Los Angeles (Sassen-Koob 1984). Labour markets in these sectors, including work in restaurants, hotels, construction, apparel and small workshops, commonly have low wages, high job and personnel turnover, informal recruiting and other irregular or intermittent characteristics. Waldinger (1985) likens them to spot markets, in which there is a high degree of uncertainty and a low level of standardisation. Under such conditions it is convenient for both employees and job-seekers to gravitate towards each other and cluster. The tendency for such types of production to do so has been demonstrated by Scott (1984) for the women's dress industry. This situation has the additional advantage of securing labour in immigrant enterprises through ethnically homogeneous networks. Independently of the operation of the housing market, the form of the labour market is the economic cement of the community. It is not inevitable that there will be dispersal and assimilation, because this is dependent upon opportunities for vertical occupational mobility into more capital-intensive sectors, in addition to the problems of financing housing mobility. Neither is the supply of peripheral jobs certain. They may be relocated to newly urbanising areas or even abroad, ironically sometimes to the very countries immigrants have left. If the communities formed by such labour processes become the bases for communal organisations, either political or workplace, the immigrant workers may lose the very qualities which made their employment attractive in the first place, submissiveness and flexibility. Put together these possibilities suggest that the dissolution of these immigrant communities is not definite. Sassen-Koob (1982) has suggested that such communities act as 'holding operations', postponing the devalorisation of areas of the city. The employment that they generate, the housing they occupy, the cash and tax flows they provide and the small businesses they run effectively mobilise immigrant resources. This is done at a low cost to both public and private capital. In central Los Angeles the Latino immigrant community is literally keeping the area turning over until downtown businesses require the land for expansion or residence.

Not all ports-of-entry are central to metropolitan areas. Hernandez (1985) identifies Union City and Jersey City as older industrial areas which have experienced multi-ethnic succession. In Los Angeles there are outlying immigrant areas, in Pacoima, San Pedro and Wilmington. The Vietnamese communities in Orange County and San Jose are further variants of this type. In both cases the cluster of high-technology industries associated with semiconductor manufacture provide semi-skilled assembly work, while the newly urbanising areas around them supply service employment. These industries are also contingent upon international locational processes and the internal operations of large multinational companies. Already San Jose, which includes Silicon Valley, has declined as a low-wage assembly region (Saxenian 1983).

The third and final type has no recognisable antecedents in earlier periods of immigration, because it is the product of the internationalisation of the urban economy. All immigrant communities generate businesses in labour-intensive sectors. However, some are more developed and integrated than others. Two facts in particular have encouraged the creation of a new type of ethnic community. First, the interpenetration of the Pacific and Caribbean national economies, achieved through international finance and business. Secondly, the arrival of immigrants with an established adaptation to urban conditions, middle-class characteristics and sometimes directly connected to transnational business or the homeland government. This type may be termed a 'transnational business enclave' or a 'nonterritorial community', phrases used by Kim (1981) with reference to the Koreans of New York City.

The Cuban enclave economy in Miami as described by Portes and Bach (1985) is partly integrated into the international financial functions of the urban economy through construction, banking, capital flight and trade. Miami became the financial capital of Latin America because of its position and the stability of the dollar. The enclave bridges primary and secondary sectors of the economy, has a degree of vertical integration and a distinctive labour market. Its role is more than just local or ethnic, as might have been the case with earlier urban villages. The transnational business enclaves announce their presence with investment in hotels, shopping malls, churches and cultural centres, newly constructed and not adapted from other uses. In Los Angeles, Little Tokyo and Koreatown are two such places, while in the suburban city of Monterey Park a business and residential community of Chinese and Taiwanese is emerging. It has none of the tourist functions associated with the older Chinatowns.

These enclaves are not necessarily the main residential districts of the ethnic groups. The appropriate locations for business are not necessarily desirable residential areas, while the decline in housing market discrimination has opened up alternative residential areas. Modern cities are characterised by a widespread dispersal of retail functions which also encourages residential diffusion. The majority of Koreatown's residential population is Latino, while Little Tokyo is only the residence of some elderly persons and some young professional Japanese. The majority of the Japanese population reside in suburban areas, the non-territorial community resembling the Jewish model. A cohesive community is maintained by social networks, language, suburban malls and businesses rather than residential proximity. The city of Gardena (once a Japanese agricultural settlement) and parts of the South Bay area describe the community. The separation of the social and spatial aspects of community must cast doubt on the assumptions of spatial models of assimilation. For the first time some immigrant groups have a socio-economic status as high or even higher than the native population. What significance for the plural nature of American societies does residential location retain in the contemporary metropolis?

The purpose of this typology is more than descriptive. It focusses research of the interrelationships between work and residence, production and reproduction. Katznelson (1981) argues that the 'schizophrenic' nature of American class relations, i.e. classes at work and ethnic groups at home, derived from the geographical separation of these two spheres. When combined with the history of migration and a close connection between nationality and occupation this created space for distinct ethnic identities. Once our understanding of ethnicity goes beyond a catalogue of cultural traits, then the particular separation and nature of work and community is central to appreciating its maintenance and negotiation. The urban economy requires differentiated labour. The possibility that there are ecological foundations to the social reproduction of labour supply means that ethnicity and ethnic communities are more than incidental to its development.

Conclusion

Although the fourth wave of immigration is possibly as large as the second wave in numerical terms, in relative numbers it is less pervasive. In fact, the impact is highly localised, concentrated in the great metropolitan regions which are the focal points of the international and national economies. Some of these regions, such as New York, Los Angeles and Chicago, are established urban areas with a history of immigration. Others are urbanising around new industrial or economic activities, such as Miami, San Jose and Anaheim–Santa Ana–Garden Grove. Where the new immigration differs most from its predecessors is in the internationalisation of capital alongside labour. This implies that particular combinations of capital and labour in specific locations are contingent upon shifts in the world economy and not just local factors. There are many possibilities for capital and labour switching geographically, which imperils the economic survival of new immigrant communities. The opportunities for upward mobility are no longer just suburban, but global in nature. The discontinuities in the urban economy are such that some new immigrants are likely to be trapped by them, while others will be able to exploit them. The future of ethnic minorities in the USA is implicated deeply in contemporary processes of immigration and urbanisation.

JOHN D. KASARDA, JÜRGEN FRIEDRICHS AND
KAY E. EHLERS

11

Urban industrial restructuring and minority problems in the US and Germany*

Similar processes have been shaping the demographic and economic structure of US and German cities during the past three decades. These processes include the urban exodus of middle- and upper-income Caucasian residents and their partial replacement by lower-income minorities (e.g. blacks and Hispanics in US cities and Turks in German cities); suburbanisation of traditional central-city manufacturing, retail, and wholesale trade and simultaneous expansion in the cities of administrative, financial, professional, and other high-order services; corresponding declines in blue-collar and other jobs requiring less education and increases of white-collar information processing jobs requiring substantial education; a growing mismatch between the education levels of minority groups expanding in the cities and educational requirements of new urban growth industries.

As a consequence of these conflicting urban demographic and employment shifts, unemployment rates in most large US and German cities have risen faster than their respective national averages. Among urban minorities, unemployment has grown precipitously and has remained intractably high even under conditions of national economic recovery. This chapter analyses the structural determinants of the rapid rise of urban minority unemployment in the two nations and discusses public policy responses to the problem.

Our working thesis is that industrial transformations of US and German cities from centres of goods processing to centres of information processing have reduced the role these cities were once able to play as employment opportunity ladders for disadvantaged persons. This appears especially so for cities in America's northern industrial belt and cities in Germany's Rhine–Ruhr and Saar regions where economic transformation and resulting blue-collar job declines have been most severe in recent decades. Unfortunately, many of these same cities have concurrently experienced large increases of minority residents whose educational backgrounds are not appropriate for knowledge intensive jobs in administration, finance, the professions, and other white-collar services that have partially replaced blue-collar jobs these cities have lost.

We thus propose that a growing demographic-employment opportunity mismatch is a fundamental reason why central city unemployment rates in the US and Germany tend to be well above their national averages and inordinately high among inner-city racial and ethnic minorities. We further propose that current public policies in both countries, though well-meaning, may be aggravating demographic-employment opportunity mismatches by providing a subsistence infrastructure that tends to encourage displaced labour to remain in localities of severe blue-collar job decline. Let us elaborate this thesis.

Spatial mismatch, unemployment and public policy

Central to our frame of reference and working thesis is the term 'mismatch'. Mismatch may be defined as a discordant distribution of labour qualifications vis-à-vis qualifications required for jobs available at a point in time. Two processes of mismatch can be discerned: a non-spatial (or nationwide) one and a spatially specific (or local community) one.

The *non-spatial* process corresponds with the overall changes in the nation's economic structure from primary industry via secondary to tertiary (cf. Clark 1940, Fourastie 1949). Much current discussion of post-industrial society builds on this model, with further differentiation and specification applied to the tertiary (service) sector (e.g. Abler 1977, Bell 1973, La Porte and Abrahams 1976, Noyelle and Stanback, 1984). Whereas the industrial transition model is a straightforward description of the historical changes that have taken place in economic sectors, it is not without limitations (cf. Huebl and Schepers 1983) and, especially for our purposes, it is not sufficiently diagnostic regarding unemployment, i.e. the conditions of incomplete labour-force adaptation (cf. Kleber 1983).

Fourastie, when discussing the unemployment problem, assumes that by the interplay of market forces, unemployed labour will adapt to the changing economy by 'shifting' from one sector to the next. He, however, underestimates the difficulties of worker retraining/adaptation as well as the role emigration played in demographically relieving the European labour surplus in the last century when masses of displaced labour migrated to the New World.

Moreover, Fourastie did not foresee the technological innovations leading to such rapid changes in educational requisites for employment in the tertiary sector and declining demands for low-skill labour that many advanced industrialised countries are currently experiencing (cf. Fels and Schmidt 1981). Thus, we actually do not know whether the high unemployment rates currently confronting many Western economies are a relatively permanent structural feature or whether they simply reflect temporarily incomplete adaptation; if the latter, then appropriate labour-force skills will eventually be acquired or substantial new service sector jobs (both high and low skill) will be created, relieving the mismatch.

Just as critical to structural unemployment is the problem of shrinkages and transformations in local employment bases, which are occurring at too fast a pace for local labour to be able to adapt geographically. There are many personal, economic, and structural constraints that impede spontaneous outmigration of the unemployment from declining or trans-forming local labour markets. These include, among others, lack of information about job opportunities elsewhere, discrimination, local social and economic ties, and low expected marginal utility of migration relative to opportunity costs (cf. Morrison 1973). Thus, spatially specific mismatches and corresponding rising local unemployment can occur simultaneously with national job growth.

Extending our model further, rising local unemployment often results in programmes providing additional welfare assistance to the unemployed and government subsidies to local industries to stimulate employment growth (or to stem decline). In the US, these latter subsidies (such as targeted tax credit programmes and 'Urban Development Action Grants') are requested as incentives to attract businesses and industry to certain locations facing high unemployment. In Germany, along with this type of intervention, subsidies are given to existing central-city industries to ensure they will retain their labour force (e.g. shipbuilding and steel industries). Moreover, localised high unemployment rates result in tech-nical eligibility or requests for more spatially targeted public assistance to aid the unemployed in distressed areas (e.g. extension of unemployment compensation, government subsidised health insurance and additional welfare benefits). An illustrative case is the ongoing efforts of the mayors of German cities to get additional federal funds for welfare aid (which now come largely from city budgets) to supplement direct aid to the unemployed, which the federal government provides.

Spatially targeted industrial and welfare subsidies are likely to have short-term beneficial effects by generating some local jobs and relieving social pains created by high unemployment. Apropos the former, however, it is becoming increasingly clear that industrial subsidies will not reverse continuing blue-collar job declines in most urban and regional economies. Indeed, both Kasarda (1980) and Hicks (1982) for the US and Fels and Schmidt (1981) for Germany suggest the locally specific industrial interventions may impede longer-term employment growth in targeted cities by inappropriately sheltering old, declining industries and thus hindering the adaptation of cities to their emerging service sector roles. Apropos the latter, spatially uneven welfare subsidies may contribute to longer-term demographic-employment mismatches at the local level by providing a subsistence infrastructure that acts as a disincentive for disadvantaged persons to leave areas of severe blue-collar job decline. For example, many well-intentioned welfare services have understandably been concentrated in inner-city areas of greatest economic distress, with the unintended, yet possible, consequence of bonding distressed people to distressed places (Kasarda 1985).

Comparative differences

Comparing urban restructuring in the US to Germany has several advantages. Cities in both countries face common problems of adapting to their new service roles in advanced market economies and reducing unemployment. However, the political programmes and conditions of the labour markets in the two countries differ in a number of important respects. First, German programmes are more directed toward a 'jobs to the people' strategy, whereas in the US a tacit 'strategy' of laissez-faire redistribution (i.e. 'people-to-jobs') has predominated. Second, Germany has a tighter social web with respect to unemployment assistance and public assistance. This may account for the lower migration rates of unemployed persons. Third, the US economy is less dependent on exports, while exports account for over 30 per cent of the GNP of Germany. This puts pressure on Germany to keep up with international competition, especially with low-wage countries. Fourth, the US has a more dynamic economy as indicated by much higher job growth during the 1980s.

A final, important difference should be noted. Most of the minorities in Germany are still made up of foreign labour (*Gastarbeiter*), usually Turkish workers, not of immigrants, as in the US and Great Britain. They came to Germany by governmental contracts to alleviate a shortage of labour in the 1960s, and were *supposed* to 'rotate' back to their home countries. However, the majority did not leave Germany. This is documented by the fact that in 1984, 64.7 per cent of all foreigners had lived in Germany longer than eight years (*Statistisches Jahrbuch der Bundesrepublik Deutschland* 1985: 69).

Despite these significant cross-national differences, we nevertheless find

254   *John Kasarda, Jürgen Friedrichs and Kay Ehlers*

many similarities in urban demographic and employment transformations in the two nations, resulting in analogous mismatches between the labour force and job opportunities. In the sections which follow, we shall document these similarities and discuss their consequences for cities and their disadvantaged residents.

Selection of cities

We noted above that US cities most affected by conflicting demographic and functional transformation are the original industrial cities of the North. We have selected twelve of the largest of these cities for analysis: Baltimore, Boston, Chicago, Cleveland, Detroit, Milwaukee, Minneapolis/St Paul, Newark, New York, Philadelphia, Pittsburgh, and St Louis. Our analyses of the rise of the information processing sector in US cities and changing educational requirements for employment require us to use detailed *County Business Pattern* data that are available for five of these cities where county and city boundaries correspond. These cities are Baltimore, Boston, New York, Philadelphia and St Louis.

West German cities selected include Bremen, Duisburg, Düsseldorf, Frankfurt, Hamburg, Munich, Saarbrücken and Stuttgart. Since many readers may be less familiar with a number of these German cities than with the major cities of the US, we will briefly comment on each.

Hamburg was the largest in the former FRG after Berlin. In recent decades, Hamburg's manufacturing and port status has slipped. The city has lost almost all of its shipbuilding to Third World countries, with a significant portion of the repair work and cargo going to ports in The Netherlands and Belgium. Some of Hamburg's losses in manufacturing and port employment were compensated by expansion of the city's mass media industry which may eventually become its most important industry.

The city of Bremen, located 100 km from Hamburg, likewise experienced major declines in port activities and manufacturing. Bremen is currently struggling with very high rates of unemployment and expenditures for public assistance.

Economic transformation has severely hit cities in the traditional mining and steel region of Rhine–Ruhr. Two cities were selected from this formerly flourishing area: Düsseldorf and Duisburg. Düsseldorf is the capital city of the largest Bundesland (i.e. state), North Rhine–Westphalia. Its current significance stems from administrative functions namely trade and congresses. Nevertheless, it is affected by economic decline of the entire region. While Düsseldorf may have sufficient industrial diversity to overcome regional contraction, Duisburg may not. It represents the typical old industrial city, severely hit by its declining industries.

Similarly, Saarbrücken, the capital city of the small Bundesland, the Saarland, depends on the major industries of the region, mining and steel. Due to its peripheral location adjacent to France and a low industrial diversity, it exhibits all the problems of cities dominated by old, declining industries. The economy is kept alive by massive federal subsidies to the steel industry.

Frankfurt was selected for two reasons: it is the financial capital of Germany, if not of Europe (competing with London), and is expected to transform further in this direction. Moreover, among the large cities, it has the highest percentage of foreign population, 21.4 per cent in 1984.

Two cities from the south of Germany were included, both the capital cities of their respective Bundesland: Stuttgart of Baden-Württemberg and Munich of Bavaria. During the past decade, economic growth has shifted from the formerly strong north to the south. Both Baden-Württemberg and Bavaria have experienced growth rates in their state GNP above the national average, and are viewed as having a more favourable investment than northern regions.

Changes in urban employment

Table 11.1 describes employment changes in the twelve US cities by major industrial sector, between 1972 and 1982. The two largest cities, New York and Chicago, each lost over 200,000 manufacturing jobs during this ten-year period. For Chicago, this constituted nearly 50 per cent of its manufacturing jobs. On a percentage basis, Baltimore, Detroit and Philadelphia also lost more than one-third of their manufacturing jobs between 1972 and 1982. Observe further that wholesale employment also declined in all cities. Particularly sharp declines were experienced by Baltimore, Boston, Chicago, Detroit, Newark, Philadelphia and St Louis. The retail employment picture in these cities is not much brighter, with all cities but Pittsburgh losing retail employment between 1972 and 1982. Cities with major losses of retail employment, on a proportional basis, include Chicago, Cleveland, Detroit and Newark, all declining 25 per cent or more.

In contrast to sharp declines in the retail, wholesale and manufacturing sectors of these cities, service sector employment has expanded in all but two – Detroit and St Louis. Boston more than doubled its employment in the service sector between 1972 and 1982, whereas Chicago, Minneapolis/St Paul and Pittsburgh increased their service sector employment by at least one third. Boston's economy, in fact, added more service sector jobs than it lost employment in other sectors, making this city the only net job gainer between 1972 and 1982.

Table 11.1 *Change in employment, by industrial sector, in major US northern central cities, 1972–82*

City	Manufacturing Absolute[a]	%	Wholesale Absolute[a]	%	Retail Absolute[a]	%	Services Absolute[a]	%	Total Absolute[a]	%
Baltimore	-32	-35	-6	-25	-11	-20	2	6	-47	-19
Boston	-12	-20	-7	-28	-5	-9	32	57	7	4
Chicago	-203	-47	-30	-29	-53	-26	58	37	-228	-25
Cleveland	-39	-29	-4	-15	-13	-29	1	2	-55	-22
Detroit	-75	-41	-16	-45	-29	-41	-10	-18	-129	-38
Milwaukee	-28	-27	-1	-4	8	21	8	29	-13	-7
Minneapolis/St Paul	-29	-27	-2	-5	-5	-9	19	42	-17	-7
Newark	-13	-28	-4	-35	-10	-49	1	1	-27	-28
New York	-228	-30	-39	-15	-75	-18	113	26	-229	-12
Philadelphia	-78	-38	-14	-28	-21	-20	9	12	-104	-24
Pittsburgh	-10	-16	-2	-11	1	3	10	33	-1	-1
St Louis	-29	-29	-7	-26	-7	-19	-5	-14	-48	-24

Note: [a] Figures in thousands
Source: US Bureau of the Census, Economic Censuses, 1972 and 1982

Note the dire straits facing Detroit. During the same ten-year period, this city lost 41 per cent of its manufacturing jobs, 45 per cent of its wholesale jobs, 41 per cent of its retail jobs *and* 18 per cent of its service sector jobs. These figures will become particularly telling (given our mismatch thesis) when we describe demographic changes that have occurred in Detroit and other large northern cities between 1970 and 1980.

Data for the German cities shown in Table 11.2 exhibit similar patterns of employment change, by sector. All eight cities lost manufacturing jobs between 1970 and 1980 with Hamburg, Bremen, Düsseldorf and Stuttgart each losing over 20 per cent of their manufacturing bases. The 1980–4 data show that manufacturing employment declines have continued into this decade.

In terms of commerce (retail and wholesale trade), all cities but Bremen and Munich lost jobs between 1970 and 1980. During the 1980s, every city we examined lost jobs in commerce, with the more recent rates of employment decline exceeding those of the 1970s.

As with the United States, German cities partially compensated for their losses in manufacturing and trade with increasing employment in their service sectors. All cities for which we obtained data show a growth of at least 20 per cent in service sector employment between 1970 and 1980. Service sector employment growth continued during the 1980s in these German cities, but at a reduced pace. Like Boston, Munich's growth in service sector employment exceeded that city's losses in the remaining industrial sectors during the 1970s, so that it is the only major city in Germany to show an overall net employment gain during the 1970s.

New urban growth industries

When one examines the components of service sector employment, it becomes immediately apparent that substantial diversity exists. This sector includes maids, parking-lot attendants, financial analysts and medical doctors. Such diversity in aggregated employment statistics clouds more than it clarifies significant transformations taking place in the employment basis of cities.

Appraising transforming city economies requires decomposition of selected service employment. In the case of the US, this can be done by using detailed industrial sector breakdowns provided in US Bureau of the Census *County Business Patterns* for selected cities where city and county boundaries correspond. These industry data were further cross-classified by the occupations of workers in each industry using US Bureau of the Census industry-by-occupation matrices (1978). Those service sector industries where more than half the employees were classified as

Table 11.2 *Change in German employment,[a] by industry, 1970–80 and 1980–4*

City	Manufacturing		Commerce		Services		Other		Total	
	Absolute	%	Absolute	%	Absolute	%	Absolute	%	Absolute	%
Bremen										
1970–80	−24,314	−23.9	1,950	4.5	13,292	23.5	−9,125	−13.4	−18,197	−6.7
1980–4	−9,894	−12.8	−3,447	−7.6	106	0.7	−7,092	−12.1	−20,327	−8.1
Hamburg										
1970–80	−78,556	−30.8	−8,433	−5.3	44,184	20.1	−2,444	−1.4	−45,249	−5.6
1980–4	−23,612	−13.4	−15,938	−10.5	3,576	1.4	−15,876	−9.0	−51,850	−6.8
Düsseldorf[b]										
1970–80	−38,211	−27.8	−4,671	−6.6	21,337	21.1	−5,672	−9.4	−27,217	−7.4
1980–4	−8,866	−8.9	−4,550	−6.9	1,632	1.3	−191	−0.4	−11,975	−3.5
Duisburg[c]										
1970–80	n/a	n/a	n/a	n/a	n/a	n/a	n/a	n/a	n/a	n/a
1980–4	−17,069	−17.5	−2,783	−10.4	1,703	4.3	−12,493	−21.4	−30,588	−3.8
Saarbrücken[c]										
1970–80	n/a	n/a	n/a	n/a	n/a	n/a	n/a	n/a	n/a	n/a
1980–4	−3,297	−12.1	−2,231	−12.5	343	1.0	−1,444	−6.5	−6,629	−6.5
Frankfurt[b]										
1970–80	−29,578	−19.1	−7,756	−9.5	30,113	23.0	2,294	2.3	−4,927	−1.1
1980–4	−16,407	−13.1	−9,194	−12.4	913	0.6	−5,520	−5.5	−30,208	−6.6
Stuttgart										
1970–80	−42,571	−24.1	−3,731	−6.5	21,429	23.1	−1,496	−2.4	−26,370	−6.8
1980–4	−11,047	−8.3	−3,420	−6.4	2,420	2.1	−114	−0.2	−12,161	−3.3

Munich										
1970–80	−39,983	−16.4	16,541	18.8	55,034	30.3	10,759	9.0	42,352	6.9
1980–4	−22,644	−11.1	−4,979	−4.8	6,708	2.8	−3,170	−2.8	−24,085	−3.6
67 cities										
1970–80	−620,128	−16.2	2,069	0.1	710,565	30.9	51,510	3.0	144,016	1.5
1980–4	−400,177	−12.4	−136,891	−9.0	75,239	2.5	−80,725	−4.6	−542,554	−5.7
Germany										
1970–80	−1,032,521	−10.7	92,180	3.3	1,417,657	33.5	140,746	3.9	618,062	3.0
1980–4	−912,947	−10.6	−148,785	−5.1	287,703	5.1	−139,497	−3.7	−913,526	−4.4

Note: [a] 1970: Employed, excluding civil servants; 1980 and 1984: Employed only, who are obliged to participate in Social Security, therefore civil servants and self-employed are excluded.
[b] Minor incorporations between 1970 and 1980.
[c] Due to major incorporations no data are given.
Data refer to 27.5.1970, 30.6.1980, 30.6.1984

Source: Special analyses of the Federal Agency of Labor; ANBA 5/1985: 701. Statistisches Bundesamt: Arbeitsstättenzählung vom 27.5.1970, vol. 5.

Table 11.3 *Employment in information processing industries^a in major US cities, 1970–83*

City	1970 Absolute^b	%	1983 Absolute^b	%	Change 1970–83 Absolute^b	%
Baltimore	108	29.1	115	41.2	7	6
Boston	914	41.6	279	58.0	85	44
New York	1,172	35.0	1,328	46.3	156	13
Philadelphia	220	28.5	279	47.3	59	27
St Louis	96	25.5	107	42.8	11	11

Note: ^{a} Information processing industries are those service industries in which more than 50 per cent of the employees are classified as executives, managers, professionals or clerical workers.
^{b} Figures in thousands

Source: US Bureau of the Census, *County Business Patterns*, 1970 and 1983
US Bureau of the Census, *Industry by Occupation Matrices*, 1978.

managers, executives, professionals, or clerical workers were designated as information processing industries. For Germany, a similar classification of industries was used. The following industries were counted as 'information processing': banking/insurance (no. 69), arts/sciences (nos. 74–7), law counselling (no. 79) and public administration (nos. 91–4). 'Transport and communication' (no. 63–8) was not included, because the majority of those employed in this industry work for the federal railway.

Our working thesis, one will recall, is that both US and German cities are structurally transforming from goods processing to information processing. The data presented in Table 11.3 clearly illustrate the growth in information processing jobs in major northern cities of the US. Between 1970 and 1983, Baltimore added 7,000 jobs in its information processing industries, St Louis 11,000, Philadelphia 59,000, Boston 85,000 and New York City 156,000. The percentage increases range from 6 in Baltimore to 44 in Boston. By 1983, 58 per cent of Boston's employment was in information processing industries, with the other four above named cities all exceeding 40 per cent.

Data for the German cities presented in Table 11.4 reveal similar increases in employment in their information processing industries. Like in US cities, considerable growth in information processing industries in German cities occurred simultaneously with declines in total city employment (see Table 11.2). By 1984, six of the eight German cities analysed had more than 20 per cent of their employment in information processing.

Another important dimension of new urban growth industries is the educational characteristics of their jobholders. Table 11.5 presents US

Table 11.4 *Employment^a in German information processing industries, 1970–84*

City	1970 Absolute	%^{b}	1980 Absolute	%^{b}	1984 Absolute	%^{b}
Bremen	33,725	12.4	38,068	15.1	38,483	16.6
Hamburg	130,976	16.1	147,082	19.2	151,473	21.1
Düsseldorf^c	61,916	16.8	72,197	21.1	72,802	22.1
Duisburg^c	12,855	7.1	17,477	7.9	17,934	9.4
Saarbrücken^c	16,725	19.4	20,862	20.6	20,999	22.2
Frankfurt^c	83,056	17.9	98,150	21.4	98,497	22.9
Stuttgart	59,585	15.3	74,196	20.4	75,876	22.8
Munich	106,784	17.3	135,358	20.5	136,518	21.5
67 cities	1,372,740	14.7	1,739,797	18.3	1,760,680	19.8
Germany	2,441,595	12.0	3,122,742	14.9	3,221,745	16.1

Note: ^{a} 1970: Employed, excluding civil servants; 1980 and 1984: Employed obliged to participate in Social Security
^{b} In percentage of all employed
^{c} Incorporations between 1970 and 1980

Source: Sources and dates: See Table 11.2

employment data for city industries classified by the mean years of schooling completed by their jobholders. Industries where jobholders (in 1982) had an average education level of less than twelve years were classified as low-qualification industries. Those industries whose job holders had, on average, completed more than thirteen years of schooling (e.g. some college education) were classified as high-qualification industries.[1] Employment within each city was aggregated (based on 1982 educational criteria) for 1970 and 1983 to document changes in high and low educational qualification industries between 1970 and 1983.

The results in Table 11.5 reveal that, between 1970 and 1983, New York city lost 508,000 jobs in its low-qualification industries while adding 204,000 jobs in its high-qualification industries. Philadelphia lost 175,000 jobs in low-qualification industries while gaining 45,000 in the high category. Boston added more jobs to its high-qualification industries than it lost in its low-qualification industries, contributing to that city's overall employment growth. St Louis lost 94,000 low-qualification industry jobs and remained constant in the high category, while Baltimore lost 74,000 from the low category and added 10,000 jobs to the high-qualification industry.

To analyse changes in industrial jobs in German cities by the qualifications of the employed, industries were classified according to the years of schooling into 'low' (average education of jobholders less than ten

Table 11.5 *US central-city employment in industries, by educational qualifications, 1970–83*

City	1970 Absolute	%	1983 Absolute	%	Change 1970–83 Absolute	%
Baltimore						
Low	187	50	113	40	− 74	− 39
High	90	24	100	36	10	11
Boston						
Low	168	36	124	26	− 44	− 26
High	185	40	252	52	67	36
New York						
Low	1,445	43	936	33	− 509	− 35
High	1,002	30	1,206	42	204	20
Philadelphia						
Low	396	51	221	37	− 175	− 44
High	205	27	250	42	45	22
St Louis						
Low	198	53	104	42	− 94	− 47
High	98	26	98	39	0	0

Source: US Bureau of the Census, *County Business Patterns*, 1970 and 1983; US Bureau of the Census, 1982 Current Population Survey (machine-readable file)

years), 'medium' (ten to twelve years) and 'high' (thirteen or more years). Table 11.6 provides the job changes in the low and high categories for the 1980–4 period. As with large cities in the US, there was an overall decline in jobs requiring low qualifications, and a rise in jobs with high qualifications. Moreover, the increase in high-qualification jobs was not sufficient to compensate for the decrease of jobs needing only low qualifications. In fact, between 1980 and 1984, the majority of German cities lost at least three jobs in their low-qualification industries for each job added in their high-qualification industries.

As Table 11.6 shows, the large German cities on the whole exhibit transforming economic structures requiring higher employment qualifications than the nation: 25.4 per cent low qualifications compared with 29.7 per cent, and 9.5 per cent high compared with 6.8 per cent having high qualifications (1984). Cities with a large share of employment in manufacturing in 1980 (Duisburg, Saarbrücken) have lost more low-qualification jobs than the other cities, which perhaps is due to the fact that they had more such jobs to lose. Even in 1984, two mining and steel cities, Duisburg and Saarbrücken, still have a comparatively large percentage of jobs with low qualifications. The most 'advanced' cities with relatively large percentages of high-qualification jobs are Stuttgart,

Table 11.6 *Employment in Germany by qualification, 1980 and 1984*

City	1980 Absolute	%	1984 Absolute	%	Change 1980–4 Absolute	%
Bremen						
Low	58,830	23.4	51,619	22.3	−7,211	−12.3
High	17,571	7.0	19,782	8.6	2,211	12.6
Hamburg						
Low	173,520	22.6	151,855	21.2	−21,665	−12.5
High	61,970	8.1	70,447	9.8	8,477	9.8
Düsseldorf						
Low	83,371	24.4	75,043	22.8	−8,328	−10.0
High	31,647	9.3	35,196	10.7	3,549	11.2
Duisburg						
Low	74,449	33.5	56,975	29.7	−17,474	−23.5
High	10,913	4.9	11,801	6.2	888	8.1
Saarbrücken						
Low	29,479	29.1	25,672	27.1	−3,807	−12.9
High	7,319	7.2	7,798	8.2	479	6.5
Frankfurt						
Low	104,226	22.7	87,922	20.5	−16,304	−15.6
High	60,550	13.2	65,398	15.2	4,848	8.0
Stuttgart						
Low	97,839	26.9	85,331	24.3	−12,508	−12.8
High	40,264	11.1	44,692	12.7	4,428	11.0
Munich						
Low	175,983	26.6	152,527	24.0	−23,456	−13.3
High	76,116	11.5	83,222	13.1	7,106	9.3
67 cities						
Low	2,613,508	27.5	2,276,505	25.4	−337,003	−12.9
High	763,386	8.0	853,647	9.5	90,261	11.8
Germany						
Low	6,812,463	32.5	5,961,067	29.7	−851,396	−12.5
High	1,207,819	5.8	1,365,001	6.8	157,182	13.0

Note: Data refer to 30 June of respective year.

Source: Special analyses by the Federal Agency of Labor; Statistisches Bundesamt: Fachserie 1, Reihe 4.2, Sozialversicherungspflichtig beschäftigte Arbeitnehmer 1980 and 1984: authors' own calculations.

Munich and Frankfurt. In these cities, the percentage of employees in higher qualification industries is twice the figure for the country as a whole.

The requirement for higher educational qualifications in Germany no doubt will continue to grow. A recent projection to the year 2000 indicates that even under conditions of status quo, the share of jobs requiring only low qualifications will drop from 30 per cent in 1982 to 20 per cent in 2000, whereas jobs requiring high qualifications will increase their share from 8.5 per cent to 15 per cent over the same period (von Rothkirch and Tessaring 1986). These projections assume an economic growth rate of 2.5 per cent, with jobs in manufacturing further declining and jobs in offices, research and other information processing services continuing to increase.

Changing demographic compositions

A rather clear picture emerges from the above analysis. There have been substantial declines in employment in US and German urban industries that traditionally sustained large numbers of less-educated persons. The job losses have been partially replaced by growth in white-collar service industries with substantially higher educational requirements. This has implications for the expansion in these cities of population groups whose typical educational backgrounds place them at a serious disadvantage as the economies of these cities transform.

Table 11.7 summarises the racial and ethnic compositional changes between 1970 and 1980 within the four largest northern US cities (New York City, Chicago, Philadelphia and Detroit). New York City, which experienced an overall population decline of over 823,000 during the decade, actually lost 1,393,000 non-Hispanic whites. Approximately 40 per cent of the loss of non-Hispanic whites in New York City were replaced by an infusion of over 570,000 Hispanics, blacks and other minorities during the 1970s.

Chicago's demographic experience during the 1970s was similar to New York City's. Approximately 50 per cent of Chicago's minority population increase during the decade consisted of Hispanics. However, it is important to point out that Chicago also gained more than 100,000 blacks between 1970 and 1980. By 1980, 57 per cent of Chicago's resident population was composed of minorities.

Philadelphia had the smallest aggregate population decline of the four cities. Philadelphia's decline in non-Hispanic whites, together with its net increase of 23,000 minority residents during the 1970s, raised its minority percentage to 43 per cent in 1980.

Detroit experienced the highest rate of non-Hispanic white residential decline of any major city in the country. Between 1970 and 1980, Detroit lost more than one half of its white residents while it added 102,000 blacks to its resident base. Combined with modest increases in both non-Hispanics and other minorities, Detroit's large increase in black residents and sharp drop in non-Hispanic white residents transformed the city's

Table 11.7 Total and minority populations of the four largest northern cities in the US, 1970–80

City	1970			1980			Change 1970–80		
	Total Absolute	Minority[a] Absolute	% Minority	Total Absolute	Minority[a] Absolute	% Minority	Total Absolute	Minority[a] Absolute	% Minority
New York	7,895	2,833	36	7,072	3,403	48	−823	570	20
Chicago	3,363	1,364	41	3,005	1,706	57	−358	342	25
Philadelphia	1,949	702	36	1,688	725	43	−261	23	3
Detroit	1,511	691	46	1,203	801	67	−308	110	16

Note: [a] Minority population is composed of non-Hispanic blacks, Hispanics and Asians

Source: US Bureau of the Census, 1970 and 1980 Census of Population (machine-readable files)

residential base from 46 per cent minority in 1970 to 67 per cent minority in 1980. (More detailed data on demographic change in these and other large US cities along with education completed is provided in Kasarda 1984 and 1985.)

Analogous demographic change figures for German cities are presented in Table 11.8. Most cities experienced a loss in German population, with Saarbrücken and Duisburg growing only through annexation. Total population losses in the majority of German cities would have been even greater had they not been compensated by the influx of foreign population.

Labour force shortages during the 1950s and 1960s led the German government to sign labour import agreements with a number of southern European countries, starting with Spain (1960), Greece (1960) and Turkey (1961), followed by Portugal (1964), Italy (1965) and, finally, Yugoslavia (1968). These foreign labourers were called 'guestworkers' since they were supposed to work in Germany for a limited time only and then 'route' back to their home countries. The number of foreign residents therefore increased from 170,000 in 1952 to 2,600,000 in 1973 and up to 4,363,600 in 1984. By 1984, the foreign population (33 per cent of whom were Turks) made up for 7.1 per cent of the entire population of Germany.

Foreign labour gravitated to large cities where blue-collar job opportunities had traditionally been the greatest. Thus, between 1970 and 1980, foreign proportions increased by over 110 per cent in the large cities. As may be observed in Table 11.8, cities such as Bremen, Hamburg, Duisburg and Saarbrücken grew by a much larger percentage.

The policy of rotation was clearly based upon economic rationality. However, it turned out that this rationality applied only to Germany as a space economy and not to foreign labourers as human beings. For them, recession conditions in Germany proved more attractive than the best of economic times in their native countries (this pertains in particular to the Turks). Despite rising anti-guestworker prejudice in the German population, the social-political climate made expulsion virtually impossible when Germany's economy slowed in the early 1970s. On the contrary, a policy to unite families of foreign labourers in Germany was implemented, resulting in a doubling or more of the foreign population in many large cities. The idea that foreigners are 'rotating guests' is no longer pertinent. They have, for all intents and purposes, become immigrants. Even the 1983–4 federal programme to promote returns to home countries by a 'return subsidy' of 10,000 DM and a refund of workers' social security payments have resulted only in 13,600 agreed return subsidies and 114,000 agreed refundings, with an estimated total of 300,000 guest-

Table 11.8 Demographic change in Germany by ethnicity, 1970–84

City	1970			1980			1984			1970–80		1980–4	
	Total Absolute	Foreign Absolute	Foreign %	Total Absolute	Foreign Absolute	Foreign %	Total Absolute	Foreign Absolute	Foreign %	Total % change	Foreign % change	Total % change	Foreign % change
Bremen	582,277	12,798	2.2	555,118	35,796	6.4	530,520	33,849	6.4	-4.7	179.7	-4.4	-5.4
Hamburg	1,793,823	59,196	3.3	1,645,095	147,964	9.0	1,592,447	152,777	9.6	-8.3	150.0	-3.2	-3.3
Düsseldorf	663,586	45,743	6.9	590,479	72,517	12.3	565,843	72,295	12.8	-11.0	58.5	-4.2	-0.2
Duisburg[a]	454,839	22,105	4.9	558,089	68,242	12.2	522,829	60,785	11.6	22.7	208.7	-6.3	-10.9
Saarbrücken[a]	127,989	5,602	4.4	193,554	14,742	7.6	188,763	13,598	7.2	51.2	163.2	-2.5	-7.8
Frankfurt	669,625	70,555	10.5	629,375	128,765	20.5	599,634	128,421	21.4	-6.0	82.5	-4.7	-0.3
Stuttgart	633,158	77,394	12.2	580,648	102,959	17.7	561,567	99,042	17.6	-8.3	33.0	-3.3	-3.8
Munich	1,293,590	123,398	9.5	1,298,941	213,108	16.4	1,267,451	202,718	16.0	0.4	72.7	-2.4	-4.9
67 cities	20,254,881	1,040,521	5.1	20,981,937	2,209,602	10.5	20,331,436	2,157,401	10.6	3.6	112.4	-3.1	-2.4
Germany	60,650,599	2,438,580	4.0	61,566,000[b]	4,453,300[c]	7.2	61,175,000	4,363,600	7.1	1.5	82.6	-0.6	-2.0

Note: [a] Major incorporations between 1970 and 1980
 [b] Annual average
 [c] Data refer to 30 September
Data refer to 27.5.1970, 31.12.1980, 31.12.1984

Source: Statistisches Jahrbuch deutscher Gemeinden, diverse vols.; personal communication from Statistical Agencies of Länder; Statistisches Jahrbuch der Bundesrepublik Deutschland 1983

workers (including their families) having left Germany. Over 4.3 million foreign 'guests' remained in the country.

Since 1985, the policy of the federal government no longer explicitly stresses the goal of return, but neither does it promote an active citizenship-integration strategy. For the most part, the responsibility for the welfare of foreign labour and their families rests upon the local administrations.

Consequences of demographic-employment mismatches

We argued that one major consequence of the expansion of low-skill minority populations in cities experiencing contractions in low-skill jobs is rising minority unemployment. Table 11.9 provides the unemployment rates for white and black males in the four US cities whose demographic changes were described in Table 11.7. Observe that, while unemployment rates for both whites and blacks increased between 1969 and 1982, the absolute racial gap in rates widened substantially over the period. In 1969, white–black differences were negligible for all cities but Philadelphia. By 1982, black unemployment rates exceeded white rates by 10 points or more. Moreover, all cities registered exceptionally high minority unemployment rates, ranging from 20 in New York City to 37 in Detroit. The precipitous rise in black unemployment in Detroit corresponds to that city's heavy losses in blue-collar jobs during the 1970s and early 1980s documented in Table 11.1.

Table 11.9 *Male unemployment rates (for ages sixteen to sixty-four) in selected US cities, 1969, 1977, 1982*

City	1969	1977	1982
New York			
White	2.0	9.3	8.8
Black	3.8	18.7	19.8
Philadelphia			
White	2.2	10.8	11.2
Black	8.2	16.5	21.7
Chicago			
White	2.2	6.5	9.2
Black	4.5	19.8	20.0
Detroit			
White	2.4	10.0	26.0
Black	1.7	19.7	37.3

Source: Current Population Survey 1969, 1977 and 1982 (machine-readable files)

Table 11.10 *Unemployment rates^a in Germany by ethnicity, 1970–84*

	Total			German			Foreign		
City	1970	1980	1984	1970	1980	1984	1970	1980	1984
Bremen	0.6	4.1	11.2	n/a	3.8	10.5	n/a	8.2	23.4
Hamburg	0.3	2.5	9.7	n/a	2.4	8.8	n/a	4.1	20.5
Düsseldorf	0.2	2.8	7.7	n/a	2.8	6.9	n/a	4.4	14.2
Duisburg	0.7	5.8	15.2	n/a	5.8	14.1	n/a	6.4	26.5
Saarbrücken	0.6	5.0	10.5	n/a	4.8	10.5	n/a	7.7	12.1
Frankfurt	0.2	1.4	4.1	n/a	1.4	3.6	n/a	1.9	7.3
Stuttgart	0.1	1.3	4.1	n/a	1.0	3.3	n/a	2.1	8.4
Munich	0.3	2.0	5.3	n/a	2.0	4.8	n/a	1.9	8.4
67 cities	1.4^b	3.2	8.8	n/a	3.1	8.3	n/a	4.5	14.1
Germany	0.5	3.6	9.5	n/a	3.5	9.1	n/a	4.5	16.5

Note: [a] Unemployment rate (Verleichsquote) = unemployed/employed + unemployed
[b] Fifteen missing values

Source: Bundesanstalt für Arbeit: Strukturdaten für die Dienststellen; special analyses; ANBA 8/1980, 11/1980, 11/1984

Table 11.10 shows similar rises in urban minority (foreign) unemployment in Germany between 1980 and 1984. In 1980, Duisburg, Saarbrücken and Bremen had unemployment rates above the national average, reflecting contractions of their traditional goods processing industries. Unemployment in these three cities rose rapidly between 1980 and 1984, as it did in Hamburg. What is especially noteworthy in Table 11.10 is the disproportional increases in unemployment rates among foreign labour, with a number of these cities (e.g. Duisburg, Hamburg and Bremen) exhibiting foreign resident rates comparable to the exceptionally high rates for blacks in US cities. Likewise, the absolute gap in unemployment rates between German and foreign labour rose sharply in all German cities. By 1984, unemployment rates of foreign labour were at least three times those of German labour in all cities described.

Interestingly, a few cities with a high percentage of foreign population have somewhat lower unemployment rates (Frankfurt, Stuttgart, Munich), despite the fact that foreign labour has relatively low qualifications. To account for this finding, three suggestions are offered. First, foreign labour is more mobile than German labour and more willing to migrate to regions were there are more jobs – even if these are low-paid jobs. Third, the differences in foreign labour unemployment rates reflect differences in the ethnic composition of the cities' foreign labour force. The Turks, making up for about one third of the foreign labour force in all cities, account for only 20 per cent of foreign labour in Frankfurt,

Table 11.11 *Welfare assistance (AFDC) recipients per 1,000 residents in the US, 1970–80*

SMSA central county	1970	1980	Percentage change 1970–80
New York City (five boroughs)	98.60	107.78	9.3
Chicago (Cook)	49.42	90.58	83.2
Philadelphia (Philadelphia)	84.82	158.69	73.87
Detroit (Wayne)	43.93	123.79	181.79
Cleveland (Cuyahoga)	44.04	69.74	58.36
Boston (Suffolk)	109.25	136.74	25.16
St Louis City	87.46	143.24	63.78
Milwaukee (Milwaukee)	34.54	80.73	133.73
Baltimore City	102.87	168.15	63.46
Pittsburgh (Allegheny)	39.86	52.62	32.01
Newark (Essex)	n/a	136.29	-
Minneapolis/St Paul (Hennepin and Ramsey)	31.68	43.96	38.76

Source: US Bureau of the Census, *State and Metropolitan Data Book*, 1970 and 1980

Stuttgart and Munich. Turks tend to have lower qualifications and, since they are not members of the European Community, they have more difficulties obtaining employment than foreign labour from the European Community, e.g. Italians. Moreover, social acceptance of Turks is lower than those of other minorities, increasing the probability that they will be discriminated against. In this regard, Turkish guestworkers have been characterised as 'the blacks of West Germany' (Hoffmeyer-Zlotnik 1982).

Another consequence of the growing demographic-employment mismatch in US and German cities is the rise in urban welfare expenditures. Table 11.11 documents the growth between 1970 and 1980 in persons residing in twelve of the largest northern cities (or central metropolitan counties) who received 'Aid for Families with Dependent Children' subsidies. During the decade, AFDC assistance rates increased by more than 50 per cent in Baltimore, Cleveland and St Louis; by more than 70 per cent in Chicago and Philadelphia; and by well over 100 per cent in Detroit and Milwaukee. By 1980, more than one out of every ten persons residing in New York, Philadelphia, Detroit, Boston, St Louis, Baltimore and Newark were being supported by this public assistance programme. Corresponding welfare assistance figures for the period of 1972 to 1982 are provided in Table 11.12 for the eight large German cities in our study. As in the United States, there is general expansion of welfare assistance with some differences in relative scope across cities. Typically, cities with high unemployment rates have high percentages of persons on public assistance. However, there are exceptions which are due to local differ-

Table 11.12 *Welfare recipiency rates (per 1,000 residents) in Germany by ethnicity, 1972 and 1982*

City	Total 1972	Total 1982	German 1982	Foreign 1982
Bremen	n/a	84.2	81.6	118.7
Hamburg	39.7	66.6	62.6	104.3
Düsseldorf	32.5	59.5	61.5	46.5
Duisburg	40.5	56.6	62.2	19.4
Saarbrücken[a]	34.6	42.3	44.3	19.2
Frankfurt	29.3	59.2	63.9	41.8
Stuttgart	27.9	41.4	43.0	34.0
Munich	22.5	29.7	27.8	39.9
67 cities[b]	n/a	50.2	49.3	64.9
Germany	24.4	37.6	n/a	n/a

Note: [a] 1982 data refer to 1980
[b] Six missing values

Source: Statistisches Jahrbuch deutscher Gemeinden, diverse vols.; Statistisches Jahrbuch der Bundesrepublik Deutschland, diverse vols.

ences in the implementation of public assistance programmes. Except for Munich, rates are above the national average in both 1972 (24) and 1982 (37.6). The rank order of the cities of public assistance rates has remained unchanged in the ten years under study, but the differentiation between the cities increased, with Bremen having the highest, and Munich the lowest rate. Note also the exceptionally high percentage increases in welfare recipiency rates in Bremen, Hamburg, Düsseldorf and Frankfurt.

Because of the increase in persons on welfare, expenditures of German cities for public assistance rose considerably after 1980. By 1984, some of the most distressed cities, such as Bremen where 8.5 per cent of the total population received public assistance, had to spend a large share of their municipal budget for welfare, limiting their investment in urban public infrastructure and other basic urban services.

Summary and commentary

Comparing the transformation of selected US and German cities revealed striking parallels. First, the number of blue-collar jobs has been steadily declining. These jobs have been partially replaced by service sector jobs. We thus observed a widespread rise in educational qualifications required for employment in the urban economies of both countries.

Second, the minority populations of large US and German cities increased substantially since 1970. Government programmes to stem immigration to Germany and entice foreign labour to return to their home countries have had only a small impact. In the US, minority concentrations continue to increase in the cities, despite overall city population decline and entry level job losses.

The seemingly dysfunctional growth of underprivileged populations in US and German cities, at a time when these cities are experiencing serious contractions in lower-skill jobs, raises two interrelated questions: What is it that continues to attract and hold underprivileged persons in inner-city areas of distress? How are the underprivileged able to stay economically afloat?

Answers to these questions may be found in the dramatic rise of two alternative economies that increasingly dominate the livelihood of the urban disadvantaged: the *welfare economy* and the *underground economy* (illegal activities and unreported cash and barter transactions). These alternative economies have mushroomed in cities, functioning as institutionalised surrogates for the declining goods-producing economies that once attracted and sustained large numbers of disadvantaged residents.

Yet, while the expanding goods-producing economies of the urban past provided substantial numbers of the disadvantaged with a means of entry into the mainstream economy as well as with opportunities for mobility, today's urban welfare and underground economies often have the opposite effects – limiting options and reinforcing the urban con-centration of those without access to the economic mainstream. Many urban welfare services, for example, have been disproportionately con-centrated to inner-city areas of greatest distress. Dependent on place-oriented public housing, nutritional assistance, health care, income main-tenance and other such programmes, large numbers of urban minorities have become anchored in areas of severe employment decline (for documentation, see Kasarda 1985). Racial discrimination and insuffi-cient low-cost housing in outlying areas of employment growth further obstruct mobility and job acquisition by the disadvantaged, as do deficiencies in their technical and interpersonal skills so necessary to obtain and hold jobs. The upshot is that increasing numbers of potentially productive persons find themselves socially, economically and spatially isolated in segregated areas of decline, where they subsist on a combination of government handouts and their own informal economies. Such isolation, dependency and blocked mobility breed hopelessness, despair and alienation which, in turn, foster drug abuse, family dissolution and other social malaise disproportionately afflicting the urban disadvantaged.

Implications of demographic and industrial restructuring

Conflicting demographic and industrial transformations in large cities in the US and Germany have a number of implications that go beyond those noted above. We will briefly comment on each.

Inequality and discrimination

Increasing demographic- employment mismatches and spatial isolation of low-income minorities have increased social differentiation. In Germany, this is a reversal of an urban trend following World War II when a growing middle class evolved. For the first time in German history, only a small percentage of the population was in the very low and in the very high income – or social status – bracket. The impact of the present differentiation and the formation of a new urban underclass in Germany remains to be analysed. Yet, it is clear that the relative deprivation of those who cannot participate in transforming urban economies will result in growing frustrations. This, in turn, leads to feelings of resentment, which may be channelled – or 'scapegoated' – by unemployed Germans towards minorities whom they perceive as exacerbating the scarcity of blue-collar jobs. It is, therefore, not surprising to find an increase in discrimination manifesting itself in Germany (and in other western European countries undergoing industrial restructuring).

Distrust in political programmes

Continuing high unemployment rates and rising relative deprivation of large numbers of urban residents have already led to numerous and controversial social programmes by local and national governments. Since those programmes have not coped sufficiently with the problems associated with structural transformation, the public has developed an opinion that none of the programmes work. Increasing public distrust in government programmes, combined with high rates of unemployment, persons on public assistance, and relative deprivation, could eventually lead to urban unrest in the US and Germany as has already occurred in Liverpool and in Brixton in the UK.

Trade unions

Urban structural transformation and increased international competition in goods production will have debilitating effects on unions. Employment growth in both the US and Germany is concentrated largely in service sector industries where unionisation is low and declining in goods producing industries where unionisation rates are higher. Since international competition is far greater in goods producing than service industries, the former industries will be under further pressure to introduce labour-saving technologies. At the same time, goods producing industries affected by increased foreign competition will continue to seek modifications in existing wage, work and hiring agreements under the threat of possible mass lay-offs or closures. With the tacit support of elected conservative governments, there may well be increasing public calls to abolish unions entirely and subject all production labour to market forces. In short, there seems little prospect for trade unions to play a significant role in economically upgrading today's urban disadvantaged in a manner that they did in an earlier industrial era. Unions, rather than opening options to new members, will be on the defensive, trying to protect the job security of the current membership.

Industrial subsidies

We have argued that a major cause of urban structural unemployment has been the decline in blue-collar jobs. To improve blue-collar employment prospects, two strategies have been implemented: subsidising existing 'old' industries (often accompanied by national import restrictions) and subsidising new industries. The former represents a holding strategy at best. The latter, such as attracting high technology, will require higher employee qualifications than the majority of the existing local blue-collar labour force can offer. Moreover, there are fewer high-technology companies available than needed for this strategy to have an impact. In Germany, for example, the transformation of urban economies has resulted in increased competition among German and other European cities to attract high-tech companies, preferably those in the micro-electronics industry. Unfortunately, in this competition, cities with the greatest employment losses have the fewest resources to entice the newer industries. In fact, social and fiscal problems associated with disproportionately high unemployment rates create negative externalities that tend to dissuade new businesses from locating in these cities.

Education, migration and opportunity

There is little doubt that as long as large numbers of lesser educated minorities remain concentrated in economically transforming cities, their employment prospects will not improve. Despite a variety of public policy efforts to slow the departure of blue-collar jobs from these cities, the exodus continues apace. Government subsidies, tax incentives, and regulatory relief contained in existing and proposed urban policies are not nearly sufficient to overcome technological and market-driven forces redistributing blue-collar jobs and shaping the economies of major US and German cities.

Those cities that are able to adapt to their emerging service sector roles should experience renewed vitality and net job increases in the years ahead. However, lacking appropriate skills for advanced service sector jobs, those on the bottom rungs of the socio-economic ladder are unlikely to benefit. Indeed, their employment options could further deteriorate.

The new stark reality of rising urban minority unemployment in transforming and possibly even growing city economies, together with the improbability of government programmes (or the private sector) stimulating sufficient blue-collar job generation in the cities, call for greater policy emphases on education and resident skill upgrading. There is also a need for greater appreciation of the instrumental role migration plays in reducing localised unemployment problems and resulting social overhead burdens.

To assist migration, revised policies should be considered that would partially underwrite more distant job searches and subsidise relocation expenses of the structurally disadvantaged. Among the displaced are older workers who should not be expected either to migrate or to embark on extensive retraining programmes. These, mainly elderly, blue-collar workers are the true victims of economic transformation. Their situation may be helped by subsidising earlier retirement (e.g. at the age of fifty-five). Additional policies must be aimed at increasing the supply of lower income housing in outlying areas of job growth and stricter enforcement of antidiscriminatory housing and hiring to enhance mobility options of urban minorities. Finally, existing public assistance programmes should be reviewed to ensure that they are not inadvertently bonding large numbers of disadvantaged persons to inner-city areas which offer limited opportunities for employment.

All of the above must be complemented by broader economic development policies fostering sustained private sector job generation. Retraining and/or relocation of disadvantaged urban minorities and fair hiring and housing practices will be of limited use unless new and enduring jobs are available at the end of the training programmes and/or moves.

Note

* This chapter refers to the position in West Germany before unification. Unless otherwise indicated, 'Germany' should be taken to mean the Federal Republic.
1 For a discussion of the data and methodology used to classify industries by educational qualifications, see Kasarda 1983.

12

The urban underclass and mismatch theory re-examined

Scholarship in the sixties stressed the ways in which American blacks maintained caste-like qualities in a class society. More recent diagnoses have argued for the declining significance of race, shifting attention away from the black population as a whole and toward its lowest stratum, which comprises an 'urban underclass'. According to these analyses, the underclass suffers from many problems, one of which is a 'skills mismatch' with the employment structure in an economy of declining manufacturing – and growing knowledge-based industries. An influential version of this underclass/mismatch diagnosis also claims that poor urban blacks are victims of the welfare state, whose programmes reduce incentives to work and to move from cities with high benefit levels but poor employment prospects. Depending on the politics of the analyst, quite divergent policy prescriptions may follow. All agree, however, on the relative unimportance of race-oriented programmes aimed specifically at combating discrimination.

It is time to take a careful look at how well the underclass/mismatch diagnosis holds up against a decade of accumulated evidence. In this chapter I first examine the concept of the urban black underclass and show that the black poor are sinking economically, while the black middle class is not rising; in fact, the weight of evidence points to the strength of racial differences at every income level. Next, I argue that as an explanation for the economic disadvantages of lower-income blacks, the mismatch diagnosis is inadequate and misleading. Urban blacks are not particularly dependent on a declining manufacturing sector; rather, they suffer from segmentation into low-wage employment in growth industries. In the final section, I suggest that the economic problems of blacks stem at least as much from the 'ghettoisation of employment' as from human capital shortfalls and that ghettoisation is mainly a product of racial discrimination. In contrast to the underclass/mismatch diagnosis, this explanation in terms of employment segmentation and racial segregation stresses the continuing disadvantages suffered across the black class structure – albeit in a variety of forms – and thereby the continuing significance of race.

The underlass/mismatch diagnosis

There is no necessary linkage between the concepts of (a) an urban black underclass increasingly pathological and separated from the rest of the black population and (b) a mismatch between job requirements and urban lower class education or skills. Indeed, mismatch arguments are not always racially specific and, when they are, they often talk about the urban black population as a whole. Similarly, the identification of a black underclass may place little emphasis on opportunity structures as the main causal agent, instead putting the blame on cultural or psychological factors (for example, Banfield's definition of the lower class (1968)). Perhaps because most blacks are urban and because urban problems are still so closely identified with blacks, a marriage of convenience between the hypotheses has been effected. The two sets of ideas are so commonly intertwined that it is not unreasonable to view them as a single diagnosis. Thus, Glenn Loury, a Harvard economist, recently advanced the underclass/mismatch diagnosis in a widely read column on the 'Economic Scene' in *The New York Times*:

> A history of racism and discrimination has helped to create an inner-city underclass that, because of economic and technological developments in American society at large, has become much more difficult to integrate into the economic mainstream than the urban poor of previous years.
>
> For blacks with job skills or a high level of educational attainment, many if not all of the historic barriers to achieving parity with whites have been removed. For those blacks who remain poorly educated and trapped in urban ghettoes, however, enormous problems remain. This distinction, between the economic positions of the black middle class and the black underclass, has great importance for the formulation of public policy.
>
> (Loury 1985: D2)

In the latest versions of their many scholarly articles on, respectively, the underclass and mismatch phenomena William Julius Wilson (1985: 129–69) and John Kasarda (1985: 33–68) share Loury's diagnosis of the economic causes of black poverty. Indeed, Wilson and Kasarda have arguably become the two leading academic proponents – at least among sociologists – of 'the new urban reality' which the Brookings Institution identifies in a book of that name (Peterson 1985). An assessment of this interpretation of black reality requires us to disentangle the overall diagnosis into its components, to unpack the claims of each concept and see how well they fit the available evidence. In doing so, I shall rely heavily on the work of Wilson and Kasarda, evaluate their evidence, and bring my own to bear.

The urban black underclass

During the last decade, Wilson has developed and refined his thesis of a bifurcated black class structure and of an increasingly isolated and pathological underclass. Looking back over the first three-quarters of the century, he concludes in his important and controversial book (1978: 152) – *The Declining Significance of Race* – that 'a deepening economic schism seems to be developing in the black community, with the black poor falling further and further behind middle- and upper-income blacks.' These 'talented and educated blacks' are experiencing rapid upward mobility, 'opportunities that are at least comparable to those of the whites with equivalent qualifications' (p. 151). In contrast, 'poorly trained and educationally limited blacks of the inner city' fall behind, unable to compete economically and are increasingly unemployed or relegated to low-wage jobs. The problem is particularly acute for young black males, some of whom turn to crime, and for young females who have children out of wedlock. These individuals at the bottom of the class structure, 'about one-third of the entire black population' (p. 154), constitute the black underclass. Its members have more in common with similarly situated whites than with blacks of the higher classes (Wilson 1987).

After documenting sharply increasing rates of black crime and of families headed by a female, along with black joblessness, Wilson (1985: 133) stresses the importance of differentiating the urban black population along class lines:

> Although these problems are concentrated in urban areas, it would be a serious mistake to assume that they afflict all seg-ments of the urban minority community. Rather, (they) dis-proportionately plague the urban underclass – that hetero-geneous grouping of inner-city families who are outside the mainstream of the American occupational system. Included in this population are persons who lack training and skills and either experience long-term unemployment or have dropped out

of the labor force altogether; who are long-term public assistance recipients; and who are engaged in street criminal activity and other forms of aberrant behavior.

Leaving aside 'criminal activity and other forms of aberrant behavior', I would like to assess this picture of black social stratification. One way to do so is to see whether differences among blacks are growing more important than differences between blacks and whites. We should also look for discontinuities between worse-off blacks and those with better education, jobs and incomes. Indicators germane to this analysis are provided by data about (1) household composition and welfare dependency, (2) employment, (3) education, and (4) occupation and income.

Family structure and welfare dependency

Lower-income blacks suffer from a litany of interrelated problems. Some part of this population is undoubtedly locked in a syndrome of welfare dependency, female-headed families, more or less permanent withdrawal from legal employment, and, of course, poverty. To the extent that this core group is reproduced intergenerationally, it constitutes a permanently marginal stratum. In this sense, Wilson is correct in calling it an underclass. The analytic problem lies, however, in distinguishing this underclass from a lower-income population which comprises considerably more than half of all blacks. To complicate matters further, disaggregating the concept of an underclass into component dimensions shows that generalisations about a single 'type' may be misleading.

Wilson links welfare dependency (and the even stronger concept of permanency) with the sharp increase in the proportion of black families headed by a female. The connection is important for his concept of a marginalised underclass, since he rejects the notion that a matriarchal family as such is pathological, particularly where the female head participates in the labour force (a point with which I strongly concur):

> The problem for female-headed families is not simply the absence of fathers. There is considerable research documenting the important role of the extended family pattern ... in rearing and socializing black children. The problem is that an overwhelming number of these families are impoverished. Given the fact that most of [them] are more-or-less permanent recipients of welfare ... the odds are extremely high that the children in these families will be trapped in welfare.
>
> (Wilson 1982: 123; see also Wilson 1984: 84–90)

Table 12.1 *Proportion of families at selected income levels by head of household in the US, 1978*

	All families at level	Families at level with female heads	All families at level in metropolitan areas	Metropolitan families at level with female heads
Black				
Under $4,000	15.9	80.3	70.7	85.1
$4,000–$6,999	16.2	63.8	70.1	71.2
$7,000–$10,999	18.3	46.2	74.8	50.7
$11,000–$15,999	16.7	28.9	76.3	31.8
$16,000–$24,999	19.2	15.3	82.7	15.4
$25,000 and over	13.4	7.7	88.5	7.6
White				
Under $4,000	4.3	42.2	52.4	51.0
$4,000–$6,999	4.7	27.6	56.2	33.7
$7,000–$10,999	12.7	19.5	57.7	21.8
$11,000–$15,999	16.9	13.4	59.9	16.7
$16,000–$24,999	28.8	7.2	66.0	8.5
$25,000 and over	29.5	2.9	75.4	3.1

Source: Wilson (1985: 140)

There has been an enormous expansion in the proportion of female-headed families among the black population. In part, this is a somewhat ironic result of falling birthrates among all black women, but of much sharper declines among married women (28 per cent between 1970 and 1980) than among unmarried (13 per cent), and in part a result of a declining marriage rate among black women (Wilson and Neckerman 1985). Whatever the causes, the outcome was an increase between 1972 and 1980 of nearly 20 per cent in the number of black children living in female-headed families (Ellwood and Summers 1985: 27). Table 12.1 shows Wilson's data as of 1978, when about 39 per cent of all black families were female-headed, a sharp escalation from the 28 per cent figure of a decade earlier (Wilson 1985: 138). By 1983, 43 per cent of black families were female headed (Table 12.2).

Female-headed families, both black and white, have lower incomes than families with both husband and wife present, and the poorest black families are almost all headed by a female. Yet female-headed households are not necessarily poor. While a majority of black female-headed families were impoverished in 1983, a very large fraction were not. Of about 2.9 million black female-headed families, 1.7 million had income of $10,000 or less, a level comparable to the official government poverty line and equivalent to about 40 per cent of the median family income in 1983 (US

Table 12.2 *Proportion of families at selected income levels with female householder (no husband present) in the US, 1983*

	Black (%)	White (%)
Income of Family		
Under $5,000	81.9	46.0
$5,000–$12,499	57.0	25.2
$12,500–$19,999	39.2	16.9
$20,000–$24,999	25.9	10.3
$25,000 and over	14.0	5.2
All families	43.0	12.6

Source: US Bureau of the Census 1985b: Table 23

Bureau of the Census 1985b: Table 23). By this definition, 41 per cent of female-headed black families were not poor. Wilson interprets the 1978 data (as reproduced in Table 12.1) to emphasise the concentration of female-headed families among low-income blacks (evidence for his under-class diagnosis), but his figures also show rather high proportions of female-headed households at levels above $7,000 (an amount close to the 1978 poverty line). Moreover, by 1983, female-headedness had become much less associated with poverty. Almost 40 per cent of black families with income in the $12,500–$19,999 range were headed by a female (Table 12.2). These families fell into the middle quintile of the black income distribution, not the underclass.

Both Wilson's evidence and my own also show the pervasive and growing importance of inter-racial differences. Although his discussion emphasises variations among black families, his data (Table 12.1) indicate that the proportion of black families with female heads is about twice that of whites at every income level. By 1983 the inter-racial gap had grown larger, except for the very poorest group. Thus, the middle-quintile black rate of 39.2 per cent was 2.3 times the white rate at the same income level, and this ratio increased to almost three to one for families above $25,000 (Table 12.2). In conclusion, evidence about household composition pro-vides scant support for the notion that black female-headed households are limited to an underclass; it points instead to increasing racial differences.

Facts about welfare dependency raise equally troublesome questions for the underclass diagnosis. We know that a very high proportion of the poorest black families with female heads are on welfare and that about half of all families in the biggest programme – 'Aid to Families with Dependent Children' (AFDC) – are black, even though blacks constitute only about one-ninth of the general population. But the claim of a largely permanent, welfare-dependent population appears to be unfounded. Longitudinal studies have shown that fewer than half of welfare families use benefits continuously for long time periods; a majority move regularly on and off the rolls into the labour market; and the children of 'welfare' households are only little more likely to use welfare than children with comparable backgrounds who were never enrolled (Duncan 1984). If the underclass were really coterminous with permanently welfare dependent families (and with an equivalent number of males receiving no government support), it would be much smaller than Wilson's estimate of one-third of the black population.

Labour force participation and unemployment

Employment data for blacks present a picture of uneven decline. Teenagers and young adults have increasingly poor employment records in comparison to whites. Wilson may be correct in suggesting that many unemployed young black males will never be incorporated in the labour market, and instead fall into the demi-monde of the underclass. But the situation is different for females (who are commonly ignored in these discussions): they have higher labour force participation rates than whites once they reach adult status. Moreover, black/white differences in employment cut across the class structure and are growing.

Labour force participation rates indicate the proportion of the civilian, non-institutional population aged sixteen and over which is either employed or seeking employment. Table 12.3 shows that male participation rates have declined among both black and white adults, with black

Table 12.3 *Civilian labour force participation rates for the US, 1972–85*

	Males of twenty and older		Females of twenty and older		Males of sixteen to nineteen		Females of sixteen to nineteen	
	White	Black	White	Black	White	Black	White	Black
1972	82	79	43	51	60	46	48	32
1975	81	76	45	51	62	43	52	34
1978	80	76	49	56	65	45	57	37
1981	80	75	52	56	62	42	55	34
1984	79	75	53	58	59	42	55	34
May 1985[a]	79	74	54	59	–	–	–	–

[a]Not seasonally adjusted
Source: Economic Report of the President, February 1985, Table B34; Bureau of Labor Statistics, *Employment and Earnings*, June 1985: 31

Table 12.4 *Civilian unemployment rates in the US, 1972–85*

	Males of twenty and older		Females of twenty and older		Males of sixteen to nineteen		Females of sixteen to nineteen	
	White	Black[a]	White	Black[a]	White	Black[a]	White	Black[a]
1965	3	6	4	7	–	–	–	–
1972	4	7	5	9	14	32	14	41
1975	6	13	8	12	18	38	17	41
1978	4	9	5	11	14	37	14	41
1981	6	14	6	13	18	41	17	42
1984	6	14	6	14	17	43	15	43
May 1985[b]	5	13	6	13	17	40	17	40

[a]Blacks and other races
[b]Seasonally unadjusted estimate
Source: *Economic Report of the President*, February 1985, Table B34; Bureau of Labor Statistics, *Employment and Earnings*, June 1985: 31, Bureau of the Census, *Current Population Reports*, Series P–23, No. 80 (1979)

adult participation 3 to 5 points below white. For male teenagers, the inter-racial gap was large in 1972 and grew bigger in the next decade, amounting to about 20 points by the early eighties. Recent evidence points, moreover, to the extension of the teenage participation gap into the twenty to twenty-four year-old cohort. For this group, the inter-racial difference in labour force participation rates stood at 8 or 9 points in 1983 (Wilson 1985: 154). Black adult females, in contrast to males, have exhibited consistently higher participation rates than their white counterparts. But black female teenagers have increasingly fallen behind whites, largely because of increased participation rates for the latter.

The unemployment rate – the proportion of the work-age population actively seeking employment – has been substantially higher among blacks than whites regardless of gender or age cohort, with inter-racial differences most extreme among teenagers (Table 12.4). The inter-racial gap among adults of about 3 points in the mid-sixties grew to 7 or 8 points by 1985. The exceptionally high figures among black teenagers increased during the seventies for males. White teenage unemployment rates did not change at all (a point to be noted, given the restructuring of the economy during these years). By 1985, 40 per cent of black teenagers were unemployed, compared to 17 per cent of whites.

Employment to population ratios show us the proportion of the population of employment age that is actually working. They are sensitive to both non-participation rates and unemployment rates, and may reflect cyclical economic trends as well as structural ones. Table 12.5 reduces the

Table 12.5 *Civilian employment to population ratios by age cohort in the US, 1972–82*

	Males						Females					
	18–19		29–24		25–34		18–19		20–24		25–34	
	Black	White	Black	White	Black	White	Black	White	Black	White	Black	White
1972–4[a]	44.8	64.2	71.0	79.0	85.7	93.0	28.3	51.8	47.3	56.9	56.0	46.0
1975–7[a]	36.1	62.5	60.5	76.6	79.9	90.5	26.3	52.5	43.6	59.7	57.2	51.9
1978–80[a]	38.6	65.3	62.9	79.7	80.8	91.7	28.9	56.9	47.5	64.4	61.8	59.3
1981–2[a]	31.3	58.9	56.1	74.5	73.7	88.6	24.4	53.8	43.6	64.5	58.7	62.3

[a]The figures given are averages for the periods
Source: US Bureau of Labor Statistics, *Handbook of Labor Statistics* (December 1983): Table 15

cyclical effect by using two- and three-year averages. When viewed in conjunction with Table 12.3, it confirms the inference that the growing employment gap between black and white male teenagers is 'spreading' upward into the young adult population, but that extreme racial differences in non-employment among women have remained confined to the youngest age cohorts.

So far I have shown the importance of inter-racial differences in employment, especially among teenagers. Essential to evaluation of the underclass diagnosis is comparison of these inter-racial differences with differences among blacks at various class levels. Both Wilson and Kasarda present evidence directly germane to this issue. Table 12.6, columns (1)–(3), is used by Wilson (1985: 156) as evidence of a black underclass:

> Increasing joblessness during youth is a problem primarily experienced by lower-income blacks – those already in or near the underclass. To illustrate this fact [Table 12.6] provides data on unemployed teenagers living at home. Of the unemployed teenagers living at home in 1977, 67 per cent were from families with incomes below $10,000. And among those unemployed teenagers living at home and not enrolled in school, 75 per cent were from families with less than $10,000 income and 41 per cent from families with less than $5,000.

There are several problems with Wilson's interpretation of this evidence as support for the underclass diagnosis. First, any inference must be about lower-income blacks, since the categories do not identify behavioural or other attributes which might define an underclass. For this reason, Wilson refers to 'those already in or near the underclass'. This formulation begs the question altogether. Because many blacks have low incomes relative to whites, a large proportion of blacks is bound to be 'near' the underclass. But if the term is not to mean simply being hard-up economically, then its user must specify a boundary between the underclass population and the lower-income population. This Wilson cannot do. Second, a large proportion of unemployed youths lived in families which were not poor in 1977. At that time, the official poverty line for a family of four was $6,191 (US Bureau of the Census 1985a: Table 758). Even if we add half of the unemployed youths in the $5,000 to $9,999 category to the 32.1 per cent under $5,000, we can account for less than 50 per cent of unemployed black teenagers. In other words, more than 50 per cent lived in non-poor families in 1977.

Third, merely showing the distribution of unemployed teenagers across income categories cannot demonstrate that teenage joblessness is

Table 12.6 *Unemployment of blacks aged sixteen to nineteen living at home, 1977*

		Unemployed youth		
	Total (1)	Enrolled in school (2)	Not in school (3)	Distribution of all black families (4)
Family income				
Under $5,000	32.1	23.6	41.0	24.0
$5,000–$9,999	34.7	35.7	33.6	28.2
$10,000–$14,999	16.8	20.0	13.4	17.9
$15,000–$24,999	12.0	15.0	9.0	20.9
$25,000 or more	4.4	5.7	3.0	9.0
Total	100.0	100.0	100.0	100.0

Source: Wilson (1985); col. (4): *Current Population Reports*, Series P–60, No. 146 (1985), Table 14

'primarily experienced' by lower-income blacks, except in the trivial sense that more of them are unemployed than upper-income blacks. After all, a much smaller proportion of upper-income black youth is likely to be in the labour market at all. Without being in the labour market, they cannot be unemployed. But an even more serious problem stems from the causal implication which Wilson attaches to the data. He wishes to suggest that unemployment is associated with attributes found primarily in lower-income black families, rather than in all black families, or in the treatment of all black youths by employers. In order to show this, he must at the least demonstrate that the incidence of unemployment is much higher among black youths from poor families than among those from better off families. The absence of an especially strong correlation would, in fact, come as a considerable surprise and undermine his argument for an underclass explanation of youth unemployment.

To examine the incidence of black youth unemployment by income stratum, we must compare the distribution of unemployed youths with the distribution of all youths. In the absence of data on the distribution of black youths by income in 1977, I have supplied figures for the distribution of black families by income in that year (column (4), Table 12.6). Because lower-income black families have more children than do upper-income families, the distribution of families instead of teenagers by income leads us to underestimate the proportion of all black teenagers in the lowest-income categories. Nonetheless, column (4) is quite revealing. It shows that while 68 per cent of unemployed black youths lived in families with incomes under $10,000, at least 52 per cent of all black youths did so as well; thus lower-income black youths were not disproportionately unemployed. In the next income category, $10,000–$14,000, all of whose families were above the black median income, the proportion of unemployed youths is virtually identical to the proportion of families (16.8 per cent versus 17.9 per cent). Indeed, the evidence from Table 12.6 points overall to a surprising uniformity of youth unemployment across the black family income distribution. Compared with the

Table 12.7 *Unemployment rates for central-city males aged sixteen to sixty-four in the US, 1969–82*

Region and schooling	White			Black		
	1969	1977	1982	1969	1977	1982
All regions						
Did not complete high school	4.3	12.2	17.7	6.6	19.8	29.7
Completed high school only	1.7	8.0	11.0	4.1	16.2	23.5
Attended college one year						
or more	1.6	4.7	4.4	3.7	10.7	16.1
All education levels	2.6	7.7	9.5	5.4	16.5	23.4
North-east						
Did not complete high school	3.7	13.9	17.2	7.6	20.9	26.2
Completed high school only	1.7	9.4	10.3	3.4	18.2	21.9
Attended college one year						
or more	1.4	6.0	4.8	7.1	13.9	18.6
All education levels	2.4	9.6	10.2	6.1	18.6	22.6
North central						
Did not complete high school	4.9	12.8	24.3	8.3	26.2	34.8
Completed high school only	1.1	8.0	14.5	3.3	18.0	35.8
Attended college one year						
or more	1.3	3.5	3.8	1.4	12.3	22.2
All education levels	2.6	7.6	12.2	6.0	20.6	32.0
South						
Did not complete high school	3.4	9.9	13.2	3.8	14.5	28.2
Completed high school only	0.8	5.9	6.8	3.6	13.5	16.6
Attended college one year						
or more	1.7	3.1	2.9	3.6	6.2	13.6
All education levels	2.0	5.7	6.4	3.7	12.6	19.9
West						
Did not complete high school	6.4	12.0	17.3	11.6	22.2	32.9
Completed high school only	4.2	8.6	13.4	9.6	17.7	15.9
Attended college one year						
or more	1.9	6.4	6.0	2.9	13.2	9.9
All education levels	3.9	8.2	10.1	8.3	17.0	16.5

Source: Kasarda (1985: 57)

enormous differences in unemployment between black and white youths, the 'class' variations among black youths are small.

Table 12.7 presents Kasarda's evidence on how education affected unemployment in the entire male population of central cities from 1969 to 1982. Like Wilson, he stresses variation within the black population to argue that better educated blacks fare much better than less well-educated blacks. For our purposes, we will presume that the underclass includes some, perhaps a large, fraction of high school dropouts, but few grad- uates and none of those who attended college. The data show that there has indeed been considerable variation between black 'class' categories in unemployment rates. More interesting, however, is a comparison of differences by education among blacks and whites. Variation among whites was considerably greater than among blacks in each period. In other words, 'class' mattered more for whites than for blacks – a finding contrary to the underclass diagnosis. For example, the national unemployment rate for white college attendees in 1982 (4.4 per cent) was 25 per cent of the rate for white high school dropouts; yet for blacks, the ratio was 54 per cent (16.1/29.7). Furthermore, comparison of the unemployment rates of black college attendees with white high school dropouts shows that well-educated blacks are hardly better off than poorly educated whites. In 1982, the 16.1 per cent national unemployment rate among black college attendees differed little from the 17.7 per cent rate for white high school dropouts. Kasarda's unpublished data (1983b: Table 9A) demonstrate, in fact, that among central city teenagers and young adults (aged sixteen to twenty-four), both male and female blacks with one or more years of college attendance had higher rates of unemployment nationally in 1982 than male and female whites who failed to complete high school.

Education

The post-war years have witnessed an extraordinary convergence in the educational attainment of blacks and whites, even as the education of the entire population increased sharply. Table 12.8 provides three indicators of educational attainment: median years of schooling, high school dropout rates and college graduation. Since sex differences prove to be relatively small, the table aggregates males and females. The first row shows that blacks and whites had nearly identical median years of schooling by 1983, 12.6 versus 12.2, and that more than half of blacks had graduated from high school. The gap closed from 2.9 years to 0.4 since 1960, largely because of improvements in black education. As a result, it is no longer possible to think of blacks as appreciably less educated than whites.

Table 12.8 *Racial differences in educational attainment for the population aged twenty-five and older (except as specified) in the US, 1960–83*

		1960	1970	1980	1983
1.	Median years of school completed				
	Black	8.0	9.8	12.0	12.2
	White	10.9	12.1	12.5	12.6
2.	Percentage with less than four years high school				
	Black	79.9	68.6	48.8	43.2
	White	56.9	45.4	31.2	26.2
3.	25–9 year olds				
	Black	62.3	44.6	24.8	20.6
	All	39.3	26.2	15.5	14.0
4.	Percentage of 18–21 year old high school dropouts				
	Black	30.5	23.0	19.5	
	White	14.3	14.7	14.4	
5.	Percentage with four years or more college				
	Black	3.1	4.4	8.4	9.5
	White	8.1	11.3	17.1	19.5
6.	25–9 year olds, four years or more college				
	Black	4.8	6.0	11.4	12.9
	All	11.1	16.3	22.1	22.5

Source: US Bureau of the Census 1985a: Tables 213, 214, 243

Despite evidence from some places pointing to an escalating black high-school dropout problem, national trends show otherwise. In 1960, about 80 per cent of blacks failed to complete high school; by 1983 the proportion was 43 per cent. The difference between black and white rates declined from 20 points to 17, at the same time as fewer whites dropped out of high school. These numbers are extraordinary for an entire population, which after all, includes many people who completed their formal education years ago. In fact, the convergence among young adults was much greater. For twenty-five to twenty-nine year olds, the difference in dropout rates between blacks and the general population moved from 23 points in 1960 to less than 7 points in 1983. The most recent post-high school cohort, eighteen to twenty-one year olds, shows identical trends. These data do not, of course, demonstrate that the black dropout problem is a thing of the past. A national rate of even 20 per cent is a serious problem. Moreover, reports of dropout rates exceeding 50 per cent in cities like New York (Tobier 1985: 94) suggest the aggregate figures may well mask important geographical variations. Nonetheless, it is simply impossible to reconcile national trends of decreasing high school dropout rates with the notion of increasing inequalities among blacks.

To the contrary, the variance in educational attainment among blacks seems to be declining. The educational bottom of the black population is converging toward the centre, while the top is not diverging nearly as rapidly as is the case for whites. For example, in 1960, 62 per cent of young blacks (twenty-five to twenty-nine year olds) had not completed high school, while 5 per cent were college graduates. In 1983, 21 per cent had not completed high school, while 13 per cent were college graduates. The decline in the high school dropout rate was 41 points, while the gain in the college graduate rate was 8 points. For the population as a whole during the same period, the decline in the dropout rate was 25 points, while the gain in college graduates was 11 points. A rapidly rising floor in black educational attainment had reduced educational inequality among blacks and brought the black median very near the white, even though blacks have made no progress since 1960 in closing the gap with whites in college graduates.

Moreover, current evidence indicates little likelihood of improvement in the near future. In 1983, 45.6 per cent of white high school graduates were enrolled in college, compared with 30.3 per cent of blacks (US Bureau of the Census 1985a: Table 254). And these percentage differences extended over the entire income distribution. Whatever the black high school dropout problem, the inter-racial gap in educational attainment, far from being mainly associated with the underclass bottom, is most striking at the better-off top.

Occupation and income

Wilson (1982: 123) sees increasing bifurcation among blacks in occupation and income. Economic growth in the post-war years and the migration of the southern, rural, black population 'to the industrial centers of the nation created job opportunities leading to greater occupational differentiation within the black community'. By the 1960s, government 'reversed itself' and attacked racial discrimination instead of supporting it. As a result, a large proportion of blacks experienced economic mobility.

> [But] recent structural shifts in the economy have diminished mobility opportunities for others. And whereas antidiscrimination legislation has removed many racial barriers, not all blacks are in a position to benefit from them. Indeed, the position of the black underclass has actually deteriorated during the very period in which the most sweeping antidiscrimination legislation and programs have been enacted and implemented. The net effect is a growing bifurcation between the haves and have nots in the black community.   (Wilson 1982: 124)

Leaving for later discussion on the causes of black economic performance, what can we say about Wilson's description? The evidence shows
that (1) Wilson exaggerates the bifurcation in the economic fortunes of
blacks, (2) income inequality among blacks did grow somewhat after
1975, but it increased among whites as well, (3) in this most recent period
the black middle class did not close the gap with whites either in income
or occupation, while lower-income blacks fell further behind their white
counterparts. The end result has been an overall deterioration in the
economic position of the black population, a more important development than the small increase in inequality among blacks.

Blacks at every class level made significant earnings and occupational
gains in relation to whites until the mid-seventies. Freeman (1981: Table
8.1) demonstrates that the black/white earnings ratio of male workers
improved steadily from 1959 through 1976. His analysis also compares
progress among blacks at different occupational levels. It shows that black/
white income ratios improved the most for those in professional occupations: 2.6 per cent annually between 1964 and 1975 (the decade after
passage of federal anti-discrimination legislation covering many areas of
employment). But the second greatest rate of improvement was among
labourers (1.7 per cent annually), and the next was among service workers
(1.3 per cent annually). By 1976, fully employed black males received 84 to
85 per cent of white male income in every occupation except managers and
craftsmen, where the ratios were, respectively, 0.72 and 0.78. At least until
1976, therefore, the evidence on earnings and incomes does not support the
assertion of increasing bifurcation within the black community. To the
contrary, blacks in low-status occupations did at least as much catching up
to whites as those in higher-status occupations and in two cases did better.

Earnings, however, do not tell the whole story. As we have seen,
inter-racial differences in employment mean that income trends among
population groups may differ substantially from trends in earnings
among employed workers. Historical evidence about the distribution of
income in the US shows a relatively unchanged curve in the post-war
period, a 'bell' with a long right tail extending to the extremely high
incomes of a small fraction of the population. Black and white distributions have both maintained this uni-modal shape, with inequality
among blacks consistently higher than among whites. Since the mid-
seventies, inequality among blacks has increased somewhat, though much
less than Wilson's language suggests. Moreover, the black distribution
has not become bifurcated. Instead, the income distribution has shifted a
few points in favour of the two upper quintiles, to the disadvantage of the
bottom three. There has been a similar marginal movement toward more
inequality in the white distribution (see Tables 12.9 and 12.10).

Table 12.9 *Income inequality within racial groups in the US, 1960–83*
(Percentage share of aggregate family income within racial groups)

	Lower-income families (poorest 40 per cent)		Upper-income families (best-off 20 per cent)	
	White	Black[a]	White	Black[a]
1983	16.7	12.4	42.0	46.8
1982	16.8	12.8	42.1	46.2
1981	17.1	13.4	41.2	45.1
1978	17.6	13.8	41.0	44.7
1975	17.8	14.8	40.7	43.3
1970	18.3	15.1	40.5	43.4
1965	18.2	15.5	40.3	43.2
1960	17.9	13.4	40.7	44.9

[a]Blacks and other races
Source: Bureau of the Census 1985b: Table 17

Table 12.10 *Aggregate income shares to quintiles of black[a] families in the US, 1974–83*

	(Poorest) First	Second	Third	Fourth	(Best off) Fifth
1983	3.6	8.8	15.6	25.3	46.8
1982	3.8	9.0	15.8	25.3	46.2
1981	4.0	9.4	16.0	25.5	45.1
1980	4.1	9.5	16.0	25.2	45.3
1979	4.1	9.5	15.9	25.3	45.2
1978	4.2	9.6	16.3	25.1	44.7
1977	4.4	9.6	15.9	25.2	44.9
1976	4.6	9.9	16.5	25.3	43.7
1975	4.7	10.1	16.7	25.1	43.3
1974	4.7	10.0	16.4	26.0	43.9

[a]Blacks and other races
Source: US Bureau of the Census 1985b: Table 17

Table 12.11 provides a set of income classes defined in constant (1983) dollars. Since median income dropped slightly for both races between 1970 and 1983, a distribution which remained fixed in shape would show slight declines in upper categories and increases in lower ones for both races. In fact, however, there is a more substantial shift of families in both races toward the lower income categories than would be predicted by the decline in median real income. Distributions across the middle categories show an erratic pattern, while there is growth in the percentage of black and white families above $35,000, with whites outdistancing blacks.

Table 12.11 *Distribution of families across income categories expressed in constant (1983) dollars in the US, 1970–83*

	Under $5,000	$5,000 to $9,999	$10,000 to $14,999	$15,000 to $19,999	$20,000 to $24,999	$25,000 to $34,999	$35,000 and over	Total	Median income
White									
1970	3.7	8.0	10.1	15.3	9.8	28.8	24.3	100.0	26,263
1975	3.2	8.7	10.9	11.6	12.3	27.8	25.5	100.0	26,412
1980	4.1	8.3	10.7	11.8	11.7	21.7	31.8	100.0	26,484
1982	4.5	8.9	11.7	11.9	12.3	20.3	30.5	100.0	25,394
1983	4.4	8.8	11.3	11.9	11.8	20.3	31.5	100.0	25,757
Black									
1970	11.3	18.3	17.0	16.6	9.2	18.3	9.4	100.0	16,111
1975	10.5	20.7	15.4	13.7	11.2	18.9	9.6	100.0	16,251
1980	13.7	20.1	15.5	12.5	10.1	14.0	14.1	100.0	15,324
1982	16.6	20.4	15.6	11.1	10.5	14.3	11.5	100.0	14,035
1983	16.2	20.4	14.7	11.8	9.7	14.0	13.2	100.0	14,506

Source: US Bureau of the Census 1985a: Table 742

Overall, therefore, these data are consistent with the previous tables. They show some increasing inequality within each race, with the main beneficiaries the very highest income group (almost a third of whites but less than one-seventh of blacks). The greater mobility of whites into the highest income class, combined with relatively larger shifts among blacks into the lowest categories, suggests, furthermore, that income inequality between the races must have increased.

Inter-racial economic inequality is, in fact, large and on the rise (Table 12.12). The aggregate picture shows that the ratio of black/white median family income stood at 0.56 in 1983, compared with 0.62 in 1975, the closest the gap has ever been. The median white family received $25,757, while the median black family received $14,506, an income level only slightly above the boundary of the lowest white quintile, $12,878. The best-off quintile of blacks, those with 1983 incomes above $29,100, stood in a position comparable to the middle quintile of whites, those above $30,255 (US Bureau of the Census 1985a: Table 745). Viewed within the context of the white income distribution, about 40 per cent of blacks are poor, 40 per cent working class, and the remainder middle- and upper-middle class.

The poor have got poorer relative to whites. In 1974 (the best year for the black poor), 8.6 per cent of white persons lived in poverty, according to the restrictive government definition, while 30.3 per cent of blacks were poor. In the next decade, the white poor increased 3.5 percentage points

Table 12.12 *Income inequality between black and white families in the US, 1960–83*

	1960	1965	1970	1975	1978	1981	1982	1983
Ratio between black[a] and white families of boundary incomes for respective quintiles of income distribution								
Fifth quintile (highest 20%)	0.67	0.66	0.73	0.75	0.76	0.75	0.73	0.75
Third quintile	0.59	0.60	0.68	0.69	0.69	0.67	0.68	0.67
Second quintile	0.50	0.54	0.60	0.61	0.59	0.57	0.56	0.56
First quintile (lowest 20%)	0.43	0.50	0.54	0.55	0.51	0.51	0.49	0.48
Ratio of black to white median family income	–	–	0.61	0.62	0.59	0.56	0.55	0.56[b]
Ratio of black to white median family income for two-earner families with head employed year round, full-time	–	–	0.78	0.84	–	0.87	0.85	0.84

[a]Blacks and other races
[b]$14,506 for black families and $25,757 for white families
Source: US Bureau of the Census 1985a: Tables 743, 745, and comparable tables 1981–4; Bureau of the Census 1985b: Table 17

to 12.1 per cent for 1983; the black poor increased 5.2 points, to 35.7 per cent in 1983. As of 1982, 44 per cent of blacks and 17 per cent of whites had incomes less than 125 per cent of the government poverty line (US Bureau of the Census 1985a: Tables 758 and 759). Data on income shares indicate that the poorest blacks are slipping further behind the poorest whites. The black/white ratio of family incomes which defined the first (lowest) quintile declined from 0.55 in 1975 to 0.48 in 1983, with a similar trend also evident in the second quintile (Table 12.12).

The relative income position of blacks at the middle and upper ends of the distribution has failed to improve (Table 12.12). The income level defining the third (middle) quintile of black families remained fixed at about 0.68 of the white level after 1970, while the ratio for the fifth (highest) quintile of families held constant at 0.75 after 1975. Even among black families with the best economic prospects – two-earner households with a fully employed, presumably male, head – relative economic disadvantage in 1983 was identical to the situation in 1975. On balance, then, the evidence indicates that inter-racial differences outweigh inequalities among blacks, that the so-called black middle class is very small when defined by income relative to whites, and that it has not improved its relative position in more than a decade.

Table 12.13 *Employed civilians by occupation in the US, 1985ᵃ*

	Men		Women	
	White	Black	White	Black
Total sixteen years and over (in thousands)	52,143	5,105	40,491	5,171
Managerial and professional speciality	26.4	12.4	24.7	16.8
Executive, administrative and managerial	14.2	6.7	9.7	6.2
Professional speciality	12.2	5.6	15.0	10.7
Technical, sales and administrative support	20.1	14.9	46.8	38.9
Technical and related support	2.9	2.0	3.1	3.8
Sales occupations	11.6	4.7	13.4	8.1
Administrative support, including clerical	5.6	8.3	30.3	26.9
Service occupations	8.5	20.7	16.6	29.2
Private household	ᵇ	0.1	1.6	5.6
Protective service	2.3	4.3	0.4	0.7
Service, except private household and protective	6.1	16.2	14.6	22.9
Precision production, craft and repair	21.1	14.6	2.3	2.5
Operators, fabricators and labourers	19.5	33.3	8.5	12.6
Machine operators, assemblers and inspectors	7.5	11.5	6.2	9.7
Transportation and material moving occupations	6.7	11.4	0.8	0.9
Handlers, equipment cleaners, helpers and labourers	5.3	10.4	1.4	2.0
Farming, forestry and fishing	4.4	4.1	1.2	0.1

ᵃMarch
ᵇLess than 0.05 per cent
Source: Bureau of Labor Statistics, *Employment and Earnings* April 1985: Table A–23

Occupation is, of course, the most proximate and powerful determinant of income level and class position. It should come as no surprise, therefore, that the rapid occupational gains of blacks during the sixties slowed greatly in the seventies. While the number of blacks in middle-class occupations continued to expand slowly (in this sense there was a growing black middle class), the increase was significantly greater for whites. Table 12.13 describes the occupational profile of the employed population as of early 1985, broken down by race and sex. On the whole, blacks are underrepresented in the higher-status occupations. The inter-racial gap is greatest among males in the managerial, professional group. It is also substantial in the sales category – an occupation type, it should be noted, with only middling educational requirements – but relatively small among women clericals, a very important white-collar occupation for black women. Blacks of both sexes are overrepresented among service workers and other blue-collar occupations.

Table 12.14 *Occupational distributions of individuals aged twenty-five to thirty-four in the US, 1973 and 1982*

	Young white males		Young white females	
	1973	1982	1973	1982
Professional, technical	19.6	20.8	22.1	24.7
Managers, administrators	13.5	20.3	4.3	8.3
Sales	6.5	6.7	5.3	5.9
Clerical	6.3	5.0	37.0	34.0
Crafts	22.8	21.8	1.4	2.3
Operatives except transport	12.4	8.2	12.2	7.2
Transportation operatives	6.0	52	0.6	0.7
Labourers except farm	4.8	3.3	0.8	1.1
Services, including private household	5.5	5.8	16.1	14.9
Farm labourers	2.5	2.9	1.2	0.9

	Young black males		Young black females	
	1973	1982	1973	1982
Professional, technical	9.4	12.0	15.0	17.5
Managers, administrators	5.0	6.3	2.5	3.8
Sales	2.3	3.3	2.0	2.8
Clerical	8.0	8.7	30.0	37.9
Crafts	17.2	17.9	1.6	1.5
Operatives except transport	20.5	16.1	18.2	13.7
Transportation operatives	10.6	8.1	0.4	1.1
Labourers except farm	12.8	10.8	1.6	1.3
Services, including private household	10.9	15.0	28.0	20.0
Farm labourers	3.1	1.8	0.7	0.4

Source: Stafford (1983: 18)

By singling out a cohort of younger black and white workers, Table 12.14 eliminates the inertial force of older workers. The table shows upward occupational mobility for both male and female young black workers. Black percentages in the four white-collar categories increased, with the biggest gain among women clerical workers, who constituted 38 per cent of young black women workers in 1982. A bit more than 18 per cent of young black males were in the professional/managerial occupations in 1982, compared with 14.5 per cent a decade earlier. But whites, and especially white males, experienced much greater occupational mobility. By 1982, more than 41 per cent of young white males held professional-managerial jobs. Whereas the increase among blacks was about 4 percentage points, it was 8 points among whites. Black women did better compared with white women. But even here the gap increased at the top. These data on occupational performance suggest that the relatively unchanged ratios in black to white incomes among the highest-income black families may actually deteriorate in coming years, since blacks are falling behind whites in the best-paid occupational categories.

In summary, the underclass diagnosis is inconsistent with the evidence we have reviewed. A concept which necessarily encompasses almost half of the black population is *prima facie* suspect. Beyond that, the facts do not support the idea of black bifurcation. The expanding black middle class barely exists. The central conundrum of American race relations is the economic gulf between blacks and whites at every class level. Thus, even broadening the definition of the problem to include lower-income blacks is not enough. For most blacks are 'lower-income' in white terms. What must be explained is the continuing economic significance of race.[1]

The cause of economic disadvantage for blacks: the mismatch diagnosis

Rejecting ongoing discrimination as a central explanation for the economic situation of the black underclass, Wilson turns instead to the mismatch diagnosis, a thesis which has long occupied 'a venerable place in the literature on black poverty' (Bailey and Waldinger 1984: 12). More than twenty years ago the Kerner Commission developed the identical argument:

> Since World War II, especially, America's urban-industrial society has matured; unskilled labor is far less essential than before, and blue-collar jobs of all kinds are decreasing in number and as a source of new employment. The Negroes who migrated to the great urban centers lacked the skills essential to the new economy; and the schools of the ghetto have been unable to provide the education that can qualify them for decent jobs. The Negro migrant, unlike the immigrant, found little opportunity in the city; he had arrived too late, and the unskilled labor he had to offer was no longer needed.
>
> (Report of the National Advisory Commission on Civil Disorders 1967: 278)

The plausibility of the argument has probably contributed to its longevity, in spite of thin evidence on its behalf. John Kasarda, in his recent formulation (1983a, 1983b, 1985), has sought to substantiate the analysis empirically.

Underlying Kasarda's explanation is a logic of premises and claims:

(1) the economic problem of blacks is mainly unemployment, rather than low wages;

(2) jobs with relatively low educational requirements are disappearing in central cities because of the decline in goods-producing and -distributing industries;

(3) central city blacks are particularly dependent on employment in such industries;

(4) they do not have the educational qualifications for employment in urban knowledge-intensive growth industries;

(5) they cannot get to suburban low-skill jobs for want of automobiles; and

(6) they are unwilling to move to the south and south-west, where they might find unskilled work, because of welfare dependency in the high-benefit cities of the North-east and the Midwest.

One of Kasarda's key findings is provided by analysis of employment change during the 1970s in a sample of central cities. Table 12.15 shows employment availability through net job growth (premise 1) and employment suitability for urban blacks through average educational 'requirements' by industry (premise 2). According to this exhibit, central city 'entry-level' jobs have declined everywhere except in the newer cities of the west, while 'knowledge intensive' jobs have actually expanded even in cities with sharp downturns in total employment. A second element in the diagnosis rests on evidence of lower average levels of education for central city blacks (aged sixteen to sixty-four) compared with whites (premise 4). Together, these findings lead Kasarda (1985: 53) to conclude that

> racial minorities are at a serious structural disadvantage in central cities that are losing entry-level industry jobs because substantially larger proportions of city minority residents lack the formal schooling to take advantage of information-processing jobs that are expanding in the cities.

Kasarda's analysis is weakened by the following methodological and substantive problems:

1 The labels 'entry-level' and 'knowledge-intensive (Table 12.15) are misleading. Kasarda's methodology is to classify jobs according to the mean years of schooling of employed central city residents by industry (i.e. type of business: durable goods manufacturing and professional services). Industries with mean years of schooling of less than 12.0 are designated 'entry-level', while those with more than 14.0 are called 'knowledge-intensive'. From this methodology we know little about the character of occupations and jobs within each type of industry. In

Table 12.15 *Employment changes, by industry's average educational requirements for nine US cities, 1970–80*

City and industrial categorisation	Number of jobs, 1980	Change, 1970–80 Number	%
New York			
Entry-level	763	−472	−38.2
Knowledge-intensive	462	92	24.9
Philadelphia			
Entry-level	208	−102	−32.9
Knowledge-intensive	91	25	37.8
Baltimore			
Entry-level	108	−52	−32.4
Knowledge-intensive	32	5	20.6
Boston (Suffolk County)			
Entry-level	115	−34	−22.6
Knowledge-intensive	75	19	33.3
St Louis			
Entry-level	103	−23	−18.2
Knowledge-intensive	21	−8	26.3
Atlanta (Fulton County)			
Entry-level	136	−19	−12.1
Knowledge-intensive	41	11	35.6
Houston (Harris County)			
Entry-level	457	194	73.8
Knowledge-intensive	152	83	119.4
Denver			
Entry-level	110	14	14.5
Knowledge-intensive	44	21	91.4
San Francisco			
Entry-level	142	13	−10.2
Knowledge-intensive	65	21	46.8

Source: Kasarda (1985: 50)

fact, other things being equal, internal variance in mean employee education is greater within industries than between them, since industries usually incorporate a wide range of possible occupations and types of jobs.

2 'Entry-level' and 'knowledge-intensive' are completely different dimensions, the one characterising, presumably, ease of access to 'unskilled' employment and the other, a type of production involving information or knowledge. In fact, many jobs in 'entry-level' industries like construction, printing and restaurants are difficult for blacks

to penetrate because of exclusionary craft unions and/or employer discrimination, while 'knowledge-intensive industries' like education and health care offer relatively easy access to their large proportion of 'low-skill' jobs (e.g. kitchen worker in an infant school).

3   Mean years of schooling for all industry employees is an inadequate surrogate for 'employers' educational requirements' (see item 1, above, and Table 12.15). Moreover, employers' requirements cannot be equated with necessary entry-level education. 'The idea that specific jobs require specific skills which aspiring workers either possess or lack is misleading. The real world job requirements and hiring standards are far more flexible than the model implicit in the mismatch explanation' (Brecher 1977: 9).

4   The entire distribution of employment across industries with varying mean years of schooling is not shown. Jobs which fall between 12.0 and 14.0 years of schooling (the mean is 12.64), about half of central city employment, are excluded (based on calculations from Tables 6A and 6B (Kasarda 1983b)), resulting in incorrect inferences about job availability. For example, hospitals (13.55 mean years of schooling) are omitted, although they are a growth industry with huge central-city employment (1.5 million in 1982). Doctors' and dentists' offices (14.50 years) are included as knowledge-intensive industries, though they provide only about 175,000 jobs (Kasarda 1983b: Table 5).

5   The analysis is based on an arbitrary sample of fifty-two industries at various levels (2, 3 and 4 'digits') of the 'Standard Industrial Classification'. For example, all of manufacturing is treated as a single industry, while services are represented by '4 digit' industries like museums and chiropractors' offices with low internal variance in employee education (Kasarda 1983b: Table 5). Such a methodology does not permit generalised inferences about net job growth and decline at a constant level of industrial differentiation; it is equivalent to comparing, say, the education of all American men with that of twenty-four-year old women living in affluent suburbs of Boston.

6   Kasarda (1985: Table 6) presents the educational levels of the entire central city population aged sixteen to sixty-four in tabular form, trichotomised by numbers of blacks and whites who have failed to complete high school, graduated from high school, or at least attended college. He notes that blacks are overrepresented in the first category and underrepresented in the third. As we have seen, however, had he compared younger adult blacks and whites, those entering the job market, he would have found much smaller educational differences. Even among the entire work-age population, his published data indicate only about 10 percentage points difference between races in the

lowest and highest categories, hardly sufficient to account for the employment problems of urban blacks which he documents at length. But Kasarda's unpublished data are more revealing (1983b: Table 4). They show that the inter-racial difference in mean years of schooling for employment-age central-city residents is less than 0.75 years, with the average black a high school graduate (12.03 years). These numbers greatly weaken the 'inadequate education' half of the mismatch argument.

Beyond these methodological difficulties, the mismatch diagnosis is inconsistent with the actual structure of employment of the black population. Kasarda appears to accept implicitly the premise that blacks are particularly dependent on employment in declining 'entry-level' industries – in his industry sample, mainly construction, manufacturing and retail trade. The facts show otherwise. Blacks (see Table 12.16) are no more dependent than whites on manufacturing (a long-standing historical

Table 12.16 *Employed civilians by industry in the US, 1980*

	Blacks		Whites	
	Absolute (in thousands)	%	Absolute (in thousands)	%
Total	9,333	100	84,927	100
Agriculture	152	1.6	2,417	2.8
Forestry, fisheries and mining	51	0.5	1,086	1.3
Construction	404	4.3	5,106	6.0
Manufacturing				
Non-durable goods	940	10.0	7,063	8.4
Durable goods	1,224	13.1	11,642	13.9
Transportation, communication and other public utilities	827	8.9	6,004	7.1
Wholesale trade	258	2.8	3,796	4.5
Retail trade	1,036	11.1	13,992	16.7
Finance, insurance and real estate	450	4.8	5,231	6.2
Services	3,288	35.2	23,488	28.0
Private household	(275)	(2.9)	(385)	(0.5)
Hospitals and healthcare	(980)	(10.5)	(5,871)	(7.0)
Schools and colleges	(879)	(9.4)	(6,852)	(8.1)
Public administration	702	7.5	4,202	5.0

Source: US Census of Population and Housing 1980, Vol. 1, part D–1–A

trend) and are considerably underrepresented in retail trade and construction. They are overrepresented, however, in services, including 'knowledge-based' hospitals and health care, schools and colleges.

Black employment patterns in New York, the quintessential 'converting' city (Fainstein and Fainstein 1982) with 'knowledge-based' growth industries, are inconsistent with the mismatch diagnosis (Bailey and Waldinger 1984). Blacks are underrepresented compared with whites in manufacturing and other contracting sectors. They are overrepresented in the major white-collar growth industries of finance, insurance and real estate, and significantly over-represented in service industries, including banking and hospitals (Stafford 1985: Table 8). Sassen-Koob (1984: 155) shows that the highest incidence of very low-skilled jobs in New York City is found in 'business services', the fastest growing employment sector locally and nationally, and a centre of black employment. Finally a study by the Federal Reserve Bank of New York (Chall 1985) concludes that black employment problems cannot be explained by recent changes in industrial composition.

Before leaving the mismatch diagnosis, we should touch briefly on Kasarda's final two premises. Along with Kasarda, we believe that suburban racial integration is an important goal. Nonetheless, more integration would have only modest effects in mitigating the black employment problem. As we have shown (note 1), suburban blacks are not much better off in terms of employment or income than those who live in central cities. Freeman and Holzer (1985: 25) conclude:

> Although the increase of black youth joblessness is often attributed to the movement of jobs from cities to suburbs, a careful assessment of the relation between location and employment in Chicago does not find this to be a major factor. The black youth employment problem there is one of 'race, not space'.

In contemporary America, workplace and residence are commonly separated geographically; workers commute within an entire metropolitan economy. Most manufacturing growth may have been in the suburbs, but 'simply living near the manufacturing jobs does not insure a black worker that he will get one' (Brecher 1977: 8). Kasarda asserts that central city blacks cannot get to suburban low-skill jobs for want of automobiles, and many of those with low wages ride in car pools. In fact, a low-paid worker without a car who works in a suburb may be better off living in a central city than in another suburb. Car-pooling is obviously more difficult if neither the destination nor the origin of a work-related trip is centrally located.

Because much of the growth in 'entry-level' employment has occurred in the south and south-west, Kasarda advocates that unskilled blacks move in that direction from northern central cities. He believes, however, that welfare reduces incentives to move, or indeed to take low-wage jobs which may be available nearby.[2] Logic and facts say he is wrong. First of all, black males – whose non-employment problems are discussed at length – almost never receive welfare benefits, so they must be supported clandestinely on the meagre allotments handed to females with dependent children. Thus, it must be women who are the primary victims. Indeed, Kasarda, believes that welfare encourages black females to have children, rather than work. In the absence of strong supporting evidence, it is difficult to take this argument seriously. Ellwood and Summers (1985: Table 4), demonstrate, in fact, that there is no correlation whatsoever between AFDC benefit levels by states and the incidence of female-headed black households. As to the claim of work disincentive, they conclude (1985: 31) that the wide variety of studies which have addressed this issue show that the AFDC programme has but 'modest negative effects' on female labour supply. Moreover, during the very period of the seventies when Kasarda claims welfare was taking blacks out of the labour market and tying them to declining cities, the welfare rolls actually contracted. Between 1972 and 1980, the number of black children on AFDC dropped nationally by 5 per cent (Ellwood and Summers 1985: 27). In New York City, the average number of persons on AFDC went from 840,000 in 1975 to 737,000 in 1985 (New York City Human Resources Administration – personal communication with the Division of Policy).

Conclusion

We find that the mismatch diagnosis compounds the difficulties of the underclass interpretation, with its misplaced focus on the poorest of urban blacks. Far from being a legacy of 'historic discrimination', inter-racial economic inequality is continually reproduced through the processes of capital accumulation and labour allocation. Thus, the economic situation of blacks is rooted more in the character of employment opportunities in growing industries, than in the disappearance of 'entry-level' jobs in declining industries. Unlike for the immigrants of yesterday, the problem for blacks is not so much inadequate education, as the channelling of the educated into relataively poor jobs, and the exclusion of many of the uneducated from work altogether.

Racial employment segregation

It would be difficult to argue that the plight of the black underclass is solely a consequence of racial oppression, that is, the
explicit and overt efforts of whites to keep blacks subjugated, in
the same way that it would be difficult to explain the rapid
improvement of the more privileged blacks by arguing that traditional forms of racial segregation and discrimination still char-
acterize the labor market ... In the economic realm, then, the
black experience has moved historically from economic racial
oppression experienced by virtually all blacks to economic sub-
ordination for the black underclass ... The ultimate basis for
current racial tension is the deleterious effect of basic structural
changes in the modern American economy on black and white
lower-income groups.   (Wilson 1978: 152–3)

Wilson's formulation of the economic situation of blacks is problematic
both empirically and theoretically. In the first section of this chapter, I
reviewed evidence which points to the continuing significance of race, and
concluded that Wilson exaggerates the economic differences among
blacks and minimises those between races. The 'deleterious effect' of
economic restructuring, which I too see, harms blacks at every class level,
not just the underclass as he claims, and differentially hurts blacks more
than whites at the lowest level.

Empirical evidence of continuing racial differences does not necessarily
contradict a class analysis. From my theoretical perspective, such an
analysis would demonstrate how race becomes employed in conflicts
between labour and capital; how racial identities and conflicts are produced and utilised as resources by white employers and workers who
advance their respective economic interests. Of course, this is not
'economic racial oppression' of the kind experienced by sharecroppers, or
even by black urban workers earlier in the century. But racial discrimination is omnipresent in the economy, built into the routine decisions of
employers: the ways they organise the division of labour, how they
allocate men, women, blacks and whites among jobs, what they decide to
pay different kinds of workers, and the explicit and implicit criteria they
utilise in hiring and promotion. Combined with virulent racism in
housing markets, which keeps blacks concentrated in residential ghettos
in central cities and increasingly in suburban jurisdictions, outright discrimination along with more subtle forms of channelling in labour
markets goes a long way toward explaining black economic disadvantage.
Accordingly, I agree completely with Wilson that this is a class society

and that class differences among blacks matter; yet, I also believe that a model of labour markets which begins with group differences and institutional processes is essential to correct theorising about contemporary capitalism:

> The institutional approach to understanding labor markets ... provides a basis for viewing discrimination as both an integral part of labor market processes and their outcomes. The labor market, incorportaing a range of political, social, and economic forces, is seen to create an institutional context in which groups with different interests attempt to stabilize or enhance their positions. In this context, discrimination can be understood to be one of the important mechanisms that have contributed historically to the creation of segmented labor markets ... (Usually) discrimination would be expected to take the form of segregation into different jobs rather than lower pay for identical jobs.
>
> (Treiman and Hartmann 1981: 63)

Without taking the analogy too far, we can view employment in much the same way as housing. In labour markets, blacks offer skills and educational credentials to employers, the equivalent of wealth in housing markets. They receive jobs with particular characteristics – authority, working conditions and pay – just as they would receive housing units. As in housing markets, blacks may well have to offer more than whites for equivalent jobs. But of greater significance, they are segregated into particular places in the employment market, and kept from other opportunities. Within these employment ghettos, which overlap those into which women of all races are segregated, blacks may be able to compete on relatively fair terms for jobs available. But outside of them, jobs are kept monopolised by whites. These monopolised jobs are as likely to be 'good' low-skill work as high-level managerial positions. Moreover, in white-only industries, firms and jobs, white workers may be stronger opponents of racial integration than employers, just as white tenants may resist residential integration more strongly than landlords. Finally, in both housing and labour markets, it is capital, not labour, which determines the amount and character of goods available – housing units or jobs. When new housing stock or new jobs are shoddier or more expensive than those previously available, parvenue groups striving for upward mobility, whether in housing or employment, have a more difficult time succeeding.

In the remaining portion of this chapter, I first present some suggestive evidence about the character of jobs being produced in the economy and of how they are allocated to blacks and women. Next I review findings on segmented labour markets in New York City. I then explain, briefly and hypothetically, the situation of major sub-groups within the black population. I conclude with an observation on the politics of 'the declining significance of race'.

Economic restructuring

Blacks are positioned differently from whites in the labour market. Historically, they have shown relatively low levels of self-employment (3 per cent versus 8 per cent for whites in 1985) and 'ethnic' entrepreneurship (Freedman 1985). Disproportionate numbers of black-run businesses have in fact been supported through government contracts (Collins 1983). Most critically, blacks have shown much higher levels of government employment compared to whites – 23 versus 15 per cent in 1985 (US Bureau of Labor Statistics 1985: Table A60). And blacks in managerial and administrative occupations are more likely than whites to be government workers (Collins 1983: 374). The contraction in the public sector in the mid-seventies and stagnation thereafter, along with withdrawal from affirmative-action hiring, was one 'macro' factor which slowed black economic mobility.

The second, and perhaps more important, impediment to continued economic gains was a sharp decline in the standard of living associated with a restructuring of the economy. A new economic terrain took shape in the private economy, upon which blacks were forced to compete with whites. Real income hardly changed after 1970, while a greater proportion of the work-aged population was employed; as a result, real wages per worker declined. Associated with a great expansion of female employment was a downgrading of jobs: employers restructured work to create more part-time jobs and more low-paying jobs. Even among male workers, the proportion of low-paid jobs increased in relation to high-paid work. The greatest decline, however, was in the middle – the decently paid jobs for which black men with average education could most effectively compete were disappearing (Sassen-Koob 1984).

While there has been much debate about the causes of this redistribution in job quality, particularly about whether expanded service or high-tech employment is to blame, the fact of redistribution seems clear enough. Robert Lawrence (1984: Table 1) compares wage distributions by industry in 1983 and 1969 for full-time year-round workers. He finds that regardless of industry sector, females are concentrated in low-wage jobs compared with males (though significantly, the differences are smallest in public employment). Moreover, the male earnings distribution exhibits over the same time period a disappearing middle, with poorly paid jobs becoming better paid on the average compared with the previous female distribution.

Table 12.17 *Growth in job equivalents by annual earnings level in the US,*
1970–83[a]

	1970	1983	Jobs added 1970–83
All jobs (in thousands)			
Low wage (less than $8,000)	48,331	72,647	24,316
Middle wage ($8,000–$19,999)	40,226	54,420	14,194
High wage ($20,000 and more)	28,098	37,672	9,574
Jobs allocated to males (in thousands)			
Low wage (less than $8,000)	17,292	24,110	6,818
Middle wage ($8,000–$19,999)	23,078	27,510	4,432
High wage ($20,000 and up)	24,638	29,289	4,651
Jobs allocated to females (in thousands)			
Low wage (less than $8,000)	31,039	48,537	17,498
Middle wage ($8,000–$19,999)	17,148	26,910	9,762
High wage ($20,000 and up)	3,460	8,383	4,923

[a]1983 constant dollars
Source: Derived from US Bureau of the Census, 'Money Income of Households, Families,
and Persons in the United States: 1983', *Current Population Reports*, Series P–60, No. 146
(1985): Table 40

In Table 12.17 we show net changes in the distribution of earnings by
earning level for all employed workers, including part-time. In effect, this
analysis allows us to see how annual earnings are allocated to 'job
equivalents'. Our categories are similar to Lawrence's, except for a
broader definition of middle-wage jobs. We find that low-wage jobs
comprised half of all jobs added to the economy, and that about 75 per
cent of these 'poor' jobs went to women. Even though they did better in
middle- and high-pay work, their earnings distribution compared with
men in 1983 remained skewed sharply toward the bottom. Using the same
analysis, we can see how the black situation changed over the period
(Table 12.18). In general, the wage pattern for black and white men
changed only slightly, with both exhibiting small declines in middle-wage
jobs. The overriding inter-racial difference remained the much greater
probability of black men holding low-wage, rather than high-wage, jobs
compared to whites. In contrast, both black and white women showed
small improvements at the upper end. Most strikingly, the two patterns of
distribution are almost identical. Black women hold their own against
white women.

In themselves, these aggregate data do not demonstrate racial channelling, much less employer discrimination. But in combination with more
detailed local studies, they support the idea of racially segmented labour

Table 12.18 *Inequality in earnings in the US, 1970–83*

	Males				Females			
	1970	1975	1983	Difference 1983/70	1970	1975	1983	Difference 1983/70
Blacks and other races								
Distribution (%)								
Low (less than $8,000)	39	40	44	+5	65	62	62	−3
Middle ($8,000–$19,999)	43	37	39	−5	30	31	30	0
High ($20,000 and up)	18	23	22	+4	5	7	8	+3
White								
Distribution (%)								
Low (less than $8,000)	25	25	28	+3	59	59	58	−1
Middle ($8,000–$19,999)	35	32	34	−1	34	33	32	−2
High ($20,000 and more)	40	43	38	−2	7	8	10	+3
Black/white median	0.60	0.63	0.63	–	0.92	0.93	0.89	–

Source: US Bureau of the Census, 'Money Income of Households, Families, and Persons in the United States: 1983', *Current Population Reports*, Series P–60, No. 146 (1985): Table 40

markets. Walter Stafford has recently examined employment patterns in New York City. His findings indicate that blacks are excluded from whole sectors of the economy (see Table 12.19). Many four-digit industries have very low levels of black employment, and employment segregation is on the rise. Moreover, Stafford shows how blacks are segregated into particular kinds of jobs when they are hired. In fact, only those private firms which have been closely regulated by government (e.g. the telephone company) show good distribution of black workers across job types. In a more specific study, Bailey (1985) finds that blacks are highly segmented into the worst jobs in the restaurant industry; entry-level jobs with career ladders (waiters and cooks in full-service restaurants) are largely unavailable to them. Even in the public sector, blacks are severely underrepresented in the male-dominated uniformed services (police, fire, sanitation) and are concentrated in agencies which service low-income and minority clienteles (Stafford 1983). The racially segmented employment situation in New York is typical.

Subgroups

Employment segregation in an increasingly inegalitarian economy establishes the conditions under which major subgroups of the black population must compete economically. Both white and black teenagers lack adequate educational credentials. Yet white teenagers do much better in

Table 12.19 *Representation of whites, blacks and Hispanics in specific industries compared to their representation in the labour forces in New York City, 1982*

Industrial divisions	Total number of industries[a]	Industries in which whites were 70% or more of employees[b]	Industries in which blacks were 23% or more of employees[b]	Industries in which Hispanics were 16% or more of employees[b]
Manufacturing	78	44	9	39
Wholesale	18	18	–	1
Retail	14	11	5	4
Finance, insurance and real estate (FIRE)	16	15	2	–
Transportation, public utilities and communications	17	14	2	1
Service	42	24	13	6
Construction	7	4	1	1
Total	192	130	32	52

[a]Only those industries with 500 or more employees were included in the analysis
[b]The 23 per cent and 16 per cent represent the respective labour force representation of blacks and Hispanics. The labour force representation for whites was 65 per cent in 1980. However, 70 per cent is used to demonstrate white predominance in a variety of industries.
Source: Unpublished EEOC Private Sector Employment, 1982; from Stafford (1985: 72)

the labour market. Of the factors which might account for gross inter-racial differences at every level of family income, two stand out. White teenagers, in part because of where they live and go to school, are integrated into informal employment networks of adults and adolescents. These networks not only overcome the imperfections of the labour market, but may actually help employers determine who should be hired (Freeman and Holzer 1985). Without referees considered reliable by employers – of whom current good workers are the best – black youth cannot overcome the second factor, employer prejudice and discrimina-tion. Precisely because all youth lack educational credentials or skills which certify employability, employers make judgements which are extremely susceptible to racial bias.

In sharp contrast to teenagers, black and white adult women look increasingly alike in their employment situations. Women of both races are segregated into low-wage, pink-collar ghettos. Therefore, even though black women have higher labour force participation rates than white women, and nearly comparable wages, their low earnings in 'women's work' are insufficient to improve the relative income position of black families. The primary basis of occupational segregation of black women may well be gender discrimination, which makes racial channelling unnecessary except for that small stratum of black women who have entered elite jobs.

Black adult men have lower labour-force participation rates than white men. But their main economic disadvantages are in much higher unemployment and much lower earnings. Black men with poorer edu-cational credentials suffer from isolation in secondary labour markets, where employment turnover and low wages are endemic (Rumberger and Carnoy 1980: 129–30). They are prevented by racial discrimination from gaining high-paying – often unionised – jobs with only modest entry-level educational requirements. Black men with better credentials can penetrate core industries only in so far as they are relegated to relatively low-paying subordinate jobs. Thus, while large numbers of women of both races and some black men fill subordinate jobs in the core of the economy, white men disproportionately occupy supervisory positions. There is extraordinary employer and worker prejudice against allowing black men to supervise whites. Unable on average to penetrate the managerial stratum or to land 'protected' jobs with lower edu-cational requirements, black men at each 'class' level face severe obstacles to catching up with white males. Because male earnings are so much greater than female, the continuing inter-racial gap in male earning militates against an improved economic situation for the entire black population.

The politics of diagnosis

Let me conclude by stating my political concern with the underclass/mismatch diagnosis, and more generally with arguments for the declining significance of race. William Julius Wilson argues eloquently that black economic problems are contained within an underclass victimised by class domination rather than by racial discrimination, and that governmental programmes to end employment discrimination have benefited mainly the black upper classes. Through this line of argument, Wilson is apparently trying to fashion a class-base programme, having – I think correctly – recognised the contradictions of previous 'racial' formulations. Thus, he concludes a recent publication (Wilson 1985) with a call for 'fundamental economic reform' achieved by a 'broad-based coalition':

> And since an effective political coalition will in part depend upon how the issues are defined, it is essential that the political message underline the need for economic and social reform that benefits all groups in the United States, not just poor minorities.

While I agree with Wilson's objective, I am troubled by the actual effects of tying this political strategy to a social-scientific analysis of the black situation. In fact, conservatives, with whom Wilson is completely at odds, have taken up the cry, saying we now know that only the black underclass is suffering, that its problems result from economic changes which no one can control, that discrimination is a thing of the past, and that affirmative action programmes benefit only privileged blacks. The Reagan administration concluded – perhaps cynically – that affirmative action fails to help 'the most needy' and should be ended:

> The White House Staff has drafted an executive order repealing requirements that Federal contractors set numerical goals to remedy possible job discrimination ... [An Administration report says that] 'while the rules may have helped skilled black men, they have done little to benefit white women, low-paid blacks or other intended beneficiaries'.
>
> (*The New York Times*, 15 August 1985: 1)

Race continues to be of significance, no less in national politics than in the economy. At a time when not only the welfare state, but all forms of civil rights legislation are under attack, it is impossible to ignore the political implications of sociological discussions of race and class. Wilson seeks to advance a non-racial diagnosis in a racist society to achieve social democracy. Thus far, the political results have not been promising.

Notes

1 In concluding our discussion of the underclass diagnosis, we should comment briefly on the term 'urban', in the phrase 'the urban underclass' (Wilson 1984). The urban dimension adds relatively little to an analysis. For one thing, almost all blacks are today urbanised. In 1980, 82 per cent of blacks lived in metropolitan areas, and 60 per cent of blacks in central cities (US Bureau of the Census 1985a: Table 20). The 22 per cent who lived in metropolitan 'suburbs' were mainly segregated into jurisdictions contiguous to the black ghettos of inner cities or into satellite cities (Lake 1984). Most blacks outside metropolitan areas resided in rural towns; very few lived on farms. For the great majority of blacks, the term 'urban' is a redundancy.

More important, however, is the fact that aggregated data simply do not show gross differences among blacks by degree of 'urbanisation'. For example, in 1982, 20 per cent of central city blacks were unemployed, but so were 16 per cent of suburban blacks and 19 per cent of those who lived in non-metropolitan towns. While the variation in black unemployment was greater than white, which ranged between 8 and 9 per cent, blacks in every type of location had much more in common with each other than with whites in the same residential situation, since the black unemployment rate was consistently twice the white rate (US Bureau of Labor Statistics 1983: Table 8). The identical geographical pattern was exhibited by teenage employment data. In 1980, 32 per cent of out-of-school black youths living in inner cities were employed, as were 38 per cent in the suburbs and 35 per cent in non-metropolitan towns. This minor variation was trivial when compared with the inter-racial difference in youth employment: in the same year, about 62 per cent of white youths were employed in each type of urban location (Ellwood and Summers 1985: 39). Another economic indicator, median family income, shows that while suburban blacks have higher incomes than their central-city counterparts, their relative advantage has changed little since the mid-seventies. Moreover, the income of suburban black families declined in relation to suburban white families, from 68 per cent in 1976 to 63 per cent in 1983 (US Bureau of the Census 1985a: Table 744, and previous editions).

Such admittedly crude evidence does not demonstrate that it matters little where blacks live. To the contrary, there is every reason to believe that blacks would benefit immensely from residential racial desegregation. It does suggest, however, that so long as the great majority of blacks live in ghetto situations – with all that means in terms of housing quality, schooling and community social structure – we should not expect to find major differences between the economic condition of central city and suburban blacks. Blacks are severely disadvantaged relative to whites everywhere. The addition of an urban dimension to the underclass diagnosis does little to enhance its explanatory power.

2 Incidentally, Kasarda (1985: Table 10) defines welfare to include not only AFDC, but the provision of foodstamps and subsidised housing. Doing so seems unfortunate for his mobility argument. Foodstamps is a national programme with uniform benefit levels across the country. Calling subsidised, lower-income housing 'welfare' opens for analysis the Pandora's box of the much larger subsidies which go to middle-income homeowners and discourage them from moving freely to optimise employment opportunities.

References

Abler, R. 1977 'The Telephone and the Evolution of the American Metropolitan System' in I. de Sola Pool (ed.) *The Social Impact of the Telephone*, Cambridge, MA: MIT Press

Amersfoort, van H. 1982 'Immigrant Housing in a Welfare State: The Case of The Netherlands in the 1970s', *Race and Ethnic Research* 3: 49–77

Amersfoort, J. M. M. van 1974 *Immigrants en minderhejds Vorming: Een Analyse van de Nederlandse Situatie 1945–73*, Alphen A. D. Rign: Sanson; translated by R. Lyng as: *Immigration and the Formation of Minority Groups: The dutch Experience 1945–75*, Cambridge University Press, 1982

Amersfoort, J. M. M. van and C. Cortie 1973 'Het Patroon van de Surinaamse vestiging in Amsterdam de Periode 1968 T/M 1970', *Tijdschrift voor Economische en Sociale Geografie* 64: 283–94

Amin, S. 1974 *Accumulation on a World Scale*, 2 vols., New York: Monthly Review Press

Anderson, J., S. Duncan and R. Hudson (eds.) 1983 *Redundant Spaces in Cities and Regions*, London: Academic Press

Anderson, K. 1983 'The New Ellis Island', *Time*, 13 June

Anthias, F. 1983 'Sexual Divisions and Ethnic Adaptation: The Case of Greek-Cypriot Women' in A. Phizacklea (ed.) *One Way Ticket*, London: Routledge & Kegan Paul

Babson, S. and R. Alpern, D. Elsila and J. Revitte 1984 *Working Detroit*, New York: Adama Books

Bagchi, A. K. 1982 *The Political Economy of Underdevelopment*, Cambridge University Press

Bailey, C. 1984 'The Seaway: At 25 It Looks Towards Larger Link To The World', *Detroit News*, 24 June

1985 'Black Workers and the Auto Industry: An Uncertain Future', *Detroit News*, 9 June

Bailey, T. 1985 'A Case Study of Immigrants in the Restaurant Industry', *Industrial Relations*, Spring

Bailey, T. and R. Waldinger 1984 'A Skills Mismatch in New York's Labor Market', *New York Affairs* 8(3): 3–19

Banfield, E. C.   1968   *The Unheavenly City*, Boston: Little, Brown
Banton, M.   1955   *The Coloured Quarter*, London: Jonathan Cape
Barker, M.   1981   *The New Racism: Conservatives and the Ideology of the Tribe*, London: Junction Books
Barou, J.   1978   *Travailleurs Africains en France*, Grenoble: Presses Universitaires de Grenoble
Bartels, D.   1968   'Türkische Gastarbeiter aus der Region Izmir', *Erdkunde* 22(4): 313–24
Batley, R.   1984   'A Historical Sketch of Industrial Change and its Social Impact in West Midlands County', Working Paper No. 12, Birmingham: JCRULGS
Beauftragte der Bundesregierung für Ausländerfragen   1986   *Daten und Fakten zur Ausländersituation*, Bonn
Begg, I. and D. Eversley   1986   'Deprivation in the Inner City, Social Indicators from the 1981 Census', in V. Hausner (ed.) *Critical Issues in Urban Development*, I, Oxford: Clarendon Press
Begg, I., M. Moore and J. Rhodes,   1986   'Economic and Social Change in Urban Britain and the Inner Cities' in V. Hausner (ed.) *Critical Issues in Urban Development*, I, Oxford: Clarendon Press
Bell, D.   1973   *Coming of Post-Industrial Society*, New York: Basic Books
Bennett, R. B.   1982   *Central Grants to Local Governments*, Cambridge University Press
Berger, S. and M. J. Piore   1980   *Dualism and Discontinuity in Industrial Societies*, Cambridge University Press
Birks, J. S. and G. A. Sinclair   1980   *International Migration and Development in the Arab Region*, Geneva: International Labour Organisation
Birmingham Inner City Partnership   1985   *Birmingham Inner City Profile 1985*, Birmingham ICP
Bisset, L. and L. Harding   1981   *Poor Hackney: Low Pay and Unemployment in a London Borough*, Low Pay Unit and London Borough of Hackney
Blackaby, F. (ed.)   1979   *De-industrialisation*, London: Heinemann
Bluestone B. and B. Harrison   1982   *The Deindustrialisation of America*, New York: Basic Books
Bluestone, B., B. Harrison and L. Gorham   1984   *Storm Clouds on the Horizon: Labor Market Crisis and Industrial Policy*, Brookline, MA: Economic Education Project
Boddy, M., J. Lovering and K. Bassett   1986   *Sunbelt City? A Study of Economic Growth in Britain's M4 Growth Corridor*, Oxford: Clarendon Press
Böhning, W. R.   1970   'Foreign Workers in Post-War Germany, *New Atlantis* 2: 12–38
  1972   *The Migration of Workers in the United Kingdom and the European Community*, Oxford University Press
Braverman, H.   1974   *Labor and Monopoly Capital*, New York: Monthly Review Press
Brecher, C.   1977   'The Mismatch Misunderstanding', *New York Affairs* 4(1): 6–12
Brettell, C. B.   1981   'Is the Ethnic Community Inevitable? A Comparison of

the Settlement Patterns of Portuguese Immigrants in Toronto and Paris', *The Journal of Ethnic Studies* 9(3): 1–17

Budzinski, M. 1979 *Gewerkschaftliche und betriebliche Erfahrungen ausländischer Arbeiter*, Frankfurt: Campus

Bundesminister des Innern 1983 *Kommission 'Ausländerpolitik' aus Vertretern von Bund, Ländern und Gemeinden*, Bonn

Butcher, I. J. and P. E. Ogden 1984 'West Indians in France: Migration and Demographic Change' in P. E. Ogden (ed.) *Migrants in Modern France: Four Studies*, Occasional Paper No. 23, London: Department of Geography and Earth Studies, Queen Mary College

Cable, V. 1982 'Cheap Imports and Jobs: The Impact of Competing Imports from Low Labour Cost Countries on UK Employment' in P. Maunder (ed.) *Case Studies in Economic Development*, London: Heinemann

Carley, M. 1981 *Social Measurement and Social Indicators, Issues of Policy and Theory*, London: Allen and Unwin

Castells, M. 1983 *The City and the Grassroots: A Cross Cultural Theory of Urban Social Movements*, London: Edward Arnold

Castles, S. with H. Booth and T. Wallace 1984 *Here for Good: Western Europe's New Ethnic Minorities*, London: Pluto Press

Castles, S. and G. Kosack 1985 *Immigrant Class Structure in Western Europe*, London: Oxford University Press

Centre for Contemporary Cultural Studies 1982 *The Empire Strikes Back*, London: Hutchinson

Chall, D. E. 1985 'New York City's "Skills Mismatch"', *Federal Reserve Bank of New York Quarterly Review*, Spring: 20–7

City of Liverpool 1986 *Urban Deprivation: Liverpool's Relative Position: A Technical Study*, City of Liverpool Planning Department

Clark, C. 1940 *The Conditions of Economic Progress*, London: Macmillan

Cockburn, C. 1985 *Machinery of Dominance: Women, Men and Technical Know-How*, London: Pluto Press

Cohen, R. 1981 'The New International Division of Labor, Multinational Corporations, and Urban Hierarchy' in M. Dear and A. Scott (eds.) *Urbanisation and Urban Planning in Capitalist Societies*, New York: Methuen
1987 *The New Helots: Migrants in the International Division of Labour*, Aldershot: Gower

Cohen, R. and J. Henderson 1982 'The International Restructuring of Capital and Labour: Britain and Hong Kong', Paper presented to ISA Tenth World Congress of Sociology, August

Collins, S. M. 1983 'The Making of the Black Middle Class', *Social Problems* 30(4), April 369–82

Commission of the European Communities 1981 *Commission Communication to the Council on the Situation and Prospects of the Textile and Clothing Industries in the Community*, Com (81) 388 Brussels

Conk, M. 1985 'Immigration Reform and Immigration History: Why Simpson–Mazzoli Did Not Pass' in L. Maldonado and J. W. Moore (eds.) *Urban Ethnicity in the United States*, Beverly Hills: Sage

Conseil Economique et Social   1982   'Le Devenir des industries du textile et de l'habillement', *Journal Officiel*, 25 February

Council of Great Lakes Governors   1983   *Great Lakes Governors' Economic Summit Report*, Ann Arbor, MI: Great Lakes Commission

Crewdson, J.   1983   *The Tarnished Door: The New Immigrants and the Transformation of America*, New York: Times Books

Cross, M.   1983   'Racialised Poverty and Reservation Ideology: Blacks and the Urban Labour Market', Paper presented at the Fourth Urban Change and Conflict Conference, Essex

Cross, M. and M. Keith (eds.)   1992   *Racism, the City and the State*, London: Routledge

Cross, M. and R. Waldinger   1991   'Migrants, Minorities and the Ethnic Division of Labour' in S. Fainstein, J. Gordon and M. Harloe (eds.) *Divided Cities: London and New York*, Oxford, Blackwell

Danson, M. W., W. F. Lever and J. F. Malcolm   1980   'The Inner City Employment Problem in Great Britain, 1952–76: A Shift-Share Approach', *Urban Studies* 17(2): 193–210

Darden, J. T.   1985   'The Housing Situation of Blacks in Metropolitan Areas of Michigan' in Urban Affairs Program, *The State of Black Michigan, 1985*, East Lansing, MI: Urban Affairs Programs and the Council of Michigan Urban League Executives

De Lannoy, W.   1975   'Residential Segregation of Foreigners in Brussels', *Bulletin Belge d'Etudes Géographiques* 44: 215–38

Denby, C.   1968   'Black Caucuses in the Unions', *New Politics*, Summer: 548–77

Department of the Environment,   1976   *Final Reports of the Birmingham, Liverpool and Lambeth Inner Area Studies*, 3 vols., London: HMSO
   1977   *Policy for the Inner Cities*, Cmnd 6845, London: HMSO
   1980   *National Dwelling and Housing Survey* 2, 3, London: HMSO

Desai, R.   1963   *Indian Immigrants in Britain*, London: Oxford University Press for the Institute of Race Relations

Doeringer, P. and M. Piore   1971   *Internal Labor Markets and Manpower Analysis*, Lexington, MA: Lexington Books

Dohse, K.   1981   *Ausländische Arbeiter und bürgerlicher Staat*, Königstein: Hain

Dohse, K. and K. Groth,   1983   'Ausländerverdrängung – zur Verschärfung des Ausländerrechts', *Kritische Justiz* 16(13)

Dollars and Sense   1986   'Hard Time for Black America', April: 5–7

Drewe, P.   1981   *Structure and Composition of the Population of Urban Areas with Special Reference to Inner City Areas*, Strasbourg: Council of Europe

Duffield, M.   1981   'Racism and Counter-Revolution in the Era of Imperialism: A Critique of the Political Economy of Migration', Paper presented to the Conference of Socialist Economists, Bradford, July

Duncan, G.   1984   *Years of Poverty, Years of Plenty*, Ann Arbor: Institute for Social Research, University of Michigan

Duncan, O. D. and B. Duncan   1957   *The Negro Population of Chicago*, Chicago University Press

Duncan, O. and S. Lieberson 1959 'Ethnic Segregation and Assimilation', *American Sociological Review* 64: 364–74

Economic Development Unit (EDU) 1985 *The West Midlands Economy in 1985*, Research Paper No. 4, Birmingham: EDU

Ellwood, D. and L. Summers 1985 'Poverty in America: Is Welfare the Answer or the Problem?', Conference Paper, Institute for Research on Poverty, University of Wisconsin at Madison

Elson, D. and R. Pearson 1981 '"Nimble Fingers Make Cheap Workers": An Analysis of Women's Employment in Third World Export Manufacturing', *Feminist Review* 7

Ernst, D. (ed.) 1980 *The New International Division of Labour, Technology and Underdevelopment*, Frankfurt: Campus Verlag

Ernst, D. 1981 *Restructuring World Industry in a Period of Crisis: The Role of Innovation*, Vienna: UNIDO

Esser, J. and J. Hirsch 1984 'Der CDU-Staat: Ein politisches Regulierungs-modell für den "nachfordistischen" Kapitalismus', *Prokla* 56, September

Evans, D. J. 1984 *The Segregation of the New Commonwealth Population in Wolverhampton Municipal Borough 1961–1981*, North Staffordshire Poly-technic Department of Geography and Recreation Studies, Occasional Paper 3

Eversley, D. 1978 'A Question of Numbers?' in M. Bulmer (ed.) *Social Poicy Research*, London: Macmillan

    1990a 'Regional and Housing Policies and their Impact on Internal Migra-tion', in H. Birg and R. Mackensen (eds.) *Demographisthe Wirkungen politis-chen Handelns*, International Conference 1986, Deutsche Gesellschaft für Bevölkerungswissenscahft and European Association for Population Studies, Frankfurt and New York: Campus Verlag

    1990b *Religion and Employment in Northern Ireland*, London: Sage

Eversley, D. and L. Bonnerjea 1980 *Changes in the Resident Population of Inner City Areas: The Inner City in Context 2*, London: SSRC

Fainstein N. I. and S. S. Fainstein 1982 'Restructuring the American City: A Comparative Perspective' in N. I. Fainstein and S. S. Fainstein (eds.) *Urban Policy under Capitalism*, Beverly Hills, CA: Sage, pp. 161–90

Fels, G. and K. D. Schmidt 1981 *Die deutsche Wirtschaft im Strukturwandel*, Tübingen: Mohr

Flaim, P. and E. Sehgal 1985 'Displaced Workers of 1979–83: How Well Have They Fared?', *Monthly Labour Review*, June: 3–16

Flett, H. 1977 'Council Housing and Allocation of Ethnic Minorities', *Working Papers on Ethnic Relations* 5, SSRC Research Unit on Ethnic Relations

Flynn, N. and A. Taylor 1984 *De-industrialization and Corporate Change in the West Midlands*, ESRC Inner City in Context Research Programme, Working Paper No. 8, Birmingham: JCRULGS

Fossett, M. A. *et al.* 1986 'Racial Occupational Inequality, 1940–1980: National and Regional Tends', *American Sociological Review* 15, June: 421–9

318   *References*

Fothergill, S. and C. Gudgin 1983 *Unequal Growths: Urban and Regional Employment Change in the U.K.*, London: Heinemann

Fourastié, J. 1949 *Le Grand Espoir du XXe siècle*, Paris

Fox, A. and E. Grundy 1985 'A Longitudinal Perspective on Recent Socio-Demographic Change' in OPCS, *Measuring Socio-Demographic Change*, Occasional Paper No. 34

Freedman, M. 1985 'Urban Labor Markets and Ethnicity: Shelters and Segments Reexamined' in L. Maldonado and J. Moore (eds.) *Urban Ethnicity in the United States*, Beverly Hills: Sage, pp. 145–66

Freeman, R. B. 1981 'Black Economic Progress after 1964: Who has Gained and Why?' in S. Rosen (ed.) *Studies in Labor Markets*, University of Chicago, pp. 247–94

Freeman, R. B. and H. J. Holzer 1985 'Young Blacks and Jobs – What We Know Now', *The Public Interest* 72 (Winter): 18–31

Frey, W. H. 1985 'Mover Destination Selectivity and Changing Suburbanisation of Metropolitan Whites and Blacks', *Demography* 22: 223–43

Friedman, J. 1985 'The World City Hypothesis', Unpublished Paper, Conference on the International Division of Labour, Centre of Urban Studies and International Sociological Association, University of Hong Kong, August

Friedmann, J. and G. Wolff 1983 'World City Formation: An Agenda for Research and Action', *International Journal of Urban and Regional Research* 6: 309–44

Friedrichs, J. 1982 *Spatial Disparities and Social Behaviour: A Reader in Urban Research*, Hamburg

Fröbel, F., J. Heinrichs and O. Kreye 1980 *The New International Division of Labour: Structural Unemployment in Industrialised Countries and Industrialization in Developing Countires*, Cambridge University Press

Frost, M. and N. Spence 1984 'The Changing Structure and Distribution of the British Workforce', *Progress in Planning* 21(2)

Gans, P. 1984 'Innerstädtische Wohnungswechsel und Veränderungen in der Verteilung der Bevölkerung in Ludwigshafen: eine empirische Untersuchung über Wohnungsteilmärkte und Mobilitätsbarrierren', *Geographische Zeitschrift* 72(2): 81–98

Geiger, F. 1975 'Zur Konzentration von Gastarbeitern in alten Dorfkernen', *Geographische Rundschau* 27: 61–71

Geissler, H. 1976 *Die neue soziale Frage*, Freiburg: Herder

Gertler, M. 1986 'Discontinuities in Regional Development', *Society and Space* 4: 71–81

Glyn, A. and J. Harrison 1980 *The British Economic Disaster*, London: Pluto Press

Good, D. 1984 *Social Processes at Work in Space: The Distribution of Immigrants in Lucerne, Switzerland 1980*, Dissertation for part of BA Degree, Oxford University, unpublished

Gordon, D. M., R. Edwards and M. Reich 1982 *Segmented Workers, Divided Workers: The Historical Transformation of Labour in the United States*, Cambridge University Press

Gordon, M. M. 1964 *Assimilation in American Life*, Oxford University Press
Greater London Council 1983 *Office Work and Information Technologies*, Economic Policy Group Strategy Document No. 10, Greater London Council
   1985 *The London Industrial Strategy*, Greater London Council
Green, N. 1985 *Les Travailleurs immigrés juifs à la Belle Epoque*, Paris: Fayard
Gregory, K. D. 1985 'Toward a Strategy for Economic Development in the Black Community' in Urban Affairs Programs, *The State of Black Michigan, 1985*, East Lansing, MI: Urban Affairs Programs and the Council of Michigan Urban League Executives
Guillon, M. 1974 'Les Repatriés d'Algérie dans la région parisienne', *Annales de Geographie* 83: 644–75
Guilbert, M. and V. Isambert-Jamati 1956 *Travail féminin et travail à domicile. Enquête sur le travail à domicile de la confection féminine dans la région parisienne*, Paris: Centre National de la Recherche Scientifique
Guillon, M. and I. Taboada 1986 *Le Triangle de Choisy*, Paris: L'Harmattan
Hall, S. 1988 *The Hard Road to Renewal*, London: Verso
Halliday, F. 1977 'Labour Migration in the Middle East', *MERIP Reports* 59: 1–17
Hamnett, C. 1983 'The Conditions in England's Inner Cities on the Eve of the 1981 Riots', *Area* 15(1): 7–13
   1984 'Housing the Two Nations', *Urban Studies* 43: 389–405
Hamnett, C. and W. Randolph 1986 *Socio-Tenurial Polarization in London*, Social Statistics Research Unit Working paper No. 45, University of London
Hamnett, C., W. Randolph and C. Evans 1985 'Racial Minorities in the London Labour Market', Working Paper No. 37, Social Statistics Research Unit Working Paper No. 45, University of London
Harris, C. 1984 'The Magnitude of Job Loss from Plant Closings and the Generation of Replacement Jobs: Some Recent Evidence', *Annals of the American Academy of Political and Social Science* 475: 15–27
Harris, R. 1983 'Space and Class: A Critique of Urry', *International Journal of Urban and Regional Research* 7(1): 115–21
Harrison, B. 1982 'Rationalisation, Restructuring and Industrial Reorganisation in Older Regions: The Economic Transformation of New England since World War II', Working Paper No. 72, Joint Center for Urban Studies of MIT and Harvard University
Hausner, V. and B. Robson 1986 *Changing Cities: An Introduction to the Economic and Social Research Council's Inner Cities Research*, London: ESRC
Henderson, J. 1985 'The New International Division of Labour and Urban Development in the Contemporary World-System' in D. Drakasis-Smith (ed.) *Urbanisation in the Developing World*, London: Croom Helm
Henderson, J. and R. Cohen 1982 'The International Restructuring of Capital and Labour: British and Hong Kong', Unpublished Paper, World Congress of Sociology, International Sociological Association, Mexico City, August
Herbers, J. 1983 'Burdens Shed by Washington Fall Unequally on States, *The New York Times*, 3 July

Hernandez, J.   1985   'Improving Data: A Research Strategy for New Immigrants' in L. Maldonado and J. W. Moore (eds.) *Urban Ethnicity in the United States*, Beverly Hills: Sage

Hershberg, T., E. P. Burstein, E. P. Eriksen, S. Greenberg and W. L. Yancey   1979   'A Tale of Three Cities: Blacks and Immigrants in Philadelphia, 1850 to 1880, 1930 and 1970', *Annals* 441: 55–81

Hicks, D. A. (ed.)   1982   *Urban America in the Eighties*, New Brunswick, NJ: Transaction Books

Hill, H.   1969   'Black Protest and the Struggle for Union Democracy', *Issues in Industrial Democracy*: 19–29

Hill, R. C.   1982   'Race, Class and the State: The Metropolitan Enclave System in the United States', *The Insurgent Sociologist* 10(2): 45–59

Hill, R. C. and M. Indergard   1987   'Downriver: Deindustrialization in Southwest Detroit' in S. Cummings (ed.) *Business Elites and Urban Development: Case Studies and Critical Perspectives*, Albany, NY: State University of New York Press

Hill, R. C. and C. Negrey   1985   'The Politics of Industrial Policy in Michigan', in S. Zukin (ed.) *Industrial Policy: Business and Politics in the United States and France*, New York: Praeger

'Deindustrialisation in the Great Lakes', *Urban Affairs Quarterly* (forthcoming)

Hodgeson, M.   1984   'Economic Statistics from the 1981 Census', *GLC Statistical Series*, No. 31

Hoel, B.   1982   'Contemporary Clothing Sweatshops, Asian Female labour and Collective Organisation' in J. West (ed.) *Work, Women and the Labour Market*, London: Routledge & Kegan Paul

Hoffman, K. and H. Rush   1983   *Microelectronics and Clothing – the Impact of Technical Change on a Global Industry*, Draft Report, Science Policy Research Unit, Sussex University

Hoffman-Nowotny, H.   1982   *Soziologie des Fremdarbeiterproblems: Eine theoretische und empirische Analyse am Beispiel der Schweiz*, Stuttgart: Ferdinand Enke Verlag

Hoffmeyer-Zlotnik, J.   1980   'Gastarbeiter im Sanierungsgebiet, *Universität Hansestadt Hamburg Forschung* 12, Soziologische Stadtforschung in Hamburg

    1982   'Community Change and Invasion: The Case of Turkish Guest Workers' in J. Friedrichs (ed.) *Spatial Disparities and Social Behaviour: A Reader in Urban Research*, Hamburg

Holzner, L.   1982   'The Myth of Turkish Ghettos: A Geographic Case Study of West German Responses towards a Foreign Minority', *The Journal of Ethnic Studies* 9(4): 65–85

Horton, R.   1986   'Human Resources' in C. Brecher and R. Horton, *Setting Municipal Priorities, 1986*, New York University Press: 170–203

Hottes, K.   1975   'Die Integration der Gastarbeiter in die Stadt als soziales System' in M. G. Eisenstadt and W. Kaltyefleiter (eds.) *Minoritäten in Ballungsräumen*, Bonn: Forschungsinstitut; pp. 77–100

Hottes, K. and U. Mayer   1977   'Siedlungsstrukturelle Auswirkungen der Verteilung von Ausländern in den Gemeinden. Integration ausländischer Arbeitnehmer. Siedlungs– Wohnungs- und Freizeitwesen', *Studien zur Kommunalpolitik, Schriftenreiher des Instituts für Kommunalwissenschaften* 16: 283–435

Hottes, K. and P. M. Potke 1976 'Herkunft und Verteilung ausländischer Arbeitnehmer im Ruhrgebiet und Bergisch-Märkischen Lande, *Bochumer Geographische Arbeiten*, Sonderreihe, 6

Houston, M. F. 1983 'Aliens in Irregular Status in the United States: A Review of their Numbers, Characteristics and Role in the U.S. Labor Market', *International Migration* 21: 372–413

Huebl, L. and W. Schepers 1983 *Strukturwandel und Strukturpolitik*, Darmstadt: Wissenschaftliche Buchgemeinschaft

Hunt, H. 1969 *The Intermediate Areas*, Report of a Committee under the Chairmanship of Sir Joseph Hunt, London: HMSO, Cmnd 3998

Hwang, S., S. H. Murdock, B. Parpia and R. R. Hamm 1985 'The Effects of Race and Socio-Economic Status on Residential Segregation in Texas, 1970–80', *Social Forces* 63: 732–47

Illinois Advisory Committee to the US Commission on Civil Rights 1981 *Shutdown: Economic Dislocation and Equal Opportunity*, Washington, DC: Government Printing Office, June

Institut National de Statistiques et des Etudes Economiques (INSEE) 1982 *Recensement général de la population*, 1982 Statistiques des Enterprises (fichier interne) trimestriel

International Labour Office 1981 *Employment Effects of Multinational Enterprises in Industrialised Countries*, Geneva: ILO

1984 *World Labour Report*, Geneva: ILO

Jacobs, Jane 1984 *Cities and the Wealth of Nations*, New York: Random House

Jacobs, Jim 1981 'Suburbs and Disinvestment', Unpublished Manuscript, Macomb Community College, Center for Community Development, Detroit, MI

Jenkins, R. 1984 'Divisions over the International Division of Labour', *Capital and Class* 22, Spring

Jones, A. M. 1980 'Spatial and Social Mobility of Foreign Immigrants in Marseille, 1962–1975', Unpublished D.Phil, thesis, Oxford University

Jones, P. N. 1978 'The Distribution and Diffusion of the Coloured Population in England and Wales, 1961–71, *Transactions of the Institute of British Geographers* 3: 315–32

1983 'Ethnic Population Succession in a West German City 1974–80: The Case of Nuremberg', *Georgraphy* 68: 121–32

Jones, T. P. and D. McEvoy 1978 'Race and Space in Cloud Cuckoo Land', *Area* 10: 162–6

Kantrowitz, N. 1969 'Ethnic and Racial Segregation in the New York Metropolis, *American Journal of Sociology* 74: 685–95

Karn, V., J. Kemeny and P. Williams 1985 *Home Ownership in the Inner City*, Aldershot: Gower

Kasama 1983 Newsletter of the Philippines Support Group, Issue No. 2

Kasarda, J. D.   1980   'The Implications of Contemporary Redistribution Trends for National Urban Policy', *Social Science Quarterly* 61(3 and 4): 373–400

1983a   'Entry Level Jobs, Mobility and Urban Minority Unemployment', *Urban Affairs Quarterly* 19(1), September: 21–40

1983b   'Urban Industrial Transformation and Minority Opportunity', Paper prepared for the Office of Policy Development and Research, US Department of Housing and Urban Development (HC–5482)

1984   'Hispanics and Urban Change', *American Demographics*, November: 24–9

1985   'Urban Change and Minority Opportunities' in Paul Peterson (ed.) *The New Urban Reality*, Washington, DC: The Brookings Institution

Katznelson, I.   1981   *City Trenches*, New York: Oxford University Press

Keeble, D.   1978   'Industrial Decline in the Inner City and Conurbation', *Transaction of the Institute of British Geographers* 3: 101–14

Keely, C. B. and P. J. Elwell   1981   'International Migration: Canada and the United States' in M. M. Kritz *et al.* (eds.) *Global Trends in Migration: Theory and Research on International Population Movements*, New York: Center for Migration Studies

Keesing, D. R. and M. Wolf   1980   *Textile Quotas against Developing Countires*, Thames Essay No. 23, Trade Policy Research Centre, London

Keinath, W. F. Jr   1985   'The Spatial Component of the Post-Industrial Society', *Economic Geography* 61: 223–40

Kennedy-Brenner, C.   1979   *Foreign Workers and Immigrant Policy*, Paris: Development Centre of the OECD

Kerner Commission   1967   *Report of the National Advisory Commission on Civil disorders*, Washington, DC: Government Printing Office

Kidron, M. and R. Segal   1981   *The State of the World Atlas*, London: Heinemann Educational Books

Kim, I.   1981   *The New Urban Immigrants: The Korean Community in New York*, Princeton University Press

Kindleberger, C. P.   1967   *Europe's Postwar Growth – The Role of Labour Supply*, Cambridge, MA: Harvard University Press

King, R.   1976   'The Evolution of International Labour concerning the EEC', *Tijdschrift voor Economische en Social Geographie* 67: 66–82

Kleber, W.   1983   'Die sektorale und sozialrechtliche Umschichtung der Erwerbsstruktur in Deutschland 1962–1970' in M. Haller and W. Mueller (eds.) *Beschäftigungssystem im gesellschaftlichen Wandel*, Frankfurt and New York: Campus

Knight, D. R. W., A. Trapatsaris and J. Jaroszek   1977   'The Structure of Employment in Greater London, 1961–81', GLC Research Memorandum (RM 501)

Kritz, M. M. (ed.)   1983   *U.S. Immigration and Refugee Policy: Global and Domestic Issues*, Lexington, MA: D. C. Heath

Kuehne, P.   1982   'Die ausländischen Arbeiter in der Bundesrepublik Deutschland – eine Herausforderung für die deutschen Gewerkschaften', *WSI Mitteilungen* No. 7

La Brecque, R. 1983 'Welcome to Sunny Salvador North', *Los Angeles*, October

Lake, R. W. 1984 'Changing Symptoms, Constant Causes: Recent Evolution of Fair Housing in the United States', *New Community* 11(3): 206–13

La Porte, R. and C. Abrahams 1976 'California as a "Post-Industrial" Society: a Test Case?' Paper at the Annual Meeting of the American Political Science Association, New Orleans, 4–8 September

Lawrence, R. A. 1984 'Sectoral Shifts and the Size of the Middle Class', *The Brookings Review*, Fall: 3–11

Lebon, A. 1984 'La Population estrangère au recensement de 1982', *Problèmes économiques*, Documentation française 16, août, no. 1886

Lee, T. R. 1973 'Ethnic and Social Class Factors in Residential Segregation', *Environment and Planning*: 5: 447–90

1977 *Race and Residence: The Concentration and Dispersal of Immigrants in London*, Oxford Research Studies in Geography, Oxford: Clarendon Press

Ley, D. 1980 'Liberal Ideology and the Post-Industrial City', *Annals of the American Association of Geographers* 70: 238–58

Lichtenberger, E. 1984 *Gastarbeiter: Leben in zwei Gesellschaften*, Vienna: Hermann Bohlaus

Lieberson, S. 1963 *Ethnic Patterns in American Cities*, New York: Free Press of Glencoe

1980 *A Piece of Pie*, Berkeley: University of California Press

Lin, V. 1985 'Health, Women's Work AND Industrialisation: Women Workers in the Semi-Conductor Industry in Singapore and Malaysia', Unpublished Paper, Conference on the International Division of Labour, Centre for Urban Studies and International Sociological Association, University of Hong Kong, August

Logan, J. R. and M. Schneider 1984 'Racial Segregation and Racial Change in American Suburbs, 1970–1980', *American Journal of Sociology* 89: 874–88

Lomas, G., assisted by N. Deakin and L. Donnelly 1975 *The Inner City*, London Council of Social Service

Loury, G. 1985 'Wage Patterns among Blacks', *The New York Times*, 9 August, Section D: 2

Lovett, D. and B. Ham 1983 'Class Formation, Wage Formation and Community Protest in a Metropolitan Control Centre', *International Journal of Urban and Regional Research* 8 (3): 354–87

Low Pay Unit 1984 *Below the Minumum: Low Wages in the Clothing Industry*, Birmingham: West Midlands Low Pay Unit

Marie, C. G. 1983 'L'immigration clandestine et travail clandestine', Ministère des Affaires Sociales et de la Solidarité Nationale, Paris

Markusen, A. 1985 *Steel and Southeast Chicago*, Center for Urban Affairs and Policy Research, Evanston, IL: North-Western University

Martin, R. and B. Rowthorne. (eds.) 1985 *De-industrialisation and the British Space Economy*, London: Macmillan

Marx, K. 1954 *Capital*, I, London: Lawrence and Wishart

Massey, D. 1984 *Spatial divison of Labour: Social Structures and the Geography of Production*, London: Macmillan

1986 'The International Division of Labour and Local Economic Strategies: Thoughts from London and Managua, Unpublished Paper, ESCR Conference on Localities in an International Economy, Cardiff, September

Massey, D. and R. Meegan 1982 *The Anatomy of Job Loss: The How, Why and Where of Employment Decline*, London: Methuen

Massey, D. S. 1981 'Dimensions of the New Immigration to the United States and Prospects for Assimilation', *Annual Review of Sociology* 7: 57–85

Massey, D. S. and K. M. Schnabel 1983 'Recent Trends in Hispanic Immigration in the United States', *International Migration Review* 17: 212–44

McCormick, M. 1984 'Labor Relations' in C. Brecher and R. Horton (eds.) *Setting Municipal Priorities: American Cities and the New York Experience*, New York University Press: 301–2

Mik, G. 1983 'Residential Segregation in Amsterdam: Background and Policy', *Tijdschrift voor Economische en Sociale Geographie* 74: 74–86

Miles, R. 1982 *Racism and Migrant Labour*, London: Routledge & Kegan Paul
    1986 'Labour Migration, Racism and Capital Accumulation in Western Europe since 1945: An Overview', *Capital and Class* 28

Montagne-Vilette, S. 1981 'Le Pret-à-porter à Paris: de l'artisanat à l'industrie', Unpublished thesis, Paris–Nanterre

Morokvasic, M. 1984 'Birds of Passage are also Women', in Morokvasic (guest editor) 'Women in Migration', *International Migration Review* 68 (18), Winter: 886–907
    1986 'Recours aux immigrés dans la confection parisienne. Elements de comparaison avec la ville de Berlin Ouest', Ministère du Travail et Mission de Liaison Interministerielle pour la lutte contre le traffic de main d'ôeuvre, Document de Travail No. 12, Groupe de recherches et d'analyse des migrations internationales (GRAMI), fevrier

Morrison, P. A. 1973 *Migration from Distressed Areas: Its Meaning for Regional Policy*, Santa Monica, CA: Rand Corporation

Moynihan, D. P. 1965 *The Negro Family: The Case for National Action*, Washington, DC: Office of Policy Planning and Research, US Department of Labor
    1970 *Maximum Feasible Understanding*, New York: The Free Press

Mühlgassner, D. 1984 'Der Wanderungsprozess' in E. Lichtenberger (ed.), *Gastarbeiter*, Vienna: Böhlau

Muller, T. 1985 *The Fourth Wave: California's Newest Immigrants*, Washington DC: The Urban Institute Press

Murray, C. 1984 *Losing Ground: American Social Policy, 1950–1980*, New York: Basic Books
    1990 *The Emerging British Underclass*, Choice in Welfare Series No. 2, London: Institute of Economic Affairs

Nash, J. and M. P. Fernandez-Kelly (eds.) 1983 *Women, Men and the International Division of Labour*, Albany: State University of New York Press

National Union of Tailors and Garment Workers 1979 'Executive Board's Report', General Conference, April

Netherlands Central Bureau of Statistics 1984 *Statistical Yearbook of The Netherlands 1983*, The Hague: Staatsuitgeverij

Nilsson, N. 1983 'Figarma – Fully Integrated Garment Manufacture: An Extension of the Concept of Flexible Manufacturing Systems (FMS)' in R. H. Hollier (ed.) *Automated Materials Handling*, Proceedings of an International Conference, April 20–2, London; IFS Publications Ltd, and North Holland Publishing Co.

Northeast-Midwest Institute 1979 *The Regional Impact of the Crisis at Chrysler*, Washington, DC

Northrup, H. 1968 *The Negro in the Automobile Industry*, Philadelphia, PA: University of Pennsylvania Press

Noyelle, T. and T. Stanback 1984 *The Transformation of American Cities*, Totowa, NJ: Rowman and Allanheld

Office of Management and Budget 1972 *Standard Industrial Classification Manual*, Washington, DC: Government Printing Office

Office of Population Censuses and Surveys 1974 *Census 1971 Great Britain, Age, Marital Condition and General Tables*, London: HMSO

1975 *Population Trends*, 2, London: HMSO

1982 *Great Britain: Summary and Review*, CEN 81 CM 58

1985 'Labour Force Survey 1984: Country of Birth, Year of Entry and Nationality', *OPCS Monitor*, LFS 85/1 and 85/3, London: HMSO

1986 *Births by Birthplace of Mother, 1985 (FMI 86/4): And Births by Birthplace of Parents, 1985 (FMI 86/5)*, London: OPCS

Ogden, P. 1977 'Foreigners in Paris: Residential Segregation in the Nineteenth and Twentieth Centuries', Occasional Paper 11, Department of Geography, Queen Mary College, University of London

O'Loughlin, J. and G. Glebe 1981 'The Location of Foreigners in Düsseldorf: A Causal Analysis in a Path-analytic Framework', *Geographische Zeitschrift* 69: 81–97

1984a 'Residential Segregation of Foreigners in German Cities', *Tijdschrift voor Economische en Sociale Geografie* 74(4): 373–84

1984b 'Intra Urban Migration in German Cities', *Geographische Zeitschrift* 74(1): 1–23

Oriol, M. 1981 *Report on Studies of the Human and Cultural Aspects of Migration in Western Europe 1918–1979*, Strasbourg: European Science Foundation

Osterman, P. 1983 'The Mismatch Hypothesis and Internal Labor Markets', *Proceedings of the 36th Annual Meeting of the Industrial Relations Research Association, 1982*, Madison, WI: Industrial Relations Research Association

Pahl, R. 1984 *Divisions of Labour*, Oxford: Basil Blackwell

Paine, S. 1974 *Exporting Workers: The Turkish Case*, Cambridge University Press

1977 'The Changing Role of Migrant Workers – the Advanced Capitalist Economies in Western Europe' in R. T. Griffiths (ed.) *Government, Labour and Business in European Capitalism*, London: Europotentials Press, pp. 195–225

Parker, J. and K. Dugmore   1976   *Colour and Allocation of GLC Housing*, The Report of the GLC Lettings Survey 1974–5, Research Report 21, Greater London Council

1977/8   'Race and Allocation of Public Housing – GLC survey', *New Community* 6: 27–40

'Part-time Workers: Rising Numbers, Rising Discord', *Business Week*, 1 April 1985: 62–63

Patterson, S.   1963   *Dark Strangers*, London: Tavistock Publications

Peach, C.   1965   'West Indian Migration to Britain: The Economic Factors', *Race* 7: 31–47

1966   'Factors Affecting the Distribution of West Indians in Great Britain', *Transactions of the Institute of British Geographers* 38: 151–63

1968   *West Indian Migration to Britain: A Social Geography*, London: Oxford University Press for the Institute of Race Relations

1974   'Ethnic Segregation in Sydney and Intermarriage Patterns', *Australian Geographical Studies* 12: 219–29

1975   'Immigrants in the Inner City', *Geographical Journal* 141: 372–9

1978–9   'British Unemployment Cycles and West Indian Immigration, 1955–74', *New Community* 7: 40–4

1981   'Conflicting Interpretations of Segreation' in P. Jackson and S. Smith (eds) *Social Interaction and Social Segregation*, London: Longman

1982   'The Growth and Distribution of the Black Population in Britain 1945–80' in D. A. Coleman (ed.) *The Demography of Immigrant and Minority Groups in the United Kingdom*, London: Academic Press: 23–42

1983   'The Dissolution and Growth of Ethnic Areas in American Cities', in C. Peach, V. Robinson and S. Smoth (eds.) *Ethnic Segregation in Cities*, London: Croom Helm

1986   'A Geographical Perspective on the 1981 Riots in England', *Ethnic and Racial Studies* 9(31): 396–411

Peach, C., V. Robinson and S. Smith (eds.)   1983   *Ethnic Segregation in Cities*, London: Croom Helm

Peach, C. and S. Shah   1980   'The Contribution of Council House Allocation to West Indian Desegregation in London, 1961–71', *Urban Studies* 17: 333–41

Peach, C. and S. W. C. Winchester   1974   'Birthplace, Ethnicity and the Enumeration of West Indians, Indians and Pakistanis', *New Community* 3: 386–93

Peach, C., S. W. C. Winchester and R. Woods   1975   'The Distribution of Coloured Immigrants in Britain', *Urban Affairs Annual Review* 9: 395–419

Peach, C. *et al.* (eds.)   1975   *Urban Social Segregation*, London: Longman

Peil, M.   1971   'The Expulsion of West African Aliens', *Journal of Modern African Studies* 9(2): 205–29

Perry, D. C. and R. J. Watkins   1981   'Contemporary Dimensions of Uneven Urban Development in the U.S.A.' in M. Harloe and E. Lebos (eds.) *City, Class and Capital: New Developments in the Political Economy of Regions*, London: Edward Arnold, pp. 115–42

Peterson, P. E. (ed.) 1985 *The New Urban Reality*, Washington, DC: The Brookings Institution

Phillips, D. 1986 *What Price Equality? A Report of the Allocation of GLC Housing in Tower Hamlets*, Housing Research and Policy Report No. 9, London: Greater London Council

1986 'Race and Housing in London's East End: Continuity and Change', *New Community* 14(3): 356–69

Philpott, S. 1977 'The Montserratians: Migration, Dependency and the Maintenance of Island Ties in England', in J. L. Watson (ed.) *Between Two Cultures: Migrants and Minorities in Britain*, Oxford: Blackwell Scientific Press

Philpott, T. L. 1978 *The Slum and the Ghetto*, New York: Oxford University Press

Pierson, D. K. 1984 'Michigan Fears "Raids" on Lakes', *Detroit News*, 2 December

1985 'Great Lakes Charter Signed but it is Nonbinding', *Detroit News*, 5 February

Pinch, S. and A. Williams 1977 *Changes in the Distribution of Immigrants in the British Urban System, 1961–71*, Paper presented to the Urban Studies Group, Institute of British Geographers, King's College, London, 13 May

Piore, M. J. 1979 *Birds of Passage: Migrant Labour in Industrial Societies*, Cambridge University Press

1980 'Dualism as a Response to Flux and Uncertainty' in S. Berger and M. J. Piore, *Dualism and Discontinuity in Industrial Societies*, Cambridge University Press: 23–54

Portes, A. and R. L. Bach 1985 *Latin Journey: Cuban and Mexican Immigrants in the United States*, Berkeley: University of California Press

Power, J. 1979 *Migrant Workers in Western Europe and the United States*, Oxford: Pergamon Press

Price, C. 1969 'The Study of Assimilation' in J. A. Jackson (ed.) *Migration*, Cambridge University Press

Reimers, D. 1985 *Still the Golden Door: The Third World Comes to America*, New York: Columbia University Press

Report of the National Advisory Commission on Civil Disorders 1968, New York: Bantam

Rex, J. 1982 'The 1981 Urban Riots in Britain', *International Journal of Urban and Regional Research* 6(1): 99–113

Rex, J. and R. Moore 1967 *Race, Community and Conflict*, Oxford University Press

Rist, R. C. 1978 *Guestworkers in Germany: The Prospects for Pluralism*, New York: Praeger

Robinson, V. 1979 *The Segregation of Asians within a British City: Theory and Practice*, Research Paper 22, Oxford: School of Geography

1980 'Correlates of Asian Immigration, 1959–74', *New Community* 8: 115–22

Rothkirch, Chr. v. and M. Tessaring 1986 'Projektionen des Arbeitskraftsbedarfs nach Qualifikationsebenen bis zum Jahre 2000', *MittAB* 1/1986, IAB

Rumberger, R. W. and M. Carnoy 1980 'Segmentation in the U.S. Labor Market: Its Effects on the Mobility and Earnings of Whites and Blacks', *Cambridge Journal of Economics* (4): 117–31

Runnymede Trust 1975 *Race and Council Housing in London*, London: Runnymede Trust

Rutter, M. and N. Madge 1976 *Cycles of Disadvantage*, London: Heinemann

Salah, A. 1973 *La Communauté algérienne dans le Département du Nord*, Paris: Editions Universitaire

Sassen-Koob, S. 1979 'Economic Growth and Immigration in Venezuela', *International Migration Review* 13(3): 455–71

1982 'Recomposition and Peripheralisation at the Core', *Contemporary Marxism* 5: 88–100

1983 'Capital Mobility and Labour Migration: Their Expression in Core Cities' in R. Timberlake (ed.) *Urbanisation in the World Economy*, New York: Academic Press

1984 'The New Labor Demand in Global Cities' in M. Smith (ed.) *Cities in Transformation*, Berkeley, CA: Sage Publications, pp. 139–71

Saunders, P. 1990 *A Nation of Home Owners*, London: Unwin Hyman

Sawers, L. and W. K. Tabb (eds.) 1984 *Sunbelt/Snowbelt: Urban Development and Regional Restructuring*, New York: Oxford University Press

Saxenian, A. 1983 'The Urban Contradictions of Silicon Valley: Regional Growth and the Restructuring of the Semiconductor Industry', *International Journal of Urban and Regional Research* 7: 237–62

Scarman, Lord 1981 *The Brixton Disorders, 10–12 April 1981, Report of an Inquiry by the Rt. Honourable the Lord Scarman, OBE*, Cmnd 8247, London: HMSO

Schober, K. 1982 'Les Immigrés de la seconde génération en RFA: Problèmes et Prospective', *Documentation Française* 1(803), 22 December: 18–23

Schweke, W. and L. Webb 1984 'A National Industrial Policy – States Seize the Initiative', *Ways and Means* 7: 1–6

Schwinges, U. 1980 'Zur Integration von Zuwanderern: Aussiedler in Hamburg', *Universität hansestadt Hamburg Forschung*, 12, Soziologische Stadtforschung in Hamburg: 52–7

Scott, A. J. 1984 'Industrial Organisation and the Logic of Intra-Metropolitan Location III: A Case Study of the Women's Dress Industry in the Greater Los Angeles Region', *Economic Geography* 60: 3–27

1986 'Industrialization and Urbanization: A Geographical Agenda', *Annals of the American Association of Geographers* 76: 25–37

Serrin, W. 1986 'Growth in Jobs since '80s is Sharp, but Pay and Quality are Debated', *The New York Times*, 8 June

Shah, S. 1980 *Aspects of the Geographical Analysis of Asian Immigrants in London*, Unpublished D.Phil. thesis, Oxford University

Shulman, S. 1984 'Competition and Racial Discrimination: The Employment Effects of Reagan's Labour Market Policies', *Review of Radical Political Economics*, 16(4): 111–28

Shyllon, F. P.   1974   *Black Slaves in Britain*, London: Oxford University Press for the Institute of Race Relations

Sidel, R.   1986   *Women and Children Last: The Plight of Poor Women in Affluent America*, New York: Viking

Simon, G.   1979   *L'Espace des travailleurs tunisiens en France*, Poitiers: Simon

Singh, A.   1977   'U.K. Industry and the World Economy: A Case of De-Industrialisation', *Cambridge Journal of Economics*: 113–36

Smith, D. J.   1977   *Racial Disadvantage in Britain*, Harmondsworth: Penguin
   1984   *Ethnic Minorities in Britain*, London: Policy Studies Institute

Soja, E. W., R. Morales and G. Wolff   1983   'Urban Restructuring: An Analysis of Social and Spatial Change in Los Angeles', *Economic Geography* 59: 195–230

SOPEMI   1984   *Continuous Reporting System on Migration, Report 1984*, Paris: OECD

Squires, G. D.   1981   'The Flight of Capital Hit Minorities the Hardest', *The Chigaco Sun Times*, 24 May

Staeck, K. and I. Karst, (eds.)   1982   'Racial and Ethnic Stratification and Affirmative Action Planning in New York City's Public and Private Sector', Unpublished draft report to the US Commission on Civil Rights
   1985   *Closed Labor Markets*, Community Services Society of New York

Stafford, W.   1983   'Racial and Ethnic Stratification and Affirmative Action Planning in New York City's Public and Private Sector', Unpublished draft report to the US Commission on Civil Rights
   1985   *Closed Labor Markets*, Community Services Society of New York

Stanback, T. M. and T. J. Noyelle   1981   *Metropolitan Labor Markets in Transition: A Study of Seven SMSAs*, Final Report, Washington, DC: US Department of Commerce

State of Michigan   1984   *The Path to Prosperity: Findings and Recommendations of the Task Force for a Long-Term Economic Strategy for Michigan*, Lansing, MI

Statistisches Bundesamt   1966   *Bevölkerung und Kultur*, Volks- und Berufszählung vom 6. Juni, Heft 3, Stuttgart und Mainz: V. Kohlhammer

Statistisches Bundesamt Wiesbaden   1984   *Statistisches Jahrbuch der Bundesrepublik Deutschland*, Stuttgart und Mainz: V. Kohlhammer
   1985   *Statistisches Jahrbuch der Bundesrepublik Deutschland*, Stuttgart and Mainz: V. Kohlhammer

Sternlieb, G. and J. W. Hughes (eds.)   1976   *Post-Industrial America: Metropolitan Decline and Inter-Regional Jobs Shifts*, New Brunswick, NJ: Center for Urban Policy Research
   1983   'The Uncertain Future of the Central City', *Urban Affairs Quarterly* 18(4): 455–72

Storper, M. and R. Walker   1984   'The Spatial Division of Labor: Labor and the Location of Industries' in L. Sawers and W. K. Tabb (eds.) *Sunbelt/Snowbelt: Urban Development and Regional Restructuring*, New York: Oxford University Press

Taeuber, K. E.   1983   *Racial Residential Segregation, 28 Cities, 1970–80*, CDE

Working Paper 83–12, Madison: Center for Demography and Ecology, University of Wisconsin

Taeuber, K. E. and A. F. Taeuber 1965 *Negroes in Cities*, Chigaco: Aldine

Thirwall, A. P. 1982 'De-industrialisation in the United Kingdom', *Lloyds Bank Review* 144: 22–37

Thomas, B. 1954 *Migration and Economic Growth*, Cambridge University Press

Thomas, E. 1982 *Immigrant Workers in Europe: Their Legal Status*, Paris: The Unesco Press

The Times (London) 1984 'Generating Jobs', *The Times 'Special Report'*, 24 February

Tobier, E. 1982 'Foreign Immigration' in C. Brecher and R. Horton (eds.) *Setting Municipal Priorities, 1983*, New York University Press
    1984 *The Changing Face of Poverty: Trends in New York City's Population in Poverty: 1960–1990*, Community Service Society of New York
    1985 'Population' in C. Brecher and R. Horton (eds.) *Setting Municipal Priorities: American Cities and the New York Experience*, New York University Press: 19–42

Treiman, D. J. and H. I. Hartmann (eds.) 1981 *Women, Work and Wages*, Washington, DC: Academy Press

United Nations 1984 *Concise Report on the World Population Situation in 1983*, Department of International Social and Economic Affairs Population Studies 85, New York

United Nations Economic Commission for Europe 1979 *Labour Supply and Migration in Europe: Demographic Dimensions 1950–75 and Prospects*, New York: United Nations

United States Bureau of Labor Statistics 1983 *Geographic Profile of Employment and Unemployment, 1983*, Bulletin 2216, Washington, DC: Government Printing Office

United States Bureau of the Census 1983 *1980 Census of Population* Volume 1, *Characteristics of the Population*, Chapter C, 'General Social and Economic Characteristics', Part 1: United States Summary, Washington, DC: Government Printing Office
    1985a *Statistical Abstract of the United States*, Washington, DC: Government Printing Office
    1985b *Statistical Abstract of the United States*, Washington, DC: Government Printing Office

United States Bureau of Labor Statistics 1983 *Handbook of Labor Statistics*, Washington, DC: Government Printing Office
    1985 *Employment and Earnings*, June, Washington, DC: Government Printing Office

United States Department of Health and Human Services 1985–6 *Report of the Secretary's Task Force on Black and Minority Health* (Margaret Heckler, Secretary, Katrina W. Johnson, Study Director), Government Printing Office

United States Department of Justice 1980 *1979 Statistical Yearbook of the Immigration and Naturalization Service*, Washington, DC: Government Printing Office

1986a *1982 Statistical Yearbook of the Immigration and Naturalization Service*, Washington, DC: Government Printing Office

1986b *1984 Statistical Yearbook of the Immigration and Naturalization Service*, Washington, DC: Government Printing Office

United States Department of Labor 1983 *Time of Change: 1983 Handbook on Women Workers*, Washington, DC: Goverment Printing Office

United States Equal Employment Opportunity Commission 1981 *1979 Report: Minorities and Women in Private Industry*, Washington, DC: Government Printing Office

Urry, J. 1981 'Localities, Regions and Social Class', *International Journal of Urban and Regional Research* 5(4): 455–74

Vanneeste, D. 1981 'Sociaal-Ruimtelijke in een Stad: Betekenis Van de Indicator "Gestarbeiders": een Onderzoek van de Gentse Situatie', *Tijdschrift van de Belgische Vereniging voor Aardrijkskundige Studies* 2: 161–74

Van Valey, T., K. A. Woods and W. G. Marston 1982 'Patterns of Segregation among Hispanic-Americans: A Base-line for Comparison', *California Sociologist* 5: 27–40

Veyne, P. 1984 *Writing History*, New York: Wesleyan University Press

Waldinger, R. 1985 'Immigration and Industrial Change in the New York City Apparel Industry', in G. J. Borjas and M. Tienda (eds.) *Hispanics in the U.S. Economy*, Orlando: Academic Press

Wallerstein, I. 1979 *The Capitalist World Economy*, Cambridge University Press

Walraff, G. 1986 *Lowest of the Low*, London: Pluto Press

Ward, D. 1982 'The Ethnic Ghetto in the United States: Past and Present', *Transactions of the Institute of British Geographers* n.s. 7: 257–75

Warren, B. 1980 *Imperialism: Pioneer of Capitalism*, London: Verso

Washington, T. 1985 'The Great Lakes: A Blueprint for their Protection', *Detroit News*, 10 March

Weisbach, H. J. 1984 'Humanisation Problems with Regard to Advanced Machinery Technologies in the Clothing Industries', Statement to the Tripartite Conference on 7 September in Sunningdale

Weisz, R. and M. Anselm 1981 'L'Industrie de l'habillement en région Provence–Alpes–Cote d'Azur, Stratégies d'enterprises et organisation de la production', Aix-en-Provence: CERFISE

White, P. 1984 *The West European City*, London: Longman

Wilson, W. J. 1978 *The Declining Significance of Race*, Chicago and London: University of Chigaco Press

1982 'Race-oriented Programs and the Black Underclass', in C. Cottingham (ed.) *Race, Poverty and the Urban Underclass*, Lexington, MA: Lexington Books, pp. 113–32

1984 'The Urban Underclass' in L. W. Dunbar (ed.) *Minority Report*, New York: Pantheon; pp. 75–117

1985 'The Urban Underclass in Advanced Industrial Society', in P. E. Peterson (ed.) *The New Urban Reality*, Washington, DC: The Brookings Institution, pp. 129–60

1987   *The Truly Disadvantaged: The Inner City, the Underclass and Public Policy*, University of Chicago Press

Wilson, W. J. and K. M. Neckerman   1985   'Poverty and Family Structure: The Widening Gap between Evidence and Public Policy Issues', Conference Paper, Institute for Research on Poverty, University of Wisconsin at Madison

Winchester, S. W. C.   1975   *Spatial Structure and Social Activity: A Social Geography of Coventry*, Oxford University, Unpublished D.Phil, thesis

Wisconsin Advisory Committee to the United States Commission on Civil Rights   1982   *Business Incentives and Minority Employment*, Washington, DC: Government Printing Office

Wolin, S.   1972   'Political Theory as a Vocation', in M. Fleisher (ed.) *Machiavelli and the Nature of Political Thought*, New York: Atheneum

Wong, M. G.   1985   'Post-1965 Immigrants: Demographic and Socioeconomic Profile' in L. Maldonado and J. W. Moore (eds.) *Urban Ethnicity in the United States*, Beverly Hills: Sage

Woods, R.   1979   'Ethnic Segregation in Birmingham in the 1960s and 1970s', *Ethnic and Racial Studies* 2: 455–76

Wright, E. O.   1978   *Class, Crisis, State*, London: New Left Books

Yancey, W. L., E. P. Ericksen and R. N. Juliani   1976   'Emergent Ethnicity: A Review and Reformulation', *American Sociological Review* 41: 391–403

Yancey, W. L. and G. H. Leon   1985   'The Structure of Pluralism: "We're all Italian Around Here, Aren't We, Mrs. O'Brien?"' *Ethnic and Racial Studies* 8: 94–116

Index